Apple Pro Training Series
OS X Lion Support Essentials

Kevin M. White

Apple
Certified

Apple Pro Training Series: OS X Lion Support Essentials
Kevin M. White
Copyright © 2012 by Peachpit Press

Published by Peachpit Press. For information on Peachpit Press books, contact:

Peachpit Press
1249 Eighth Street
Berkeley, CA 94710
(510) 524-2178
http://www.peachpit.com
To report errors, please send a note to errata@peachpit.com. Peachpit Press is a division of Pearson Education.

Apple Series Editor: Lisa McClain
Production Coordinator: Kim Elmore, Happenstance Type-O-Rama
Technical Editor: John C. Welch
Apple Reviewer: Shane Ross
Apple Project Manager: Judy Lawrence
Copy Editor: Peggy Nauts
Proofreader: Gail Nelson
Compositor: Maureen Forys, Happenstance Type-O-Rama
Indexer: Jack Lewis
Cover Illustration: Kent Oberheu
Cover Production: Chris Gillespie, Happenstance Type-O-Rama

ISBN 13: 978-0-321-77507-8   ISBN 10: 0-321-77507-4
9 8 7 6 5 4 3 2 1
Printed and bound in the United States of America

Acknowledgments In addition to the amazing Peachpit staff members who were instrumental in completing this work, I would like to thank the development team for their hard work: Judy Lawrence, Shane Ross, Gordon Davisson, and Adam Karneboge. Additional thanks go to John Signa, Arek Dreyer, Ben Greisler, John Soward, Shoun Regan, Jason Bruder, and Brian Gupton. Finally, I could not have made this journey without the support of my family and loving wife, Michelle.

This book is dedicated to the newest member of my family, Sawyer Martin White.

Contents at a Glance

Getting Started xi

Chapter 1   Installation and Configuration 1
Chapter 2   User Accounts 59
Chapter 3   File Systems 121
Chapter 4   Data Management 213
Chapter 5   Applications and Processes 285
Chapter 6   Network Configuration 353
Chapter 7   Network Services 423
Chapter 8   Peripherals and Printing 523
Chapter 9   System Startup 575
Appendix A   General Mac Troubleshooting 601
Appendix B   Command-Line Essentials 609

Index 637

Table of Contents

Getting Started............................ xi

Chapter 1 Installation and Configuration 1

About OS X Lion........................... 2

Before Upgrading a Previous System...................... 4

Preparing the System Drive........................... 10

Upgrade or Install Lion 12

Installer Troubleshooting............................. 18

Using Lion Recovery................................. 21

Using Setup Assistant................................ 30

Configuring System Settings........................... 41

Install Software and Updates.......................... 47

What You've Learned 54

References.. 54

Review Quiz....................................... 56

Chapter 2 User Accounts 59

Understanding User Accounts 60

Managing User Accounts.............................. 64

Managing User Home Folders 71

Managing Login and Fast User Switching................. 80

Essential Account Security 86

Managing Keychains................................. 98

Resetting Account Passwords 104

What You've Learned 116

References.. 117

Review Quiz....................................... 117

Chapter 3 File Systems. 121

Understanding File System Components 122

Managing File Systems. 126

Using Software RAID. 146

Using Optical Media. 154

Using FileVault 2. 163

Understanding File System Permissions 171

Managing Permissions via the Finder 183

Managing Permissions via Terminal 189

Troubleshooting File Systems 196

What You've Learned 207

References. 207

Review Quiz. 209

Chapter 4 Data Management 213

Understanding the System File Structure 214

Managing Font Resources 220

Managing Hidden Items 223

Using Aliases and Links. 228

Understanding File System Metadata 234

Managing Launch Services 240

Using Spotlight and Quick Look 245

Using File Archives and Disk Images. 255

Managing Time Machine. 265

What You've Learned 279

References. 280

Review Quiz. 280

Chapter 5 Applications and Processes 285

Understanding Applications and Processes 286

Installing and Updating Applications 295

Managing Application Accessibility. 312

Using Auto Save, Versions, and Resume 315

Monitoring Applications and Processes 324

Application Troubleshooting. 331

Managing Dashboard. 341

What You've Learned 347

References. 347
Review Quiz. 349

Chapter 6   Network Configuration 353
Understanding Network Concepts. 354
Understanding Networks in Action 359
Configuring Basic Network Settings 365
Using Network Locations. 367
Using Network Service Interfaces. 370
Using Virtual Network Services 376
Using Network Protocols. 388
Troubleshooting Network Configuration 408
What You've Learned 416
References. 417
Review Quiz. 418

Chapter 7   Network Services 423
Understanding Network Services. 424
Using Network Applications 430
Using File Sharing Services 438
Using Host Sharing Services 468
Securing Network Services 486
Troubleshooting Network Services. 490
Understanding Directory Services 497
Configuring Network Directory Services 500
Managing Network Authentication 507
Troubleshooting Directory Services. 513
What You've Learned 515
References. 516
Review Quiz. 517

Chapter 8   Peripherals and Printing. 523
Understanding Peripherals 524
Using Bluetooth Peripherals 534
Troubleshooting Peripherals 539
Understanding Printing, Scanning, and Faxing. 544
Configuring Printing, Scanning, and Faxing 547
Managing Print Jobs. 557

Sharing Printers. 565
Advanced Printing Management 568
Troubleshooting the Print System 570
What You've Learned 572
References. 572
Review Quiz. 573

Chapter 9   System Startup 575
Understanding the Startup Sequence. 576
Sleep Modes, Logout, and Shutdown. 587
Troubleshooting Startup. 590
What You've Learned 596
References. 597
Review Quiz. 598

Appendix A   General Mac Troubleshooting 601
Troubleshooting Workflow 602
Quick Fixes 603
Diagnostic Tools 605
Binary Search. 606
Research Resources. 606

Appendix B   Command-Line Essentials 609
Command-Line Basics. 610
Command-Line Navigation. 616
Command-Line File Manipulation 622
Command-Line Administration. 630
Command-Line Tips and Tricks. 634

Index 637

Getting Started

This book is based on the same criteria that are used for Apple's official training course, Lion 101: OS X Support Essentials 10.7, an in-depth exploration of troubleshooting on OS X Lion. It serves as a self-paced tour of the breadth of functionality of Lion and the best methods for effectively supporting users of Lion systems.

The primary goal is to prepare help desk specialists, technical coordinators, service technicians, system administrators, and others who support Macintosh users to knowledgeably address customer concerns and questions. This includes the ability to return a Lion computer to normal operation using the proper utilities, resources, and troubleshooting techniques.

Whether you are an experienced system administrator or just want to dig deeper into Lion, you'll learn in-depth technical information and procedures used by Apple-certified technicians to install, configure, maintain, and diagnose Macintosh computers running Lion.

This book assumes a basic level of familiarity with Mac OS X. Unless otherwise specified, all references to OS X Lion refer to version 10.7.0, which was the most current version available at the time of writing. Due to subsequent upgrades, some screens, features, and procedures may be slightly different from those presented on these pages.

Learning Methodology

This book is based on lectures and exercises provided to students attending Lion 101: OS X Support Essentials 10.7, a three-day, hands-on course that provides an intense and in-depth exploration of how to troubleshoot on OS X Lion. For consistency, we follow the basic structure of the course material, but you may complete it at your own pace.

Each chapter is designed to help experienced users become experts who are able to support other Lion users by:

▶ Providing *knowledge* of how Lion works

▶ Showing how to use diagnostic and repair *tools*

▶ Explaining troubleshooting and repair *procedures*

For example, in Chapter 6, "Network Configuration," you'll learn basic networking concepts (knowledge). You'll acquire network configuration and troubleshooting techniques using the Network preferences and Network Utility (tools). And you'll explore methods for troubleshooting networking issues (procedures). In addition, each chapter includes troubleshooting techniques for dealing with common issues related to the topic at hand.

Each chapter focuses on a different aspect of Lion:

▶ Chapter 1, "Installation and Configuration"—Preparing and partitioning the drive; installing OS X Lion; using the installer log files to verify a successful installation; using Lion Restore; configuring Lion with the Setup Assistant; updating software with Software Update and Installer; learning tips and techniques for troubleshooting an installation problem.

▶ Chapter 2, "User Accounts"—Creating and managing user and administrator accounts; locating directory attributes; implementing security; selecting passwords; managing the keychain.

▶ Chapter 3, "File Systems"—Identifying the file systems supported by Lion; using FileVault 2; managing file and directory ownership and permissions; using Disk Utility; repairing files; using the command line for file management.

▶ Chapter 4, "Data Management"—Exploring the system volume, file system layout, preferences, frameworks, and file types unique to Lion (that is, file system metadata and packages); using Spotlight, file archives, and disk images; archiving and restoring data with Time Machine; managing backup data; accessing data outside of Time Machine.

▶ Chapter 5, "Applications and Processes"—Understanding applications supported in Lion, applications created with different developer APIs, the UNIX concept of a process, and the relationship of processes to applications; using tools to monitor and manage processes; setting application preferences; troubleshooting.

▶ Chapter 6, "Network Configuration"—Configuring basic networks; setting up TCP/IP networking, Ethernet, and Wi-Fi; connecting multiple networks; using network locations; isolating and troubleshooting network elements.

▶ Chapter 7, "Network Services"—Connecting to common network resources; enabling network services on a Lion client; accessing AFP, SMB, SSH, FTP, and WebDAV connections; using Bonjour, NetBIOS, and the network browser; sharing files between Macs and Windows; sharing web documents; taking advantage of screen sharing and remote login; using firewalls; isolating sharing issues from network issues; configuring and troubleshooting network directory services.

▶ Chapter 8, "Peripherals and Printing"—Connecting peripherals to a Mac; identifying cabling, connections, and device drivers for common peripherals; managing printers and print jobs; understanding printer PPDs and PDF workflow; learning techniques for isolating cabling, driver, or application issues.

▶ Chapter 9, "System Startup"—Troubleshooting boot issues with a Mac at startup; understanding the phases of the startup process; identifying the active part of the system during each phase; exploring issues that can arise; launching processes automatically with the launchd and loginwindow startup items.

In addition to the chapters listed here, this book includes; Appendix A, "General Mac Troubleshooting," a collection of general Apple troubleshooting information; and Appendix B, "Command-Line Essentials," an introduction to the command-line environment in Lion. These appendices may be valuable to you, but they are not essential for the coursework or certification.

Chapter Structure

Each chapter begins with an opening page that lists the learning goals for the chapter and an estimate of time needed to complete the chapter. The explanatory material is augmented with hands-on exercises essential to developing your skills. For the most part, all you need to complete the exercises is a Macintosh computer running OS X v10.7 or later. If you lack the equipment necessary to complete a given exercise, you are still encouraged to read the step-by-step instructions and examine the screen shots to understand the procedures demonstrated.

NOTE ▶ Some of these exercises can be disruptive—for example, they may turn off network services temporarily—and some exercises, if performed incorrectly, could result in data loss or damage to system files. As such, it's recommended that you perform these exercises on a Mac computer that is not critical to your daily productivity. Apple, Inc., and Peachpit Press are not responsible for any data loss or any damage to any equipment that occurs as a direct or indirect result of following the procedures described in this book.

We refer to Apple Knowledge Base documents throughout the chapters, and close each chapter with a list of recommended documents related to the topic of the chapter. The Knowledge Base is a free online resource (www.apple.com/support) containing the very latest technical information on all of Apple's hardware and software products. We strongly encourage you to read the suggested documents and search the Knowledge Base for answers to any problems you encounter.

You'll also find "More Info" resources throughout the chapters, and summarized at the end of each chapter, that provide ancillary information. These resources are merely for your edification, and are not considered essential for the coursework or certification.

At the end of each chapter is a short chapter review that recaps the material you've learned. You can refer to various Apple resources, such as the Knowledge Base, as well as the chapters themselves, to help you answer these questions.

Apple Certification

After reading this book, you may wish to take the OS X Support Essentials 10.7 Exam to earn the Apple Certified Support Professional 10.7 certification. This is the first level of Apple's certification programs for Mac professionals:

▶ Apple Certified Support Professional 10.7 (ACSP)—Ideal for help desk personnel, service technicians, technical coordinators, and others who support OS X Lion customers over the phone or who perform Mac troubleshooting and support in schools and businesses. This certification verifies an understanding of Lion's core functionality and an ability to configure key services, perform basic troubleshooting, and assist end users with essential Mac capabilities. To receive this certification, you must pass the OS X Support Essentials 10.7 Exam. This book is designed to provide you with the knowledge and skills to pass that exam.

▶ Apple Certified Technical Coordinator 10.7 (ACTC)—This certification is intended for Mac OS X technical coordinators and entry-level system administrators tasked with maintaining a modest network of computers using Lion Server. Since the ACTC certification addresses both the support of Mac clients and the core functionality and use of Lion Server, the learning process is correspondingly longer and more intensive than that for the ACSP certification, which addresses solely Mac client support. This certification requires passing both the OS X Support Essentials 10.7 Exam and the OS X Server Essentials 10.7 Exam.

NOTE ▶ Although all of the questions in the OS X Support Essentials 10.7 exam are based on material in this book, simply reading it will not adequately prepare you for the exam. Apple recommends that before taking the exam, you spend time actually setting up, configuring, and troubleshooting Lion.

Apple hardware service technician certifications are ideal for people interested in becoming Macintosh repair technicians, but also worthwhile for help desk personnel at schools and businesses, and for Macintosh consultants and others needing an in-depth understanding of how Apple systems operate:

▶ Apple Certified Macintosh Technician (ACMT)—This certification verifies the ability to perform basic troubleshooting and repair of both desktop and portable Macintosh systems, such as iMac and MacBook Pro. ACMT certification requires passing the Apple Macintosh Service exam and the Mac OS X Troubleshooting Exam. To learn more about hardware certification, visit http://training.apple.com/certification/acmt.

About the Apple Training Series

Apple Training Series: OS X Lion Support Essentials is part of the official training series for Apple products developed by experts in the field and certified by Apple. The chapters are designed to let you learn at your own pace. You can progress through the book from beginning to end, or dive right into the chapters that interest you most.

For those who prefer to learn in an instructor-led setting, Apple also offers training courses at Apple Authorized Training Centers worldwide. These courses are taught by Apple Certified Trainers, and they balance concepts and lectures with hands-on labs and exercises. Apple Authorized Training Centers have been carefully selected and have met Apple's highest standards in all areas, including facilities, instructors, course delivery, and infrastructure. The goal of the program is to offer Apple customers, from beginners to the most seasoned professionals, the highest-quality training experience.

To find an Authorized Training Center near you, visit http://training.apple.com.

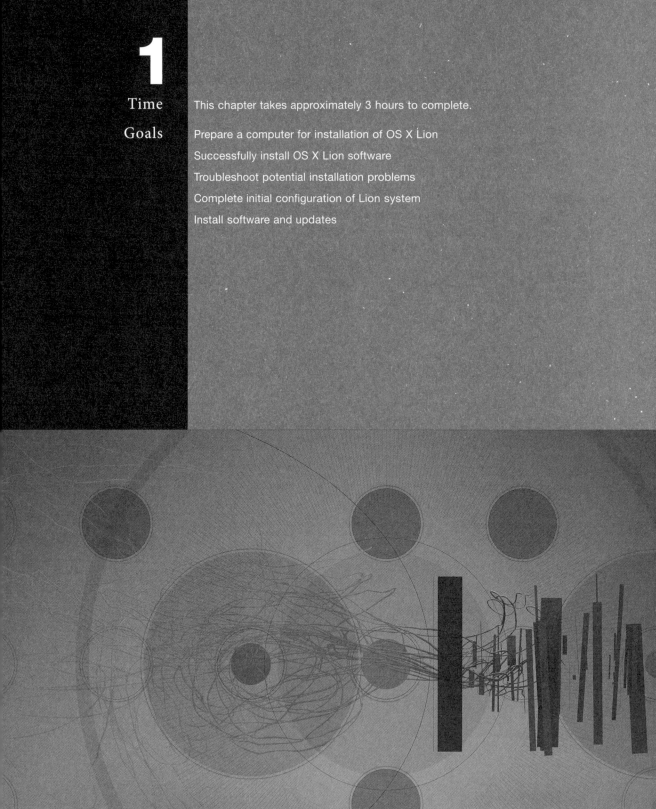

1

Time   This chapter takes approximately 3 hours to complete.

Goals   Prepare a computer for installation of OS X Lion

Successfully install OS X Lion software

Troubleshoot potential installation problems

Complete initial configuration of Lion system

Install software and updates

Chapter 1

Installation and Configuration

Those unfamiliar with Mac computers may look upon their design and assume that beauty is only skin deep. After all, it's true that today's Macs use much of the same technology found in other Intel-based computers. So it could seem that elegant design is all that sets Apple's computers apart from the competition. Yet, for the Mac, what's on the inside makes it special as well. Seasoned Mac users know the true differentiator is the software that transforms hardware into a functional computer: the operating system, the true soul of a computer.

Every Mac computer has some version of the Mac OS preinstalled when built. The version of Mac OS X that ships with a computer is usually the latest available at the time. Thus, every Mac will at some time need a later version of the operating system to have the latest features and bug fixes. This chapter starts with a brief introduction to OS X Lion, then guides you through the installation, initial configuration, and updating of the operating system. This will also include troubleshooting issues that may arise during these processes.

NOTE ▶ Several of the operations that you will learn about in this chapter involve significant changes to your Mac's setup. Many of them are difficult to reverse, if not irreversible. If you plan to experiment with the topics discussed in this chapter, you should do so on a spare computer or the external hard drive that does not contain critical data.

About OS X Lion

OS X Lion is the latest version of Apple's primary operating system. Since its introduction in 2001, Mac OS X has become an increasingly attractive alternative to other operating systems because of its combination of innovative technologies. Mac OS X is the only operating system that combines a powerful open-source UNIX foundation with a state-of-the-art user interface, offering all the ease of use for which Apple is known. Furthermore, the Mac is an exceptional development platform, as evidenced by the large selection of high-quality third-party software titles available for it.

In addition to the features found in previous versions of Mac OS X, Lion includes over 250 new features. The central theme in Lion is the marriage of the best features in iOS with the flexibility of the Mac operating system. Those familiar with iOS will immediately recognize its influence in Lion. Key new features in Lion include Multi-Touch gestures, full-screen applications, a new application launcher dubbed Launchpad, application resume, document autosave, and versions. In addition, Lion shows the same refinement that's present iOS, in even in the small details.

MORE INFO ▶ A full list of Lion's new features can be found at www.apple.com/macosx/whats-new/features.html.

Integration Through Standards

Much of the success of Mac OS X can be attributed to Apple's wholehearted embrace of industry-standard formats and open-source software. The historic perception of the Macintosh platform being closed or proprietary is far from today's reality. Nearly every technology in Lion is based on well-known standards. Adoption of common standards saves engineering time and allows for much smoother integration with other platforms. Even when Apple developers must engineer a technology for a new feature, Apple often releases the specs to the developer community, fostering a new standard. An example of this is the Bonjour network discovery protocol, which Apple pioneered and has maintained as an open standard for others to develop and use.

Some examples of common standards supported by Mac OS X are:

▶ Connectivity standards—Universal Serial Bus (USB), IEEE 1394 (FireWire), Thunderbolt, Bluetooth wireless, and the IEEE 802 family of Ethernet standards

▶ File system standards—UNIX File System (UFS), File Allocation Table (FAT), New Technology File System (NTFS), ISO 9660 optical disc standard, Universal Disk Format (UDF)

▶ Network standards—Dynamic Host Configuration Protocol (DHCP), Domain Name System (DNS), Hypertext Transfer Protocol (HTTP), Internet Message Access Protocol (IMAP), Simple Mail Transfer Protocol (SMTP), File Transfer Protocol (FTP), Network File System (NFS), and Server Message Block/Common Internet File System (SMB/CIFS)

▶ Application and development standards—Single UNIX Specification v3 (SUSv3), Portable Operating System Interface (POSIX), C and C++, Ruby, Python, and Perl

▶ Document standards—ZIP file archives, Rich Text Format (RTF), Portable Document Format (PDF), Tagged Image File Format (TIFF), Portable Network Graphics (PNG), Advanced Audio Coding (AAC), and the Moving Picture Experts Group (MPEG) family of media standards

Using This Chapter Wisely

Depending on the state of your Mac, not all of this chapter will be appropriate for you. Of course, you could simply read the entire chapter, but it might not be the best idea to attempt all the techniques described here on your working Mac. Odds are, your Mac falls into one of the following general categories:

▶ Your Mac already has Lion—If this is the case, you probably don't want to reinstall the operating system. You can still explore most of the utilities covered in this chapter, but you should avoid instructions that will erase or reinstall your system.

▶ You want to repair or reinstall an existing Lion system—If this is the case, you'll want to proceed directly to the section of this chapter entitled "Using Lion Recovery."

▶ Your Mac is currently running Mac OS X v10.6.x and you want to upgrade—If this is the case, you'll want to proceed directly to the next section of this chapter, "Before Upgrading a Previous System."

▶ Your Mac is currently running a version of Mac OS X prior to v10.6 and you want to upgrade—If this is the case you will need to acquire a drive containing the Lion Recovery media.

▶ Your Mac is currently running a previous version of Mac OS X but it's not working very well—If this is the case, you will want to back up important data, erase the system drive, and perform a "clean" install. Simply upgrading a previous system that has problems often makes for a Lion system with problems. In this case, you will also need access to a drive containing the Lion Recovery media.

NOTE ▶ If you don't know what version of Mac OS X your Mac is running, simply select About This Mac from the Apple menu.

NOTE ▶ You can purchase an OS X Lion Recovery Drive from Apple. Or, if you're more technically inclined, you can make your own Lion Recovery media as covered in the "Using Lion Recovery" section of this chapter. This process, however, requires access to a Mac running v10.6.6 or later.

Before Upgrading a Previous System

Because every Mac ships with Mac OS X preinstalled, the majority of installations of Lion are upgrades. An upgrade installation implies that there is an operating system that the Installer will be replacing. There will probably also be user data on this system that is important to the user. The Lion installation process is designed to retain non-system data during an upgrade installation.

Upgrading an operating system is a complicated process that isn't entirely free from issues. Apple has worked hard to improve the Mac OS X upgrade experience through the years, but other variables involved could still lead to issues. For instance, a hardware failure issue could prevent a successful upgrade installation. For these reasons, you should take some preparatory steps to prevent Installer issues and data loss.

Verifying Installation Requirements

It's important to understand the installation requirements for the copy of Mac OS X you plan to use and also the requirements of the particular Macintosh you intend to install it on. If you're not sure what the intended Mac's specifications are, use the System Profiler application to view the computer's status.

If the Mac is already running a previous version of Mac OS X, you can simply open System Profiler (in the /Applications/Utilities folder). You can also get to System Profiler by choosing About This Mac in the Apple menu, then More Info. Within System Profiler, verify the computers' specifications by selecting and viewing the various content areas in the Hardware section.

NOTE ▸ If your Mac lacks the /Applications/Utilities/System Profiler but instead has /Applications/Utilities/System Information, congratulations—you already have Lion installed. You can still reinstall the system, but you probably don't have to check for these requirements as you are already running Lion.

Upgrading OS X Lion requires:

▶ Mac computer with an Intel Core 2 Duo, Core i3, Core i5, Core i7, or Xeon processor

▶ 2 GB of memory

▶ Mac OS X v10.6.6 or later (v10.6.8 recommended)

▶ 7 GB of available space

▶ Some features require an Apple ID; terms apply

▶ Some features require a compatible Internet service provider; fees may apply

> **MORE INFO** ▶ Some Lion features have additional requirements beyond these minimum system requirements. You can learn more about feature-specific requirements at the Lion technical specifications website: www.apple.com/macosx/specs.html.

Preparing for an Upgrade Installation

While you could jump right into the Lion upgrade installation without any preparation, completing some preliminary steps will reduce the chances of upgrade problems or losing important data. There are four crucial steps you should take before any system upgrade installation: Check for firmware updates, verify application compatibility, back up important files and folders, and back up critical settings.

Plug Portable Macs into AC Power

This may seem like a no-brainer, but obviously you don't want to lose power halfway through an upgrade installation. Plug any portable Mac into AC power for the duration of the installation process to ensure its completion.

Run Apple Software Update

As mentioned previously, Mac OS X v10.6.8 is the recommended version to upgrade to Lion. Furthermore, there have been numerous updates to other Apple software in preparation for Lion's release. For example, both iLife and iWork received updates for Lion. Finally, older Macs may require a firmware update to properly access all of Lion's features. You should ensure that the Mac you're going to upgrade has all available Apple software updates.

Assuming the Mac is connected to the Internet, choose Software Update from the Apple menu. You should install all available updates. If no updates are found, your Mac is running the latest software, which will ensure a smooth Lion upgrade.

> **MORE INFO** ▸ You can find out more about the Apple Software Update mechanism and running Apple updates manually in the "Install Software and Updates" section of this chapter. Although the section is written for Lion, the behavior is similar to that of previous versions of Mac OS X.

Check for Firmware Updates

Firmware is low-level software that facilitates the startup and management of system hardware. Though rare, Apple may release firmware updates that older Macintosh computers need to operate properly with new system software. Often these updates are caught by the Apple Software Update mechanism. However, some Macs may require manual firmware updates. It's always best to check for firmware updates prior to installing a later version of Mac OS X.

Assuming the Mac is running Mac OS X v10.6, you can identify the firmware version by opening /Applications/Utilities/System Profiler. The default view for System Profiler will identify the versions of the two types of firmware on Intel-based Macs. The first, listed as Boot ROM Version, is for the Extensible Firmware Interface (EFI), which is responsible for general hardware management and system startup. The second, listed as SMC Version, is the System Management Controller (SMC) firmware responsible for managing hardware power and cooling. Once you have located your computer's firmware versions, you can determine if you have the latest updates by accessing Knowledge Base document HT1237, "EFI and SMC firmware updates for Intel-based Macs."

If you determine that your Mac requires a firmware update, you will need to find the correct update at the Apple Support Download website, http://support.apple.com/downloads. Installing a firmware update is similar to other system software updates in that it requires administrative user authorization and a restart. However, some older Macs have an extra requirement for firmware updates: After the initial installation process, you must shut down and restart the computer, holding down the power button until you hear a long tone. This will initiate the remainder of the firmware update process. Be sure to carefully read any instructions that come with a firmware updater! Failure to properly update a Mac's firmware could lead to hardware failure.

NOTE ▶ If you experience an unsuccessful update you can restore your Mac's firmware with a Firmware Restoration CD. You can find out more about acquiring and using this CD from Knowledge Base document HT2213, "About the Firmware Restoration CD (Intel-based Macs)."

Verify Application Compatibility

When moving to a new operating system, third-party applications may require updates to function properly. Assuming your Mac is running Mac OS X v10.6, you can easily collect a list of installed applications by opening /Applications/Utilities/System Profiler.app. In System Profiler, you will need to verify that View > Full Profile is selected, to reveal the Applications section in the Contents list. Selecting Applications from the Contents list causes System Profiler to scan the current system for all available applications.

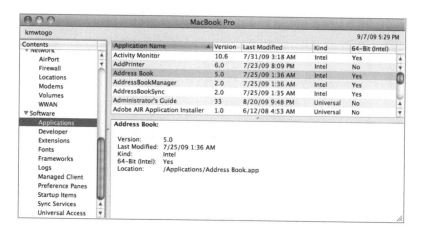

You don't have to worry about the applications installed as part of the operating system. Those will be replaced when you install the new system. However, you may have to do your own research to determine if third-party applications require updates.

Lion also includes a list of known incompatible software. If the Lion Installer detects known incompatible software during an upgrade installation, it will move incompatible software to a folder named Incompatible Software. In some cases the incompatible software isn't moved, but the operating system prevents you from opening the software. Instead, it displays a warning dialog stating that the software is known to be incompatible. You can find out more about this new feature of Mac OS X from Knowledge Base document HT3258, "Mac OS X v10.6, OS X Lion: About Incompatible Software."

Back Up Important Files and Folders

Experienced computer users already know to keep backups of their important files and folders. Having a current backup is important before making significant changes to the computer. Installing a new operating system is a significant change that if done improperly could result in catastrophic data loss.

If the system is already running Mac OS X v10.5 or later, you can use the built-in Time Machine software to easily create a backup before you start your installation. Using Time Machine and other archival tools is covered in Chapter 4, "Data Management."

Document Critical Settings

Apple has designed Migration Assistant and the Lion Installer to help ensure that previous settings are not lost when you are upgrading Mac OS X. Nonetheless, some settings are so critical to your computer's function that you would be well served to document them in case something should go wrong.

Specifically, network settings are critical and should be documented before a system upgrade is attempted. Network settings for all previous versions of Mac OS X can be located in the Network pane of System Preferences, accessed from the Apple menu. Avoid missing settings by navigating through all the available network interface and configuration tabs.

> **TIP** ▶ You can quickly document your settings by using the screen capture keyboard shortcut, Command-Shift-3, to create picture files of the dialogs onscreen.

Keeping Up-to-Date

For the most recent information regarding the installation process, your best source is the Apple Support page and Knowledge Base. A good place to start is the Lion page at http://www.apple.com/support/lion. Anytime you intend to install Lion, you should visit these resources to catch any recently discovered issues. The Apple Knowledge Base documents are sprinkled throughout this guide for a reason: They are the best source for official, up-to-date support information.

Preparing the System Drive

Again, because most Lion installations are of the upgrade variety, further system drive preparation isn't necessary. Any drive containing any version of Mac OS X for Intel-based Macs is already properly formatted for Lion. In other words, if "upgrade installation" describes your situation, then you should move right to installing Lion as covered in the next section.

However, if you need to perform an erase and install for a "clean" system or you are planning on repartitioning the drive, you will have to prepare the system drive prior to installing Lion. Specifically, Lion only supports installation on drives that are partitioned via the GUID Partition Table (GPT) scheme and contain at least one Mac OS X Extended (Journaled) formatted volume.

Erasing the system drive before a system installation may be necessary for various reasons. Obviously erasing the system drive will erase any existing data, but sometimes this may be necessary. For example, if you are upgrading the Mac's internal drive to a bigger or faster drive, it must be formatted for Lion. Another instance is when the operating system has serious issues; in this case, erasing and installing a "clean" copy of Lion may resolve the situation.

The reasons to repartition your system drive are a bit more complex, so they are covered in the next section. Nevertheless, the process of repartitioning may require erasing data on the disk, and thus is often done prior to installing Lion. You will use Disk Utility for both erasing and repartitioning the disk. Disk Utility can be found on any Mac in the / Applications/Utilities folder or, as covered later in this chapter, from the Utilities menu when using Lion Recovery from external media. If you're going to make changes to the system drive before you install Lion, you must do so while started up from a system on another physically different drive.

> **MORE INFO ▶** This chapter does not include details about erasing or repartitioning disk drives; these procedures are covered extensively in Chapter 3, "File Systems."

Understanding Partitioning Options

Before selecting a destination drive, you may want to pause and consider the various partition methodologies that are available as installable Lion destinations. Most Macs have a single hard drive formatted as a single partition that defines the entire space on that hard drive. This is the Apple default partition setup. However, by repartitioning the hard drive, you can choose to break up that single large partition into separate smaller partitions. This allows you to treat a single physical storage device as multiple separate storage destinations.

Just as installing a new operating system will have long-lasting ramifications on how you use your computer, so does your choice of partition options. Thus, before you install a new operating system you should consider your partition philosophy. The following lists present the pros and cons of various partition options. Again, many of these concepts will be further discussed in Chapter 3, "File Systems."

Single Partition

▶ Pros—Most drives are formatted with a single partition by default, so no changes are necessary and no data will be lost. Also, a single partition is the most efficient use of space on your drive, as you won't have wasted space due to having separate partitions.

▶ Cons—Having only a single partition severely limits administrative flexibility. Many maintenance and administrative tasks require multiple partitions, so you will have to use an additional physical storage device to accommodate those needs. Further, because system and user data are combined on a single drive, administration can be more difficult.

Multiple Partitions

▶ Pros—Multiple partitions allow you to have multiple operating systems and multiple storage locations on a single device. Having multiple operating systems allows you to run different versions of Mac OS X from one drive or create utility systems that can be used to repair the primary system. With multiple storage locations, it's much easier to replace a damaged operating system because all the user's data resides on another partition.

▶ Cons—Most drives need to be repartitioned to use multiple partitions. While Lion supports dynamic partitioning without losing data, it can only do so when working within the free space of a drive. Therefore certain partition configurations may require you to completely erase the drive. Any future partition changes may require you to sacrifice data on the drive as well. Additionally, Boot Camp Assistant, used to configure a partition for Windows or another non-Apple operating system, does not support multiple-partition drives. Finally, multiple partitions can be very space inefficient if you don't plan carefully, as you may end up with underused partitions that run out of space too soon.

Upgrade or Install Lion

Apple is well known for designing every operation to be as easy as possible, and the Lion installation process is an example of this. It's so well-engineered that most users can easily complete it with no training. However, anyone tasked with supporting Lion computers should be more familiar with all the necessary procedures to ensure a smooth installation.

> **NOTE** ▶ New Macs usually come with a computer-specific release of Mac OS X that was engineered for that model and may include additional bundled software. This book assumes that you will be using a standard copy of the OS X v10.7 Lion Installer, so you may find that some details vary if you are using a computer-specific install. For more information, see Knowledge Base document HT2681, "What's a 'computer-specific Mac OS X release'?"

Acquiring the Lion Installer

One of the significant changes in Lion is the new system Installer. The big news is that Lion is available for download from the Mac App Store. You can also purchase an OS X Lion Recovery Drive from Apple, but most people will download their copy of Lion, as it's cheaper and easier than buying physical media. That said, once you have downloaded the Lion Installer, you can also create your own Lion Recovery drive by following the instructions in the "Using Lion Recovery" section later in this chapter.

NOTE ▶ If you already have Lion installed on your Mac, then you can't download the Installer again. This is because you can download and run the full Installer from the Lion Recovery system, covered later in this chapter.

If you are acquiring Lion for the first time, the process is as simple as buying a song in iTunes or a new game from the App Store. Using the Mac App Store does have a few prerequisites, though:

▶ You must be running Mac OS X v10.6.6 or later.

▶ You must be connected to the Internet, ideally at broadband speeds. The Lion Installer is around 4 GB, so it can take a while to download even on "fast" connections.

▶ You must have an Apple ID associated with valid credit card information. If you have purchased items from Apple via iTunes or the Mac App Store previously, then you are already set. If you have yet to purchase products online from the Apple App Store or iTunes, then you can set up your information within the Mac App Store.

Assuming you meet this criteria, simply open /Applications/App Store. Lion will likely remain as one of the featured items on the store, so it should be easy to find. Purchase Lion and it will automatically download the Install Mac OS X Lion application to your Mac. Once the download is complete, the Lion Installer will automatically open and run.

MORE INFO ▶ Details regarding the Mac App Store are covered in Chapter 5, "Applications and Processes".

Install Mac OS X Lion

There are two primary types of installations; upgrade installs that replace an existing Mac OS X system, and new installs that place a new copy of Lion on a drive without a system. The Installer will automatically choose the appropriate installation type based on your selected destination. For installation destinations, the Lion Installer can upgrade the system that your Mac is currently running from, or you can install to another drive attached to your Mac.

NOTE ▶ If you want to perform an erase and install, you must manually erase the destination system drive using Disk Utility before running the Lion Installer. If the destination is another system drive, this can be done from your currently running Mac. However, if you want to erase the system drive your Mac is currently running from, then you will need to do this from an external Lion Recovery system, as covered later in this chapter.

NOTE ▶ You cannot install Lion if any other users are currently logged into the Mac via Fast User Switching. You will either need to have those users log out of their session or restart the computer to forcibly end the other user sessions.

The installation process itself involves just a few simple choices up front, followed by the actual installation. This allows the user to spend only a few moments choosing the installation destination, and then leave the computer unattended while the installation completes.

TIP ▶ The Lion installation process can be safely restarted after a power loss or drive disconnection. If this occurs, simply restart the installation.

To upgrade or install Lion:

1 If the Lion Installer isn't already running, open the /Applications/Install Mac OS X Lion application.

2 Continue through the Welcome screen.

3 Agree to the Apple Software License Agreement.

4   At this point, you can select the install destination.

The default selection is the current startup disk; to select other drives or partitions, click the Show All Disks button. Details regarding this step are covered in the next section of this chapter.

NOTE ▶ If you are upgrading or installing while running from a standard Mac system, you will have to authenticate as an administrative user.

5   Click the Install button to start the installation.

NOTE ▶ If you run the Lion Installer from the Lion Recovery system, the screenshots may not look exactly like those presented here.

The installation will complete automatically without further interaction. First, the Installer will create a Lion Restore system on the destination drive. This step will only take a few minutes, as the Lion Restore system is only around 700 MB. When this first stage is complete, the Mac will restart to the freshly minted Lion Restore system.

NOTE ▶ The Lion Recovery system partition, dubbed Recovery HD, is a hidden partition that will never appear in the graphical interface when running Lion. The Recovery HD partition is created out of the last 700 MB or so of the primary Lion installation destination.

Once started from the Lion Restore system, the Installer will automatically continue with the remainder of the install process. This second stage, when the "real" copy of Lion is installed to the destination drive, will take quite a while, as it must install over 4 GB of data. When this is complete, the Mac will restart once more, into the installed copy of Lion.

If you installed a new copy of Lion, the system will restart into the full Setup Assistant experience, as covered later in this chapter. On the other hand, if you installed an upgrade, you will be greeted by a shorter Setup Assistant experience. This is because an upgraded Mac already has the required initial configuration. In this case, you will only see the Setup Assistant Registration and Finishing Up screens, again covered later in this chapter.

> **NOTE ▶** If you install Lion to the system drive hosting the Install Mac OS X Lion application (as is typical of a standard upgrade installation), the Installer will delete the original installation assets to save space. This, however, renders the Install Mac OS X Lion application useless unless it's allowed an Internet connection to reacquire the installation assets.

Selecting the Install Destination

After you have passed the initial installation screens, you will be prompted to select the installation destination. You are simply selecting the disk partition where Lion will be installed. This can be an internal or an external drive as long as it's properly formatted. The default selection is the current startup disk; you will have to click the Show All Disks button to choose an alternate destination.

NOTE ▶ The Customize button is for installing OS X Lion Server. This button will only illuminate when running the Lion Installer from a Lion Server system.

You may notice that the Installer will not let you select certain drives or partitions. This is because the Installer has determined that your Mac cannot start from that item. Possible reasons are:

▶   The disk does not use the proper partition scheme for your Macintosh. Intel Macs use GPT. You can resolve this issue by repartitioning the drive using Disk Utility.

▶   The specific partition is not formatted properly. Lion requires a partition formatted as a Mac OS Extended (Journaled) volume. You can resolve this issue by erasing the partition using Disk Utility.

▶   The Lion Installer can't create the Lion Recovery HD. This issue can be resolved by adjusting the destination partition size. For more information, see Knowledge Base article TS3926, "OS X Lion: Installer reports 'This disk cannot be used to start up your computer.'"

▶   The Lion Installer does not support installing to a drive containing Time Machine backups. For more information, see Knowledge Base article TS2986, "Mac OS X v10.6, OS X Lion: Cannot install Mac OS X v10.6 or later on a volume used by Time Machine for backups."

Again, the system automatically determines if there is an existing version of Mac OS X on the selected destination. If there is an existing system, the Installer will upgrade the system to the version of Lion included with the Installer.

Lion supports hardware a few years older than the latest version of the operating system. However, previous versions of Mac OS X do not support hardware that is newer than the operating system release. In other words, you may come across a Mac that's newer than the Lion Installer you're trying to use. If this is the case, the installation will fail to start up the Mac or simply refuse to install. You should then use the Lion Recovery system that came with the Mac.

MORE INFO ▶ See Knowledge Base document HT2186, "Don't install a version of Mac OS X earlier than what came with your Mac."

Installer Troubleshooting

Apple has worked hard to make Lion's installation as painless and reliable as possible. Yet, as with any complicated technology, problems may arise. The good news is that the Lion Installer has the ability to "back out" of an installation and restart to the previous system.

If this is the result, then obviously the installation did not complete, but at least you still have a functioning Mac.

Thoroughly verifying that your computer meets the requirements for Lion and completing the installation preparation steps outlined earlier in this chapter will go a long way toward preventing or resolving any serious problems.

Beyond, appropriate preparation, the most common installation failures arise from problems with the destination disk. Here are a few specific issues regarding this:

▶ The Installer was unable to verify the selected drive or partition. This indicates serious drive problems. You should refer to the troubleshooting steps in Chapter 3, "File Systems," to resolve this issue.

▶ The Installer may give you an error message saying that some features of Lion are not supported on the selected drive. You will see this message if your system drive is a software RAID set or uses nonstandard Boot Camp partitioning. If this is the case, the Installer will not be able to create a Lion Restore HD, but you will still be able to install Lion.

   MORE INFO ▶ See Knowledge Base document HT4649, "OS X Lion: 'Some features of Mac OS X Lion are not supported for the disk (volume name)' appears during installation."

▶ In some cases, even when a drive is partitioned and formatted properly, the Installer will not let you select that disk. This error most often occurs when there is also a Boot Camp partition on the drive. The resolution in this case involves slightly decreasing the size of the Mac partition to make room for the Lion Restore HD.

   MORE INFO ▶ See Knowledge Base document TS3926, "OS X Lion: Installer reports 'This disk cannot be used to start up your computer.'"

Using the Installer Log

The granddaddy of all troubleshooting resources for Lion is the log file. Nearly every process writes entries in a log file, and the Installer is no different. The Installer log contains progress and error entries for nearly every step of the installation process, including steps not shown by the standard interface. Information in the Installer log will allow you to more precisely pinpoint problems or verify installation.

   TIP ▶ You can also use this technique to check on the progress of any general software installation via the Installer application.

TIP ▶ After installation you can access the Installer log on a normally running Mac from the /Applications/Utilities/Console application. Once Console is open, select /private/var/log/install.log.

Anytime during the installation process, you can bring up the Installer log by following these steps:

1 If the Installer is running in full-screen mode, you will not see the menu bar. Move your mouse to the top of the screen to reveal the menu bar.

2 Choose Window > Installer Log from the menu bar or hold down the Command-L keyboard shortcut.

3 Choose Show All Logs from the Detail Level pop-up menu to view the entire contents of the Installer log.

4 Use the Spotlight search field in the toolbar to isolate specific entries in the Installer log.

5 To save the Installer log, choose File > Save or click the Save button in the toolbar.

TIP ▶ The Mac will not automatically restart during the system installation process as long as the Installer Log window is the foremost window.

You can leave the Installer Log window open during the entire installation process to monitor progress. You may find that, even during a successful installation, the Installer reports many warnings and errors. Many of these reported issues are benign, and you should only concern yourself with them if you are trying to isolate a show-stopping problem. When the installation successfully completes, you should see summary entries in the Installer log that look similar to the screenshot above.

Using Lion Recovery

From a troubleshooting viewpoint, one of the biggest additions to Lion is the new Lion Recovery system. Lion Recovery replaces functionality previously accessed via the Mac OS X Installation DVD. This includes not only the ability to install Lion but also the ability to access a variety of administration and troubleshooting utilities. The primary difference is that the Lion Recovery system is, by default, located on the primary system drive. This allows easy "anytime" access to recovery utilities without the need for additional media.

This move stemmed from the fact that for many, Lion will be acquired via download from the Mac App Store, thus necessitating a non-DVD-based recovery solution. Furthermore, as more and more Mac users have access to broadband Internet, the need for an optical drive diminishes every year. Some new Mac models even ship sans optical drive.

In this section you will learn how to access Lion Recovery on both new Macs that came with Lion preinstalled and on systems that were upgraded to Lion. You will also briefly explore the utilities available from Lion Recovery. As long as you don't make any permanent changes using the utilities in Lion Recovery, you can safely explore without damaging your primary Lion system.

Startup from Lion Recovery

There are several methods for starting up from Lion Recovery:

▶ If your Mac was upgraded to Lion—The Lion Recovery HD should have been installed as part of the Lion upgrade installation. To access Lion Recovery, simply restart the Mac while holding the Command-R keyboard shortcut. If Lion Recovery doesn't start, then your best choice is to start up from an external drive containing a Lion Recovery HD.

▶ If your Mac came preinstalled with Lion—The Lion Recovery HD came as part of the Mac's default system image. To access Lion Recovery, simply restart the Mac while holding the Command-R keyboard shortcut. If Lion Recovery is missing or doesn't otherwise start, and your Mac model was released after July 19, 2011, your Mac should automatically engage Lion Internet Recovery. As the name implies, your late-model Mac will attempt to re-download the Lion Recovery system from Apple's servers. After a fresh Lion installation, you can then open the Mac App Store to download and install any other software that came with your new Mac, like the iLife suite.

MORE INFO ▶ For more about the requirements for using Lion Internet Recovery, see Knowledge Base article HT4718, "OS X Lion: About Lion Recovery."

▶ If you have Lion Recovery on an external drive—Connect the Lion Recovery drive to your Mac and restart the Mac while holding the Option key. This will invoke the Mac's Startup Manager, where you can use the arrow and Return keys or the mouse and trackpad to select the Lion Recovery HD.

Once the Lion Recovery system fully starts, you will be presented with the Mac OS X Utilities window. From there you can install (or reinstall) Lion and choose from a variety of maintenance applications.

Lion Recovery Utilities

Lion Recovery is a useful administrative and troubleshooting resource. When you start up from this system, you will have access to several system administration and maintenance tools. There are even a few utilities in this system that you cannot find anywhere else in Lion. Again, when you first start the Lion Recovery system, you are greeted with the Mac OS X Utilities window.

TIP ▶ It's also worth noting that, when started up from Lion Recovery, Ethernet and Wi-Fi networking is available if the network provides DHCP services. While Ethernet is automatically enabled if physically connected, you can connect to a wireless network from the Wi-Fi menu item.

From the Lion Recovery Mac OS X Utilities window, you can access:

▶ Restore From Time Machine Backup—You can use this to restore a full-system Time Machine backup from either a network or a locally connected drive. Time Machine will be further discussed in Chapter 4, "Data Management."

▶ Reinstall Mac OS X—As the name implies, this will open the Lion Installer. If you are running from a full Lion Restore system, like the OS X Lion Recovery Drive purchased from Apple, the drive contains the Lion installation assets. However, the hidden local Lion Restore HD and drives created with Lion Recovery Disk Assistant do not contain the installation assets and thus require Internet access to reinstall Lion. Further, for these systems to download the Lion installation assets, they must verify the Mac is authorized to run Lion. For Macs that shipped with Lion, this authorization is automatic. For Macs upgraded to Lion, you will have to authenticate with the Apple ID used to purchase Lion.

▶ Get Help Online—This will open Safari, directed to Apple's support site.

▶ Disk Utility—This application is responsible for storage-related administration and maintenance. It is especially useful when the Mac has started up from Lion Restore, because Disk Utility can be used to manage a system disk that otherwise can't be managed when in use as the startup disk. Specifically, Disk Utility can be used to prepare a drive for a new installation of Lion or to attempt repairs on a drive that fails installation. Disk Utility usage is further discussed in Chapter 3, "File Systems."

NOTE ▶ While running from Lion Recovery, if the Mac's system drive is protected by FileVault 2, then you will need to unlock the drive to access its content. This can be done via Disk Utility.

▶ Click the close button or Quit to access Startup Disk—If you attempt to quit the Mac OS X Utilities window, it will prompt you to start the Startup Disk utility. This utility will allow you to select the default system startup disk. The default startup disk can be overridden using any of the alternate startup modes discussed in Chapter 9, "System Startup."

Wait, there's more. Lion Recovery has a few extra utilities hidden in the Utilities menu at the top of the screen.

From the Utilities menu you can access:

► Firmware Password Utility—This utility will allow you to secure the Mac's startup process by disabling all alternate startup modes without a password. You can disable or enable this feature and define the required password. You can find out more about Firmware Password in Chapter 2, "User Accounts."

► Network Utility—This is the primary network and Internet troubleshooting utility in Mac OS X. The Network utility will be further discussed in Chapter 6, "Network Configuration."

► Terminal—This is your primary interface to the UNIX command-line environment of Lion. The most useful command you can enter from here is simply resetpassword followed by the Return key.

► Reset Password opened via Terminal—This utility will allow you to reset the password of any local user account, including the root user, on the selected system disk. Obviously, this is a dangerous utility that can pose a serious security threat. Because of this, the Reset Password utility will only run from Lion Recovery. You can find out more about Reset Password in Chapter 2, "User Accounts."

If you are accessing Lion Recovery from a full Lion Recovery drive, you may also see the following additional Utilities menu items:

▶ Disk Utility (see description above).

▶ System Information—This application allows you to inspect the status of both the hardware and software on your Mac. You will be using this application throughout this guide, including a later section of this chapter.

▶ Restore From Time Machine Backup (see above).

> **NOTE** ▶ The utilities available from Lion Recovery can certainly be used to compromise system security. Then again, any system whose default startup disk can be overridden during startup is wide open to compromise. Therefore, in secured environments it's often necessary to use the Firmware Password utility to help protect your systems.

Create a Lion Recovery Drive

In some cases, a Mac with Lion installed does not have a local Lion Recovery HD. For example, if you just replaced the internal hard drive with a new drive, there will be nothing on the new drive. Also, Lion systems on software RAID sets and drives with nonstandard Boot Camp partitioning will not have a local Lion Recovery HD. In these cases, you would need to start up from an external Lion Recovery drive. One solution is to purchase an OS X Lion Recovery Drive from Apple. Two do-it-yourself solutions exist to convert a standard drive into a Lion Recovery drive. The first involves creating a minimal Lion Recovery drive using Lion Recovery Disk Assistant. The second solution creates a full Lion Recovery drive using the contents inside the Install Mac OS X Lion application.

> **NOTE** ▶ To use either of the following methods for creating a Lion Recovery drive, the drive must first be partitioned using the GUID partition scheme. Most external drives do not start out partitioned with GUID, so before creating the Lion Recovery drive, you may need to repartition the destination drive. Repartitioning a drive is detailed in Chapter 3, "File Systems."

Create a Minimal Lion Recovery Drive

The advantage to creating a Lion Recovery drive with this method is that it only requires a 1 GB USB flash drive. This method is also fully supported by Apple as it's initiated through the Lion Recovery Disk Assistant, available on Apple's support downloads website. The downside to this method is that the resulting Lion Recovery drive will not contain the Lion installation assets. Thus, when running Lion Recovery from this drive, if you need to reinstall Lion, the system will have to download the Lion Recovery assets from the Internet.

NOTE ▶ You must run the Recovery Disk Assistant from a Mac system that contains a local hidden Lion Recovery HD.

To create a minimal Lion Recovery drive:

1 Direct a web browser to the following website, http://support.apple.com/kb/DL1433, and download the Lion Recovery Disk Assistant.

By default the Lion Recovery Disk Assistant disk image should automatically mount and open in a new Finder window. If it does not, simply double-click on the disk image file, RecoveryDiskAssistant.dmg, in the Downloads folder.

2 If you wish to keep the Lion Recovery Disk Assistant application on your Mac, drag and drop the icon in a convenient location like the /Applications or /Applications/ Utilities folder.

3 Open the Recovery Disk Assistant application by double-clicking on it.

Because this file was downloaded from the Internet, the system will prompt you to verify that you want to open this application. Click the Open button to continue.

4   Recovery Disk Assistant will open with a software license agreement. Click the Agree
button to continue.

5   The Recovery Disk Assistant will wait for you to connect a small (1 GB or larger) USB
flash disk.

Once you connect a USB flash disk, click the icon representing the disk, and then
click the Continue button. Finally, authenticate as an administrative user to create a
Lion Restore drive.

The restore process should only take a few minutes to complete, depending on the speed
of your external drive. Note the amount of time it takes to create the Lion Restore disk.
If it takes more than a few minutes, the drive you've selected is relatively slow and ultimately not a good choice for this task. When complete, you should quit the Recovery Disk
Assistant.

You should also test your Lion Recovery drive before you put it into "rotation." When you
create a Lion Recovery drive using this method, it will be named Recovery HD. However,
the drive will never show up in the Finder interface. To test, simply restart the Mac and
hold the Option key during startup. This will start the Mac into Startup Manager. One of
the options should be Recovery HD. If you select the Recovery HD drive, it should then
start up just like a normal Lion Recovery system by presenting you with the Mac OS X
Utilities window. To return to your primary system, close the Mac OS X Utilities window
to reselect your primary startup disk.

Create a Full Lion Recovery Drive

The advantage to creating a Lion Recovery drive with this method is that it will include the Lion installation assets on the drive. However, this method requires an 8 GB drive and is not fully supported by Apple.

To create a full Lion Recovery drive:

1 In the Finder, right-click or Control-click on /Applications/Install Mac OS X Lion. From the pop-up menu, choose Show Package Contents.

2 In the new Finder window, navigate to the Contents/SharedSupport/ folder. Inside this folder you should see a disk image file named InstallESD.dmg. This is a disk image containing a copy of the Lion Recovery drive and the Lion Installer assets.

NOTE ► If InstallESD.dmg is missing, you will need to re-download the Install Mac OS X Lion application. To do so, throw the current one in the Trash and empty the Trash. Next, open the Mac App Store, navigate to your items under Purchased, and you will be able to reinstall the OS X Lion item.

3 If you haven't already connected the destination external drive to the Mac, do so now.

4 Open /Applications/Utilities/Disk Utility and select the destination external drive from the drive list.

NOTE ► If the destination external drive isn't already partitioned via the GPT scheme, then you must repartition the drive as covered in Chapter 3, "File Systems."

5 Click the Restore tab to the far right of the Disk Utility window.

6 Drag the destination external drive from the drive list to the Destination field. In the example screenshot, the destination drive is named External Drive 1.

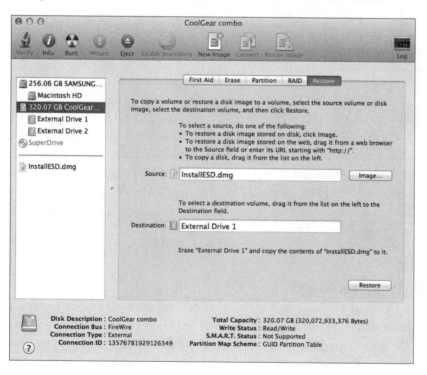

7 Drag the InstallESD.dmg file from the Finder to the Source field in the Disk Utility window. Again, the example screenshot shows this.

8 Click the Restore button and then the subsequent Erase button. Finally, authenticate as an administrative user to create a Lion Restore drive.

The restore process can take anywhere from just a few minutes to half an hour depending on the speed of your external drive. Note the amount of time it takes to create the Lion Restore HD. If it takes more than a few minutes, the drive you've selected is relatively slow and ultimately not a good choice for this task.

Again, you should test your Lion Recovery drive before you put it into "rotation." When you create a Lion Recovery drive using this method, it will be named Mac OS Install ESD. To test, simply select it in the Startup Disk preferences and then restart the Mac. Upon startup, it should behave just like a normal Lion Recovery system by presenting you with the Mac OS X Utilities window. To return to your primary system, close the Mac OS X Utilities window to reselect your primary startup disk.

Using Setup Assistant

If you are using a brand-new Mac for the first time or you have just installed Lion on a drive or partition with no previous system, you will be presented with the Setup Assistant. The Setup Assistant will guide you through the preliminary configuration required to use a new system. Any of the configurations made while using the Setup Assistant can be easily changed later by accessing the appropriate preferences.

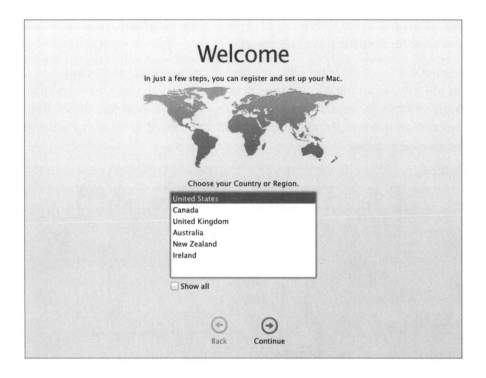

NOTE ▶ If you pause for a few moments at the Startup Assistant Welcome screen, the VoiceOver tutorial will begin. This is an optional tutorial that explains how to use the VoiceOver assistance technology designed for people who are visually impaired. VoiceOver will be further discussed in Chapter 5, "Applications and Processes."

First you will choose the primary language. This ensures that the applications on your system use appropriate language and dialect. At the Setup Assistant Welcome screen, you'll need to choose a country or region to continue. This information is used to complete the registration process. At this point you will also select the primary keyboard layout.

TIP ▶ Both language and keyboard layout settings can be changed later from the Language & Text preferences.

Setup: Network Settings

The Setup Assistant will attempt to establish a connection to the Internet by automatically configuring the Mac's network settings. It will first attempt to automatically detect the network settings via DHCP on a wired Ethernet network. If it finds an Internet connection via wired Ethernet, you won't be prompted to set up networking, and the Setup Assistant will move on to the Migration Assistant process.

If you are not connected via wired Ethernet, you will see a configuration screen. The assistant will try to figure out which type of network connection you need to set up first and present you with the appropriate configuration screen. On most Macs this will be the Wi-Fi network setup screen. From here you can select a wireless network and authenticate to that network if required.

For other network types, you can click the Other Network Options button and choose a different connection type to configure. Only one active network connection needs configuration to enable the Setup Assistant to move on with the setup. If you decide to manually configure one of the network settings, your choices will vary depending on your Mac's hardware capabilities. Alternatively, you can select the "My computer does not connect to the Internet" button, which also enables the Setup Assistant to move on. You don't have to set up networking at this point, and you can do so at any time from the Network preferences.

> **MORE INFO** ▶ Network configuration concepts will be further discussed in Chapter 6, "Network Configuration."

Migration Assistant

After you select an appropriate language and network configuration, the Setup Assistant switches to the Migration Assistant. If you are migrating from a previous system, the Migration Assistant is a huge time-saver. It enables you to easily transfer all the settings, user accounts, and data from another system to your new system. While previous versions of Mac OS X could migrate from other Macs, Lion's Migration Assistant can also migrate data from a Windows PC.

> **NOTE** ▶ You can use the Migration Assistant at any time after the initial setup by opening /Applications/Utilities/Migration Assistant.

> **NOTE** ▶ When using the Migration Assistant after setup, you cannot migrate Legacy FileVault-protected home folders; to migrate them with Migration Assistant, you must do it during the initial system setup.

> **NOTE** ▶ Always run Apple Software Update on computers you are about to migrate from. This ensures they have the latest copy of the Migration Assistant application.

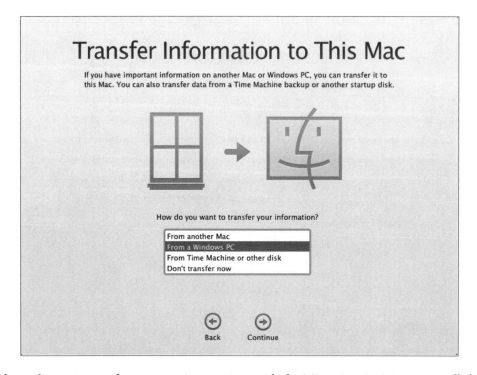

If you choose to transfer your previous settings with the Migration Assistant, you will skip several steps of the Setup Assistant configuration process. If you do not have a previous system to migrate from, simply leave the default choice of "Do not transfer my information now" and click Continue to proceed with the Setup Assistant.

However, if you choose to use Migration Assistant, you can migrate:

▶   From another Mac—This option will scan the local network looking for other Macs running Migration Assistant and ready to transfer their information. If you don't have a local network, you can directly connect two running Macs via Ethernet or FireWire, and they will create a local network, with each other. You will find Migration Assistant in the /Applications/Utilities/ folder on Macs running Mac OS X v10.4 Tiger or later. To migrate from any previous version of Mac OS X, you should always install all available Apple software updates to ensure they include the latest version of Migration Assistant.

MORE INFO ▶ See Knowledge Base document HT4413, "How to use Migration Assistant to transfer files from another Mac."

▶   From a Windows PC—This option will scan the local network looking for other Windows PCs running Migration Assistant and ready to transfer their information.

Lion can migrate from Windows XP SP3 or greater, assuming those systems have Windows Migration Assistant installed; it can be downloaded from Apple's support website.

MORE INFO ▶ See Knowledge Base document HT4796, "OS X Lion: About Windows Migration Assistant."

▶ From Time Machine or another disk—This option will scan all locally mounted drives and the local network looking for Time Machine backups. It will also scan all locally mounted drives for a previous system. This includes external drives or other Macs in target disk mode connected via USB, FireWire, or Thunderbolt.

MORE INFO ▶ To engage target disk mode on your previous Mac, start the Mac up while holding the T key. Using target disk mode is further detailed in Chapter 3, "File Systems."

When the Migration Assistant finds another system or Time Machine backup, it scans the contents and presents you with a list of available items to migrate. If the Migration Assistant discovers multiple system drives or archives, you must select the specific system you wish to migrate from the Information pop-up menu.

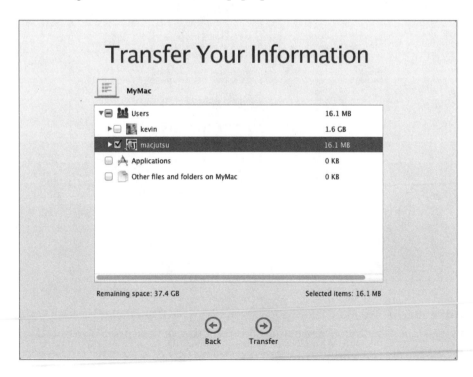

NOTE ▶ If multiple drives are available on a system, you can choose to migrate that data as well. However, the migration process does not create new partitions on the new system; instead, it creates folders on the new system with the contents of the migrated drives.

Once you make your selections, you can begin the transfer process. The more data you have selected to transfer, the longer the process will take. Mature systems with lots of data can take several hours to migrate. After completing the migration, you will be presented with the Setup Assistant Registration and Finishing Up screens, as covered in this section.

Setup: Registration Process

The registration process, though not required, is an important part of system setup. If you're connected to the Internet at this point, the registration process will send the registration information to Apple. An Apple ID is the login you will use for all Apple online services, including access to the Apple Support pages and the iTunes and Mac App stores. An Apple ID is free to set up.

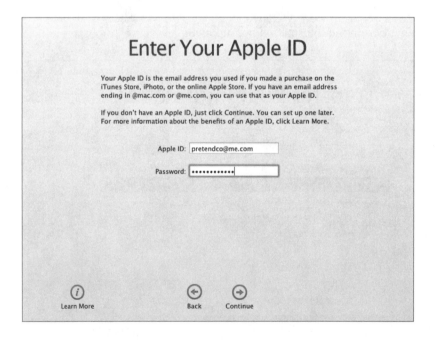

MORE INFO ▶ For more information about the Apple ID or the registration process, click the Learn More button. You can also visit the Apple ID website at https://appleid.apple.com/.

If you do not want to complete the registration process during the initial setup, you can skip it now by leaving the fields blank and clicking the Continue button through the next few screens. You can also cancel the registration process at any point with the keyboard shortcut Command-Q, and then click the Skip button when the Cancel Registration dialog appears. Remember, you can always complete it later by visiting www.apple.com/register.

NOTE ▶ Attempting to use the Command-Q keyboard shortcut while viewing non-registration screens in the Setup Assistant will not allow you to skip those screens. Instead, you will be forced to shut down or continue.

Setup: Initial Account Creation

After registration you will be presented with the most important part of the setup process, the Create Your Account screen. From this screen you must create the initial administrative user account to continue the Setup Assistant process. The account you create here will be the only administrative user account initially allowed to modify all system settings, including the creation of additional user accounts. Therefore, until you create additional administrative user accounts, it is important that you remember the authentication information for this first account.

MORE INFO ▶ User accounts will be further discussed in Chapter 2, "User Accounts."

Create Your Computer Account

Enter a name and password to create your computer account. You need this password to administer your computer, change settings, and install software.

Full Name: Local Admin

Account Name: ladmin

This will be used as the name for your home folder and can't be changed.

Password: ••••••••

Verify: ••••••••

☑ Require password when logging in.

Password Hint:

Enter a hint to help you remember your password. Anyone can see the hint, so choose a hint that won't make it easy to guess your password.

Back   Continue

To create the initial administrative user account:

1   Enter a long user name. This name can contain nearly any alphanumeric character.

2   Enter an account name. This name cannot contain any spaces, capitals, or special characters.

3   Enter the password twice (not three times) to verify it was typed correctly.

4   Only enter a password hint if you think you may forget this password.

The password hint should not match your password.

5   Once you have double-checked your work, click the Continue button to create the new account.

If you didn't set a password hint, the system will advise you to set one. You can set one now or simply leave it blank and click the Continue button.

6   If your Mac is attached to or includes an iSight camera, you will be prompted to take a snapshot as a picture for the account.

You can also choose a picture from the library if you're camera shy.

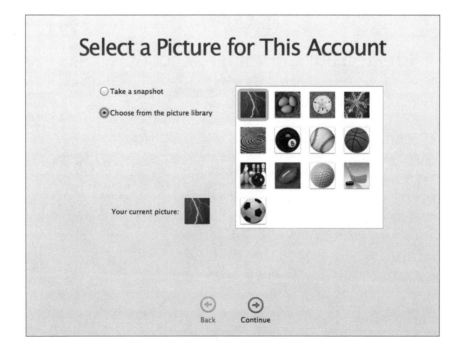

Setup: Time Zone

You're almost done; at this point in the Setup Assistant process you must configure your Mac's time zone settings. Lion features automatic time zone selection if your Mac includes a Wi-Fi card and is connected to the Internet. Select the checkbox at the top of the Select Time Zone screen and the Mac will automatically locate your closest time zone by connecting to an Internet database that tracks networks and their geographical location. If the system is able to locate your closest city and time zone, click Continue to complete the setup. The Mac will also automatically connect to Apple's time servers to set the date and time.

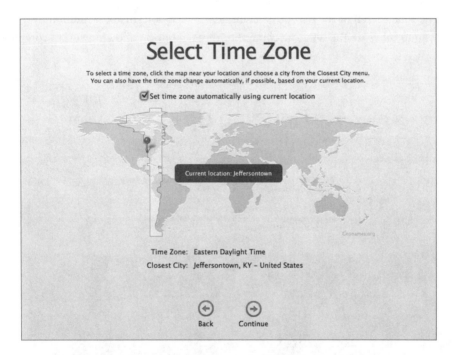

If your Mac isn't connected to the Internet at this point, you will have to manually select a time zone. Even when not connected to the Internet, Lion features a time zone selector with a large database of locations. You can either approximate your location by clicking on the map, or you can enter a city name in the field. Try your closest city first, as even small cities are part of the database. If your first choice isn't found, try a larger city in your time zone but still try to stay as local as possible.

TIP Time zone, date, and time settings can all be reconfigured via the Date & Time preferences.

Setup: Finishing Up

One final Setup Assistant screen will appear if your Mac has a Multi-Touch trackpad or Magic Mouse. In what may be considered the ultimate homage to iOS in Lion, scrolling now mimics that on Apple's touch devices. Moving your finger(s) up moves the scrolling content up as well, and vice versa for down. If you think about this new method from the perspective of "imagine your finger is pushing the screen content around," Apple's new "natural" scrolling makes sense. With the legacy method, you scroll down to move the content up; thus the traditional scroll wheel has actually always been vertically inverted.

At any rate, Apple clearly wants you to adopt "natural" scrolling, as Lion defaults to this method. The final screen of the Setup Assistant helps teach you this new method by requiring you to move up the window content to reveal a button allowing you to complete the setup process.

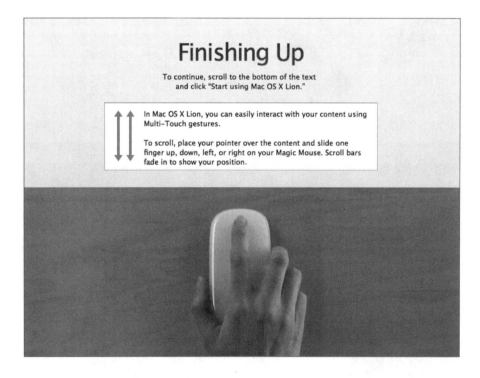

TIP ▶ You can revert scrolling back to the legacy method in the Mouse and Trackpad preferences.

Configuring System Settings

Once your Mac has completed its initial configuration via Setup Assistant, you will rely on various system tools for administration and troubleshooting. In this section you will learn about the fundamental Lion configuration application, System Preferences, and how to gather essential system information with the About This Mac dialog and the System Information application.

Using System Preferences

The System Preferences application is the primary interface for adjusting user and system settings. (In other operating systems these settings would be accessed using control panels.) You will use System Preferences throughout this book and any time you are setting up a new Mac. The quickest access to System Preferences is via the Apple menu, because it's always available from any application that shows the menu bar.

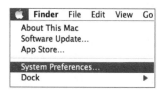

TIP ▶ The System Preferences application can also be found in the /Applications folder. You can use any shortcut method you like to access the System Preferences application, including using its icon in the Dock and placing it in the Finder sidebar.

The first time you access System Preferences, you'll notice it is divided into four separate rows representing the four main categories of System Preferences: Personal, Hardware, Internet & Wireless, and System. Any third-party preference panes you install will appear automatically in a fifth row categorized as simply Other.

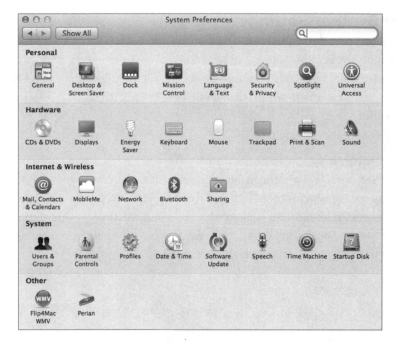

The categorization of the individual System Preferences is deliberate:

▶ Personal—These preferences panes will generally only affect settings for the active user account. In other words, for most of the System Preferences in this category, each user has his own discrete settings.

▶ Hardware—These preferences panes are specific to hardware settings. For example, the Energy Saver and Print & Scan preferences in this category can affect every user on the Mac, and thus they require administrator user access to make changes.

▶ Internet & Wireless—These preferences panes are used to configure various network-related services. The Network preferences pane is the primary interface for managing your Mac's network and Internet configuration. Also, the Network and Sharing preferences in this category can affect every user on the Mac, and thus they require administrative access to make changes.

▶ System—These preferences panes have a systemwide effect when changed. Consequently, all of the preferences in this category require administrative access.

▶ Others (optional)—There is no Apple-imposed order to the classification of these preferences panes other than they are not part of the standard Lion installation. The developers of third-party preferences decide whether their preferences require administrative access.

Accessing a set of preferences is as simple as clicking once on the icon. Most System Preferences changes are instantaneous and don't require you to click an Apply or OK button. Clicking the Show All button in the upper-left corner returns you to the view of all System Preferences. Clicking and holding this button will reveal a pop-up menu of all the System Preferences.

If you're not sure where a specific feature setting is located in the various preferences, you can use the Spotlight search field in the upper-right corner to quickly locate the hidden setting.

You'll notice that some preferences have a lock in the bottom-left corner. These can be accessed only by an administrative user account. If a set of preferences you need to access is locked from editing, simply click the lock icon, and then authenticate as an administrative user to unlock it.

NOTE ▶ The lock icon is a general indication that access to the item requires administrative authentication. The lock icon shows up in a variety of places, not just in System Preferences.

Information About Your Mac

Knowledge of your Mac's specifications is always important when installing new software, updating installed software, performing maintenance, or troubleshooting a problem. Your first stop to discovering a Mac's specifications is the About This Mac dialog. You can open this dialog at any point by choosing About This Mac from the Apple menu.

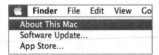

Initially, the About This Mac dialog will show you the Mac's system software version, processor type and speed, total system memory, and current startup disk. You can also find the system build identifier and hardware serial number by repeatedly clicking the system version number directly below the bold "Mac OS X" text:

▶ System version number—This number represents the specific system software version currently installed on the Mac. The first part, 10, obviously represents the tenth generation of the Mac operating system. The second digit, 7, represents the seventh major release of Mac OS X. The final digit, if any, represents an incremental update to the operating system. Incremental updates generally offer very few feature changes but often include a number of bug fixes.

▶ System build number—This is an even more granular representation of the specific system software version currently installed on the Mac. Apple engineers create hundreds of versions of each system software release as they refine the product. The build number is used to track this process. Also, you may find that the computer-specific builds of Mac OS X that come preinstalled on new Mac hardware will differ from the standard installation builds. This is an important detail to note if you are creating system images for mass distribution, as computer-specific builds of Mac OS X may not work on other types of Mac hardware.

▶ Hardware serial number—The hardware serial number is also located somewhere on the Mac's case. However, Apple has a tendency to choose form over function, so the serial number may be quite difficult to find. As with many other complicated products, the Mac's serial number is a unique number used to identify that particular Mac for maintenance and service issues.

TIP ▶ This information, along with other useful information, is also available at the login screen by clicking just below the words "Mac OS X." This allows you to check a Mac's vital statistics quickly, without even having to log in first.

TIP ▶ Macs that have had their logic boards replaced may not properly display the serial number in the About This Mac dialog.

Examining System Information

The information in the About This Mac dialog is only the tip of the iceberg compared with what can be found via the System Information (formerly System Profiler) application. From the About This Mac dialog, click the More Info button to open System Information. If you open System Information via this method, you will be presented with a more informative About This Mac window, a new feature of Lion.

From the System Information About This Mac window, you can view a bit more detail about your Mac, including its primary specifications, display configuration, storage allocation, and installed memory. Quite possibly the best feature of this new window is the Support and Service buttons to the far right that link directly to specifically useful areas of Apple's support and service websites.

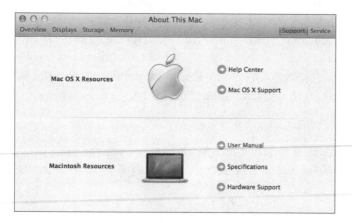

To examine the full gamut of what System Information offers, return to the Overview section of the About This Mac window and click the System Report button. This will open a new System Information window revealing all available reporting options.

You will use System Information to locate critical system details in nearly every chapter of this book. Additionally, one of the most important uses of System Information is as a documentation tool. Anytime you need to document the current state of a Mac, you can use System Information to create a detailed system report. To create this report while in System Information, simply choose Export As Text from the File menu.

> **TIP** The System Information application can also be found in the /Applications/ Utilities folder. You can use any shortcut method you like to access the System Information application, including placing it in the Dock and the Finder sidebar.

> **TIP** You can also directly access System Information from the Apple menu by holding the Option key. This changes the About This Mac Apple menu choice to System Information.

> **TIP** When opening System Information directly, you will skip the summary About This Mac window and instead be presented with the full system report.

Install Software and Updates

Adding new capabilities is the very reason "software" exists. It's expected that you will add new applications to increase the capabilities of your Mac and, as products are refined, new software updates as well. In this section you will look at the primary installation technology in Lion, the Installer application. This application can be used to install Apple software and updates and many third-party software titles. You will also look at the built-in Apple software update technology, which is an automatic method to keep all your Apple software up-to-date.

Using the Installer Application

A great feature of Lion is the relative ease with which most new software is installed. In fact, many applications require only that the user copy a single application file to the local system drive. At the same time, more complicated software may require multiple resources placed at a variety of specific locations on your Mac. A prime example of a complicated software installation is any system software update.

> **TIP** ▶ You have the option of manually downloading and installing Apple software updates. You can find all Apple updates at http://support.apple.com/downloads/. Once downloaded, you will use the Installer application to apply the update.

The Installer application makes complicated application installations simple. Often, software developers will create an "installer package" with all the instructions necessary for the Installer application to set up the new software on your system.

> **MORE INFO** ▶ Though covered briefly here, installing applications will be further discussed in Chapter 5, "Applications and Processes."

BrotherPrinter
Drivers.pkg

Double-clicking one of these software installer packages will open the Installer application and begin the installation process. Much like the Lion installation process, the Installer application will guide you through the steps necessary to install or update software.

This may include agreeing to software licenses, selecting a destination, selecting package options, and authenticating as an administrative user.

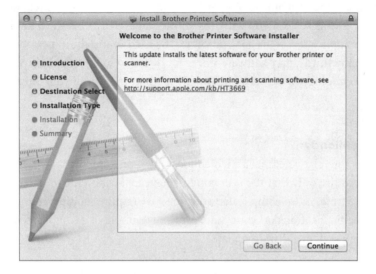

NOTE ▶ Third-party software developers may choose to use a proprietary non-Apple installer for their product. These installers will behave differently than the Apple Installer.

NOTE ▶ Proceed with caution if an installer requires you to authenticate as an administrative user. These installers need administrative access so they can make changes that modify parts of the system that may affect all users.

Advanced Installer Features

If you're curious about what an installation package is actually doing to your Mac, you have two ways to find out. First, you can view the Installer log at any time while using the Installer application by choosing Window > Installer Log or using the Command-L keyboard shortcut. The Installer log is a live view of any progress or errors reported during the installation process.

MORE INFO ▶ Accessing the Installer log is covered in the "Using the Installer Log" section earlier in this chapter.

If you want to inspect an installer package before installing the application, you can do so, but not using the Installer log. After passing the initial installation welcome screens and agreeing to any software license agreements while using the Installer application, you can preview the list of files to be installed by choosing File > Show Files from the menu bar or using the Command-I keyboard shortcut.

TIP ▶ Save time looking for what you need by using the Spotlight search field in the toolbar when examining the Installer log or file list.

With Mac OS X v10.5, Apple introduced a few new significant Installer application features. For starters, users may specify their home folder as the installation destination for applications that allow it. Apple also introduced a dynamic installation package that remains up-to-date as long as the Mac has Internet access. Network-based installation packages automatically download the latest software from a vendor's servers during the installation process.

Finally, Apple increased the security and reliability of software installation packages by supporting signed packages. These packages contain special code used to validate the authenticity and completeness of the software during installation. This makes it nearly impossible for nefarious hackers to insert illegitimate files in trusted installation packages. You can identify a signed installer package by a small certificate icon in the far right of the installer window title bar. Clicking this icon reveals details about the signed package, including its certificate status.

Using Apple Software Update

Keeping current with software updates is an important part of maintaining a healthy Mac. Fortunately, Lion includes an easy-to-use Software Update application that automatically checks Apple's servers via the Internet to make sure you're running the latest Apple software. Automatic Software Update checking is enabled by default the first moment you start using your Mac. If an update is detected, it will be downloaded in the background, and you will be presented with a Software Update dialog.

You have three choices when presented with this dialog:

▶   Click the Show Details button to open the full Software Update, so you can further inspect all the available updates, as covered in the next section of this chapter.

▶   Click the Not Now button to dismiss the automatic update until the next scheduled update check.

▶ Click the Install button, and then authenticate as an administrative user to have the updates install immediately.

NOTE ▶ An Internet connection is required to use Software Update for both automatic and manual updates. Also, the Software Update application checks only for updates of currently installed Apple software. Finally, some software updates require that you also agree to the Apple Software License Agreement.

You can manually open the Software Update application to check for updates at any time via any of the following methods:

▶ Choose Software Update from the Apple menu.

▶ Click the Check Now button in the Software Update preferences.

▶ Click the Software Update button in the About This Mac dialog.

TIP ▶ The Software Update application can also be found in the /System/Library/ CoreServices folder. You can use any shortcut method you like to access the Software Update application, including placing it in the Dock and the Finder sidebar.

When you choose to have Software Update install new software for you, it will do so in one of two ways. First, if the new software does not require a restart for installation, the software will automatically install without any further user interaction. But if the new software requires a restart after the install process, you will be presented with a dialog featuring a Log Out and Install button. You can, of course, choose to install these updates later, but you will eventually have to restart to take advantage of the new software.

Software Update Details

When Software Update opens to show you new updates, selecting the Show Details button reveals its full interface. This allows you to individually inspect all the available Apple software updates. The information provided includes the update name, version, file size, and a detailed description. You will also be able to deselect and ignore updates that you do not wish to install.

TIP ▶ Updates in the list that require a restart will have a small gray icon of a triangle inside a circle next to their name.

If you don't want to be reminded of a particular update again, you can choose to ignore the update by selecting it from the list of available updates and then choosing Update > Ignore Update from the menu bar. You can bring back all ignored updates by choosing Software Update > Reset Ignored Updates, which appears only after you have ignored an update.

Also from this menu you can open a web browser to Apple's downloads website. With Lion, this is the only official method for saving an Apple update installer. This is unlike previous versions of Mac OS X, which allowed you to download updates from within Software Update. Updates downloaded from Apple can be installed by the Installer application or any other application that can process Apple installation packages, such as Apple Remote Desktop.

Software Update Preferences
The Software Update preferences, accessed via System Preferences, enable you to adjust the schedule of automatic software updates and review previously installed updates.

The default view is the Scheduled Check pane; from here you can:

▶ Click the Check Now button to manually open Software Update.

▶ Enable or disable automatic software updates by toggling the "Check for updates" checkbox.

▶ Adjust the frequency of automatic updates using the Check for Updates pop-up menu.

▶ Enable or disable the automatic download of updates by toggling the "Download updates automatically" checkbox.

> **NOTE** ▶ The Software Update schedule is saved separately for each user of a Mac. Thus another user's account may automatically download updates even when your account has them disabled.

> **NOTE** ▶ Software Update requires authentication as an administrative user to complete the installation of any automatically downloaded updates. In other words, standard user accounts are not allowed to install updates from Software Update.

When you select the Installed Software tab, you can investigate previously installed Apple software updates. You will be able to view the name, version, and date installed for any software update. It's important to know that this interface shows only Apple software that was installed after the system installation, although it shows both manually and automatically installed Apple software. You can view the full Installer log from the Console application as covered in the "Using the Installer Log" section of this chapter.

What You've Learned

▶ Upgrading to Lion requires a Mac computer with an Intel Core 2 Duo, Core i3, Core i5, Core i7, or Xeon processor, 2 GB of memory, Mac OS X v10.6.6 or later (v10.6.8 recommended), and 7 GB of available disk space.

▶ The Lion Installer guides you through system installation.

▶ The Lion Recovery system includes a variety of administration and troubleshooting utilities.

▶ The Setup Assistant guides you through the initial configuration of your Mac system.

▶ The Migration Assistant can be used to easily transfer user accounts, settings, and data from a previous system.

▶ Apple provides updates to Lion through the Software Update service. To ensure that your system is up-to-date, run Software Update on a regular basis.

References

You can check for new and updated Knowledge Base documents at www.apple.com/support.

Firmware and Startup

HT2568, "Determining BootROM or firmware version"

HT1237, "EFI and SMC firmware updates for Intel-based Macs"

HT2213, "About the Firmware Restoration CD (Intel-based Macs)"

HT1352, "Setting up firmware password protection in Mac OS X"

HT1310, "Startup Manager: How to select a startup volume"

System Installation

TS3925, "OS X Lion: Unable to download OS X Lion wirelessly from Mac App Store – 'Your device or computer could not be verified' "

HT2681, "What's a 'Computer-Specific Mac OS X Release'?"

HT2186, "Don't install a version of Mac OS X earlier than what came with your Mac"

HT3258, "Mac OS X v10.6, OS X Lion: About incompatible software"

TS2986, "Mac OS X v10.6, OS X Lion: Cannot install Mac OS X v10.6 or later on a volume used by Time Machine for backups"

HT4649, "OS X Lion: 'Some features of Mac OS X Lion are not supported for the disk (volume name)' appears during installation"

TS3926, "OS X Lion: Installer reports 'This disk cannot be used to start up your computer'"

HT4718, "OS X Lion: About Lion Recovery"

HT4796, "OS X Lion: About Windows Migration Assistant"

DL1433, "Lion Recovery Disk Assistant"

HT1222, "Apple security updates"

URLs

Full Lion features list: www.apple.com/macosx/whats-new/features.html

Lion detailed technical specifications: www.apple.com/macosx/specs.html

Apple's software downloads: http://support.apple.com/downloads

Main Lion support website: www.apple.com/support/lion

Apple ID website: https://appleid.apple.com/

Apple product registration: www.apple.com/register

Review Quiz

1. What are the minimum hardware requirements for upgrading a system with Lion?

2. What seven preparation steps must you take before upgrading a system with Lion?

3. How can you identify if a Mac requires a firmware update?

4. What are the advantages and disadvantages of using a single-partition drive with Mac OS X? How about a multiple-partition drive?

5. What utilities are available when started up from Lion Recovery?

6. Where can you locate the system version number, build number, and serial number? What is the significance of these numbers?

7. How do the four default System Preferences categories differ?

8. How do you ensure that you have the latest Apple software?

Answers

1. The minimum requirements for upgrading Lion are:

    A Mac with an Intel Core 2 Duo, Core i3, Core i5, Core i7, or Xeon processor

    2 GB of memory

    Mac OS X v10.6.6 or later (v10.6.8 recommended)

    7 GB of available disk space

    Some features require an Apple ID; terms apply

    Some features require a compatible Internet service provider; fees may apply

2. Seven steps you should take before upgrading a system to Lion are to plug portable Macs into main power, run Apple Software Update, check for firmware updates, verify application compatibility, back up important files and folders, document critical settings, and keep up-to-date by visiting Apple's Lion support website.

3. You can identify a Mac's firmware version by opening the full system report in the System Information application. You can verify if a Mac's firmware is up-to-date by visiting Apple's support website, which maintains a list of available firmware updates.

4. Single-partition drives are easier to set up initially, but they aren't as flexible for administration and maintenance. Multiple-partition drives require repartitioning during setup but provide several separate partitions, which can be used to segregate user data and host multiple operating systems.

5. The Lion Recovery system provides access to Restore System From Time Machine Backup, Reinstall Mac OS X, Get Help Online via Safari, Disk Utility, Startup Disk, Firmware Password Utility, Terminal, Reset Password, System Information, and Network Utility.

6. The system version, build number, and hardware serial number are located in the About This Mac dialog or the login screen. The system version number defines the specific version of Mac OS X currently installed. The system build number is an even more specific identifier used primarily by developers. Finally, the hardware serial number is a unique number used to identify your specific Mac.

7. Generally, Personal preferences affect only a single user, Hardware preferences adjust hardware and peripheral settings, Internet & Wireless preferences affect personal and system network settings, and System preferences affect all users and often require administrative access.

8. The Software Update application checks for Apple software updates via the Internet. You can adjust automatic update settings or manually open the Software Update application from the Software Update preferences.

2

Time   This chapter takes approximately 2 hours to complete.

Goals   Recognize various user account types and user attributes

Create and manage user accounts and home folders

Understand and implement user security techniques

Resolve issues that prevent users from accessing their accounts

Chapter **2**

User Accounts

One of the hallmarks of a modern operating system is support for multiple user accounts. Lion delivers this in spades with a robust, secure, and highly polished multiuser environment. Lion's UNIX foundation is the root of this sophisticated multiple-user environment. UNIX operating systems have a long history of providing such services. Apple has made many improvements to the UNIX functionality by providing advanced user management features and streamlined administration tools, all with Apple's traditional ease of use.

In this chapter, you will explore the technologies that allow individuals to log in and use the Mac. You will also learn how to create and manage multiple user accounts in Lion. Finally, you will learn account security and troubleshooting techniques.

Understanding User Accounts

Mac users have been known to identify their beloved computer with a pet name; nevertheless, your Mac absolutely identifies you via a user account. With the exception of the rarely used single-user mode, you are required to log in with a user account to perform any task on the Mac. Even if the Mac is sitting at the login window and you haven't yet authenticated, the system is still using a handful of system user accounts to maintain background services. Every single file and folder on a Mac's hard drive, every item and process, belongs to some user account. Consequently, a thorough understanding of user accounts is necessary to effectively administer and troubleshoot Lion.

NOTE ▶ Unlike previous versions of Mac OS X, Lion defaults to requiring a user login even if there is only a single user account created for the system. This setting enhances security, as it requires every user to log in. Further, training the user to log in every time the computer restarts is important if the user is to enable FileVault 2, which requires the user to log in on startup.

NOTE ▶ This chapter focuses on user accounts that are available only to a single local Mac. Network user accounts, on the other hand, are available to multiple Macs and are hosted from shared servers. Network user accounts are briefly covered in Chapter 7, "Network Services."

User Account Types

The majority of home Mac users are only aware of, and therefore only use, the account created when the Mac was initially set up with the Setup Assistant. Apple has engineered Lion to mimic a single-user operating system by default. However, Lion supports multiple simultaneous user accounts. The system also supports several types of user accounts to facilitate different levels of access. Essentially, you choose a specific account type to grant a defined level of access that best meets the user's requirements. User accounts are categorized into one of five types: standard users, administrative users, the guest user, sharing only users, and the root user.

Standard Users

Ideally, standard is the account type most should use on a daily basis. Standard accounts are also commonly used when multiple people share a computer. This is because the standard account strikes the best balance between usability and security. Standard users are members of the "staff" group and have read access to most items, preferences, applications, and other users' Public and Sites folders. Yet they are only allowed to make changes to personal preferences and items inside their own home folders. Standard users are not allowed to make changes to systemwide preferences, system files, or anything that might affect another user's account.

> **TIP** ▶ Standard users can be further restricted using parental controls. The account type known as managed is a standard account with parental controls enabled, as covered later in this chapter.

Administrative Users

Administrative users aren't much different from regular users, save for one important distinction: Administrative users are part of the "admin" group and are allowed full access to almost all applications, preferences, and most system files. By default, administrative users do not have access to protected system files or other users' files outside the Public and Sites folders. Despite this, administrative users can bypass these restrictions in both the graphical environment and using Terminal if needed. For example, administrative users are allowed to update system software as long as they successfully authenticate when the installer application asks for authorization.

Because administrative access is required to make changes to the system, this is the default account type for the initial account created when Lion is set up for the first time with the Setup Assistant. Additional standard user accounts can be created for daily use, but the Mac should have access to at least one administrative account.

Guest User

Previous versions of Mac OS X use only the guest account to facilitate file sharing by allowing nonauthenticated access to users' Public folders. Starting with Mac OS X v10.5, support was added for a full guest user account. Once enabled, the guest user is similar to a nonadministrative user but without a password. Anyone with access to the Mac can use it to log in. However, when the guest user logs out, the guest user's home folder is deleted. This includes preference files, web browser history, or any other trace that the user might have left on the system. The next time someone logs in as a guest, a brand-new home folder is created for that user.

NOTE ▶ The guest user is enabled by default for file-sharing access only.

Sharing Only Users

Again, starting with Mac OS X v10.5, support was added for special user accounts that have access only to shared files and folders. Sharing only users have no home folder and cannot log in to the Mac's user interface or Terminal. Administrative users can create multiple shared users with unique names and passwords. Sharing users start out with access similar to that of the guest user, with access only to other users' Public folders. Administrative users can, however, define specific shared user access to any folder via the Sharing preferences. File sharing will be further discussed in Chapter 7, "Network Services."

Root User

The root user account, also known as System Administrator, has unlimited access to everything on the Mac. The root user can read, write, and delete any file; can modify any setting; and can install any software. To help prevent abuse of this account, by default no one is allowed to log in as root, as a password hasn't been set for the root user. Since many system processes run as the root user, it needs to exist on the system; otherwise, Lion wouldn't be able to start up. The root user is covered in greater detail in "Essential Account Security," later in this chapter.

User Account Attributes

Although the login window enables you to log in to the Mac environment, the Open Directory system is responsible for maintaining the account information. Open Directory stores local user account information in a series of XML-encoded text files located in the /var/db/dslocal/nodes/Default/users folder. This folder is only readable by the System Administrator (root) account, but if you were to inspect these files, you would discover that they are organized into lists of user attributes and their associated values. Each user has a variety of attributes that define the account details. All of the attributes are important, but for the scope of this chapter you need only be familiar with the primary user account attributes:

▶ Full name—This is the full name of the user. It can be quite long and contain nearly any character. However, no other account on the system can have the same full name. You can easily change the full name later at any point.

▶ Alias names—These names are used to associate the local Mac user account with other service accounts. For example, a user's Apple ID can be associated with a local account. This attribute is optional for Lion, but it is required for integration with Apple Internet services like iCloud and Back to My Mac.

▶ Account name—Sometimes also referred to as "short name," this is the name used to uniquely identify the account and by default is also used to name the user's home folder. A user can use either the full name or the account name interchangeably to authenticate. However, no other account on the system can have the same account name, and it cannot contain any special characters or spaces. Special characters not allowed include commas, slashes, colons or semicolons, brackets, quotes, and symbols. Allowed characters include dashes, underscores, and periods.

▶ User ID—This is a numeric attribute used to identify the account with file and folder ownership. This number is almost always unique to each account on a single system, though overlaps are possible. User accounts start at 501, while most system accounts are below 100. It's important to note that the user ID is only "unique" to other users on the local system. Every other Mac uses similar ID numbers, so between Macs this uniqueness is lost. For example, every first user created on a Mac will have the ID number 501. Further, if you delete a user, that user's ID is now up for grabs and the system will reuse the ID for new users.

▶ Universally Unique ID (UUID)—Sometimes also referred to as Generated UID or GUID, this alphanumeric attribute is generated by the computer during account creation and is unique in both space and time: Once created, no Mac system anywhere will ever create an account with the same UUID. It is used to reference the user's password and for group membership and file permissions. It's important to note that while UUIDs may be truly unique, a Mac won't be able to identify another Mac's UUIDs. In other words, UUIDs created on one Mac are not known by another Mac. Thus, locally created UUIDs cannot be used between Macs for mutual identification.

▶ Group—This is a numeric attribute used to associate the user with a default group. As covered previously, the default for most users is 20, which is associated with the staff group. This means that when you create a new file, it belongs to your user account and to the staff group.

▶ Login shell—This file path defines the default command-line shell used in Terminal by the account. Any user who is allowed to use the command line in Terminal has this set to /bin/bash by default. Both administrative and standard users are given this access by default.

▶ Home directory—This file path defines the location of the user's home folder. All users except for sharing users, who do not have home folders, have this set to /Users/<name>, where <name> is the account name.

NOTE ▶ Account passwords are stored separately from the rest of the account attributes to enhance security. Password storage is covered in greater detail in "Essential Account Security," later in this chapter.

Managing User Accounts

Now that you have an understanding of the user account types and primary attributes used by Lion, it's time to get down to the task of managing user accounts.

Creating New User Accounts

To create new user accounts:

1   Open the Users & Groups preferences by choosing Apple menu > System Preferences, then clicking the Users & Groups icon.

2   Click the lock icon in the bottom-left corner and authenticate as an administrative user to unlock the Users & Groups preferences.

3   Click the plus button below the user list to reveal the account creation dialog.

4   Choose the appropriate account type from the New Account pop-up menu.

At a minimum, complete the Full Name and Account name fields. A password is not required, but it's highly recommended that you choose a nontrivial password. Passwords and system security are covered in "Essential Account Security," later in this chapter.

Password hints are not required either, but they are recommended if you are forgetful of such things. Password hints are revealed at the login screen after three failed attempts.

5   Click the Create User button to have the system create the user account.

6   Optionally, in Lion you can associate an Apple ID with the account. This gives users who lost their login password the ability to reset their local account password with their Apple ID.

To enable this, click the Set button, and then enter or create an Apple ID for this user. After you have set an Apple ID, select the "Allow user to reset password using Apple ID" checkbox.

MORE INFO ▸ Details regarding how to reset a user account with an Apple ID are covered in the "Reset a Password at Login" section later in this chapter.

You can easily modify or add attributes at any time by simply selecting the account from the list in the Users & Groups preferences. Additional configurable attributes here include the user picture, associated Address Book card, login items, and parental controls. You can also switch an account between standard and administrative at any time with this dialog.

TIP ▸ The guest user account is also enabled and configured from the Users & Groups preferences.

Managing User Login Items

Most users will find it convenient to have their favorite files or applications open automatically as soon as they log in to the Mac. Lion features a new auto resume feature, which by default, will automatically reopen applications users had running from their last session. However, you can also configure reoccurring login items that will always automatically open after login. You can manage login items for any account that you are currently logged into.

NOTE ▸ When using the Users & Groups preferences, even as an administrative user, you cannot configure login items for other user accounts.

To manage login items:

1   Open the Users & Groups preferences and select your currently logged-in user account. This will appear at the top of the user list under My Account.

2   Click the Login Items tab.

3   Add login items either by clicking the plus button below the Login Items list to reveal a selection dialog or by simply dragging and dropping items from the Finder into the Login Items list.

4   You can delete login items by selecting them and then clicking the minus button.

TIP ▸ Drag and drop a mounted network share from the Finder to the Login Items list to have the Mac automatically connect to the share at login.

TIP ▶ You can temporarily disable the login items from automatically opening by holding down the Shift key as you log in to the Mac.

Using Parental Controls

Lion includes an extensive collection of managed preferences that enable you to further restrict what users can and cannot do. Apple puts these managed preferences under the parental controls moniker, but they are also applicable in a business or institutional setting. As parental controls are designed to further limit standard user accounts, they cannot be applied to an administrative user.

MORE INFO ▶ Parental controls is a limited subset of a much more extensive managed preferences system available when using the OS X Lion Server administration tools. You can find out more about this technology from Apple Training Series: OS X Lion Server Essentials v10.7.

Management options available via parental controls include the following:

▶ Use Simple Finder to simplify the Finder to show only the items most important to your managed user.

▶ Create a list that defines which applications or widgets a user is allowed to open. Users will not be allowed to open any application or widget not specified in the list.

▶ Enable automatic Safari website content filtering, or manually manage a list of permitted websites or a combination of both automatically and manually permitted websites.

▶ Limit Mail and iChat to allow exchanges only with approved addresses.

▶   Set weekday and weekend time usage limits.

▶   Hide profanity in the built-in Dictionary.

▶   Restrict access to printers, password changes, optical media, and the Dock.

▶   Maintain Safari, iChat, and application usage logs. Doing this logs both allowed and attempted but denied access.

   NOTE ▶ Most third-party applications will not honor parental controls' content filters and account limit settings. Examples of unsupported applications include the Firefox browser and Outlook email client. This is, however, easily remedied using the afore-mentioned parental controls application restriction list.

To enable and configure parental controls:

1   Open the Parental Controls preferences and authenticate as an administrative user to unlock its settings.

2   Select the user from the accounts list you wish to manage with parental controls, and then click the Enable Parental Controls button.

3   Select the user you wish to manage from the accounts list and use the tabs to navigate through all the options.

   TIP ▶ You can remove parental controls from a user's account by clicking the Action menu button (the small gear icon) at the bottom of the user list and selecting "Turn off Parental Controls" from the pop-up menu.

TIP ▶ Your Mac's Parental Controls preferences can be managed remotely by another Mac running Lion. To enable this feature in the Parental Controls preferences, click the Action menu button (the small gear icon) at the bottom of the user list to reveal a pop-up menu that lets you choose Allow Remote Setup. From another Mac on the local network, open the Parental Controls preferences, and any Mac allowing this remote control will automatically appear in the user list. You will have to authenticate using an administrator account on the selected Mac to be granted Parental Controls preferences access.

Managing Group Accounts

Essentially, a group account is nothing more than a list of user accounts. Groups are primarily used to allow greater control over file and folder access. Lion uses several dozen built-in groups to facilitate secure system processes and sharing. For instance, all users are members of the staff group, administrative users are also members of the admin group, and the root user has its own group, known as wheel. Using groups to manage sharing will be discussed in Chapter 3, "File Systems."

NOTE ▶ Standard accounts are always members of the staff group, and administrative accounts are always members of the admin group regardless of what is shown in the group membership of the Users & Groups preferences.

NOTE ▶ The Users & Groups preferences can only be used to manage local nonsystem users and groups.

Creating new group accounts is similar to creating new user accounts:

1   Open the Users & Groups preferences and authenticate as an administrative user to unlock its settings.

2   Click the plus button below the user list to reveal the account creation dialog.

3   Choose Group from the New pop-up menu.

4   Enter a group name in the Full Name field and click the Create Group button. You cannot use the same name as that of a group that already exists.

5   Add user accounts to the group by selecting the appropriate checkboxes in the Membership list.

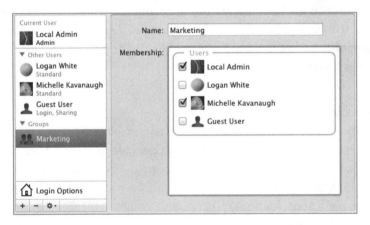

TIP ▶ In Lion, groups can contain other groups as part of their membership. This feature is known as nested groups.

Managing Additional Account Attributes

From the Users & Groups preferences, after authenticating as an administrator, you can also access normally hidden user account attributes by right-clicking or Control-clicking on a user account to reveal the Advanced Options dialog. Although you are allowed to manually edit these attributes to make a desired change or fix a problem, you can just as easily break the account by entering improper information. For example, you can restore access to a user's home folder by correcting the Home Directory information, or you can accidentally prevent a user from accessing her home folder by mistyping this information.

Managing User Home Folders

If you think of a user's account information as his mailing address, then you can think of his home folder as his house and its contents. The directions to his house are certainly important, but it's the stuff inside the house that's really valuable to the owner. The same is true on the Mac. Aside from the initial account attributes, every other item that the user is likely to create or need is stored in that user's home folder. As mentioned earlier, the default location for a locally stored user home folder is /Users/<name>, where <name> is the account name.

NOTE ▶ Network user accounts often have home folders located on a shared server or possibly even a removable disk drive. Network user accounts are briefly covered in Chapter 7, "Network Services."

Understanding Home Folder Contents

Traditional Mac users are notorious for putting personal files anywhere they like with little regard for order. Yet, with every revision of Mac OS X and its included applications, Apple has been coaxing users into a tidier home folder arrangement. Though users can still create additional folders to store their items, most applications will suggest an appropriate default folder, while other applications won't even ask users and simply use the assigned default folder.

All the contents of the default folders inside a user's home folder are only viewable by the user, with the exception of the Public folder. Other users are allowed to view the contents of the Public folder, but they are not allowed to add items or make changes. There is a Drop Box folder inside the Public folder that others are allowed to put files in, but they still cannot see inside this folder. It's important to note that if a user puts other files and folders at the root level of her home folder, by default, other users will be able to view those items. Of course, you can change all of these defaults by adjusting file and folder access permissions as outlined in Chapter 3, "File Systems."

The default items in a Lion Mac user's home folder are:

▶ Desktop—Many an old-school Mac user's files end up right here. This has been the traditional dumping ground for many users' files. Although this practice may be aesthetically unpleasing, there is no reason to stop users from keeping their items here, as it does not slow down or in any way harm the system.

▶ Documents—This is the default storage location for any document type that does not have a dedicated folder. Most famously, Microsoft Office prefers this folder as the default location for all its user documents. Certainly putting items here is the best alternative to cluttering up the desktop.

▶ Downloads—This folder made its premiere in Mac OS X v10.5 as a solution to help prevent desktop clutter. It is the default location for Internet applications to store downloaded files. Sequestering all Internet downloads to this folder also makes it much easier for virus and malware protection utilities to identify potentially harmful files.

▶ Library—Whether a user knows it or not, this folder has become a collection for many user resources. Previous versions of Mac OS X did not hide this folder. In Lion, Apple has chosen to hide this folder, as its use has been deprecated. That means future versions of Mac OS X may not include this folder. While you may not see this folder from the Finder, currently many non-document-type resources end up in the user's Library folder. This includes, but isn't limited to, user-specific preference files, fonts, contacts, keychains, mailboxes, favorites, screen savers, widgets, and countless other application resources.

> **TIP** The quickest method to reveal the user's Library folder is to manually go to the folder in the Finder. While holding the Option key, choose Go > Library from the menu to reveal the hidden user's Library folder. You can learn more about hidden items in Chapter 4, "Data Management."

▶ Movies—This is obviously the default location for movie files, and therefore it is often preferred by applications such as iMovie, iDVD, and iTunes.

▶ Music—This is, naturally, the default location for music files, and therefore it is often preferred by applications such as GarageBand, Logic, and iTunes. It is also the default location for iPhone and iPod Touch applications, which are managed by iTunes.

▶ Pictures—This is the default location for picture files, and therefore it is often preferred by applications such as iPhoto, Aperture, and, once again, iTunes.

▶ Public—This is the default location for users to share files with others. Everyone who has access to a computer locally or via network file sharing can view the contents of this folder. There is a Drop Box folder inside this folder where others can place files that only the owner of the home folder can see.

Optional items commonly found in a Mac user's home folder are:

► Applications—This optional folder must be created manually, but as you can see by its custom icon, the system recognizes this as a special folder. As the name implies, this is the preferred location for users to install their own applications.

► Sites—This is the default location for personal websites when Web Sharing is enabled. This folder was created by default in previous versions of Mac OS X, but in Lion you must create it manually via the Sharing preferences. Outside of viewing these files through a web browser, only other local users can actually browse inside this folder.

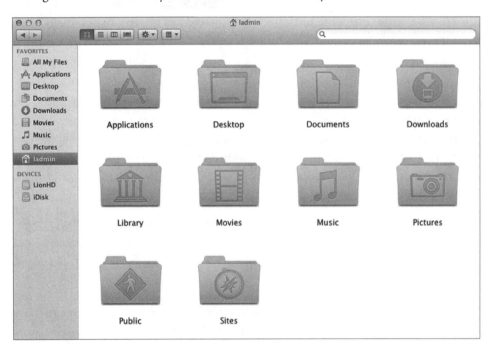

Deleting a User Account

Deleting a user account in Lion is even easier than creating one. To delete a user account, simply select it from the list of users in the Users & Groups preferences, and then click the minus button at the bottom of the list. An administrator need only make one choice when deleting a user account: what to do with the user's home folder contents.

NOTE ► If a user has a particularly large home folder, it may take several minutes for the delete options dialog to appear.

The administrator deleting the user account can choose one of three options:

▶ Save the home folder in a disk image—This option will create an archive of the user's home folder as a disk image file. The disk image file will be saved in the /Users/ Deleted Users folder with the account name as the name of the disk image file. Retaining the home folder as a disk image makes it easy to transport to other systems or import archived items to another user's home folder.

Keep in mind you must have sufficient free disk space available on the local system drive, essentially enough to duplicate the original home folder, to create the archive disk image. This process can take quite a bit of time, depending on the size of the user's home folder.

▶ Don't change the home folder—This will leave the user's folder unchanged save for its name. It will simply append "(Deleted)" to the home folder's name, letting you know the user account no longer exists. The deleted user's home folder will maintain the same access restrictions as a normal user home folder. Subsequently, even though this is a much quicker and more space-efficient method when compared to the archival option, you will have to manually adjust file ownership and permissions to access the items.

▶ Delete the home folder—This will delete the home folder contents immediately. The items will not be stored in a Trash folder before they are deleted, so they will not be easily recoverable using this method.

TIP ▶ The default method used to delete a user's home folder is equivalent to a quick erase. Thus, the contents are potentially recoverable using third-party data forensics tools. Check the "Erase home folder securely" option and the system will perform a secure erase of the user's home folder items. You can learn more about securely erasing items in Chapter 3, "File Systems."

Understanding Migration Assistant

The best method to move or restore a user's account and home folder is with Apple's Migration Assistant. This handy application will do all the hard work for you when it comes to properly moving a user account and home folder from one Mac to another. As covered in the previous chapter, "Installation and Configuration," the Migration Assistant runs as part of the Lion Setup Assistant on new or newly installed Mac systems. However, you can also run this application at any point by opening /Applications/Utilities/Migration Assistant. Once open, the Migration Assistant will walk you through a few easy steps to migrate the data.

In a nutshell, Migration Assistant automates all the steps necessary to migrate individual user accounts, non-system applications, and other non-system resources to a Mac. The migration can occur between two Macs on the same network or directly connected via a Thunderbolt or FireWire cable. Migration Assistant can also restore user accounts from Time Machine backups, either directly connected or via the network or any other drive containing a Mac OS X system. This is useful for when problematic hardware prevents a Mac from starting up but the system drive itself remains functional. In this case you could physically remove the system drive and connect it to another Mac for migration. Lastly, Migration Assistant can copy information from another Windows PC via a local network.

> **MORE INFO** ► The focus of this section is using Migration Assistant to move an account from one Mac to another. For more information about migrating from a Time Machine backup or a Windows PC, refer to Chapter 1, "Installation and Configuration."

As convenient as Migration Assistant is, at times it's not the best solution to move a user account. For example, in certain situations you may need to erase and install a new system to repair or update a Mac. Unfortunately, you can't always count on the user having a recent Time Machine backup of the system. Thus, erasing the system drive would also destroy any user accounts on the Mac. In this case, because you're only working with a single Mac, as opposed to moving from one Mac to another, and you don't have a Time Machine backup, Migration Assistant isn't going to work for you. You will have to manually move the user's home folder.

> **NOTE ▶** Migration Assistant can only migrate a Legacy FileVault-protected user account to a Mac during the initial Setup Assistant process. The Setup Assistant process is covered in the previous chapter, "Installation and Configuration."

> **NOTE ▶** Always run Apple Software Update on computers you are about to migrate from. This ensures they have the latest copy of the Migration Assistant application.

Manually Moving or Restoring a User's Home Folder

If you find yourself in a situation where Migration Assistant won't fit your needs, then you can manually move the user's home folder data. While this doesn't require another Mac, it does require that you temporarily copy the user's home folder to another "backup" storage drive. Once you have additional backup storage available, log into the user's account and, in the Finder, simply drag his home folder to the backup drive. As long as you copy the root of the user's home, the folder with the user's account name, then the Finder should copy the entirety of the user's home in one move.

> **NOTE ▶** If you are creating a copy of another user's home folder content, you will be prompted to authenticate as an administrative user to continue.

Once you are sure you have a complete copy of the user's home folder on the backup storage, you can erase the system drive and repair it. With the new system working in place, you can follow these steps to manually restore the user's home folder data.

NOTE ▶ The proper method to restore a user's home folder manually requires that the user account not yet exist on the system. This is because the system can automatically associate a manually restored home folder with a newly created account.

To manually restore a user's home folder:

1 Log in with an administrative user account that is not associated with the user home folder you're trying to restore.

You can create a temporary administrative user account to perform these steps if you plan to promote the user you're restoring to an administrator as well.

2 In the Finder, copy the user's home folder from its backup location to the Mac system drive. Depending on how the home folder data was originally saved to the backup drive, you will have to complete one of the three following procedures:

▶ **If the user's home folder is stored normally on another non-system drive:**
Simply drag and drop the user's home folder from the backup drive to the root of the /Users folder. Click the Authenticate button and enter your administrator account credentials to complete the copy.

▶ **If the user's home folder is archived as a disk image:** Double-click on the user's disk image file to mount it in the Finder. If the drive doesn't appear on the desktop, go to the Finder preferences and enable showing CDs, DVDs, and iPods on the desktop. While holding the Option key on the keyboard, drag and drop the mounted disk image drive from the desktop to the root of the /Users folder. Holding the Option key will force the Finder to make a copy of the entire disk image drive. Authenticate as an administrator to complete the copy.

▶   **If the user's home folder was from a previous account on the Mac but the data was never moved off the system drive or archived:** In this case the system left the user's previous home in the Users folder, but appended "(Deleted)" to the name of the home folder. You need to remove "(Deleted)"; simply click on the name of the folder to edit the name. You will have to authenticate as an administrator to rename this folder.

NOTE ▶ It's imperative when you copy a user's home folder root to copy any hidden items inside the folder. In other words, if you try to copy individual folders inside the user's home folder, you may end up missing hidden items at the root, or beginning, of the user's home folder.

3   From the Users & Groups preferences, create a new user account using the same account name as the restored user. This is necessary to associate the new account with the restored home folder.

MORE INFO ▶ Creating a new user is covered in the "Creating New User Accounts" section earlier in this chapter.

4   Assuming you used the same account name as the name of the home folder, the system will recognize this and prompt you to associate the two.

When this dialog appears, click the Use Existing Folder button, and the system will automatically resolve any file and folder ownership issues to ensure the new user account can access the restored home folder contents.

5   Log in to the newly restored user account and all the user's settings should take effect.

It would be wise to double-check important settings and application preferences before you erase the backup home folder.

Managing Login and Fast User Switching

The login window may look simple, but because it's the front door to each system, as an administrator you should become familiar with a variety of security options here. Primarily, these options either provide higher security or greater accessibility. You can adjust the behavior of the login window from the Users & Groups preferences by authenticating as an administrative user and then clicking the Login Options button at the bottom of the user accounts list.

Login window options include:

▶ Enable or disable automatic login as the Mac starts up. This option is disabled in Lion by default. Obviously, you can only define one account for automatic login.

▶ Choose whether the login window shows a list of available users or blank name and password fields. Not only is choosing to have name and password fields more secure, but it's also more appropriate for environments with network user accounts.

▶ Determine the availability of Restart, Sleep, and Shut Down buttons at the login window. Macs in environments that require security will not have these buttons available at the login window.

▶ Specify whether users can use the input menu. This allows users easy access to non-roman characters, like Cyrillic or Kanji, at the login window.

▶ Determine whether the login window will show password hints after three bad password attempts. This may seem to be an insecure selection, but remember that password hints are optional for each user account.

▶ Disable fast user switching and adjust the associated menu item.

▶ Enable users to take advantage of VoiceOver audible assistant technology at the login window.

▶ Configure the Mac to use accounts hosted from a shared network directory. Network accounts are covered in Chapter 7, "Network Services."

> **TIP** ▶ You can configure a short three-line message for the login window from the Security & Privacy preferences as covered later in this chapter. If your organization requires a full login banner, this can be configured via the instructions in Knowledge Base article HT4788, "How to create a Login window banner in OS X Lion."

Using Fast User Switching

It's easy to imagine a situation when two users want to use a Mac at the same time. While it's not possible for two users to use the Mac's graphical interface simultaneously, it is possible for multiple users to remain logged in to the Mac at the same time. Fast user switching enables you to quickly move between user accounts without logging out or quitting open applications. This allows users to keep their work open in the background while other users are logged in to the computer. A user can later return to his account instantly, right where he left off.

> **NOTE** ▶ Fast user switching is not recommended for network accounts.

To use fast user switching:

1 Fast user switching is enabled by default in Lion. You should see the fast user switching menu item on the far right next to the Spotlight search menu. By default this menu will appear as your user account full name. If you don't see this menu item, then you need to enable fast user switching from the Login options pane of the Users & Groups preferences.

2 Initiate the switch to another user by simply selecting her name from the fast user switching menu.

3 If the selected user account has a password, you will be presented with a Login Window dialog. You must authenticate as the selected user in order to switch to that account.

4 Once you're authenticated, the computer will switch to the other account, typically with a cube-spinning transition.

5   Click the fast user switching menu again, and you can verify that other user accounts are still active, as indicated by an orange checkbox next to their names. You can log in or return to any account, at any time, using this menu.

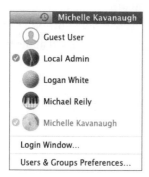

TIP ▶ You can move the fast user switching menu item, or any other menu item on the right side of the menu bar, by dragging the menu item while holding down the Command key.

Fast User Switching Issues

Apple has worked hard to make fast user switching a reliable feature. Many of the built-in Lion applications are fast user switching savvy. For instance, when you switch between accounts, iTunes will automatically mute or unmute your music, iChat will toggle between available and away chat status, and Mail will continue to check for new messages in the background. However, in some circumstances you will experience resource contention when more than one user attempts to access an item.

Examples of fast user switching resource contention are:

▶   Application contention—Some applications are designed in such a way that only one user can use the application at a time. If other users attempt to open these applications, either they are met with an error dialog or the application simply doesn't open. Most of the applications that fall into this category are professional applications, which tend to be resource hogs, so it's advantageous to keep only one copy running at a time.

▶ Document contention—These are cases where one user has a document open and remains logged in with fast user switching, often preventing other users from fully accessing the document. As an example, Microsoft Office will allow other users to open the document as read-only and will display an error dialog if the user tries to save changes. In a more extreme example, some applications will not allow other users to open the document at all. In the worst-case scenario, an application will allow two people to edit the file simultaneously, but it will only save changes made by the user who saved last. In this case, the application's developers simply didn't account for the possibility that two users might edit the same document at the same time, so you often won't even see an error message.

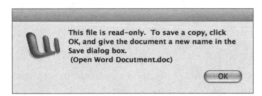

▶ Peripheral contention—Many peripherals can be accessed by only one user at a time. This becomes a fast user switching issue if a user leaves an application running that has attached itself to a peripheral. The peripheral will not become available to other applications until the original application is quit. Examples of this include video cameras, scanners, and audio equipment.

Fast user switching also has interesting ramifications for non-system drives. For example, if one user attaches an external storage device, the drive is available to all other users on the system, even if they weren't logged in when the storage was attached. Mounted disk images are handled a bit more securely. Only the user who mounted the disk image will have full read/write access to it. However, other users may still have read access to the mounted disk image.

Network shares are the only volumes that remain secure in a fast user switching environment. By default, only the user who originally connected to the share can access it. Even if multiple users attempt to access the same network share, the system will automatically generate multiple mounts with different access for each user. The exception to this rule is network home folders used by network accounts. While one network user can successfully log in, additional network users from the same server will not be able to access their network home folder. For this reason, fast user switching does not support network accounts.

Resolving Fast User Switching Issues

Unfortunately, because each resource and application can act differently, fast user switching issues are not always consistently reported or readily apparent. There is no "fast user switching is causing a problem" dialog in Lion. Still, if you are experiencing access errors for files, applications, or peripherals, your first step should be to check if any other users are still logged in. If so, you should have them log out and then reattempt access to the previously inaccessible items.

If you cannot log the other users out—perhaps because they are currently unavailable and you don't know their passwords—your options are to force the other users' suspect applications to quit or to force the other users to log out by restarting the Mac. Changing a logged-in user's password isn't an option at this point because administrators cannot manage user accounts that are currently logged in to the Mac. These accounts will be dimmed and not available in the Users & Groups preferences.

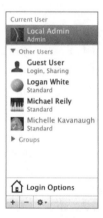

Thus, an administrator will have to force the other users' applications to quit or restart the Mac to free up any contested items or make any changes to the logged-in users. Neither option is ideal because forcing an application to quit with open files can result in data loss. Forcing an open application to quit is covered in Chapter 5, "Applications and Processes."

> **TIP** If you have already set the master password, then you can reset a currently logged-in user's password from the login window using the master password. Setting the master password and resetting a user's password is covered later in the "Using a Master Password" section of this chapter.

Attempting to restart, though, will reveal another fast user switching issue: If any other users are still logged in, an administrator will have to force those users' open applications to quit in order to restart. The system makes it easy for an administrator to force the other users' applications to quit via an authenticated restart dialog, but once again this may cause data loss to any open files.

Essential Account Security

The primary purpose of a multiple-user operating system is to provide all users with a secure work environment. Lion provides a relatively secure out-of-the-box experience for most situations. Yet some situations call for greater security than the defaults afford. Thus, the remainder of this chapter will focus on the built-in advanced security features of Lion and how best to manage and troubleshoot these features.

Understanding Account Vulnerabilities

As was discussed previously in this chapter, Lion uses a variety of user account types: standard users, administrative users, the guest user, sharing users, and the root user. Apple has made available these different account types to allow greater flexibility for managing user access. Because each account type is designed to allow different levels of access, you should be aware of each account type's potential security risk.

Standard Users

This account type is very secure, assuming an appropriate password is set. This user is allowed to use nearly all the resources and features of the Mac, but he can't change anything that might affect the system software. You can further restrict this account by using managed parental control settings, as discussed previously in this chapter.

Administrative Users

Because this is the initial account created when the Mac is set up for the first time using the Setup Assistant, many use this as their primary account type. This is advantageous because it allows the user to literally change anything on the computer, as is required for system management. The downside is that she will be allowed to make changes or install software that can render the system insecure or unstable.

Additional administrative accounts can be used for daily use, but this isn't always the best idea, as all administrative accounts are created equal. In other words, all administrative accounts have the ability to make changes to anything on the system, including deleting or changing the passwords to other administrative accounts. Administrative users can also change the administrative rights for any other user account, either disabling current administrators or changing standard users into administrators. Further, opening poorly written or intentionally malicious software as an administrative user could seriously harm the system software.

Most significantly, though, any administrative user can enable the root account or change the root account password using the Directory Utility application located in the /System/Library/CoreServices folder. For these reasons, you should seriously consider limiting the number of administrative user accounts on your Mac systems.

Guest User

Guest users are allowed, by default, to access your Mac via network file sharing without a password. Additionally, you can allow guests to log in to your Mac's graphical user interface without a password. Even though the guest home folder is deleted every time the guest logs out, the obvious security risk here is that literally anyone has access equivalent to that of a standard user account, including access to the Public, Drop Box, Sites, and Shared folders. This means he could execute some potentially nasty applications or fill your hard drive with unwanted files. The guest user can also restart or shut down your Mac, potentially allowing him to compromise the system during startup.

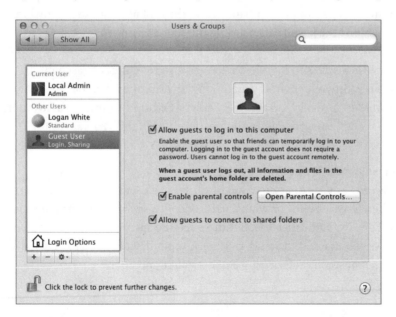

Fortunately, you can restrict the guest account using parental controls to prevent that account from running unapproved applications or restarting the Mac. Additionally, you can change the access permissions on the Shared and Drop Box folders so the guest account is not allowed to copy any items to your hard drive. Changing file and folder permissions is covered in Chapter 3, "File Systems."

Sharing Only Users

Sharing users are by default allowed file sharing access to the Public and Drop Box folders, so, like the guest user, they can potentially fill your hard drive with unwanted files. On the other hand, shared users cannot log in to the Mac otherwise and they can be required to use a password, so designating sharing users is generally much safer than using the guest account for file sharing. You can further control sharing users' access to your files by adjusting file and folder permissions. Changing permissions is a two-way street, though, and you could accidentally give a sharing user too much access. Configuring file sharing services is covered in Chapter 7, "Network Services."

Root User

The root user account, also known as the System Administrator, is disabled by default on Lion clients, and for good reason: The root account has unlimited access to everything on the Mac, and root users can do anything they want with the system. The potential for nefarious activity is literally unlimited with root account access. Remember, though, it only takes an administrative account to initially access the root account, so strictly limiting administrative usage is the key to safeguarding the root account.

> **NOTE** ▶ Anyone with access to Lion Recovery can also reset the root account. If security is a concern in your environment, it's highly recommended that you set a firmware password to prevent Lion Recovery access. Setting a firmware password is covered in the "Using Firmware Passwords" section later in this chapter.

Understanding Password Types

Lion relies on passwords as its primary method of verifying a user's authenticity. There are other more elaborate systems for proving a user's identity, such as biometric sensors and two-factor random key authentication, but these require special hardware. It's a pretty safe bet that every Mac is attached to an alphanumeric input device such as a keyboard, so passwords are still the most relevant security authentication method.

If you look closer at the security systems used by Lion, you will discover that it uses a variety of passwords at different levels to secure the computer. Most users are only familiar with their account password, but the Mac can also have a firmware password, a master password, many resource passwords, and several keychain passwords.

Each password type serves a specific purpose:

▶ Account password—Each user account has a variety of attributes that define the account. The account password is the attribute used to authenticate the user so he can log in. For security reasons, a user's account password is stored as encrypted data in the user's record. Only the root user can access the encrypted data in the user's record.

▶ Firmware password—The firmware password protects the Mac during startup. By default, anyone can subvert system security settings by simply using one of the commonly known startup-interrupt keyboard shortcuts. For example, anyone can hold down the Option key during startup to select an alternate operating system, thus bypassing your secure system. Setting the firmware password will prevent unauthorized users from using any startup-interrupt keyboard shortcuts. Setting a firmware password is covered in the "Using Firmware Passwords" section later in this chapter.

▶ Master password—The master password is used to reset standard, administrative, and Legacy FileVault user accounts if the user has forgotten his account password. Configuring and troubleshooting with the master password is covered in greater detail in the "Using a Master Password" section later in this chapter.

▶ Resource password—This is a generic term that describes a password used by nearly any service that requires you to authenticate. Resource passwords include email, website, file server, application, and encrypted disk image passwords. Many resource passwords are automatically saved for the user by the keychain system.

▶ Keychain password—Lion protects the user's important authentication assets, outside of the account password, in encrypted keychain files. Each keychain file is encrypted with a keychain password. The system will attempt to keep keychain passwords synchronized with the user's account password. However, you can maintain unique keychain passwords separate from an account password as well. Configuring and troubleshooting the keychain security system is covered in greater detail in the "Managing Keychains" section later in this chapter.

Using Security & Privacy Preferences

In addition to specific user security settings, such as account passwords and keychain items, there are systemwide security preferences that affect all users on the Mac. Many of these options are disabled by default because the average Mac user would probably consider them inconveniences. However, if your environment requires greater security, these additional security features are indispensable. Open the Security & Privacy preferences and authenticate as an administrative user to unlock the system security settings.

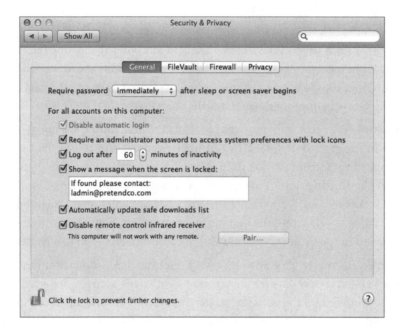

From the Security & Privacy preferences you can:

► Choose to require a password to wake the computer from sleep or screen saver mode. Both standard and administrative users can set this for their account, but an administrator cannot set this for every account from the Security & Privacy preferences.

► Disable automatic login for all accounts.

► Require administrative authentication for all lockable system preferences every single time. This way, if a logged-in administrative user leaves her Mac temporarily unattended, anonymous users cannot make any changes to system preferences.

► Automatically log out accounts after a certain amount of inactivity.

► Configure a custom message to show when the screen is locked or at the login window. You can use the Option-Return keyboard shortcut to force a new line. However, the system will only allow for three lines of text.

▶ Choose to automatically update a list of known unsafe downloads. Despite the option description of maintaining a "safe downloads list," the system actually maintains a list of unsafe items such as known malware applications.

▶ Disable the built-in infrared Apple remote sensor on equipped Mac models. By default, unless the Mac has been paired with a specific Apple remote, any Apple remote will be able to affect the Mac.

▶ Enable and configure Lion's FileVault settings and manage Legacy FileVault home folders. Legacy FileVault is covered in the "Legacy FileVault Home Folders" section later in this chapter. Lion's FileVault 2 is covered in Chapter 3, "File Systems."

▶ Enable and configure network firewall settings. The network firewall will be discussed in Chapter 7, "Network Services."

▶ From the Privacy pane of the Security & Privacy preferences, you can choose to disable the reporting of diagnostic information to Apple. The primary source of information sent with this option is application hangs or crashes. This information helps Apple resolve reoccurring issues faster. On the right side of this pane, you can choose to disable location services, which will prevent applications and services from being able to locate the Mac. New in Lion is the ability to view the items that have used location services in the past and also individually disable them. Any Mac with a Wi-Fi capabilities card can use location services.

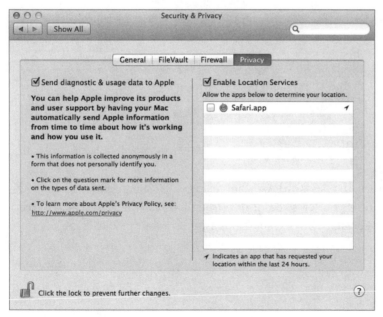

Using Password Assistant

Regardless of how sophisticated a security system is, the protection it affords is only as strong as the password you choose. For this reason, Mac OS X includes a handy Password Assistant utility that will gauge the strength of your passwords or automatically create strong passwords for you. Anytime you are creating or modifying a password that will grant access to a substantial resource, like an account or keychain password, you can use the Password Assistant.

TIP You can use the Password Assistant anytime you see the small key icon next to a password field.

To use the Password Assistant:

1   Open the Users & Groups preferences and select your user account; then click the Change Password button.

2   Enter your current account password in the Old Password field.

You can reenter the same password in the New Password field if you just want to test its strength, or you can go ahead and create a new password.

3   Click the key icon next to the New Password field to open the Password Assistant.

The Quality bar in the Password Assistant dialog will instantly show the strength of your password. If your password is not strong, the bar will be in shades of red to yellow, and you will be offered some tips as to why your password is a poor choice.

4   Try to find a stronger password by entering a different choice it in the New Password
     field.

The Password Assistant will automatically gauge your password choices as you enter
them. You know you have a strong password when the Quality bar starts turning
green.

If you're having a hard time coming up with a good password, the Password Assistant
will help you by automatically generating strong passwords. Choose a password type
from the Type pop-up menu, and use the Length slider to adjust password length.

The Suggestion pop-up menu will show a variety of password options, or you can
roll again by choosing More Suggestions.

5   Once you have found a strong password with the Password Assistant, it will be auto-
     entered in the New Password field, but you will have to enter it again manually in the
     Verify field.

6   If you are indeed changing your account password, click the Change Password button to finish; otherwise, click the Cancel button.

> **NOTE ▸** If your account password and keychain password are the same, when you change your password using the Users & Groups preferences it will automatically change both passwords.

Using Firmware Passwords

As covered previously, setting the firmware password will prevent unauthorized users from using any startup-interrupt keyboard shortcuts. This will protect your system from someone trying to circumvent an otherwise secure installation of Lion. Firmware passwords are not in any way tied to a user account. Instead, the password is saved to the Mac's firmware chip, so this password remains separate from the installed software.

> **TIP ▸** Even without setting a firmware password, enabling Lion's FileVault 2 full disk encryption will prevent unauthorized access to the encrypted system drive. FileVault 2 full disk encryption is covered in Chapter 3, "File Systems."

You set the firmware password using a utility available when the Mac is started up from a previous Mac OS X installation DVD or Lion Recovery. If you require the highest level of security for your Mac, then you must set the firmware password, as any user with access to a Mac OS X install DVD or Lion Restore can set the password if it hasn't already been set. Once the firmware password is set, only an administrative user or a user who has physical access to the internal hardware can reset the password.

To manage a Mac's firmware password:

1   Start the Mac up from a Lion Recovery system. You can use the Mac's built-in Lion Recovery HD by holding Command-R at startup or you can use the Startup Disk preferences to select an external Lion Recovery system.

> **MORE INFO ▸** Lion Recovery is detailed in Chapter 1, "Installation and Configuration."

2   Once your Mac's running from Lion Recovery, select Firmware Password Utility from the Utilities menu.

3   When the Firmware Password Utility launches, you will be presented with one of two windows:

▶   **If no firmware password is set:** Click the Turn On Firmware Password button to enable and set a firmware password for this Mac. You will then be allowed to set the password.

▶   **If a firmware password is set:** You will be presented with two choices, Change Password and Turn Off Firmware Password. Click the appropriate button for the task you wish to accomplish. Either task will require knowledge of the current firmware password to proceed.

4   Once the selected firmware password task is complete, the computer will present a confirmation window and you can then quit the Firmware Password Utility.

5   At this point you can restart your Mac back to its normal Lion system. Closing the Mac OS X Utilities application presented here will allow you to change startup drives or restart the Mac.

Again, with a firmware password set all startup-interrupt keyboard shortcuts will be disabled except for one. When you start up the Mac holding the Option key you will be presented with an authentication window where you can enter the firmware password. If you enter the correct password you will then be allowed to pick a different startup drive from the Startup Manager. This gives the administrator the flexibility to start up from another system should the need arise, but otherwise prevents users from affecting the standard Lion startup process.

MORE INFO ▶ All the available startup keyboard shortcuts are covered in Chapter 9, "System Startup."

If for some reason the Mac's firmware password becomes unknown, it can be reset. First you must remove some of the system memory from the Mac. This "proves" that you have access to the internals of the Mac. Then when you restart the Mac, hold the Command-Option-P-R keys. Continue holding until you hear the Mac restart; then you can let go of the keys. At this point the firmware password has been cleared. Unfortunately, several Mac models don't have removable system memory. If this is the case, you will need to visit an Apple Authorized Service Provider to clear the firmware password.

Legacy FileVault Home Folders

Prior to Lion, FileVault existed as a technology that secured user data by encrypting the user's home folder content. This technique, while effective, has a variety of drawbacks. For one, it did not protect data outside the user's home folder. More problematic, though, was that many system management and backup utilities simply didn't work properly with FileVault home folders. With Lion now featuring FileVault 2 full disk encryption, FileVault home folder encryption has been deprecated.

MORE INFO ▶ Lion's FileVault 2 full disk encryption is covered in Chapter 3, "File Systems."

The previous version of FileVault, now dubbed Legacy FileVault, is still supported by Lion for existing or migrated user accounts, but you can no longer enable it for new user accounts. If you are currently using a Legacy FileVault account on a Lion system, the Security & Privacy preferences will present a window prompting you to turn off Legacy FileVault.

NOTE ▶ It is strongly suggested that you turn off Legacy FileVault and switch to the much more robust FileVault 2.

NOTE ▶ You must turn off all Legacy FileVault users to enable FileVault 2.

NOTE ▶ Turning off Legacy FileVault will require a logout and a potentially lengthy copy process as the system migrates the encrypted data back to "regular" data.

NOTE ▶ Turning off Legacy FileVault requires free space on the system drive to decrypt your home folder data. If there is not enough free space, you will not be able to turn off Legacy FileVault. You may want to consider manually migrating a copy of your home folder as covered in the "Manually Moving or Restoring a User's Home Folder" section previously in this chapter.

If you dismiss this dialog, you can always decide later to turn off Legacy FileVault. Simply return to the Legacy FileVault pane of the Security & Privacy preferences. Note that you can reset the master password from this location as well.

If you decide to stick with Legacy FileVault home folders, they will behave as they did in Mac OS X v10.6. Later sections in this chapter cover techniques for managing passwords. Be sure to look for techniques pertaining to Legacy FileVault, as these accounts must be handled differently than standard user accounts.

Managing Keychains

Lion features a sophisticated system that automatically protects all your authentication assets in encrypted keychain files. Much as service workers might keep a keychain containing all the keys needed during their workday, the Mac will keep all your resource passwords, certificates, keys, website forms, and even secure notes in a single secure location. Every time you allow the Mac to remember a password or any other potentially sensitive item, it will save it to a keychain file. Only your account password remains separate from all the other items saved to your keychains.

Because so many important items end up in keychain files, the keychain files themselves are encrypted with a very strong algorithm: They are impenetrable unless you know the keychain's password. In fact, if you forget a keychain's password, its contents are lost forever. Not even the software engineers at Apple can help you—the keychain system is *that* secure. Yet, probably the single best feature of the keychain system is that it's entirely automatic using the default settings. Most users will never know just how secure their saved passwords are because the system is so transparent.

Understanding Keychain Files

There are keychain files stored throughout the system for different users and resources:

▶ /Users/<username>/Library/Keychain/login.keychain—Every standard or administrative user is created with a single login keychain. As a default, the password for this keychain matches the user's account password, so this keychain is automatically unlocked and available when the user logs in. If the user's account password does not match the keychain's password, it will not automatically unlock during login.

Users can create additional keychains if they wish to segregate their authentication assets. For example, you can keep your default login keychain for trivial items, and then create a more secure keychain that does not automatically unlock for more important items.

▶ /Library/Keychain/FileVaultMaster.keychain—This keychain is encrypted with the FileVault master password. Configuring and troubleshooting FileVault and the master password is covered later in greater detail in the "Using a Master Password" section.

▶ /Library/Keychain/System.keychain—This keychain maintains authentication assets that are not user specific. Examples of items stored here include Wi-Fi wireless network passwords, 802.1X network passwords, and local Kerberos support items. Although all users benefit from this keychain, only administrative users can make changes to it.

▶ /System/Library/Keychains/—You will find several keychain files in this folder that store root certificates used to help identify trusted network services. Once again, all users benefit from these keychains, but only administrative users can make changes to them.

NOTE ▸ Some websites will remember your password inside a web cookie, so you might not see an entry in a keychain file for every website password you save.

Using Keychain Access

The primary tool you will use to manage keychains is the Keychain Access application found in the /Applications/Utilities folder. With this application you can view and modify any keychain item, including saved resource passwords, certificates, keys, website forms, and secure notes. You can also create and delete keychain files, change keychain settings and passwords, and repair corrupted keychains.

Manage Items in a Keychain

To manage keychain items, including saved passwords:

1   As any user, open /Applications/Utilities/Keychain Access.

The default selection will show the contents of the user's login keychain, but you could select another keychain from the list to view its items.

2   Double-click a keychain item to view its attributes.

3   If the item is a password, you can reveal the saved password by selecting the "Show password" checkbox.

4   When prompted, enter the keychain password once more, and then click the Allow button to reveal the saved password. It is not advisable to click the Always Allow button.

Once you have authenticated, you can change any attribute in the keychain item dialog.

5   When you have finished making changes, click the Save Changes button.

6   Finally, you can also click the Access Control tab in the keychain item's attributes dialog to adjust application access for the selected item.

TIP   To easily search through all the keychain items, use the Categories views to the left or the Spotlight search in the top-right corner of the toolbar.

TIP The safest place to store secure text on your Mac is in keychains. In Keychain Access, you can create a new secure note by choosing File > New Secure Note Item from the menu bar.

Manage Keychain Files

To manage keychain files, including resetting a keychain's password:

1   As any user, open /Applications/Utilities/Keychain Access.

2   To create a new keychain, choose File > New Keychain from the menu bar. Next, enter a name and location for the new keychain. The default location is the Keychains folder inside your home folder. Finish by entering a nontrivial password that is six characters or longer for the new keychain and clicking the OK button.

3   To change a keychain's settings, first select it from the list, and then choose Edit > Change Settings for Keychain from the menu bar. You will be able to change automatic keychain locking settings and enable .Mac synchronization. Finish by clicking the Save button.

4   To change a keychain's password, first select it from the list, and then choose Edit > Change Password for Keychain from the menu bar. You will have to enter the keychain's current password first. Finish by entering a nontrivial password that is six characters or longer and click the OK button.

5   To delete a keychain, select it from the list and choose File > Delete Keychain from the menu bar. When the Delete Keychain dialog appears, click the Delete References button to simply ignore the keychain or click the Delete References & Files button to completely erase the keychain file.

TIP You can move keychain items between keychains by dragging and dropping an item from one keychain to another.

TIP ▶ For quick access to your keychains and other security features, you can enable the security menu item by choosing Keychain Access > Preferences from the menu bar. Then select the Show Status in Menu Bar checkbox to reveal the security menu item, as indicated by a small key icon on the right side of the menu bar.

Repair Keychain Files

To verify or repair a keychain file:

1   As any user, open /Applications/Utilities/Keychain Access.

2   If the troublesome keychain is not already in your keychain list, choose File > Add Keychain from the menu bar and you will be able to browse for it.

3   You need to unlock all the keychains you wish to check. Simply select the keychain from the list, then choose File > Unlock Keychain from the menu bar and enter the keychain's password.

4   Choose Keychain Access > Keychain First Aid from the menu bar.

5   You will have to enter your password once more, choose the Verify or Repair button, and finally click the Start button.

A log will show the keychain verification or repair process.

TIP ▶ Additional Keychain First Aid preferences can be found by selecting Keychain Access > Preferences from the menu bar.

Resetting Account Passwords

A user mistyping or forgetting her password is the primary cause of most login and access issues on any platform. The second most common issue, specific to Lion, is when a user's keychain passwords become out of sync with that user's account password. Fortunately, with a few rare exceptions, Lion provides ways to easily resolve these types of password issues.

> **TIP** ▶ If a user already knows her own password, but she wants to change it, she can do so at any time from the Users & Groups preferences. She simply selects her account, and then clicks the Change Password button to access a dialog allowing her to change her password. Further, if her account password matches her keychain password this technique will also synchronize the two passwords.

Using a Master Password

As mentioned previously, the master password can be used to reset regular account passwords and is required to reset Legacy FileVault passwords. The master password isn't tied to any local user account, so it's an effective method of providing a password reset mechanism that does not require the creation of an additional administrator account. If you are maintaining a large deployment of Macs that are using local accounts, setting a uniform master password is an easy method to ensure you always have a back door in without having your own local account.

Set or Change the Master Password

There are two cases in which the master password may already be set on a Lion system. The first is if you have upgraded a Mac from a previous version of Mac OS X where the master password was set. The second is if you used Migration Assistant to transfer a Legacy FileVault account to the Lion system. If you think you know the master password, then you can use the following instructions to change the master password. However, if you have lost the master password, then you should follow the instructions outlined in the "Resetting a Lost Master Password" section later in this chapter.

> **TIP** ▶ If you are logged into a Legacy FileVault account, you can also change the master password from the Legacy FileVault pane of the Security & Privacy preferences.

To set or change the master password:

1   Open the Users & Groups preferences and authenticate as an administrative user to unlock its settings.

2   Click the Action menu (the small gear icon) button at the bottom of the users list. This will reveal a pop-up menu allowing you to set or change the master password.

▶ If the master password has not been set, the menu choice will be Set Master Password: Select this option and you can set the Mac's master password.

▶ If the master password has been set, the menu choice will be Change Master Password: Select this option and you can change the Mac's master password. You will have to enter the existing master password first before you can set the new master password.

When setting the master password, it's strongly recommended that you choose a high-quality password. Remember, this single master password can be used to reset any other user account password.

3 With the master password set, you will be able to change account passwords from the login window.

Resetting a Lost Master Password

It is vital that the master password be properly configured and known by an administrator. If the master password is lost, an administrative user should reset it immediately for the benefit of being able to reset normal user passwords. However, just because you can set a new master password for your Mac doesn't mean you can recover a Legacy FileVault account that was created with the old master password. Only the master password created when the Legacy FileVault user was enabled can unlock an inaccessible account.

There are two distinct situations in which a master password needs to be reset. The first is when the current master password is known and an administrative user simply wants to change the password by choice. Changing a known master password is quite easy, as covered earlier in this section. Further, this method properly maintains your ability to reset passwords, be they associated with normal or Legacy FileVault accounts.

The second situation is when the current master password is lost and a new master password needs to be created. In this case, the new master password will not have the ability to reset Legacy FileVault account passwords. This is because Lion does not support re-encrypting Legacy FileVault accounts, which is a necessary step for lost master password changes. Thus, if you have lost the master password used to create a Legacy FileVault user, there is no recovery method should the user lose his password. For this reason alone you should abandon using Legacy FileVault accounts in favor of Lion's FileVault 2 full disk encryption.

MORE INFO ► Turning off Legacy FileVault encryption is covered in the "Legacy FileVault Home Folders" section earlier in this chapter. Lion's FileVault 2 full disk encryption is covered in Chapter 3, "File Systems."

To create a new master password because the previous one was lost:

1 Log out all other users on the system, and then log in as an administrative user.

2 From the Finder, locate and delete the /Library/Keychains/FileVaultMaster.cer and /Library/Keychains/FilevaultMaster.keychain files.

3 Open the Users & Groups preferences and authenticate as an administrative user to unlock its settings.

4 Click the Action menu (the small gear icon) button at the bottom of the users list. This will reveal a pop-up menu allowing you to set the master password.

Reset a Password at Login

Two methods can be used to reset a password at the login window, the master password or a user's Apple ID. The former method requires that you know a Mac's current master password, thus allowing you to reset both regular user account passwords and Legacy FileVault user account passwords at login. The latter method assumes the user account has been associated with an Apple ID, as covered previously in this chapter. However, you cannot use an Apple ID to reset a Legacy FileVault user account or any account on a system protected with FileVault 2.

These two techniques are generally only used when you don't have access to another local administrator account. If you do have access to another local administrator account, then you can reset a lost password using the instructions outlined in the next section of this chapter, "Resetting Passwords as an Administrator."

To reset an account password from the login window:

1 If you aren't already at the login window, log out of the current account.

> **NOTE ▸** In Lion you cannot reset a password from the fast user switching login window.

2 Enter the three incorrect passwords and then a pop-up menu will appear. This pop-up menu may display a password hint if one is set.

3 If the password hint doesn't help the user remember her password, you can reset the password using one of the two following methods:

▶ If you wish to reset the user's password using the master password: Click the arrow-in-a-circle icon next to Master Password. Next, enter the master password once, followed by the user's new password twice, and optionally a new password hint.

▶ If you wish to reset the user's password using an Apple ID: Click the arrow-in-a-circle icon next to Apple ID. Next, enter an appropriate Apple ID with password, and then click the Reset Password button. After the system authenticates the Apple ID, you can enter a new password twice and optionally include a new password hint.

NOTE ▶ When resetting an account password, it's strongly recommended that you choose a high-quality password.

4 Once you have entered the appropriate password information, click the Reset Password button to log the user into her existing account.

NOTE ▶ Resetting an account password with this method will not reset the user's keychain passwords. However, by default in Lion, when the user logs in, she will be prompted to fix her login keychain. This process is detailed in the "Resetting Keychain Passwords" section later in this chapter.

Resetting Passwords as an Administrator

If you have access to an administrator account, you can easily reset non-Legacy FileVault user account passwords from the Users & Groups preferences. This technique is generally only used when the user has forgotten the account password and you need to create a new one.

To reset a non-Legacy FileVault account password using administrator authorization:

1   If the inaccessible user account is still logged into the computer because of fast user switching, you will need to restart the computer to forcibly log out the user. Alternatively, you can reset the account password from the login window using the master password, as covered in the earlier "Reset a Password at Login" section.

2   Open the Users & Groups preferences and authenticate as an administrative user to unlock its settings.

3   Select the inaccessible user account from the list, and then click the Reset Password button.

4   Enter the new account password and verification in the appropriate fields.

When resetting an account password, it's strongly recommended that you choose a high-quality password.

5   Click the Reset Password button to save the new account password.

> **NOTE** ▸ Resetting an account password with this method will not reset the user's keychain passwords. However, by default in Lion, the next time the user logs in, he will be prompted to fix his login keychain. This process is detailed in the "Resetting Keychain Passwords" section later in this chapter.

Resetting Legacy FileVault Account Passwords

Legacy FileVault accounts are unique because the user's home folder is saved inside an encrypted disk image protected by that user's account password. Consequently, it is extremely important for an administrator to have the ability to reset a Legacy FileVault user's account password if the user ever wants to access her home folder files again.

A normal administrative user account is not enough to reset a lost Legacy FileVault password. Frankly, Legacy FileVault wouldn't be very secure if just any old administrative user could come along and break in. Therefore, if a Legacy FileVault user has forgotten her account password, the master password is required to reset the account.

If you have lost the master password along with the user's Legacy FileVault password, then you are completely out of luck. You must have at least one of these two passwords to recover a Legacy FileVault account. Otherwise, you are never, ever going to be able to recover the user's data. Not even Apple can help you—it designed Legacy FileVault to be as secure as possible and thus created only one method to reset a Legacy FileVault account: the master password. For this reason alone, you should abandon using Legacy FileVault accounts in favor of Lion's FileVault 2 full disk encryption.

> **MORE INFO** ▸ Turning off Legacy FileVault encryption is covered in the "Legacy FileVault Home Folders" section previously in this chapter. Lion's FileVault 2 full disk encryption is covered in Chapter 3, "File Systems."

Resetting Legacy FileVault Passwords From Users & Groups

If you do know the master password, Lion provides two methods for easily resetting Legacy FileVault user passwords. The first involves uses the login window as covered in the previous "Reset a Password at Login" section of this chapter. The second method involves resetting a Legacy FileVault account password from the Users & Groups preferences.

To reset a Legacy FileVault password from the Users & Groups preferences:

1   If the inaccessible Legacy FileVault user account is still logged in to the computer because of fast user switching, you will need to restart the computer to forcibly log out the user. Alternatively, you can reset the account password from the login window, as covered in the earlier "Reset a Password at Login" section.

2   Open the Users & Groups preferences and authenticate as an administrative user to unlock the settings.

3   Select the inaccessible Legacy FileVault account from the list; then click the Reset Password button.

4   Enter the master password in the appropriate field.

5   Enter the new Legacy FileVault password and verification in the appropriate fields.

When resetting a Legacy FileVault password, it's strongly recommended that you choose a high-quality password.

6 Finish by clicking the Reset Password button to save the new Legacy FileVault password.

> **NOTE ▶** Resetting a Legacy FileVault account password will not reset the user's keychain passwords. However, by default in Lion, the next time the user logs in, he will be prompted to fix his login keychain. This process is detailed in the following "Resetting Keychain Passwords" section.

Resetting Keychain Passwords

Only if a user knows her current account password and then decides to change her password will the system also change the user's login keychain password. So that they remain as secure as possible, keychain passwords cannot be changed by any outside password-resetting process. Apple did not design the keychain system with a back door, as doing so would render the system less secure.

Consequently, whenever an administrative user resets a user's account or FileVault password, the keychain password will remain unchanged and will not automatically open as the user logs into her account. However, by default in Lion, when a user with a recently reset password logs in, she will be prompted with a dialog to update or reset her login keychain.

> **TIP ▶** The keychain synchronization dialog can be disabled from the First Aid tab of the Keychain Access application preferences.

The default selection, Update Keychain Password, will work only if the user knows his previous keychain password. This is probably not the case if you just had to reset the password. If so, the user should click the Create New Keychain button to create a new login keychain. The system will rename his old login keychain and leave it in the user's ~/Library/Keychains folder in case he ever remembers his old password. Finally, though it's not recommended, the user can simply choose to ignore the warning by clicking the Continue Log In button.

If the automatic keychain synchronization dialog does not appear, you can still reset the user's login keychain password from the Keychain Access application, assuming the previous keychain password is known. As you'd expect, if you do not know the user's previous keychain password, then the contents of that keychain are lost forever. Using Keychain Access to manage a user's keychain is covered previously in this chapter.

Resetting the Primary Administrator Password

Many Macs intended for personal use have only the single primary administrator user account that was created when the Mac was initially set up with the Setup Assistant. Even if more than one person uses this Mac, quite often its owner is not very concerned about security. Thankfully, Lion now defaults to requiring a password at login so users are forced to enter their password at login.

However, if the computer was upgraded to Lion, it's very common for the primary user account to automatically log in during startup and to not have a master password set. This results in a high likelihood of Mac owners forgetting their primary administrator account password and not having any way to reset this password because they never enabled the master password or created another administrator account. Fortunately, Apple has prepared for these occasions by including the Reset Password utility in Lion Recovery.

> **NOTE** ▸ If the system drive is protected with FileVault 2 full disk encryption, you will have to first unlock the system drive via Disk Utility. This process is covered in Chapter 1, "Installation and Configuration." However, if there is only one account on the Mac and its password is lost, odds are you don't know the FileVault 2 password either. In this case your first move is to regain access to the FileVault 2 system drive as covered in Chapter 3, "File Systems."

To reset the primary account password:

1 Start up from a Lion Recovery system. The easiest method on a Lion system is by holding Command-R during startup.

> **NOTE** ▸ If the default Lion Recovery system doesn't work, you can use any of the alternative Lion Recovery methods detailed in Chapter 1, "Installation and Configuration."

2 Once Lion Recovery has started, choose Utilities > Terminal from the menu bar.

3 When the Terminal opens, simply type resetpassword and then press the Return key. This will open the Reset Password utility.

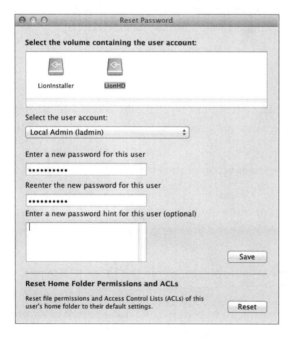

4 Select the system drive containing the inaccessible primary account you wish to reset from the row of system drive icons.

5 Choose the name of the inaccessible primary account from the pop-up menu.

6 Enter and reenter a new password and optionally a password hint in the appropriate fields.

7 Click the Save button to save the new password.

8 Quit the Reset Password utility to return to the Mac OS X Utilities window.

9 Quit the Mac OS X Utilities window to restart the Mac.

> **TIP** You can also use the Reset Password utility to repair home folder permissions and access control lists (ACLs) for the selected account by clicking the Reset button.

Obviously, the Reset Password utility is a dangerous application that can completely eliminate any of the security settings you've configured to protect your Mac. Because of this, the Reset Password utility will not run if copied off the original media, but this still doesn't prevent any user with access to Lion Recovery from using this utility. Once again, Apple prepared for this situation by providing another utility on Lion Recovery: Firmware Password Utility. As covered previously in this chapter, setting a firmware password will prevent any nonauthorized user from circumventing normal system startup.

What You've Learned

▶ There are five types of user accounts, each with its own specific access and capabilities: standard users, administrative users, the guest user, sharing only users, and the root user.

▶ Creating, managing, and deleting users is accomplished from within the Users & Groups preferences.

▶ A user's home folder can be moved or restored either using the Migration Assistant or by manually moving it to the /Users folder and creating a new account with the same account name.

▶ A variety of login and security options are available within the Users & Groups and Security & Privacy preferences.

▶ There are five types of passwords, each with its own specific use: account passwords, the firmware password, the master password, resource passwords, and keychain passwords.

▶ Lion provides robust security for protecting users' secrets via the keychain system.

▶ Legacy FileVault accounts are deprecated in Lion and should be set back to normal in favor of Lion's FileVault 2 full disk encryption.

▶ You may have to use any of a variety of password reset methods depending on the type of password you are trying to reset.

References

You can check for new and updated Knowledge Base documents at http://www.apple.com/support.

User Account Management

HT1528, "Enabling and using the 'root' user in Mac OS X"

HT4798, "OS X Lion: Apple ID can be used to reset your user account password"

HT4788, "How to create a Login window banner in OS X Lion"

Fast User Switching

TA22373, "Mac OS X 10.3 or Later: About Fast User Switching and home folders on servers"

TA22404, "Mac OS X 10.3, 10.4: Some applications only work in one account at a time"

Keychain

HT1060, "Using keychains with MobileMe, troubleshooting keychain issues"

Legacy FileVault

TA27532, "iMovie: Using FileVault can affect performance"

TA27530, "Final Cut Pro and Final Cut Express: About using FileVault"

HT2631, "Mac OS X 10.3, 10.4: FileVault—How to verify or repair a home directory image"

TS1974, "Mac OS X 10.4: FileVault—'There isn't enough space on your hard disk...' alert"

Review Quiz

1. What are the five types of user accounts in Lion? How are they different?
2. What are account attributes?
3. How can you limit a user account from having full access to all applications?
4. What are some security risks associated with each type of user account?
5. What default folders make up a user's home folder? What are some optional folders in a user's home folder?

6. What types of resource contention issues can occur when fast user switching is enabled?

7. What security risk can occur when fast user switching is enabled?

8. What does a keychain do?

9. How does Legacy FileVault secure a user's data?

10. How does resetting the master password affect existing Legacy FileVault user accounts?

11. How does resetting a user's password as an administrative user affect that user's keychains?

12. How does the Firmware Password Utility help prevent users from making unauthorized password changes?

Answers

1. Standard is the default account type; administrative users can make changes to the system; a guest user does not require a password; sharing only users can access only shared files; and the root user has unlimited access.

2. Account attributes are the individual pieces of information that are used to define a user account. Examples include full name, account name, user ID, universally unique ID (UUID), group, and home directory.

3. Parental controls can be used to further limit a user account. Examples include enforcing a simple Finder, limiting applications and widgets, setting time limits, and content filtering.

4. Standard user accounts are very secure, assuming they have good passwords. Administrative users can make changes that may negatively affect the system or other user accounts. A guest user could potentially fill your system drive with unwanted files. Sharing only users are generally very secure as long as you don't give them too much access to your items. The potential for mayhem with root user access is nearly unlimited.

5. The default folders in a user's home folder are Desktop, Documents, Downloads, Library (hidden), Movies, Music, Pictures, and Public. Optional home folder items include Applications and Sites folders.

6. Resource contention occurs when fast user switching is enabled and a user tries to access an item that another user already has open in the background. Document contention occurs when a user attempts to open a document that another user has already opened. Peripheral contention occurs when a user attempts to access a periph-

eral that is already in use by another user's open application. Application contention occurs when the second user attempts to access an application that is designed to run only once on a system.

7. When fast user switching is enabled, all users are allowed to see other users' locally connected drives.

8. A keychain is an encrypted file that is used to securely save passwords, certificates, or notes. By default, every user has a login keychain that has the same password as his account.

9. Legacy FileVault stores the user's home folder in an encrypted disk image. This disk image is accessible only by the Legacy FileVault user.

10. If a known master password is reset using the Security & Privacy preferences, Legacy FileVault accounts will not be negatively affected. On the other hand, if a master password is reset because it was lost, Legacy FileVault accounts cannot be reset by the new master password.

11. If an administrative user resets another user's account password, this process will not change any keychain passwords. Therefore, the user's keychains will not automatically open when the user logs in with her new password. The user will have to manually change her keychain passwords using the Keychain Access utility.

12. The Firmware Password Utility prevents users from starting up from another system drive. This in turn prevents them from using a Lion Recovery system to reset local passwords without authorization.

3

Time

This chapter takes approximately 3 hours to complete.

Goals

Recognize the various file systems supported by Lion

Manage and troubleshoot file systems using a variety of tools

Understand how to use FileVault 2 full disk encryption

Understand and manage file ownership and permissions

Chapter 3
File Systems

Although personal computer processor speed has increased around a thousandfold since the first Mac was introduced in 1984, storage capacity has easily increased a million times over. Compare 1984's 400 KB floppy to today's average desktop drive at 1 TB, which is roughly equivalent to 1,000,000,000 KB, or 2.5 million 400 KB floppies. Users have responded by moving thousands of pictures and hundreds of hours of music and video, historically stored in analog form, to digital storage. Likewise, enterprise customers have replaced filing cabinets and storage rooms with Redundant Arrays of Independent Disks (RAID) and backup tapes. Even though the Internet has recently changed our perception of what a computer is used for, it's clear that the computer's primary role continues to be a tool to organize, access, and store our stuff.

In this chapter, you will examine the storage technology used by OS X Lion. Storage hardware like disk drives and RAID will be covered alongside logical storage concepts like partitions and volumes. Naturally, you will learn how to properly manage and troubleshoot these storage assets as well. Finally, you will also learn to manage storage security through ownership, permissions, and access control lists (ACLs).

Understanding File System Components

Before you begin managing storage in Lion, it is important to understand the distinction between storage, partitions, and volumes. Traditionally, computer storage has been defined by disk drive hardware. After all these years, disk drive hardware still maintains the storage lead, as it has moved from removable floppy disks to enclosed hard disks. However, other more convenient removable formats have become extremely popular as they have increased in capacity. This includes optical media like CDs and DVDs and solid-state storage like solid-state disks (SSDs), USB key drives, and CompactFlash cards. All are equally viable storage destinations for Lion.

Without proper formatting, though, any storage technology is nothing more than a big empty bucket of ones and zeros, and consequently not very useful to the Mac. Formatting is the process of applying logic to storage in the form of partitions and volumes. Partitions are used to define boundaries on a storage device. You can define multiple partitions if you want the physical storage to appear as multiple separate storage destinations. Even if you want to use the entire space available on a device as a single contiguous storage location, the area must still be defined by a partition.

Once partitions have been established, the system can create usable volumes inside the partition areas. Volumes define how the files and folders are actually stored on the hardware. In fact, it's the volume that is ultimately mounted by the file system and then represented as a usable storage icon in the Finder. Obviously, a storage device with several partitions, each containing a separate volume, will appear as several storage location icons in the Finder.

Partition schemes:

- GUID Partition Table (GPT)
- Apple Partition Map (APM)
- Master Boot Record (MBR)

Most common volume formats:

- Mac OS Extended (Journaled)
- Mac OS Extended (Journaled, Encrypted)
- Mac OS Extended
- MS DOS File System (FAT32, ExFAT)
- NT File System (NTFS) *

    * read only

Partition Schemes

As mentioned earlier, drives must be partitioned in order to define and possibly segregate the drive's usable space. Every disk requires at least one partition, but Lion can support up to 16 partitions per disk. You learned the advantages and disadvantages of using single or multiple partitions in Chapter 1, "Installation and Configuration."

Lion supports three types of partition schemes. This may seem excessive, but it's necessary for Macs to support multiple partition schemes in order to start up computers using modern Intel processors, support older Mac drives, and use standard PC-compatible volumes.

The three partition schemes supported by Lion are:

▶ GUID Partition Table (GPT)—This is the default partition scheme used by Intel-based Macs. It is also the only partition scheme supported for Intel-based Macs to start up using disk-based storage. However, PowerPC-based Macs running Mac OS X v10.4.6 or later can also access this type of partitioning, but they will not be able to start up from it.

▶ Apple Partition Map (APM)—This is the default partition scheme used by previous PowerPC-based Macs. It is also the only partition scheme that PowerPC-based Macs can start up from. However, all Intel-based Macs can also access this type of partitioning.

▶ Master Boot Record (MBR)—This is the default partition scheme used by most non-Mac computers, including Windows-compatible PCs. Consequently, this is the default partition scheme you will find on most new preformatted storage drives. This partition scheme is also commonly used by peripherals that store to flash drives, such as digital cameras or smart phones. Even though no Mac can start up from this type of partitioning, all Macs can access MBR partitioning.

Obviously, if you have any additional drives formatted with APM or MBR, you will have to repartition those drives in order for them to act as a startup drive for an Intel-based Mac. But if you don't plan on ever using the additional drives as a system disk, there is no advantage to repartitioning. Also, you should keep MBR drives unmodified if you intend to keep them backward compatible with generic PCs or peripherals.

TIP Intel-based Macs can start up from USB, FireWire, and Thunderbolt external drives.

Volume Formats

The volume format defines how the files and folders are saved to the drive. To maintain compatibility with other operating systems and provide advanced features for later Mac systems, Lion supports a variety of storage volume formats.

Volume formats supported as read/write in Lion:

▶ Mac OS Standard—This is the legacy volume format used by the classic Mac OS. This format, though a precursor to Mac OS Extended, is not supported as a startup volume for Lion.

▶ Mac OS Extended—Mac OS Extended is the legacy volume format designed and supported by Apple for Macintosh computers. This format is itself an update from the earlier Mac OS Standard format. Mac OS Extended supports all the advanced features required by Lion, including Unicode filenames, rich metadata, POSIX permissions, access control lists (ACLs), UNIX-style links, and aliases.

▶ Mac OS Extended (Case-Sensitive)—This Mac OS Extended format adds case sensitivity to the file system. Normally Mac OS Extended is case-preserving but case-insensitive. This means that a normally formatted Mac volume will remember what case you chose for the characters of a file's name, but it cannot differentiate between similar filenames where the only difference is the case. In other words, it would not recognize "MYfile" and "myfile" as different filenames. By adding support for case sensitivity, Apple resolved this issue. However, this is generally an issue only for volumes that need to support traditional UNIX clients, like those shared from Macs or Xserve servers running OS X Lion Server. Further, many third-party applications exhibit significant issues when running from a case-sensitive file system. Thus, the case-sensitive option is not recommended as a default for Lion client systems.

▶ Mac OS Extended (Journaled) or Mac OS Extended (Case-Sensitive, Journaled)—This feature is an option for the Mac OS Extended format that adds advanced file system journaling to help preserve volume structure integrity. The journal records what file operations (creation, expansion, deletion, and so on) are in progress at any given moment. If the system crashes or loses power, the journal can be "replayed" to make sure operations that were previously in progress are completed, rather than left in a half-completed, inconsistent state. This helps avoid the possibility of file corruption and greatly reduces the amount of time it takes to complete the check-and-repair process on the volume after a crash. Because of these enhancements the default format for a Lion system volume is Mac OS Extended (Journaled).

NOTE ▸ While journaling protects the file structure, it cannot protect the contents of files themselves against corruption. If a large file was half-written when the system crashed, the journal will make sure that half-file is consistently entered in the volume's file-tracking databases, but it's still only half a file.

▸ Mac OS Extended (Journaled, Encrypted) or Mac OS Extended (Case-Sensitive, Journaled, Encrypted)—This feature is an option to the Mac OS Extended format that adds full disk, XTS-AES 128 encryption. This is the technology behind FileVault 2 full disk encryption. Details regarding FileVault 2 are covered in the "Using FileVault 2" section later in this chapter.

NOTE ▸ Encrypted Mac OS Extended volumes are not compatible with versions of Mac OS X prior to Lion.

▸ File Allocation Table (FAT)—FAT is the legacy volume format used by Windows PCs and by many peripherals. This format has evolved over the years, with each progressive version supporting larger volumes; FAT12, FAT16, FAT32. Apple's Boot Camp supports running Windows XP from a FAT32 volume, but Lion itself cannot start up from such a volume.

▸ Extended File Allocation Table (ExFAT)—Created specifically for large flash storage drives, ExFAT basically extends the legacy FAT architecture to support drives larger than 32 GB. Many flash-based digital camcorders use ExFAT to support the large storage volumes required for high-definition video.

▸ UNIX File System (UFS)—UFS is the legacy native volume format supported by UNIX systems. UFS served as the default UNIX file system for decades. Beginning with Mac OS X v10.5, though, UFS volumes are no longer supported as startup volumes. Further, Disk Utility does not support the creation of UFS volumes.

Volume formats supported as read-only in Lion:

▸ NT File System (NTFS)—Windows 7, Windows Vista, Windows XP, and Windows Server all use this as their native volume format. Once again, Boot Camp supports running Windows from an NTFS volume, but Lion itself cannot write to or start up from such a volume. Further, Disk Utility does not support the creation of NTFS volumes.

TIP ▸ You can add NTFS volume write support to Lion by installing the free and open source NTFS-3G and MacFUSE software bundle: http://macntfs-3g .blogspot.com.

▶ ISO 9660 or Compact Disk File System (CDFS)—This is a common standard for read-only CD media. Note, however, that "Mac formatted" CD media can contain Mac OS Standard formatted volumes.

▶ Universal Disk Format (UDF)—This is a common standard for read-only DVD media. Again, note that "Mac formatted" DVD media can contain Mac OS Standard volumes.

MORE INFO ▶ A wide variety of file systems are out there. Wikipedia has a great comparison of all file systems: http://en.wikipedia.org/wiki/Comparison_of_file_systems.

Managing File Systems

The internal disk drive originally included with your Mac is probably the only new storage device you will ever come across that is already properly formatted for full Mac compatibility. Most new storage devices are either completely blank or formatted for Windows. For the most part, you will still be able to use Windows-formatted drives on the Mac without reformatting. Conversely, if you want to install the Mac operating system on a drive or you have a new drive that is completely blank, you will have to reformat the drive.

The primary storage management tool included in Lion is /Applications/Utilities/Disk Utility. You may have already used this utility from Lion Recovery to reformat the system drive before you installed the operating system. Here you are going to explore all the aspects of this tool for managing disk and flash drives.

Disk Utility.app

MORE INFO ▶ If you prefer greater flexibility, then you can perform all the same actions of Disk Utility, plus a few more, with the diskutil command. You can also gather disk-capacity information with the df command and disk-utilization information with the du command. As always, you can find out more about these commands by reading their man pages from Terminal.

Though disk-based and solid-state drives are technologically different storage mediums, Lion treats the two similarly because they both provide dynamically writable storage. Optical media, on the other hand, is handled differently by the Mac because it's sequentially written storage. Using optical media is covered in the "Using Optical Media" section later in this chapter.

Macintosh HD   FireWire Drive   USB Key

Formatting or Reformatting a Drive

Despite all the choices Lion gives you for configuring storage, actually formatting a drive is quite easy. If you attach an unformatted device, the Mac will automatically prompt you to open Disk Utility. On the other hand, if you have a drive that is already formatted and you want to change the partition scheme or the volume structure, you can just as easily reformat the drive using the same steps.

The disk you inserted was not readable by this computer.

Initialize...   Ignore   Eject

It is important to remember that reformatting a drive will destroy any formatting that is already there; a reformatted drive is effectively losing its contents. The drive will not technically be erased—all the bits are still stored on the device. Reformatting will simply replace the previously populated volume structure with an empty volume structure. Truly erasing the contents of a drive is covered in the "Securely Erasing Files" section later in this chapter.

To format a drive:

1   Make sure the drive you wish to format is currently attached to the computer, and then open /Applications/Utilities/Disk Utility.

2 Select the drive you wish to format from the column on the left.

The size, manufacturer, and model number is usually the name of the drive. If a drive has any volumes, they will appear directly below and indented from the drive entry. If you want to reformat the entire drive, be sure to select the drive, not a volume.

3 Click the Partition tab to the right. This is the only section in Disk Utility that will allow you to change both the partition scheme and the volume format.

4 From the Partition Layout pop-up menu, choose the number of partitions you want for this drive. You must choose at least one partition.

5 Once you have selected the number of partitions you desire, click the Options button at the bottom of the partition diagram to set the partition scheme.

A dialog appears allowing you to select an appropriate partition scheme.

6   Select your partition scheme, and then click the OK button.

If you have chosen multiple partitions, you can adjust their sizes by clicking and dragging the line between partitions in the partition diagram. You can also specify a precise size by clicking in a partition area and then entering a specific size in the Size entry field to the right.

7   Choose a name and volume format for each partition.

If you have only one partition, enter an appropriate name and choose the volume format from the Format pop-up menu. If you have chosen multiple partitions, select each partition from the partition dialog first and then set the name and volume structure.

NOTE ▶ You can always change the name of a volume later in the Finder.

NOTE ▶ You cannot select any disk encryption options from Disk Utility's Partition interface. You can, however, select encryption options from the Erase interface, as covered in the "Erasing a Drive or Volume" section later in this chapter.

8   Once you have double-checked all your choices, click the Apply button.

You will be presented with a summary dialog, reminding you once again that continuing may destroy any previous volumes. If you are sure this is what you want to do, click the Partition button once more.

Partitioning and formatting takes only a few moments, and once the process is complete, you should see new volumes in the Disk Utility list and in the Finder.

Repartitioning a Drive

A previous system version, Mac OS X v10.5, introduced a new feature in Disk Utility that enabled you to dynamically repartition a drive without destroying any currently stored data on the drive. This functionality was introduced primarily to facilitate the Boot Camp setup process. Lion upgrade installations also benefit from this functionality to create the hidden Lion Recovery HD on an existing system drive.

The only downside to dynamic repartitioning is that some drives may not support the partition changes that you want to make. For instance, some drives may be too full for you to repartition. Also, Disk Utility does not support dynamically repartitioning volumes that are encrypted, like those created for use with FileVault 2, or drives formatted with the Master Boot Record partition scheme. If you come across any of these issues, you can resort to using the previous method for repartitioning a drive, which does erase any previous formatting, as outlined in the prior section of this chapter.

> **NOTE** ► Always back up important data before making changes to a drive's file system.

> **NOTE** ► Modifying a Lion system disk may also require relocating the hidden Lion Recovery HD. Fortunately, Disk Utility in Lion handles this automatically for you.

> **NOTE** ► Although Lion supports partition modifications of a currently in-use system disk, it does not support modifications of drives containing Mac OS Extended (Journaled, Encrypted) volumes. Thus, if you have enabled FileVault 2 for the system volume, you will not be able to dynamically repartition the drive.

To dynamically repartition a drive:

1   Quit all open applications, as they may crash while the file system is being changed and consequently cause data corruption or loss.

2   Make sure the drive you wish to change is currently attached to the computer, and then open /Applications/Utilities/Disk Utility.

3   Select the drive you wish to change from the column on the left.

    The size, manufacturer, and model number is usually the name of the drive. Do not select any of the drive's volumes.

4   Click the Partition tab to the right.

    Any data currently on the drive will appear as a light blue area in the partition diagram. White areas indicate free space.

5   Resize any volume, add new volumes, or delete any volume that isn't the current system drive.

▶   To resize a current volume, click and drag from the bottom-right corner until you reach the desired new size. You will not be allowed to shrink a volume past the light blue that represents data on the drive. You may choose to leave parts of the drive empty if you plan on formatting those parts later using another operating system.

▶   To add a new volume, click the small plus button below the partition diagram. Remember, you can have as many as 16 partitions per drive. Be sure to choose an appropriate name and volume format from the pop-up menu for each new volume.

▶ To delete a volume, select it from the partition diagram and click the minus button below the partition diagram. If you are deleting a preexisting partition, you will be presented with a verification dialog. If you are certain that you want to delete the selected partition, click the Remove button to finish the process. The volume will be deleted immediately, leaving free space where you will be able to resize other volumes or create new volumes.

6 Once you have made all your changes and verified your selections, click the Apply button to continue.

7 You will be presented with a summary dialog, listing what changes will be made and which (if any) volumes will be erased. If you are sure this is what you want to do, click the Partition button once more.

Depending on how much preexisting data must be moved to create your new disk structure, it may take quite a while for the repartitioning process to complete. You should not attempt to interrupt Disk Utility or open any other applications while the system is repartitioning the drive. Doing so may result in catastrophic data loss.

8   Once the process is complete, you should immediately notice the changes in the Disk Utility list and the Finder.

Erasing a Drive or Volume

You have seen earlier in this chapter how Disk Utility can be used to quickly erase an entire drive or volume by reformatting it. Yet the default reformatting process does not actually erase any files from the drive. This is because Disk Utility simply creates new blank volumes by only replacing the file and folder structure data of any volume. The old data files still remain on the drive and can be recovered using third-party recovery tools.

In fact, there is no such thing as erasing data from a drive—all you can do is write new data on top of the old data. Therefore, if you want to truly "erase" a drive or volume, you must somehow write new nonsensitive data on top of it. Disk Utility includes a variety of options that will let you securely erase old data. You can securely erase an entire drive or volume, or just a volume's remaining free space. Further, the Erase interface is the only location in Disk Utility to create a Mac OS Extended (Journaled, Encrypted) volume.

> **NOTE ▶** Encrypted Mac OS Extended volumes are not compatible with versions of Mac OS X prior to Lion.

NOTE ▶ To encrypt the system volume, you need to enable FileVault 2 as covered in the "Using FileVault 2" section later in this chapter.

NOTE ▶ Disk Utility cannot convert an existing volume to a Mac OS Extended (Journaled, Encrypted) volume. However, the diskutil command can convert an existing volume to an encrypted volume without losing the data.

NOTE ▶ Erasing or formatting a disk will not change the drive's partition scheme. To change a drive's partition scheme, you must repartition the drive, as detailed previously in this chapter.

To quickly or securely erase an entire drive or volume:

1 Make sure the drive or volume you wish to erase is currently available to the computer, and then open /Applications/Utilities/Disk Utility.

2 Select the drive or volume you wish to securely erase from the column on the left.

The size, manufacturer, and model number is usually the name of the drive. If a drive has any volumes, they will appear directly below and indented from the drive entry. If you want to reformat the entire drive, be sure to select the drive, not a volume.

3 Click the Erase tab to the right, and then click the Security Options button.

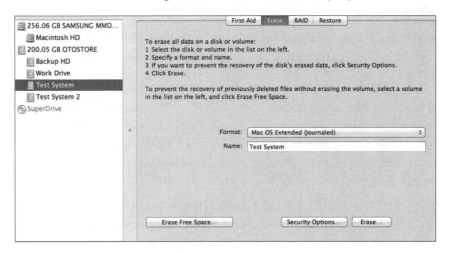

You will be presented with a dialog allowing you to choose one of the four erase options presented in a slider from Fastest to Most Secure. Drag the slide indicator to your preferred erase method and click the OK button to continue.

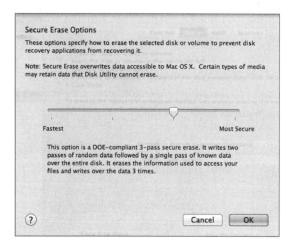

The four erase options are:

Fastest: Don't Erase Data. This is the default action that occurs when you erase or reformat a drive or volume. Obviously, this does not provide any security from drive-recovery utilities. On the other hand, this choice provides a nearly instantaneous erase option.

Second Choice: Single-Pass Erase. This option will write zeros over all the data once. This is the quickest of the secure erase options, and for most users provides an adequate level of security.

NOTE ▸ When erasing solid-state drive media, only a single-pass erase is recommended. In fact, multipass erasing of solid-state media provides no further security and can lead to degraded drive performance over time.

Third Choice: 3-Pass Erase. This is a very secure option that writes two passes of random data followed by a single pass of known data to the drive. According to Apple, this option meets U.S. Department of Defense standards for securely erasing data. The downside is that this method will take three times longer than the standard single-pass method.

Most Secure: 7-Pass Erase. This is the most secure option, which according to Apple meets U.S. Department of Defense standards for securely erasing data. The Mac will write seven different passes of random and patterned data to the drive. Obviously, this method will take seven times longer than the standard single-pass method.

4   At this point you can also change the volume's name or volume format. Again, this is the only location in Disk Utility for creating an encrypted Mac OS Extended volume.

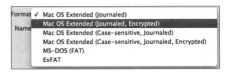

5   Double-check all your choices and then click the Erase button.

6   You will be presented with a summary dialog that varies depending on your volume format choice.

If you are not creating a new encrypted volume, the dialog simply reminds you once again that you will destroy data on any previous volumes. If you are sure this is what you want to do, click the Erase button once more.

If you are creating a new encrypted volume, a dialog will appear, allowing you to set the encrypted volume's password. Note that as the dialog states, you will not be able to recover data from the encrypted volume if you lose the password. Choose the password wisely.

Depending on the size of the selected drive or volume and the erase option you chose, this process can take anywhere from seconds to days. If the process is going to take more than a few seconds, Disk Utility will show a progress indicator with the esti- mated time required to complete the erase task.

Securely Erasing Files

Because securely erasing an entire drive or volume can take quite a bit of time, you may find it's much quicker to use a more subtle secure erase method. Also, you may not want to erase the entire contents of a volume or disk—you may just want to securely erase a few specific files or only the free space on your drive. Fortunately, Lion provides targeted secure erase options from the Finder and Disk Utility.

Use the Finder to Securely Erase Selected Items

To securely erase only select files and folders:

1   In the Finder, move the items you wish to securely erase to the Trash folder.

There are several ways to accomplish this task: You can drag and drop the items into the Trash; you can select the items and then choose File > Move to Trash; or you can select the items and use the Command-Delete keyboard shortcut.

2   Choose Finder > Secure Empty Trash from the menu bar.

The Finder's Secure Empty Trash feature is a secure erase method, which writes seven different passes of random and patterned data on top of the erased files. According to Apple, this feature even meets U.S. Department of Defense standards for securely erasing data.

3   You will be presented with a verification dialog. If you are certain you want to securely erase the items in the Trash forever, click the Secure Empty Trash button to continue.

Depending on the number and size of the files to be erased, this process can take any-where from seconds to days. The Finder will show you a progress indicator, but it will not show an estimated time.

Use Disk Utility to Securely Erase Free Space

If in the past users have neglected to securely erase their files, you can cover their tracks by erasing a volume's free space. To securely erase a volume's remaining free space, includ-ing any previously deleted files that were not securely erased:

1   Make sure the volume with the free space you wish to securely erase is available to the system, and then open /Applications/Utilities/Disk Utility.

2   Select the name of the volume with the free space you wish to securely erase from the column on the left. Make sure not to select the physical drive, only a volume of the drive.

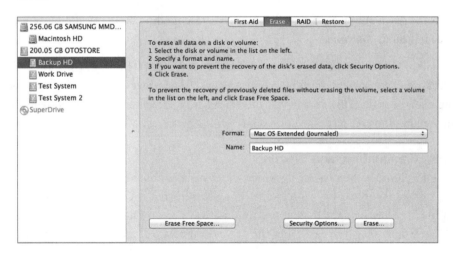

3   Click the Erase tab to the right, and then click the Erase Free Space button.

You will be presented with a dialog allowing you to choose one of the three available secure erase options, similar to those for erasing an entire volume or disk: Fastest is a single-pass erase, the second choice is a 3-pass erase, and Most Secure is a 7-pass erase.

NOTE ▶ When erasing solid-state drive media, only a single-pass erase is recommended. In fact, multipass erasing of solid-state media provides no further security and can lead to degraded drive performance over time.

4 Select the radio button next to your preferred erase method and click the Erase Free Space button to continue.

Depending on the amount of free space to erase and the erase option you chose, this process can take anywhere from seconds to days. If the process is going to take more than a few seconds, Disk Utility will show a progress indicator with the estimated time required to complete the erase task.

Mounting, Unmounting, and Ejecting

Mounting a volume is the process by which the system establishes a logical connection to a storage volume. This is not something users normally concern themselves with on the Mac, because the system will automatically mount any volume connected to the Mac. Simply plug a drive in and the drive's volumes will automatically appear in the Finder and Disk Utility. The only exception to this rule is for Mac OS Extended (Journaled, Encrypted) volumes, which require that you enter a password to unlock the drive's contents.

On the other hand, ensuring that users properly unmount and eject volumes is very important to maintaining data integrity. Unmounting is the process of having the Mac cleanly disconnect from a drive's volumes, whereas ejecting is the process of having the Mac additionally disconnect electronically from the actual hardware drive or media. When you choose to eject a drive from the Finder, the computer will actually unmount the volumes first and then eject the drive.

Ejecting Drives

There are four methods to unmount and eject a drive from the Finder:

▶ In the Finder, drag the disk icon to the Trash icon in the Dock. You'll note the Trash icon changes to an Eject icon, indicating the appropriate action.

▶ Pressing and holding the Eject key, the furthest top-right key on a Mac keyboard, for a few moments will only unmount and eject optical media. If you have more than one optical drive, press Option-Eject to unmount and eject the second optical drive.

▶ Select the volume you wish to unmount and eject from the Finder's sidebar, and then choose File > Eject from the menu bar.

▶ In the Finder's sidebar, click the small Eject button next to the volume you wish to unmount and eject.

When you use the Finder to unmount and eject a single volume that is part of a drive with several mounted volumes, you will be presented with a warning dialog giving you the choice to unmount and eject all the volumes on the drive or just the one you originally selected. You shouldn't experience any problems with a drive by having some volumes mounted while others are unmounted. Just remember to properly unmount the remaining volumes before you disconnect the drive.

TIP In the Finder, you can eject all the volumes of a drive by holding down the Option key while you click the Eject button.

Manage Volume Mounts With Disk Utility

If you need to remount volumes on a connected drive, you will have to unmount and eject the remaining volumes on the drive from the Finder, and then physically disconnect and reconnect the drive. Or you can choose to manually mount, unmount, and eject items using Disk Utility.

To manually mount, unmount, and eject items:

1   Open /Applications/Utilities/Disk Utility.

In this example screenshot, a variety of volumes are shown. Notice that the volume names from the second drive appear in dimmed text; those volumes are physically connected to the Mac but not mounted.

2   Select the volume or drive you wish to unmount or eject from the column on the left.

3   If you have selected a volume to unmount, simply click the Unmount button in the toolbar.

The volume will unmount immediately, disappearing from the Finder, although in Disk Utility the volume's name will remain but appear as dimmed text.

4   To mount an unmounted volume on a connected drive, click on the volume's dimmed name, and then click the Mount button in the toolbar. The volume should immediately mount and appear in the Finder and as normal text in Disk Utility.

If you select an unmounted Mac OS Extended (Journaled, Encrypted) volume, the Mount button is replaced by an Unlock button. Clicking the Unlock button will present a dialog where you enter a password to unlock the drive's contents. Once authenticated, the volume should immediately mount.

5 If you have selected an entire disk to unmount all its volumes and eject, click the Eject button in the toolbar.

All the disk's volumes will be unmounted, and then the disk will be disconnected from the system, disappearing from the Finder and Disk Utility. You will have to physically disconnect and reconnect the drive for its volumes to be remounted.

Ejecting In-Use Volumes

Any volume that contains files currently in use by an application or system process cannot be unmounted or ejected. The obvious reason for this is to avoid data corruption when a process attempts to write to files on that volume. If you attempt to eject a volume with in-use files, the Finder will not allow you to eject the volume, but, depending on the situation, it will try to help you eject the volume. If the application or process using the volume belongs to your account, it will let you know via the following dialog. In this case the resolution is as simple as quitting the suspect application and attempting to eject the volume again.

NOTE ▶ As the example screenshot shows, using Terminal can prevent you from ejecting a volume. Even if there is no active process, just having Terminal open with the volume as the current working directory will prevent unmounting.

If you don't own the application or process using the volume, the Finder will ask if you want to attempt to forcibly eject the volume. To take this path, you will have to click the Force Eject button twice, but the Finder will then try to quit the offending application or process to release the volume you're attempting to eject. If the volume was successfully ejected, you will be notified by the dialog.

If this doesn't work or the Finder doesn't tell you which application is suspect, you can always log out the current user to quit all her processes and log in again, or fully restart the Mac to clear the issue. While this may seem excessive, it is not advisable to physically disconnect a volume without first unmounting it, as covered in the next section.

If a volume still refuses to unmount after you've tried the previous troubleshooting steps, or you are unable to restart the computer, you can force a volume to unmount using the diskutil command. Again, it's not advisable to force the system to unmount a volume, but if you need to unmount one, this method is better than physically disconnecting the drive from the Mac.

The following command-line example shows how to forcibly unmount a volume named ExternalDrive; further, using this technique also requires administrator authentication:

```
MyMac:~ michelle$ sudo diskutil unmount force /Volumes/Backup
```

Improperly Unmounting or Ejecting

Disconnecting a volume from the Mac that you did not first unmount can lead to data corruption. If you forcibly eject a drive by physically disconnecting it before you unmount it, or if the system loses contact with the drive due to power failure, the Mac will warn you with a Device Removal dialog. You should immediately reconnect the device so the Mac can attempt to verify or repair its contents.

Anytime you reconnect a drive that was improperly unmounted, the Mac will automatically run a file system diagnostic on the drive before it remounts any volumes. Depending on the format and size of the drive, it may take anywhere from a few seconds to several hours for the system to verify the contents of the drive. Again, journaled volumes, like Mac OS Extended (Journaled), should verify quite quickly.

If you connect a drive and notice there is a fair amount of drive activity but the volumes have not mounted yet, the system is probably running a diagnostic on the drive. You can verify that the system is diagnosing a volume by opening the /Applications/Utilities/ Activity Monitor application and looking for a background process with fsck in its name. Monitoring processes is covered in Chapter 5, "Applications and Processes."

Using Software RAID

The idea behind RAID (Redundant Array of Independent Disks) is that you can combine similar drives to form large volumes with increased performance or reliability. The downside is that you have to have special hardware or software to manage the RAID. Hardware-based RAID solutions are often external to the computer because they contain many drives and include specialized hardware to manage the RAID. Conversely, software-based RAID solutions don't require any special hardware as they use software running from the computer's processor to manage the RAID.

NOTE ▶ Although Lion supports using a software RAID set as a system disk, it does not support the creation of a Lion Recovery HD volume or encrypted volumes on software RAID sets. Thus, if you choose to use a software RAID set as a system disk, you cannot enable FileVault 2.

Lion includes a software-based RAID solution as part of its file system. The advantage of using the built-in software-based RAID is that no special hardware is required. All you have to do is connect two or more similar drives to the Mac via any compatible hardware interface, and then use Disk Utility to create the RAID set. The main disadvantage is that you cannot use advanced RAID types normally available from a hardware-based RAID solution. Specifically, the popular RAID 5 and 6 implementations, which provide both increased redundancy and performance, are not available using the built-in software-based RAID solution.

TIP ▶ You can use the built-in software-based RAID to further combine hardware-based RAIDs. This technique is often used to combine the two separate sides of an Xserve RAID into a single huge volume.

Software RAID Example—1 TB Drives

Lion's built-in software-based RAID supports:

▶ RAID 0—Commonly called *striping*, RAID 0 splits up the data into multiple pieces, and then simultaneously writes each piece to a different drive in the set. This yields a single large volume, with dramatically increased read and write performance, equivalent to the cumulative size and performance of all the drives. On the other hand, RAID 0 offers zero increase in reliability since if just one drive in the set fails, then all the data is lost. In fact, RAID 0 increases your chances of data loss because you are introducing more points of failure. In short, RAID 0 is space efficient and fast but entails increased risk and provides no redundancy.

▶ RAID 1—Commonly called *mirroring*, RAID 1 writes the same data to each drive in the set. This yields a single volume that is the same size as a single drive. Write performance is no faster than with a single drive, whereas read performance is increased. The primary advantage to a RAID 1 set is that it can survive and recover from hardware failure. RAID 1 decreases your chances of data loss by providing redundancy. In short, RAID 1 is space-inefficient and partially slower but provides drive redundancy and decreased risk of data loss due to drive failure. Even so, it's very important to remember that mirroring is not a backup solution. Backup solutions create an archive of the data frozen in time and save it to another storage device. If hardware failure occurs, you can recover from a previous backup version of the data. With a mirrored RAID set, all file system changes are applied immediately to all drives in the set and no archival history is maintained.

> **NOTE** ▶ Keep in mind that with a RAID 1 set, if a drive fails, your Mac may keep running without warning you. This may leave you with only a single drive in your RAID set, effectively disabling the redundancy. You should periodically check the status of a RAID 1 set from the Disk Utility application.

▶ Nested RAID, 1+0 or 0+1—Because RAID 0 and RAID 1 offer opposed feature sets, nesting one type inside the other can provide the features of both. In other words, you can stripe data between two mirrors, or you can mirror data on two stripes. These nested configurations are certainly more complicated and require a minimum of four separate drives. However, when you combine their features, you get increased performance and redundancy.

▶ Concatenated disk set—This isn't what most would consider a true RAID configuration, as not all drives are being used simultaneously. With a concatenated disk set, the system will simply continue on to the next drive once the previous drive is filled. The only advantage here is that the user will see one large volume instead of several separate drives.

MORE INFO ▶ You can find out more about all the different RAID types by visiting Wikipedia's RAID entry, http://en.wikipedia.org/wiki/RAID.

MORE INFO ▶ Both Mac Pro and Xserve computers feature optional internal hardware RAID cards. A discussion of these cards is outside the scope of this guide, but you can find out more from the RAID Utility User's Guide available online at http://images.apple.com/server/docs/RAID_Utility_User_Guide.pdf.

Creating a RAID Set

Creating a RAID set in Lion is only slightly more complicated than formatting a standard disk or flash drive. Remember, you can use just about any combination of drives to create a RAID set. Nevertheless, you should follow a couple rules to ensure a healthy RAID set.

Here are some software-based RAID guidelines:

▶ Use identical drives if possible—This will ensure consistent size and performance for all drives in the RAID set. RAID sets are susceptible to performance degradation to the level of the lowest common denominator. In other words, all the drives in a RAID set are treated as being as large or as fast as your smallest and slowest drives. This is not an issue for a concatenated disk set.

▶ Distribute the drives across multiple interfaces to minimize contention—This often requires extra hardware, but giving the Mac multiple independent paths to the drives can dramatically increase performance.

▶ Make certain that all drives in a set are simultaneously available to the Mac— This may be a difficult criterion if the drives are using different interfaces, but it's necessary to maintain RAID consistency. If a drive in a RAID set is missing for more than a few seconds, the system will assume the drive has failed and the RAID set is damaged. In other words, make sure all the drives are turned on and plugged into the Mac at the same time.

To create a software-based RAID set:

1   Make sure all the drives for the new, unformatted RAID set are connected to the Mac, and then open /Applications/Utilities/Disk Utility.

2 Select any one of the drives from the column on the left, and then click the RAID tab to the right.

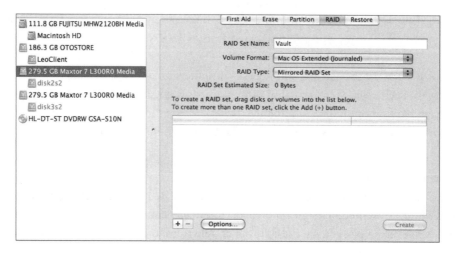

3 Click the small plus button at the bottom of the RAID diagram to create a RAID set. The new RAID set will assume some defaults that you can change at any time before you create the RAID.

4 Configure the newly created RAID set by clicking on its entry in the RAID diagram to select it. For each RAID set, you need to enter a volume name for the RAID set, choose a volume type from the Volume Format pop-up menu, and choose a RAID type from the pop-up menu. Then click the Options button at the bottom to configure the RAID block size for optimal performance or enable automatic rebuilds if the RAID set is mirrored.

NOTE ▶ Disk Utility will only create RAID sets with one volume. Further, it will not let you repartition the RAID set after it has been created.

5   If you are creating a nested RAID set, click the small plus button to create additional RAID sets.

Be sure to properly configure each new RAID set. Drag the nested RAIDs on top of the root RAID set to configure the nesting order.

6   Add the drives by dragging the drive icons from the column on the left to the RAID diagram on the right.

Each storage drive you add to your RAID set is considered a "RAID slice." To specify a particular RAID set order, continue to drag drive icons around until you set their appropriate locations in the RAID diagram.

7   Optionally, if you have added three or more drives to a mirrored RAID set, you can define a spare drive by selecting the drive from the RAID diagram and then choosing Spare from the Disk Type pop-up menu.

If you set a spare and one of the other drives becomes unreachable during the life of the RAID set, you can have the system automatically rebuild the mirrored RAID. You can enable automatic rebuilding from the RAID options dialog by clicking the Options button below the RAID diagram.

8   If you need to delete items in your RAID, select them from the RAID diagram, and then click the small minus button below the diagram.

> **TIP** If you make too many mistakes while designing your RAID, sometimes it's easier to just start over by quitting and then reopening Disk Utility.

9   Double-check all your choices and then click the Create button.

You will be presented with a summary dialog, reminding you once again that continuing may destroy any previous volumes. If you are sure this is what you want to do, click the Create button once more.

RAID set creation takes only a few moments, and once it's complete, you should see the new RAID set volume in the Disk Utility list and in the Finder. Selecting the newly created RAID set from the column on the left, and then clicking the RAID tab, should reveal that the set is "Online."

Rebuilding a RAID Set

As mentioned earlier, using multiple drives in a RAID set can introduce more points of storage failure. Fortunately, RAID 1 data mirroring configurations are designed specifically to prevent data loss when a drive fails. Lion even includes the ability to automatically repair mirrored RAID sets if you specified that option during RAID creation.

Before the system mounts a RAID volume, it will check the set for consistency. If the system finds a degraded striped RAID 0 set, you'd better have a good backup because all that data is lost. The system will report the degraded RAID set in Disk Utility, but it will not mount the volume. Only a data recovery service, such as DriveSavers, might have a chance at recovering your data.

On the other hand, if the system finds that a mirrored RAID 1 set is degraded, it will either warn you or automatically start rebuilding the RAID set if configured. Either way, the volume will still mount and be accessible to you in the Finder. You should avoid writing new data to a degraded RAID set until you have completed the rebuilding process.

There are two main failure modes for a mirrored RAID 1 set:

▶   One of the drives appears to be responding properly, but the data on the drive is not consistent with the other drives in the set. If configured, the system will automatically start rebuilding the RAID set data by recopying it from a working drive to the apparently corrupted drive. Otherwise, the system will wait for you to manually engage the rebuild process from Disk Utility.

▶   One of the drives in the set is no longer available. If a spare is configured, the system will automatically start rebuilding the RAID set data by copying it from a working drive to the spare drive. Otherwise, the system will wait for you to manually replace the drive and manually engage the rebuild process from Disk Utility.

To manually rebuild a mirrored RAID 1 set:

1   Make sure that all the drives that are part of the RAID set are connected to the Mac, and then open /Applications/Utilities/Disk Utility.

2   Select the degraded RAID set from the column on the left; it should be easy to locate as its name will show up onscreen in bright red text. Select the RAID tab to the right if it isn't already selected.

3 Depending on the failure mode of the RAID set, you will need to choose one of two resolutions:

► **Inconsistent data.** The system has discovered that one of the drives does not have the same data as the others. You will see the word "Failed" next to the drive with inconsistent data. Simply click the Rebuild button to repair the RAID set.

► **Bad or missing drive.** The system can no longer access one of the drives. You will see "Offline" next to the missing drive. Select the missing drive from the RAID dialog, and then click the small minus button below the RAID dialog to delete the missing drive. Drag the replacement drive from the column on the left to replace the missing drive from the RAID diagram. Click the Rebuild button to repair the RAID set.

Depending on the size and performance of the RAID set, the rebuild process can take anywhere from seconds to days. Disk Utility will open a progress dialog with the estimated time required to complete the rebuild task.

Using Optical Media

Over a decade ago, Apple made headlines by introducing the iMac with only an optical drive, choosing to banish the traditional floppy disk drive from the new computer's revolutionary design. It should come as no surprise, then, that Apple has already started the process of removing optical drives from new hardware designs. Both the MacBook Air and Mac mini computers have done away with optical drives to save space and weight. Usage of optical media has substantially decreased as a means of sharing files among computers, as the proliferation of high-capacity portable flash storage and high-speed wireless Internet increases. However, optical media still has value as a cheap, portable, and durable storage medium.

> **TIP** ▶ You can easily identify the capabilities of your Mac's optical drive by opening /Applications/Utilities/System Information and viewing the Disc Burning information section.

Lion provides support for reading and writing optical media, although the Mac treats optical media differently than disk or flash drives. This is because most optical media formats require that the data be sequentially and permanently written to the disc. This is why the term "burn" is often used to describe the process of writing data to an optical disc. The data is literally burned into the media, and it's common knowledge that you simply can't "un-burn" something once it's been burned.

> **NOTE** ▶ As of this writing, no Mac currently shipping includes the ability to write to Blu-ray discs. However, third-party vendors provide both the hardware and software to add this capability to Mac computers.

Several of the applications included with a new Mac are designed to burn specific types of data to optical discs. For example, iTunes can burn audio and MP3 discs, iDVD is used to create video DVDs, and iPhoto can create cross-platform photo discs. Conversely, if you simply want to burn general-purpose data files onto an optical disc, the Finder is your tool. Finally, Disk Utility rounds out the Mac's optical media functionality by providing the means to burn disk images and prepare rewritable discs for reburning.

Burning a Disc via the Finder

The Finder provides no less than three methods for burning data to an optical disc. The first enables you to quickly select and burn specific items in the Finder to an optical disc. The other two methods involve creating burn folders that let you organize the contents destined for an optical disc before you burn the data to it. This is a convenient way to burn general-purpose data discs, as you cannot change the contents of most optical discs once they have been burned.

> **TIP** ▶ The Finder will automatically burn cross-platform optical discs that can be accessed by both Macs and PCs.

Burn Selected Items

To quickly burn specific selected items:

1 Select the items you wish to burn in the Finder.

You can hold down the Shift key to quickly select contiguous lists of items, or hold down the Command key to quickly select noncontiguous items.

2 Choose File > Burn "Items" to Disc from the menu bar.

The word "Items" in the menu will be replaced by the name of the single item you have selected or the number of items you have selected.

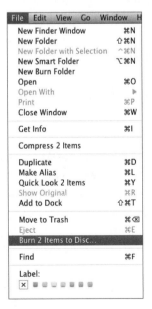

3   The Finder will present you with a dialog asking you to insert a blank disc and letting you know how much storage space will be required. Insert an appropriately sized blank recordable optical disc.

4   Once the system has verified that the inserted optical disc is adequate, it will present a dialog allowing you to select a name for the disc and a burn speed. Stick with the maximum speed unless you are experiencing problems burning discs.

5   Click the Burn button to start the burn and verification process.

Depending on the size of the data and the speed of the drive, the burn and verification process can take anywhere from minutes to hours. The Finder will show a progress dialog that will also allow you to cancel the burn by clicking the small X button on the far right.

6   Once the burn and verification is complete, the Finder will mount the completed disc. Press and hold the Eject key, the furthest top-right key on a Mac keyboard, for a few moments to eject the optical disc.

Using a Burn Folder

To use a burn folder:

1   In the Finder, choose File > New Burn Folder from the menu bar.

This will create a special new folder called "Burn Folder" in the current Finder window or desktop. You can move and rename this folder as you would any other folder.

Burn Folder.fpbf

A burn folder is special because as you drag files and folders inside this folder, they will not be moved or copied into the folder. Instead, the system creates aliases to the original items. This allows you to reorganize and rename files and folders inside the burn folder without affecting the originals or wasting drive space. You can even keep burn folders around for future use after you have burned the disc.

2   Once you have the contents of your burn folder set up correctly, click the Burn button at the top-right corner of the burn folder's Finder window, or select the burn folder and then choose File > Burn "burn folder name" from the menu bar.

The Finder will present you with a dialog asking you to insert a blank disc and letting you know how much storage space will be required. Insert an appropriately sized blank recordable optical disc.

3   Once the system has verified that the inserted optical is adequate, it will present a dialog allowing you to select a name for the disc and a burn speed. Stick with the maximum speed unless you are experiencing problems burning discs.

4   Click the Burn button to start the burn and verification process.

Depending on the size of the data and the speed of the drive, this process can take anywhere from minutes to hours. The Finder will show a progress dialog that will also allow you to cancel the burn by clicking the small X button on the far right.

5   Once the burn and verification is complete, the Finder will mount the completed disc. Press and hold the Eject key, the furthest top-right key on a Mac keyboard, for a few moments to eject the optical disc.

Burning a Specific-Size Disc

To use a burn folder for a specific disc size:

1   From within the Finder, insert a blank recordable optical disc.

If this is the first time you have inserted blank optical media in this Mac, you will be presented with a dialog that will let you choose your preferred action when blank media is inserted. Leave the default action to open the media in the Finder, and then click the OK button.

The Finder will create a new burn folder with an optical disc icon named "Untitled CD" or "Untitled DVD" on your desktop and also create a link to it in the Finder's sidebar. Creating a burn folder this way will cap the size of the burn folder to ensure it will fit once burned to the media you inserted. Note at the bottom of the following example screenshot that the Finder window shows the Untitled DVD has 4.7 GB available. Also note the Untitled DVD shows up in the Finder's sidebar with a conveniently placed burn button right next to it.

TIP ▸ If you don't see the status bar at the bottom of a Finder window, you can show it by choosing View > Show Status Bar from the menu bar.

2   Continue to reorganize, move, and ultimately burn this burn folder, as you would use a manually created burn folder (outlined in the previous steps).

> **TIP** ▶ You can adjust how the Mac reacts when you insert blank optical media from the CDs & DVDs preferences in System Preferences. For instance, when you insert a blank disc, you can have the Mac automatically open a disc-burning application instead of the Finder.

Burning a Disk Image via Disk Utility

One of Disk Utility's many features is its ability to burn the contents of a disk image to optical discs. This is extremely useful for burning backup copies of disk images you have created from original media. In other words, you can use Disk Utility to create a disk image of an original optical disc, and then burn the contents of the newly created disk image to a recordable optical disc. The burned disc will appear identical to the original media. Disk Utility supports burning both Mac .dmg files and PC .iso files to an optical disc.

> **MORE INFO** ▶ Though burning a disk image will be covered here, creating a disk image is discussed in Chapter 4, "Data Management."

To burn the contents of a disk image:

1   Open /Applications/Utilities/Disk Utility, and then click the Burn button on the toolbar.

A file browser appears that enables you to browse and select the disk image whose contents you wish to burn to an optical disc.

2   A burn options dialog appears. Click the small arrow button in the upper-right corner to reveal more burn options. The default burn options are almost always the best choice, but you can make changes here as you see fit.

3   Click the Burn button to start the burn and verification process.

Depending on the size of the disk image and the speed of the drive, the burn and verification process can take anywhere from minutes to hours. Disk Utility will open a small progress dialog that will also allow you to cancel the burn by clicking the Cancel button.

4   Once the burn and verification is complete, Disk Utility will either mount or eject the completed disc, depending on the options you chose.

Erasing Rewritable Optical Media

One last optical media trick you need to know about Disk Utility is the ability to erase rewritable optical media. Lion requires that you erase rewritable media in order to burn more data to the disc. Most of the time, though, this process takes only a few moments to complete. Only optical media bearing the RW initials can be erased and then rewritten again. Also, older optical drive hardware may not support rewritable media. You can easily identify the capabilities of your Mac's optical drive by opening /Applications/Utilities/System Information and viewing the Disc Burning information section.

To erase a rewritable optical disc:

1 Insert the rewritable optical media to be erased, and then open /Applications/Utilities/Disk Utility.

2 Select the optical drive, likely named SuperDrive, from the column on the left. If there is an Erase tab to the right, select it now if it isn't already selected.

The manufacturer and model number is usually the name of the optical drive. Do not select any disc volumes.

3 Select either the Quickly or the Completely option.

Because erasing completely takes so much longer, you should stick with the Quickly option unless the computer is having problems completing the disc-erase process.

4 Once you have made your choice to quickly or completely erase, click the Erase button to continue.

5 You will be presented with a verification dialog. If you are certain you want to erase the disc, then click the Erase button to start the process.

Depending on the erase option you selected, the erase process will either take a few seconds or up to an hour. If the process is going to take more than a few seconds, Disk Utility will show a progress dialog.

6 Once the erase process is complete, the media will remain in the drive awaiting your next move. Press and hold the Eject key, the furthest top-right key on a Mac keyboard, for a few moments to eject the optical disc.

Using FileVault 2

Prior to Lion, Apple's solution for protecting user data involved encrypting just the user's home folder content. This system, now dubbed Legacy FileVault, came with a list of caveats that prevented many system features and third-party software from behaving as expected. Further, it did not meet the security requirements of many organizations that require full-disk encryption. While third-party solutions for full-disk encryption did emerge for previous versions of Mac OS X, they often exhibited issues whenever Apple updated hardware or software. If Apple elected to make certain updates to the system, many third-party full-disk encryption schemes would simply stop working. This would leave the user literally stranded with no way to reach his encrypted data. Apple's engineers finally decided to take this problem into their own hands and introduced FileVault 2 in Lion.

> **NOTE** ▸ You cannot enable FileVault 2 if any local user is still configured to use Legacy FileVault. Details regarding Legacy FileVault, including how to disable it for a user account, are covered in Chapter 2, "User Accounts."

Understanding FileVault 2

FileVault 2 protects the entire system disk by converting it to Mac OS Extended (Journaled, Encrypted) format, which uses XTS-AES 128 encryption. This move to a full disk encryption scheme resolves all the limitations of Legacy FileVault by performing the encryption at the file system driver level of the operating system. In other words, most processes and applications don't even know the drive is encrypted, so they simply behave as normal. This was not the case with Legacy FileVault, as the system and applications were unable to access an encrypted user's home folder contents when the user was logged out of the system. Also, obviously, FileVault 2, by encrypting the entire system drive, provides better protection than Legacy FileVault. Further, because FileVault 2 is fully supported by Apple, changes to Apple's hardware and software should no longer cause compatibility issues.

Apple's FileVault 2 solution is more than just a new drive format; it's a system of new technologies that enables your Mac to transition from a standard system drive to a protected system drive. Full details of all the changes required for FileVault 2 are beyond the scope of this text, but the primary new technologies instrumental in FileVault 2 include seamless volume format conversion, user account password synchronization, secure key storage on Apple's servers for lost password recovery, Lion Recovery for initial system startup, and a new firmware login window.

You can see many of these new pieces at work during startup to an encrypted system drive. What was traditionally a straightforward task, starting up the system, takes on a new level of complexity when you can't read the system drive to start with. Thus, Apple had to devise a method to authenticate and decrypt the protected system drive during startup. When starting up from an encrypted system, the Mac actually starts from the Lion Recovery HD first in order to present the user with a login window. The user enters her account password, which is then used to access the decryption key that ultimately unlocks and decrypts the protected system volume. Once the Mac has access to the system volume, startup continues normally, with one exception: The user, having already authenticated to unlock encryption, will be automatically logged into her account.

The FileVault 2 startup process requires that the system drive contain a hidden Lion Recovery HD. So, if the system drive is missing the hidden Lion Recovery HD, you cannot enable FileVault 2. Fortunately, Lion makes it impossible to accidentally engage FileVault 2 without meeting this requirement. The following screenshot shows the dialog box presented if you try to enable FileVault 2 on a system drive lacking Lion Recovery.

MORE INFO ▶ Details regarding setup of the Lion Recovery HD are covered in Chapter 1, "Installation and Configuration."

Enabling FileVault 2

In typical Apple style, despite the underlying complexity of transitioning an existing system to a secure encrypted system, turning on FileVault 2 requires only a few simple steps.

To enable FileVault 2:

1   Log out all other users on the system, and then log in as an administrative user.

2   Open the Security & Privacy preferences and authenticate as an administrative user to unlock its settings.

3   Select the FileVault tab and then click the Turn On FileVault button.

4   If there is more than one local user on the system, a dialog will appear, allowing you to enable the ability for existing local users to unlock and decrypt the protected system drive. This grants these other users the ability to start up the system.

Click the Enable User button next to each user you wish to make unlock-capable for FileVault system drive access. Each user must then enter his account password to enable this ability. An administrator cannot override this step, as each user must each enter his (supposedly) unique password.

When you have enabled all the users, click the Continue button.

NOTE ▶ Any user not initially enabled to unlock FileVault can be enabled at a later point by clicking the Enable Users button in the FileVault pane of the Security & Privacy preferences.

NOTE ▶ Only local users or cached mobile network users can be made unlock-capable for FileVault system drive access.

NOTE ▶ New local users or cached mobile network users created after FileVault is turned on will automatically be made unlock-capable for FileVault.

NOTE ▶ Any user password changes that occur will continue to be unlock-capable for FileVault as long as those changes occur on the FileVault-protected system. In other words, if you reset the password to a cached mobile user from the network directory server, he will not be allowed to unlock the local FileVault system drive. To resolve this issue, re-enable his account by clicking the Enable Users button in the FileVault pane of the Security & Privacy preferences.

5 A dialog will appear, presenting you with an automatically generated encryption recovery key.

This key can be used later if all FileVault-enabled user passwords are lost. As the dialog insists, you should copy this key and store it someplace safe besides the computer on which you are currently enabling FileVault. Once you have copied the recovery key, click the Continue button.

6 Another dialog will appear, giving you the choice to have Apple securely store your recovery key.

Select one of the following radio buttons to choose your path:

▶ **Save the recovery key with Apple.** You will now have to pick and answer three randomly selected self-identifying questions. Only by answering these questions will Apple be able to recover the key. Once you have created the questions to your satisfaction, click the Continue button and the information will be securely sent to Apple's servers for safekeeping.

NOTE ▶ An Internet connection is, obviously, required to save the recovery key with Apple.

▶ **Do not store the recovery key with Apple.** Self-explanatory. As long as you are sure the recovery key is stored safely by your actions, click the Continue button to move on.

7 A final dialog will appear, prompting you to restart the Mac. Click the Restart button.

After a few brief moments, the system volume will be ready to convert to a Mac OS Extended (Journaled, Encrypted) volume. The system will need to restart to begin the encryption.

8 Upon restart, you should notice a login window appears much quicker than normal. This is the new FileVault login window hosted from the Lion Recovery HD. Authenticate as a FileVault-enabled user, and system startup will continue until the user is automatically logged into his account.

9 If you authenticated as the same user who turned on FileVault, the Security & Privacy preferences should automatically reopen. If not, open the Security & Privacy preferences and click the FileVault tab to reveal the encryption progress.

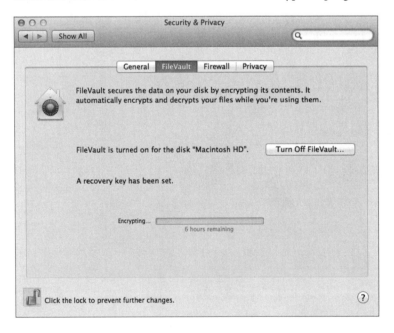

From the Security & Privacy preferences, you can view the progress of the system drive encryption as well as an estimated completion time. It may take several hours to completely encrypt a system drive. Obviously, the length of time will vary greatly based on the amount of data that must be encrypted. Amazingly, you can close the Security & Privacy preferences and continue to use the Mac as normal even though the system is slowly encrypting the drive it's running from. No notification will appear once encryption is complete, but you can always return to the Security & Privacy preferences, to check the progress.

If for some reason you wish to turn off FileVault encryption, you can do so from this same Security & Privacy pane. Doing so will require another system restart and a potentially lengthy decryption process. However, similar to the encryption process to enable FileVault, the decryption process can continue in the background without interrupting the user.

Using a FileVault 2 Recovery Key

While highly unlikely on multiuser systems, it's probably more common than you think for a single-user Mac's human to lose the login password. If by some means all unlock-capable account passwords are lost on a FileVault-protected system, you may still be able to unlock the system. The ability to unlock a FileVault-protected system lies with the recovery key. Hopefully, the user dutifully copied and saved his recovery key someplace safe.

If, however, the user has also lost his recovery key, all is not lost as long as he chose to have Apple store his key in case of a situation just like this. At this point you must contact AppleCare directly. You will have to provide the Mac's serial number, and they will have you answer the three security questions that were configured when FileVault was enabled to access the recovery key. You must successfully answer all three questions to retrieve the recovery key. Obviously, AppleCare will not make exceptions if you are unable to answer the questions, as that would seriously undermine the intended security of the FileVault solution.

> **MORE INFO ▶** You can find out more about Apple's policies regarding access to a saved recovery key from Knowledge Base article HT4790, "OS X Lion: About FileVault 2." You can find out how to directly contact AppleCare from Knowledge Base article HE57, "Contacting Apple for support and service."

If, in a worst-case scenario, you have lost all unlock-capable account passwords and the recovery key, there is no way to recover the data on the system drive. You might as well start up to Lion Recovery, as covered in Chapter 1, "Installation and Configuration," and then repartition the system drive. At that point, you could reinstall Lion or restore from a Time Machine backup, also covered in Chapter 1.

If you do have access to the FileVault recovery key:

1   At the FileVault login window, select a user and enter a bad password three times. You will be presented with a dialog suggesting you reset the user's password with the recovery key.

2   Click the triangle-in-a-circle button next to the words "Recovery Key" and the dialog will change, allowing you to then enter the recovery key.

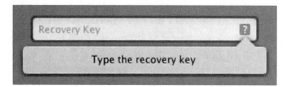

Enter the recovery key and then press the Return key.

3   Upon successfully entering the recovery key, the system will unlock and decrypt the system drive and continue the startup process.

4 You will eventually be presented with the traditional Mac login window, prompting you to set a new password for the user.

Enter a new password twice, then an optional password hint, and then click the Reset Password button to log in the user.

Understanding File System Permissions

The technologies collectively known as file system permissions are used to control file and folder authorization for Lion. File system permissions work alongside the user account technologies, which control user identification and authentication, to provide the Mac's secure multiuser environment. File system permissions—just like user accounts—permeate every level of the operating system, so a thorough investigation of this system is required to fully understand Lion.

In short, every single item on the system volume has permissions rules applied to it by the operating system. Only users and processes with root account access can ignore file system permissions rules. Thus, these rules are used to define file and folder access for every normal, administrative, guest, and sharing user. Any user can easily identify the permissions of a file or folder with the Finder's Get Info window.

NOTE ▶ The Lion interface sometimes uses the word "privileges" in place of permissions. In general, the meaning of these two terms is similar.

Viewing File System Permissions

To identify file system permissions from the Finder:

1   In the Finder, select the file or folder for which you wish to identify the permissions. You can select multiple items to open multiple Get Info windows.

2   Open the Get Info window.

There are several methods for doing this. You can choose File > Get Info from the menu bar; use the Command-I keyboard shortcut; choose Get Info from the Action pop-up menu in a Finder window toolbar; or, in the Finder, right-click or Control-click on an item and choose Get Info.

3   Once you have opened a Get Info window, click the Sharing & Permissions disclosure triangle to reveal the item's permissions.

Note that the permissions list is broken into two columns. To the left is a list of users or groups with access to this item, and to the right is the associated privilege assigned per user or group. Modifying these settings is covered in the "Managing Permissions" sections later in this chapter.

TIP ▶ You can also identify ownership and permissions from the Finder's dynamic Inspector window. This is a single floating window that will automatically refresh as you select different items in the Finder. To open the Inspector window from the Finder, use the Option-Command-I keyboard shortcut.

Ownership for Permissions

Every file and folder belongs to at least one owner and one group and also has an ownership setting for everyone else. This three-tiered ownership structure provides the basis for file system permissions:

▶ Owner—By default, the owner of an item is the user who created or copied the item to the Mac. For example, the user owns most of the items in her home folder. The system or root user almost always owns system software items, including system resources and applications. Traditionally, only the owner can change the item's ownership or permissions. Despite this, Lion makes management easier by giving every administrative user the ability to change ownership and permissions regardless of who the item's owner is.

▶ Group—By default, the group of an item is inherited from the folder it was created in. Thus, most items belong to the staff, wheel, or admin groups. Group ownership is designated to allow users other than the owner to have access to an item. For instance, even though root owns the /Applications folder, the group is set to admin so administrative users can make changes to the contents of this folder.

▶ Everyone—The Everyone setting is used to define access for anyone who isn't the owner and isn't part of the item's group. In other words, this means everyone *else*. This includes local, sharing, and guest users.

The simple three-tiered ownership structure presented here has been part of traditional UNIX operating systems for decades. However, with only three levels of permissions to choose from, it is quite difficult to define appropriate access settings for a computer with many user accounts and shared files, as is the case with many servers. Fortunately, as you'll see later, access control lists (ACLs) were developed to allow for nearly limitless ownership and permissions configurations.

Standard (POSIX) Permissions

Lion's standard file system permissions structure is based on decades-old UNIX-style permissions. This system is also sometimes referred to as POSIX-style permissions. The system may be old, but for most Mac users it is quite adequate because you can define privilege rules separately at each ownership tier. In other words, the owner, the group, and everyone else has individually specified access to each file or folder. Further, because of the inherent hierarchy built into the file system, where folders can reside inside other folders, you can easily create a complex file structure that allows varying levels of sharing and security.

A variety of privilege combinations is available from Terminal, as discussed in the "Managing Permissions via Terminal" section later in this chapter. However, Apple has streamlined the Finder to allow only the most common permissions options.

Permissions that you can assign to a file using the Finder are:

▶ Read & Write—The user or group members can open the file and save changes.

▶ Read Only—The user or group members can open the file but cannot save any changes.

▶ No Access—The user or group members have no access to the file at all.

Permissions that you can assign to a folder using the Finder are:

▶ Read & Write—The user or group members can browse and make changes to the contents of the folder.

▶ Read Only—The user or group members can browse the contents of the folder but cannot make changes to the contents of the folder.

▶ Write Only (Drop Box)—The user or group members cannot browse the folder but can copy or move items into it.

▶ No Access—The user or group members have no access to the contents of the folder.

NOTE ▶ The Finder assumes that "execute" access goes along with "read" access for folders.

Access Control Lists (ACLs)

Access control lists (ACLs) were developed to expand the standard (POSIX) permissions architecture to allow more control of file and folder access. Lion has adopted a style of

ACL similar to that available on Windows-based NTFS file systems and UNIX systems
that support NFSv4. This ACL implementation is extremely flexible but increases complexity by adding more than a dozen unique privilege and inheritance attribute types.
Further, this implementation supports an unlimited number of ACL attributes for any
user or group. Finally, it's important to note that if an ACL rule applies to a user or
group, this rule will trump standard UNIX permissions. However, any users or groups
that don't apply to a specific ACL will still be bound by the standard permissions currently in place.

Apple does not expect average users to navigate through all the options available using
ACLs, so once again the Finder has been streamlined to allow only the most common
ACL configurations. In fact, the Finder only allows you to assign ACL attributes that
match the most common permissions configurations that were previously listed in this
chapter. The only feature of ACLs that the Finder actually implements is the ability to have
an unlimited number of user or group privilege rules. In other words, the Finder uses the
ACL architecture to let you configure unique privileges for an unlimited number of users
or groups. Prior to Mac OS X v10.5, the Finder would only allow you to assign permissions using the standard three-tiered ownership style, with one owner, one group, and one
setting for everyone else.

Permissions in a Hierarchical Context

It is important to remember that permissions do not exist in isolation; rather, permissions are applied in the context of folder hierarchy. In other words, your access to an item is based on an item's permissions in combination with the permissions of the folder in which it resides. If you're still confused, it's easiest to think of permissions as defining access to an item's content, not the item itself. Remember the word "content" as you consider the following three simplified examples.

Read & Write

Read & Write

Can edit the file content
Can view or copy the file
Can move or delete the file
Can rename the file

Read Only

Can't edit file content
Can view or copy the file
Can move or delete the file
Can rename the file

Example 1: Your permissions to the folder are read and write. It's obvious that you should have full access to the first file, as your permissions here are read and write as well. You can also view and copy the second file, but you can't make changes to the file's content because your permissions are read only. Yet you can still move, delete, or rename the second file because you have read and write access to the folder's contents. Thus, the second file isn't secure in this example because you can make a copy of the original file, change the copied file's content, delete the original file, and finally replace it with the modified copy. In fact, this is how most graphical applications save document changes; thus the file can indeed be edited.

Example 2: You have read-only permission to the folder. You can edit the content of the first file because you have read and write access to it, but you can't move, delete, or rename it because you have read-only access to the folder's contents. On the other hand, you can effectively delete the file by erasing its contents. The bottom file here is the only truly secure file, as you're only allowed to view or copy the file. Granted, you can make changes to the contents of a copied file, but you still can't replace the original.

> **NOTE ▶** Many applications cannot save changes to files inside read-only folders, because these applications attempt to replace the original file during the save process, instead of revising the file's content. In other words, you may need read and write access to both the file and the folder it's inside to save changes to the file.

Read & Write

Read & Write
Locked File

Only owner can edit the file
Can copy, but copies locked
Only owner can move or delete
Only owner can rename the file

Example 3: Your permissions are identical to the first folder in the first example, with one significant change. The owner of this file has enabled the locked attribute, perhaps through Lion's new Versions document control feature. Even though you have read and write access to the example folder and file, the locked attribute prevents all users who aren't the file's owner from modifying, moving, deleting, or renaming the file. From most applications, only the owner is allowed to change the file's content or delete it, but the owner can also disable the locked attribute to return the file to normal. You can still make a copy of the locked file, but the copy will be locked as well. However, you will own the copy, so you can disable the locked attribute on the copy, but you still can't delete the original locked file unless you're the owner.

MORE INFO ▶ The locked attribute is covered in the "Managing Locked Items via the Finder" section later in this chapter.

Permissions for Sharing

Once you have an understanding of the permissions options available to you in Lion, you should explore how the local file system is set up by default to provide a secure environment that still allows users to share files.

If you don't have fast user switching enabled as outlined in Chapter 2, "User Accounts," you should enable it now to make it easy to test file system permissions as different users. Further, to aid in your exploration of the file system, you should use the Finder's Inspector window. This single floating window, which automatically refreshes as you select different items in the Finder, allows you to quickly explore the default permissions settings without having to open multiple Finder Get Info windows. Open the Inspector from the Finder by using the Option-Command-I keyboard shortcut, and then click the disclosure triangle to reveal the Sharing & Permissions section.

NOTE ▶ The Inspector window sports a different title bar than the Get Info window. Also, the Inspector window will always float on top of all other windows in the Finder.

Home Folder Sharing

Lion protects the user's files by default and allows them to be shared easily when needed. This starts with the user's home folder. You'll notice that users are allowed read and write access to their home folder, while the staff group and everyone are allowed only read access.

This means that every local user or guest can view the first level of every other user's home folder. (As a reminder, guests are allowed access to your computer without a password. This is why you can disable guest access in the Users & Groups preferences.) The default home folder permissions may seem insecure until you look at the permissions in context. Most user data is actually stored inside a subfolder in the user's home folder, and if you inspect those subfolders, you'll notice that other users are not allowed to access most of them.

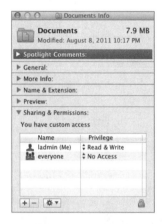

A few subfolders in a user's home folder, however, are specifically designed for sharing. The Public folder and optional Sites folder remain readable to everyone. A user can easily share files without having to mess with permissions by simply moving the files into those two folders. Others will be able to read those files, but they still cannot make any changes to them.

NOTE ▶ User-created files and folders at the root of the home folder will, by default, have permissions like the Public folder's. To secure new items at the root of the home folder, simply change the permissions as outlined in the "Managing Permissions via Finder" section later in this chapter.

Looking deeper, you'll notice a subfolder of the Public folder is the Drop Box. This folder's permissions allow all other users to copy files into the folder even though they cannot actually see other files in the Drop Box folder. This allows other users to discreetly transfer files without others knowing.

MORE INFO ▶ The permissions used to locally protect the Public and Sites folders are also used to protect these folders as they are shared over the network. Sharing files is covered in Chapter 7, "Network Services."

The Shared Folder

An additional folder set aside for sharing is the /User/Shared folder. You'll notice that this is a general sharing location that allows all users to read and write items to the folder. Normally this permissions setting would also allow any user to delete another user's item in this folder. Yet the Finder's Inspector window is not showing you the full permissions picture here. A unique permissions setting on the Shared folder prevents other users from being able to delete items that they don't own. This permission setting, known as the "sticky bit," can only be set via Terminal, as covered in the "Managing Permissions via Terminal" section later in this chapter. The sticky bit is specifically covered in the "Using the Sticky Bit" section later in this chapter.

Securing New Items

Once you understand how Lion's file system security architecture works with the folder hierarchy, it's time to consider how this technology is used to secure new items. You've learned previously in this chapter that Lion is preconfigured for secure file and folder sharing, but you will find that new items are created with unrestricted read access.

For example, when a user creates a new file or folder at the root of her home folder, by default all other users, including guest users, are allowed to view this item's contents. The same is true for new items created by administrators in local areas such as the root of the system volume and the local Library and Applications folders.

New items are created this way to facilitate sharing, so you do not have to change any permissions to share a new item. All that is required of you is to place the new item in a folder that other users can access, like the predefined sharing folders covered in the previous section. It's assumed that if you want to secure a new item, you will place it inside a folder that no one else has access to, like your home Desktop or Documents folders.

On the other hand, this default behavior is inconvenient if you want to safely store your items in an otherwise public area, like the root of the system volume. To store items in a public area so they are only accessible to the owner requires you to change the item's permissions using either the Finder or Terminal, as outlined later in this chapter.

Specifically, from the Finder's Sharing & Permissions section of the Get Info window, you must remove all other users and all group accounts from the permissions list. You cannot remove the Everyone permission, so you will have to set it to No Access. Once you have made these permissions changes, only the owner will have access to the item.

Managing Permissions via the Finder

A significantly redesigned Finder was one of the major new features in the previous Mac OS X v10.5. This included a new interface for managing ownership and permissions from the Finder's Get Info window. The redesign was necessary to incorporate support for ACLs. As covered previously in this chapter, the Finder uses the ACL architecture so you can configure unique privileges for an unlimited number of users or groups.

You may find that while the Finder makes permissions management simple, it does so through a form of obfuscation. In other words, the Finder hides the complexity of permissions by intentionally misrepresenting the full permissions of an item. If you're more comfortable with standard permissions, or you simply require full access to an item's permissions, then you're best served by managing permissions via Terminal as covered later in this chapter. However, for the most common permissions settings, the Finder's simplified permissions interface is still the quickest and easiest solution.

Modifying File Permissions via the Finder

To change permissions in the Finder:

1   In the Finder, select the file or folder for which you wish to change the permissions, and then open the Get Info window.

2   Once you have opened a Get Info window, click the Sharing & Permissions disclosure triangle to reveal the item's permissions.

3   If you aren't the owner of the item, you must click the small lock icon in the bottom-right corner of the Get Info window and authenticate as an administrative user.

4   To add new users or groups, click the small plus button in the bottom-left corner of the Get Info window.

A dialog will appear, allowing you to select a new user or group. To select an existing user or group, choose his or its name from the list and click the Select button. Alternately, you can create a new Sharing user account by clicking the New Person button or selecting a contact from your Address Book. Creating a new Sharing account in either case requires that you also enter a new password for the account.

MORE INFO ▶ Details about creating Sharing user accounts and how to create additional groups are covered in Chapter 2, "User Accounts."

5   To delete users or groups, select the account from the permission list and click the small minus button in the bottom-left corner of the Get Info window.

NOTE ▶ The Finder's Get Info window will not allow you to delete or change the original owner or delete the Everyone privilege of an item. You can use this window to seemingly delete all group privileges, but this isn't truly deleting the group privilege. Instead, it's simply removing all the privileges for the item's original group.

6   To assign different privileges, simply click on any privilege and a pop-up menu will appear, allowing you to choose another access option for that user or group. Details about the privilege options available from the Finder are covered previously in this chapter.

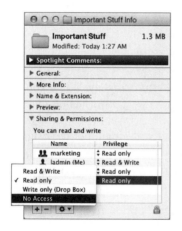

7   If you are changing the permissions of a folder, by default the Finder will not change the permissions of any items inside the folder. In many cases, you will want to apply the same permissions to the items inside the folder.

You can accomplish this quickly by clicking the Action button (the small gear icon) at the bottom of the Get Info window to reveal the Action pop-up menu, and then choosing the "Apply to enclosed items" option from this menu.

NOTE ▶ Even if you are the owner of a folder, you may still have to click the lock in the bottom-right corner of the Get Info window and authenticate as an administrative user.

NOTE ▶ Applying permissions to the enclosed folder items will apply all permissions settings to all enclosed items, not just the changes you recently made. Further, these changes cannot be easily reverted.

8 Changes made using the Get Info window are applied immediately. When you are done making ownership or permissions changes, close the Get Info window.

As long as you keep the Get Info window open, the Finder will remember the original permissions setting for the item. This is useful for testing different permissions configurations, as you can always revert to the original permissions setting. To do so, click the Action button (the small gear icon) at the bottom of the Get Info window to reveal the Action pop-up menu, and then choose the "Revert changes" option from this menu.

Managing Locked Items via the Finder

Lion includes a special file and folder attribute that trumps all write privileges and even administrative user access. Users can choose to lock a file or folder that they own from the Finder's Get Info window. They can also lock files within applications that support Lion's Auto Save and Versions document control features. Locking an item will render it completely unchangeable to all users except the item's owner. Even administrative users are prevented from making changes to another user's locked file in the graphical interface. In other words, a standard user could potentially lock an item that the administrative user would have no ability to change in the graphical interface.

> **MORE INFO** ▶ Lion's Auto Save and Versions document control features are detailed in Chapter 5, "Applications and Processes."

To lock a file or folder in the Finder:

1 In the Finder, select the file or folder you wish to lock, and then open the Get Info window.

2   Once you have opened the Get Info window, click the General disclosure triangle to reveal the Locked checkbox.

3   As long as you are the original owner of the item, you will be allowed to select the Locked checkbox.

Changes made using the Get Info window are applied immediately.

Once an item is locked, no other users can modify, move, delete, or rename it. In the graphical interface the owner can modify the content of the item or delete it, but the Finder still prevents the owner from moving, renaming, or changing ownership and permissions for the locked item. In fact, if you as the owner try to move a locked item, the Finder will default to making a copy. The owner can return the file to the normal state by disabling the locked attribute from the Finder's Get Info window. An administrative user can disable the locked attribute, but only via Terminal, as covered later in this chapter.

Permissions for External Volumes

Portable external disk and flash drives are useful tools for transferring files and folders from one computer to another. A downside to this technology, though, is that computers can't properly interpret file ownership because they don't share the same user account database. In other words, most Macs don't have the exact same user accounts, so when a drive is moved from one Mac to another, the file ownership from one Mac is meaningless to another.

NOTE ▶ The Mac considers any locally mounted volume that is not the system volume to be an external volume. Thus, other partitions on your internal system disks are considered external volumes.

Unless you plan to implement a centralized network user database so all your Macs do share the same user account database, ownership on external volumes will have to be ignored to prevent access issues. This is the default behavior in Lion for all external volumes. Keep in mind, however, that this approach introduces the security risk that all local users will have full access to the contents of external volumes. If you find this an unacceptable risk, you can disable the default behavior and force Lion to honor ownership on external volumes.

To honor ownership on external volumes:

1   In the Finder, select the external volume for which you wish the system to honor the ownership, and then open the Get Info window.

2   Once you have opened a Get Info window, click the Sharing & Permissions disclosure triangle to reveal the item's ownership and permissions.

3   Click the small lock icon in the bottom-right corner of the Get Info window and authenticate as an administrative user to unlock the Sharing & Permissions section.

4   Deselect the "Ignore ownership on this volume" checkbox.

Changes made using the Get Info window are applied immediately.

Managing Permissions via Terminal

Viewing and modifying file system permissions in Terminal's command line is both much richer and more complicated than in the Finder. The Finder has streamlined ownership, permissions, and ACLs, providing only the most common features that users require. However, Terminal offers every conceivable ownership and permissions option. Further, Terminal often provides more than one method for performing identical permissions tasks.

> **NOTE ▶** If you aren't already comfortable with navigation in the UNIX command line available from Terminal, then it's strongly recommended that you study the command-line concepts in Appendix B, "Command-Line Essentials," before reading the remainder of the section.

Viewing Standard Permissions

The ls command is your primary tool for viewing file and folder information via Terminal. The ls command has many options for viewing nearly any file or folder attribute. You can learn more about all the options available to ls from its manual entry page. Here, you will be presented with a few fundamental permissions viewing options.

The most basic ls option for viewing file and folder ownership and permissions is -l:

```
MyMac:~ michelle$ ls -l
total 0
drwx------+ 5 michelle staff 170 Aug 20 15:49 Desktop
drwx------+ 3 michelle staff 102 Aug 20 01:08 Documents
drwx------+ 3 michelle staff 102 Aug 20 01:08 Downloads
drwx------ 19 michelle staff 646 Aug 20 01:08 Library
drwx------+ 3 michelle staff 102 Aug 20 01:08 Movies
drwx------+ 3 michelle staff 102 Aug 20 01:08 Music
drwx------+ 4 michelle staff 136 Aug 20 01:08 Pictures
drwxr-xr-x+ 7 michelle staff 238 Aug 20 15:29 Public
drwxr-xr-x 5 michelle staff 170 Aug 20 01:08 Sites
```

The first string of characters at the beginning of each line is shorthand for the item type and permissions. The following information appears from left to right: the number of hard links associated with the item (for most users, this particular bit will be trivial information), the assigned owner, the assigned group, the last modification date, and, finally, the item's name.

Here is the syntax for the abbreviated information section:

▶ The first character is item type: - for file, d for folder, and l for symbolic link.

▶ The next three characters indicate the owner's permissions: - for no access, r for read access, w for write access, and x for file execute access or folder browsing access.

▶ The middle set of three rwx or - characters indicate the group's permissions.

▶ The final set of three rwx or - characters indicate everyone else's permissions.

▶ Optionally, there may be a + at the end to indicate that the item has ACL rules applied to it, or an @ at the end to indicate that the item has extended attributes.

The execute privilege attribute x has not been introduced yet, but it is the third standard privilege attribute after read and write. The execute privilege is enabled on files that are commands and applications (or folders that contain application bundles), to indicate that the item contains executable software code. The execute privilege is also required on normal folders to access the contents of the folder. The Finder doesn't show you when the execute privilege is used, but it should properly manage the execute privilege when you make permissions changes using the Get Info window.

NOTE ▶ If you are concerned with managing the execute permission, you should avoid permissions changes via Finder and instead manage execute permissions via Terminal.

Viewing Access Control Lists (ACLs)

The ACL technology is more advanced than standard permissions because it allows an arbitrary number of user and group permissions rules per item. Each permissions rule is known as an Access Control Entry (ACE). Every file and folder on the system can have an unlimited list of ACE rules, hence the "list" in ACLs.

From Terminal, Lion's ACL implementation provides more than a dozen unique privilege attribute types and lets you define each as a specific allow or deny rule. In other words, you can assign an item an unlimited number of user or group rules, or ACEs, which can be used to allow or deny any of the following privilege attributes:

▶ Administration—Administration attributes, which define a user's or group's ability to make permissions changes, include change privileges and change ownership.

▶ Read—Read attributes define a user's or group's ability to read items and include read attributes, read extended attributes, read file data or list folder contents, execute file or traverse folder, and read permissions.

▶ Write—Write attributes define a user's or group's ability to make changes and include write attributes, write extended attributes, read file data or create files in folder, append file data or create new subfolder inside folder, delete item, and delete subfolders and files.

Furthermore, each ACE for a folder can include a static inheritance rule that defines whether the folder's permissions also apply to new items placed in the folder. Inheritance attributes include the following: no inheritance, apply to just new items in this folder, apply to any new child folders, apply to any new child files, and apply to all descendants of this folder.

To view an item's ACLs alongside their permissions, simply add the -e option to the -l option:

```
MyMac:~ michelle$ ls -le
total 0
drwx------+ 5 michelle staff 170 Aug 20 15:49 Desktop
 0: group:everyone deny delete
drwx------+ 3 michelle staff 102 Aug 20 01:08 Documents
 0: group:everyone deny delete
drwx------+ 3 michelle staff 102 Aug 20 01:08 Downloads
 0: group:everyone deny delete
drwx------ 19 michelle staff 646 Aug 20 01:08 Library
```

```
drwx------+ 3 michelle staff 102 Aug 20 01:08 Movies
 0: group:everyone deny delete
drwx------+ 3 michelle staff 102 Aug 20 01:08 Music
 0: group:everyone deny delete
drwx------+ 4 michelle staff 136 Aug 20 01:08 Pictures
 0: group:everyone deny delete
drwxr-xr-x+ 7 michelle staff 238 Aug 20 15:29 Public
 0: group:everyone deny delete
drwxr-xr-x 5 michelle staff 170 Aug 20 01:08 Sites
```

Modifying File Permissions via Terminal

You will use two primary commands for changing file and folder permissions in Terminal's command line: chown for changing ownership and chmod for changing privileges.

Changing Ownership via Terminal

Short for "change ownership," chown will let you change the owner and group associated with a file or folder. Using chown often requires root access, so this command is almost always preceded by the sudo command. To use chown, enter the new owner's name, followed optionally by a colon and the new group name, and then finish with the item's path. In the following example, Michelle uses the chown command to change testfile1's ownership to the user account kevin and the group account admin.

NOTE ▶ Remember that, as covered in Appendix B, if you want to change the ownership of a folder and its contents, you must tell the chown command to run recursively by adding the -R option.

```
MyMac:~ michelle$ ls -l Desktop/
total 0
-rw-r--r-- 1 michelle staff 0 Aug 20 15:49 testfile1
drwxr-xr-x 4 michelle staff 136 Aug 20 15:47 testfolder
MyMac:~ michelle$ sudo chown kevin:admin Desktop/testfile1
Password:
MyMac:~ michelle$ ls -l Desktop/
total 0
-rw-r--r-- 1 kevin admin 0 Aug 20 15:49 testfile1
drwxr-xr-x 4 michelle staff 136 Aug 20 15:47 testfolder
```

Changing Privileges via Terminal

Short for "change file mode," chmod will let you change the privileges associated with a file or folder. Using chmod on files you don't own requires root access, so the chmod command is often preceded by the sudo command. To use chmod, enter the new privileges first followed by the item's path.

As for changing privileges, there are two basic methods when using the chmod command:

▶ Using alphanumeric abbreviations—The basic syntax goes like this: account type, modifier, and then privilege. Account types include u for owner, g for group, and o for everyone else. Modifiers include + for allow, - for deny, and = for exact setting. Privileges are as expected with r for read, w for write, and x for execute or folder access. For example, if you're using this method to allow full access for the owner and group but read-only access for everyone else, you'd enter ug=rwx,o=r.

> **TIP** ▶ As an alternative to x you can also use X for smart execute, which tells chmod to add the x permission only to items for which it makes sense—all folders and files that are already marked executable. This is especially useful for recursive operation, where x should be added to folders but not most files.

▶ Using octal notation—As you can see, chmod extensively uses shortcuts and abbreviations. To save even more keystrokes you can use octal notation, which uses numeric abbreviations for defining privileges. The basic syntax for octal notation is to use a single-digit number for the user first, followed by a single number for the group, and then a last single number for everyone else. Octal notation uses 0, for no access; 1, for execution only; 2, for write-only; and 4, for read-only. To use mixed permissions, simply add the numbers together. For example, if you were using this method to allow full access to a folder for the owner and group but read-only access for everyone else, you'd type 775.

In the following example, Michelle uses the chmod command to change the permissions of testfile1 and testfolder to allow read and write access for the owner and the group but read-only access for everyone else. She first uses alphanumeric abbreviations, and then octal privilege equivalents.

> **NOTE** ▶ Remember, if you want to change the privileges of a folder and its contents, you must tell the chmod command to run recursively by adding the -R option.

```
MyMac:~ michelle$ ls -l Desktop/
total 0
-rw-r--r-- 1 michelle staff 0 Aug 20 15:49 testfile1
drwxr-xr-x 4 michelle staff 136 Aug 20 15:47 testfolder
MyMac:~ michelle$ chmod ug=rw,o=r Desktop/testfile1
MyMac:~ michelle$ ls -l Desktop/
total 0
-rw-rw-r-- 1 michelle staff 0 Aug 20 15:49 testfile1
drwxr-xr-x 4 michelle staff 136 Aug 20 15:47 testfolder
MyMac:~ michelle$ chmod 775 Desktop/testfolder/
MyMac:~ michelle$ ls -l Desktop/
total 0
-rw-rw-r-- 1 michelle staff 0 Aug 20 15:49 testfile1
drwxrwxr-x 4 michelle staff 136 Aug 20 15:47 testfolder
```

MORE INFO ▶ The chmod command supports many other permissions settings, including full ACL management, which go beyond the scope of this guide. However, you can always find out more about chmod by reading its built-in man page.

Using the Sticky Bit

As mentioned previously in this chapter, the /Users/Shared folder has a unique permission setting that allows all local users to read and write items into the folder yet prevents other users from being able to delete files that they didn't originally put in this folder. This special permissions configuration is brought to you courtesy of the "sticky bit." Essentially, enabling the sticky bit on a folder defines it as an append-only destination, or, more accurately, a folder in which only the owner of the item can delete the item.

You can clearly see the sticky bit setting of the /Users/Shared folder when you view its ownership and permissions. Note the t on the end of the permissions information, which indicates that the sticky bit is enabled:

```
MyMac:~ michelle$ ls -l /Users/
total 0
drwxrwxrwt 7 root   wheel 238 Aug 10 18:49 Shared
drwxr-xr-x+ 16 cadmin staff 544 Aug 17 00:10 cadmin
drwxr-xr-x+ 16 logan  staff 544 Aug 19 00:06 logan
drwxr-xr-x+ 17 kevin  staff 578 Aug 17 00:14 kevin
drwxr-xr-x+ 15 michelle staff 510 Aug 20 16:43 michelle
```

You can enable sticky bit functionality similar to the /Users/Shared folder on any other folder using a special octal notation with the chmod command. In the following example, Michelle has already created a new folder named NewShared. She then uses the chmod command with +t to set sharing for all users with sticky bit functionality:

```
MyMac:~ michelle$ chmod -R +t NewShared/
MyMac:~ michelle$ ls -l
total 0
drwx------+ 5 michelle staff 170 Aug 20 15:49 Desktop
...
drwxrwxrwt 2 michelle staff 68 Aug 20 17:20 NewShared
...
```

Managing Locked Items via Terminal

As mentioned previously, Lion includes a special file system lock feature that prevents anyone but the owner of an item from making changes to that item. Any user can easily lock a file or folder he owns from the Finder's Get Info window or from any application that supports Lion's Auto Save and Versions document control features, also covered earlier in this chapter.

The problem with the file system lock is that the Finder prevents even other administrative users from making changes or unlocking items they don't own. In fact, this file system lock extends to Terminal as well. Even with sudo access, an administrator is not allowed to change a locked item—with one important exception, the chflags command. This command allows the administrator to change file system flags, which among other things allows you to lock or unlock any file or folder on the system.

In the following example, Michelle needs to change the permissions of a folder owned by another user so the folder can be shared. However, even using sudo she is denied access to doing this, indicating the file is locked. She verifies this by using ls –lO to view the file listing with file flags, which indeed returns the statement that the folder is locked, uchg. She then uses the chflags command with the nouchg option to unlock the folder. Finally, she is able to make changes to the previously locked file.

```
MyMac:Shared michelle$ sudo chmod go+rx SecureFolder/
chmod: Unable to change file mode on SecureFolder/: Operation not permitted
MyMac:Shared michelle$ ls -lO
total 0
drwx------ 7 cadmin wheel -    238 Jul 7 13:18 AnotherFolder
drwx------ 7 cadmin wheel uchg 238 Jul 7 13:18 SecureFolder
```

```
MyMac:Shared michelle$ sudo chflags nouchg SecureFolder/
MyMac:Shared michelle$ sudo chmod go+rx SecureFolder/
MyMac:Shared michelle$ ls –lO
total 0
drwx------ 7 cadmin wheel -  238 Jul 7 13:18 AnotherFolder
drwxr-xr-x 7 cadmin wheel -  238 Jul 7 13:18 SecureFolder
```

MORE INFO ▶ Using the chflags command with the uchg option will enable the file system lock on an item, thus preventing others from changing that item. Read the man page for chflags to reveal the other types of file flags that it can manipulate.

Troubleshooting File Systems

Because the operating system requires a functional file system, the software that drives the file system is very reliable. In fact, most file system failures are due to bad hardware or media. It doesn't matter how good the software is, though; if the hardware is no longer reading or writing bits, it's pretty much useless to the file system. If, during troubleshooting, you determine that catastrophic hardware failure is the problem, there really isn't anything you can do from a software perspective to repair the device. Only a data recovery service, such as DriveSavers, might have a chance at recovering your data.

MORE INFO ▶ When storage hardware suffers from catastrophic failure, DriveSavers is the most popular hard drive recovery service for Macs. You can find out more about its product at www.drivesaversdatarecovery.com.

Conversely, if you're experiencing file system issues but the storage hardware still appears to function, you may be experiencing partial hardware failure or file system corruption. In these cases, you can try some steps using Lion's built-in utilities to repair the volumes or at least recover data.

Gathering File System Information

Before attempting any fixes, you should become fully familiar with the file system configuration you're dealing with. Once again, the /Applications/Utilities/Disk Utility application will be your main tool for gathering file system information. The availability and status of storage hardware in Disk Utility will help determine if you are indeed experiencing hardware failure.

When you open Disk Utility, it will scan the file system for all attached devices and volumes. To gather detailed information about a specific drive or volume in Disk Utility, simply select the item from the column on the left and then click the Info button in the toolbar. Remember, the drive's name is its size and manufacturer information, whereas a drive's volumes appear directly below the drive name in the list.

The information gathered from these dialogs will reveal a great deal about the status of a drive or volume. Of most importance for determining hardware failure is a drive's S.M.A.R.T. (Self-Monitoring, Analysis, and Reporting Technology) status. A drive that features S.M.A.R.T. technology can automatically determine if the drive is suffering from some sort of internal hardware failure.

If a connected drive doesn't even appear in the Disk Utility list, odds are the drive has suffered a catastrophic failure. You should double-check the drive's status using /Applications/Utilities/System Information to verify that the drive is unreachable. When you open System Information, the drive's information should appear when you select the bus that the drive is connected to, such as Serial-ATA or FireWire. If a drive does not appear in System Information either, then it is not available to the Mac in its current state. At this point you should focus your efforts on troubleshooting the drive hardware. This includes simple fixes, such as looking for loose connections or replacing bad cables, as well as more complex fixes, such as having to replace bad hardware.

Verify or Repair a Drive

Disk Utility can be used to examine and attempt to repair a partition scheme or volume directory structure. The partition scheme is used to define the space where volumes exist. The volume directory structure is used by the file system to catalog where files and folders exist on the drive. To access data on the drive, the file system must first check with the partition scheme and volume directory structure in order to locate the appropriate bits on the drive that make up the requested file. Obviously, any damage to this information can lead to serious problems, including data loss.

Before any drive is mounted, the Mac will automatically perform a quick consistency check to verify the drive's partition scheme and volume directory structure. The system will also quickly scan the startup drive during the startup process. However, if the system is unable to mount a drive or its volumes, or you are experiencing issues accessing a drive's content, you can use Disk Utility to verify and repair the partition scheme or volume directory structures.

To use Disk Utility's verify and repair features:

1   If you're attempting to repair the system drive, you should first start up from Lion Recovery by holding Command-R at startup, and then choose Disk Utility from the Mac OS X Utilities window.

   NOTE ▶ If the default Lion Recovery system doesn't work, you can use any of the alternative Lion Recovery methods detailed in Chapter 1, "Installation and Configuration."

   If you are on a currently running Mac, double-check that the drive you wish to verify or repair is attached to the computer, then open /Applications/Utilities/Disk Utility.

2   Select the drive or volume you wish to verify or repair from the column on the left, and then click the First Aid tab to the right.

   By selecting a drive, you are indicating that you wish to verify or repair the selected drive's partition scheme. However, by selecting a volume, you are indicating that you wish to verify or repair the selected volume's directory structure. As a best practice, you should verify or repair all components of a single drive.

3   Verify the selected item by clicking the Verify Disk button in the bottom-right corner.

   It may take a few minutes to complete the verification process. During this time Disk Utility will show a progress indicator and log entries in the history area. Click the Show details checkbox to view more detail in the history log. You can stop the process at any time by clicking the Stop button.

4   If no problems were found, you should see an entry in the history log with green text. If problems were uncovered, they will appear in bright red text. If the drive has problems, and you haven't already started the repair process, you should do so now.

The system will continue to run the repair process until no more problems are found. This may take a while because the system may run through the repair process several times.

Using Target Disk Mode

Mac hardware has a unique ability to share its internal drives via a feature called target disk mode. Basically, when target disk mode is engaged, instead of starting up normally from the system disk, the Mac will bridge any internal drives to the FireWire and/or Thunderbolt ports. Because target disk mode is a function built into the Mac's hardware, even if the installed operating system volume is corrupted, you can still use this feature. An administrative user can enable target disk mode on a currently running Mac by clicking the Target Disk Mode button in the Startup Disk preferences. Alternately, you can engage target disk mode during system startup by holding down the T key while you turn on the Mac.

> **NOTE ▶** Certain forms of hardware failure can prevent a Mac from entering target disk mode. If you suspect this is the case, you should try using Apple Hardware Test as covered in Chapter 9, "System Startup."

> **NOTE ▶** Target disk mode is not supported on any Mac that lacks FireWire or Thunderbolt ports or that uses third-party storage interfaces.

> **NOTE ▶** Target disk mode cannot be engaged during system startup when using a Bluetooth wireless keyboard.

Once target disk mode is engaged, you will see large FireWire and/or Thunderbolt symbols on the screen, and then you can simply plug the targeted Mac into another fully functioning Mac via a FireWire or Thunderbolt cable. The targeted Mac's internal volumes should mount normally on the other Mac as if you had plugged in a normal external drive. At this point, you can do anything to the targeted Mac's internal drive that you could do to any local drive, including installations, repairs, and data migration.

Recovering Data From a Non-Starting System

If you are still stuck with a Mac that refuses to fully start up from its internal system drive, you might be able to recover important data off the drive as long as it's functional. You can use the Mac's built-in target disk mode to easily access the internal system drive and recover important data from another fully functional Mac.

> **NOTE** ▶ If your Mac doesn't support, or is unable to engage, target disk mode, then your best bet is to visit an Apple Authorized Service Provider. An alternate solution would be to remove the drive from the troubled computer and attach it to another fully functional Mac.

To recover data using target disk mode:

1 Turn on the troublesome Mac while holding down the T key to engage target disk mode.

2 Once the FireWire and/or Thunderbolt symbols appear on the targeted Mac, connect the computer to another fully functioning Mac using a standard FireWire or Thunderbolt cable.

3   If the targeted Mac's volume appears in the Finder, you should first attempt to repair the volume using Disk Utility, as detailed previously in this chapter.

4   Once repairs have been completed, you have a variety of data recovery options:

▶ **Use the Finder** to manually copy data from the targeted Mac to storage attached to the functioning Mac.

▶ **Use Disk Utility** on the functioning Mac to create a disk image archive of the targeted Mac's system volume. Creating disk images is covered in Chapter 4, "Data Management."

▶ **Use the Migration Assistant** on a functioning or newly installed Mac to easily migrate user accounts, settings, or applications. The Migration Assistant is covered in Chapter 1, "Installation and Configuration."

5   After you have migrated the data, you should use Disk Utility to reformat the targeted Mac's drive, and then attempt to reinstall the operating system.

System installation is also covered in Chapter 1, "Installation and Configuration."

Depending on the amount of corruption present on the targeted Mac's system drive, you may not be able to use Disk Utility or the Migration Assistant. The drive may simply be too corrupted to recover all that data. In this case, you will have to resort to manually copying data.

In general, the items most important to users are stored in their home folder, so you should start there. This can be a time-consuming process; as the Finder discovers damaged files, you will have to manually restart the copy process and omit the damaged files.

TIP There are several third-party drive recovery utilities available for Lion. While this text doesn't recommend one over another, it would be wise to contact an Apple Authorized Service Provider for recommendations.

TIP Use the ample spare time between manual file copies to remind the Mac's owner (or yourself) that you wouldn't have to labor over the broken drive if there was a good backup! Using Time Machine to keep backups is covered in Chapter 4, "Data Management."

Permissions Troubleshooting

Permissions issues can be caused by a variety of situations. Many are due to user error, but others can be the result of an unintentional failure elsewhere in the system. For instance, some software installers may improperly change permissions during the installation process. You may also experience permissions issues after restarting from a power loss or system freeze.

System and application errors, such as applications that will not open or an inability to empty the Trash, may occur due to incorrect permissions. Many of these permissions issues can be resolved by utilities that are part of Lion. If you are having trouble accessing an application, you should attempt to resolve the issue using Disk Utility's Repair Disk Permissions feature. Also, if you are experiencing problems trying to access home folders, you can use the Reset Password utility in Lion Recovery to reset home folder permissions. The use of these two utilities for resolving permissions issues is covered later in this section.

Most general permissions issues are revealed in obvious ways. A user attempting to access a file or folder is immediately stopped and presented with a dialog stating that he doesn't have the appropriate permissions. In this case, a permissions change on the item, or the folder it's inside, is usually all that's needed to resolve the issue. If you are going to attempt to repair the item's permissions manually, you should be familiar with the methods for managing permissions outlined previously in this chapter.

MORE INFO ▶ For further guidance on general permissions troubleshooting, you can also refer to Apple Knowledge Base document HT2963, "Troubleshooting permissions issues in Mac OS X."

Clearing ACLs via Terminal

Compared with adjusting standard permissions, adjusting file and folder ACLs is quite complicated—in fact, such detailed ACL management goes beyond the scope of this guide. Nevertheless, there is one helpful trick for resolving access issues if you think improperly set ACLs are causing the issue. You can, with a single command, clear all the ACLs for a given file or folder using the chmod command with the -RN option.

In the following example, Michelle needs to clear the troublesome ACLs of a shared folder named "SharedStuff" and its contents. She first lists the permissions with ACLs using the ls command, then uses chmod -RN to "clear" the folder's ACLs. Finally, Michelle double-checks her work by viewing the permissions again, verifying that the ACL is empty for the SharedStuff folder.

```
MyMac:Shared michelle$ ls -le
total 0
drwxr-xr-x+ 2 cadmin wheel 68 Jul 7 22:37 SharedStuff
 0: group:family allow add_file,search,add_subdirectory,delete_child,readattr,writeattr,writeextattr,rea
dsecurity
MyMac:Shared michelle$ sudo chmod -RN SharedStuff/
Password:
MyMac:Shared michelle$ ls -le
total 0
drwxr-xr-x 2 cadmin wheel 68 Jul 7 22:37 SharedStuff
```

Disk Utility's Repair Permissions

One of the most common troubleshooting techniques for Lion is to use Disk Utility's Repair Disk Permissions feature. Many novice Mac administrators use this technique every time they encounter any problem. The reality is that this process fixes only file permissions issues specific to certain installed Apple software. Further, this process will not touch any incorrect permission settings on personal or user data.

In other words, this process, though a good starting point for addressing system and application issues, will not fix every incorrect permissions issue on a problematic Mac. In fact, you can verify exactly which installed items the repair permissions process will fix from the repair_packages command. In the following example, Michelle uses this command to list the packages that will be checked. Note that the output was truncated to save space; however, you may notice the third-party printer drivers listed as part of "standard packages." This is because those drivers were installed automatically via the Apple Software Update mechanism.

```
MyMac:~ michelle$ sudo /usr/libexec/repair_packages --list-standard-pkgs
Password:
    com.apple.pkg.BrotherPrinterDrivers
    com.apple.pkg.HewlettPackardPrinterDrivers
    com.apple.pkg.ServerAdminTools
    com.apple.pkg.X11User
...
```

MORE INFO ▶ For more information, you can also reference Apple Knowledge Base document HT1452, "About Disk Utility's Repair Disk Permissions feature."

The upside is that the repair permissions process is an easy troubleshooting step that could resolve many permissions issues. Keep in mind that many default folders were also installed as part of the operating system. Thus, the repair permissions process will not only repair system items but also important folders like /Applications and /Library.

To verify or repair disk permissions:

1   Open Disk Utility on a currently running Mac by opening /Applications/Utilities/Disk Utility, or on a Mac started up from Lion Recovery, by choosing Disk Utility from the Mac OS X Utilities window.

    NOTE ▶ If the default Lion Recovery system doesn't work, you can use any of the alternative Lion Recovery methods detailed in Chapter 1, "Installation and Configuration."

2   Select the system volume you wish to repair from the column on the left.

3   Select the First Aid tab to the right.

4   Click the Verify Disk Permissions button to view a log of any potential problems.

5   Click the Repair Disk Permissions button to view and fix any permission problems.

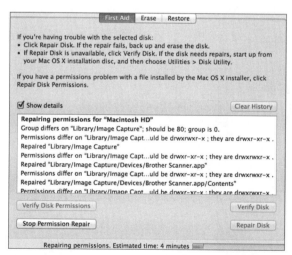

Reset Password's Reset Home Permissions

If a user's home folder becomes inaccessible due to improper permissions, you can attempt to fix the issue by manually adjusting the permissions yourself, or you can try the Reset Password utility found only in Lion Recovery. This utility was primarily designed to reset user passwords; nonetheless, this tool also has the ability to reset a user's home folder permissions and ACLs. Keep in mind that this process will reset all home folder permissions, including intentionally changed permissions that may have benefited the user.

To reset home folder permissions and ACLs:

1 Start up from a Lion Recovery system. The easiest method on a Lion system is to hold Command-R during startup.

> **NOTE** ▶ If the default Lion Recovery system doesn't work, you can use any of the alternative Lion Recovery methods detailed in Chapter 1, "Installation and Configuration."

2 Once Lion Recovery has started, choose Utilities > Terminal from the menu bar.

3 When Terminal opens, type resetpassword and then press the Return key. This will open the Reset Password utility.

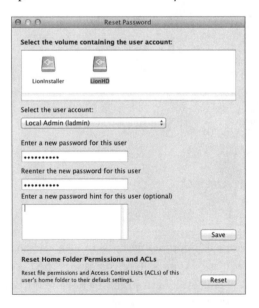

4   Select the system volume containing the account whose home folder needs resetting from the row of system volume icons.

5   Choose the user account whose home folder needs resetting from the user pop-up menu.

6   Quit the Reset Password utility to return to the Mac OS X Utilities window.

7   Quit the Mac OS X Utilities window to restart the Mac.

> **TIP** ▶ You can, obviously, also use the Reset Password utility to change a user's lost password.

What You've Learned

▶   Lion's file system supports a variety of partition schemes and volume types.

▶   Disk Utility is your primary tool for managing the Mac's file system.

▶   Lion includes robust built-in support for software-based RAID sets and burning optical media.

▶   FileVault 2 protects your Mac by providing full disk encryption for the system drive.

▶   File system permissions, in the form of standard permissions, and access control lists (ACLs) are used to control file and folder access.

▶   Terminal offers many useful tools for managing the Mac's file system that go beyond the capabilities of the graphical user interface.

References

You can check for new and updated Knowledge Base documents at www.apple.com/support.

General File System

HT2355, "Mac OS X: About file system journaling"

HT1375, "About disk optimization with Mac OS X"

HT2374, "Mac OS X 10.5: About resizing disk partitions"

RAID

HT2559, "Mac OS X, Mac OS X Server: How to use Apple-Supplied RAID software"

TA24104, "Intel-based Macs: Flashing question mark when trying to boot from RAID volume"

HT1346, "Mac Pro RAID Card and Xserve RAID Card: Frequently Asked Questions (FAQ)"

Optical Media

HT2882, "Factors that affect writing to or reading from optical media"

HT2543, "About optical disc drive burning and write speeds"

TA23476, "About default optical drive burning speeds"

HT2446, "Using nonstandard discs in optical drives"

Ownership and Permissions

TS1402, "Unable to move, unlock, modify, or copy an item in Mac OS X"

HT2963, "Troubleshooting permissions issues in Mac OS X"

HT1452, "About Disk Utility's Repair Disk Permissions feature"

File System Troubleshooting

HT1782, "Using Disk Utility to verify or repair disks"

HT1526, "You can't empty the Trash or move a file to the Trash"

HT2528, "Intel-based Macs: 'You have inserted a disk containing no volumes that Mac OS X can read' alert message"

URLs

NTFS-3G/MacFUSE software bundle provides full support for NTFS:
http://macntfs-3g.blogspot.com

Wikipedia entry comparing file systems:
http://en.wikipedia.org/wiki/Comparison_of_file_systems

Apple RAID Utility User's Guide:
http://images.apple.com/server/docs/RAID_Utility_User_Guide.pdf

Wikipedia entry comparing RAID types: http://en.wikipedia.org/wiki/RAID

DriveSavers data recovery: www.drivesaversdatarecovery.com

Review Quiz

1. What is the difference between disk drives, partitions, and volumes?

2. What are the two primary partition schemes for Mac-formatted drives? What are their differences?

3. What two volume formats are supported for a Lion system volume?

4. How does file system journaling work?

5. What are the four erase options available in Disk Utility? What are the differences between them?

6. How does the Finder's Secure Empty Trash feature work?

7. What four methods can be used to eject a volume or drive from the Finder?

8. What is the potential side effect of improperly unmounting or ejecting a drive or volume?

9. What differentiates a RAID 0 set from a RAID 1 set?

10. How do you use the Finder's Burn Folder feature?

11. How do you use Disk Utility to burn an optical disc?

12. Why is the root, or beginning, level of a user's home folder visible to other users?

13. How are the permissions on the Shared folder set to allow local user sharing?

14. How does the default organization of the file system allow users to safely share local files and folders?

15. What does it mean when you choose the option to "ignore volume ownership" in the Finder? What are the security ramifications of ignoring volume ownership?

16. How do you identify the ownership and permissions of a file or folder in the Finder?

17. What is the sticky bit?

18. What is the locked file flag?

19. How is Disk Utility's Verify and Repair feature used?

20. What is target disk mode and how is it engaged?

Answers

1. Disk drives are the actual storage hardware; partitions are logical divisions of a disk drive used to define the storage space; and volumes, contained inside partitions, are used to define how the individual files and folders are saved to the storage.

2. GUID Partition Table is the default partition scheme on Intel-based Macs, and Apple Partition Map is the default partition scheme on PowerPC-based Macs.

3. The volume formats supported as system volumes for Lion are Mac OS Extended (Journaled) and Mac OS Extended (Journaled, Encrypted).

4. File system journaling records what file operations are in progress at any given moment. This way, if a power failure or system crash occurs, after the system restarts it will be able to quickly verify the integrity of the volume by "replaying" the journal.

5. The four erase options in Disk Utility are Fastest, which simply replaces the volume's directory structure; a second choice, which provides good security by writing zeros on top of all the previous drive data; a third choice, which provides even better security by writing three separate passes of information on top of the previous drive data; and Most Secure, which provides the best security by writing seven separate passes of information on top of the previous drive data.

6. The Finder's Secure Empty Trash will perform a 7-pass erase on the contents of the Trash folder.

7. The four methods used to eject a volume or drive from the Finder are to drag the drive icon to the Trash in the Dock; press and hold the Eject key for a few moments to unmount and eject optical media; select the volume you wish to unmount and eject from the Finder and choose File > Eject from the menu bar; and, finally, in the Finder's sidebar, click the small Eject button next to the volume you wish to unmount and eject.

8. Improperly unmounting or ejecting a drive or volume may cause data corruption. The system will automatically verify and repair an improperly unmounted or ejected volume the next time it becomes available to the Mac.

9. RAID 0 uses disk striping to simultaneously write data to all drives, providing increased performance, but it increases your chances of data loss due to drive failure. RAID 1 uses disk mirroring to write the same data to multiple drives, which does not increase performance but does greatly decrease your chances of data loss due to drive failure.

10. There are two methods for using a burn folder in the Finder. First, you can create a burn folder of any size by choosing File > New Burn Folder from the menu bar. Once

you are done adding and arranging items in the burn folder, click the Burn button and then insert a blank recordable optical disc. Or you can create a burn folder of a specific optical disc size by first inserting a blank recordable optical disc; the Finder will automatically create a burn folder that matches the size of the recordable optical disc.

11. Disk Utility can burn the contents of a disk image to an optical disk. Click the Burn button in Disk Utility's toolbar, select a disk image, and then insert a blank recordable optical disc.

12. The root level of a user's home folder is visible to other users so they can navigate to the Public and Sites shared folders.

13. The Shared folder is set up to allow all users to read and write files, but only the user who owns an item can delete it from the Shared folder. This is accomplished using the sticky bit permissions setting.

14. Every home folder contains a Public folder that other users can read and a Drop Box folder that other users can write to. All other subfolders in a user's home folder (except the optional Sites folder) have default permissions that do not allow access to other users. The Shared folder is also set for all users to share items.

15. You can choose to ignore ownership on any non-system volume. This will ignore any ownership rules and grant any logged-on user unlimited access to the contents of the volume. It is a potential security risk because it will allow any local user account to have full access to the volume even if that user did not originally mount the volume.

16. An item's ownership and permissions can be identified using the Get Info or Inspector windows in the Finder.

17. The sticky bit is a special permission used to define a folder as an append-only destination or, more accurately, a folder in which only the owner of the item can move, rename, or delete the item.

18. The locked file flag prevents anyone, including the item's owner, from editing an item. Only the item's owner can unlock the item to then allow modification.

19. The Disk Utility's Verify and Repair feature is used to verify or repair the directory structure of a volume. The directory structure contains all the information used to locate files and folders on the volume.

20. Target disk mode is a Mac-specific hardware feature that, when engaged, will share the Mac's internal disk drives through the FireWire ports. Target disk mode can be engaged from the Startup Disk preferences or by holding down the T key as you turn on the Mac.

4

Time   This chapter takes approximately 3 hours to complete.

Goals   Explore and understand the Lion file layout

Discover common system files, their location, and their purpose

Leverage file metadata by using Spotlight for advanced searching

Learn file management techniques unique to Lion

Archive files and folders using technologies built in to Lion

Use Time Machine to back up and restore important data

Chapter **4**
Data Management

It is not unusual for an OS X Lion system volume to contain well over 100,000 folders and 500,000 files just to support the operating system and its applications. As you can imagine, the number of items in a user's home folder varies widely, depending on the user, but even the most frugal of users will have thousands of items in his home folder. With this many files on hand, attempting to explore and fully comprehend Lion's file layout may seem like a monumental task. To the contrary: Lion's system files have been streamlined and reorganized into an easy-to-understand layout that is both easier for the Mac administrator to manage and provides enhanced security.

This chapter builds on the previous chapter, "File Systems," to focus more specifically on the composition and organization of the files and folders that make up Lion. In this chapter you, acting as an administrator, will use the file layout to strategically allocate resources. You will also work with many Mac-specific file technologies, including resource forks, packages, Quick Look, and Spotlight. Finally, you will use the built-in features for archiving data on the Mac, and learn how to back up and restore data using Time Machine.

Understanding the System File Structure

Lion's system layout is designed to strike a balance between ease of use and advanced functionality. For the basic user, looking at the root, or beginning, of the file system from the Finder will reveal only four default folders: Applications, Library, Users, and System. The contents of these four folders represent all that most users, and many administrators, will ever need to access. Yet when advanced users look at the system root from Terminal, they will see many more items that the Finder would normally hide. Thus, the complexity and flexibility of a UNIX operating system remains for those users who require it.

MORE INFO ▶ Exploring Lion's system layout from Terminal's command-line interface is covered in Appendix B, "Command-Line Essentials."

The following describes the default system root folders you'll see from the Finder:

▶ Applications—Often called the local Applications folder, this is the default location for applications available to all local users. Only administrative users can make changes to the contents of this folder.

▶ Library—Often called the local Library folder, this is the default location for ancillary system and application resources available to all local users. Once again, only administrative users can make changes to the contents of this folder.

▶ System—This folder contains resources required by the operating system for primary functionality. Users very rarely have to make changes to the contents of this folder. Even administrative users are unable to make changes to items in the System folder without reauthenticating.

▶ Users—This is the default location for local user home folders. Specific access to home folder items is discussed in Chapter 2, "User Accounts."

▶ Developer (Optional)—This optional folder contains the Apple Xcode Developer Tools. This is not part of the standard installation, but it's still a fundamental part of the system, and its installer can be found in the Mac App Store. Like the Applications and Library folders, the Developer folder can be changed only by an administrative user.

System Resource Types

All Lion-specific system resources can be found in the various Library folders throughout the system volume. System resources can be generally categorized as any resource that is not a general-use application or user file. That's not to say that applications and user data can't be found in the Library folders. On the contrary, the Library folder is designed to keep both user and system resources organized and separated from the items you use every day. This keeps the Applications folder and user home folders free from system resource clutter.

Opening any of the Library folders will reveal several dozen categories of items. It is not necessary to explore every possible Library item, but there are a few system resources you should be familiar with:

▶ Application Support—This folder can be found in both the user and local Library folders. Any ancillary data needed by an application may end up in this folder. For example, it often contains help files or templates for an application. Once again, application resources are placed here to keep the Applications folders tidy.

▶ Extensions—Also called kernel extensions, these items are found only in the system and local Library folders. Extensions are low-level drivers that attach themselves to the kernel, or core, of the operating system. Extensions provide driver support for hardware, networking, and peripherals. Extensions load and unload automatically, so there is little need to manage them, as is common in other operating systems. Extensions are covered to greater detail in Chapter 8, "Peripherals and Printing."

▶ Fonts—Found in every Library folder, fonts are files that describe typefaces used for both screen display and printing. Font management is covered in the "Managing Font Resources" section later in this chapter.

▶ Frameworks—Found in every Library folder, frameworks are repositories of shared code used among different parts of the operating system or applications. Frameworks are similar to extensions in that they load and unload automatically, so again, there is little need to manage these shared code resources. You can view your Mac's currently loaded frameworks from the /Applications/Utilities/System Profiler application.

▶ Keychains—Found in every Library folder, keychains are used to securely store sensitive information, including passwords, certificates, keys, website forms, and notes. Keychain technology was covered previously in Chapter 2, "User Accounts."

▶ LaunchDaemons and LaunchAgents—These items can both be found in the local and system Library folders, and LaunchAgents can also be found in the user's Library folder. These Launch items are used to define processes that start automatically via the launchd process. Lion uses many background processes, which are all started by launchd. Furthermore, every single process is a child of the launchd process. LaunchAgents are for processes that need to start up only when a user is logged in, whereas LaunchDaemons are used to start processes that will always run in the background even when there are no users logged in. More about launchd can be found in Chapter 9, "System Startup."

▶ Logs—Many system processes and applications archive progress or error messages to log files. Log files can be found in every local Library folder. Log files are viewed using the /Applications/Utilities/Console application.

▶ PreferencePanes—PreferencePanes can be found in any Library folder. These items are used by the System Preferences application to provide interfaces for system configuration. System Preferences usage is covered in Chapter 1, "Installation and Configuration."

▶ Preferences—Preferences, found in both local and user libraries, are used to store system and application configuration settings. In other words, every time you configure a setting for any application or system function, it is saved to a preference file. Because preferences play such a critical role in system functionality, they are often the cause of software problems. Troubleshooting preference files is covered in Chapter 5, "Applications and Processes."

▶ Startup Items—Found in only the local and system Library folders, these are precursors to LaunchAgents and LaunchDaemons. Starting with Mac OS X 10.5, Apple is officially discouraging the use of Startup Items. In fact, you will have Startup Items only if you've installed third-party software that hasn't been updated. In Lion the launchd process will still support many Startup Items, but this may not be true for future versions.

System Resource Hierarchy

Library folders, and thus system resources, are located in each of the four domain areas: user, local, network, and system. Segregating resources into four domains provides increased administrative flexibility, resource security, and system reliability. Resource domains are more flexible because administrators can choose to allocate certain resources to all users or just specific users. Using resource domains is more secure because standard users can add resources only to their own home folder and cannot access other users' resources. In addition, it's more reliable because, in most cases, you don't have to make changes to the core system functionality in order to provide more services.

> **TIP** ▶ The quickest method to reveal the user's Library folder is to manually go to the folder in the Finder. While holding the Option key, choose Go > Library from the menu to reveal the hidden folder. You can learn more about hidden items in the "Managing Hidden Items" section later in this chapter.

The four system resource domains are, in order:

▶ User—Each user has his own Library folder in his home folder for resources. When resources are placed here, only the user has access to them. Also, a user can have his own Applications folder in his home folder. This folder is hidden in Lion as it's now deprecated and thus may not appear in future versions of Mac OS X. However, you will still find many thousands of items in this folder as developers continue to rely on this location for resources.

▶ Local—Both the root Applications and root Library folders are part of the local resource domain. This is why they are known as the local Applications and local Library folders. Any resources placed in these two folders are available to all local user accounts. By default, only administrative users can make changes to local resources.

▶ Network—Lion can access system resources and applications from a network file share. Administrators must configure an automounted share in order to enable the Network resource domain. Configuring automounted shares goes beyond the scope of this guide. However, it is covered in another reference guide, *Apple Pro Training Series: OS X Lion Server Essentials*.

▶ System—Finally, the system domain encompasses all the items necessary to provide core system functionality. There are many hidden items at the root of the system volume that make up the system resource domain, but the only one you will see in the Finder is the root System folder. In many cases, you do not need to add or manage any resources here.

With four different domains containing resources, a strong likelihood exists for overlap in resources, meaning there may be multiple copies of similar resources available to the system and user at any given time. The system is designed to handle this by searching for resources from the most specific, those in the user domain, to the least specific, those in the system domain. If multiple similar resources are discovered, the system will use the resource most specific to the user. For example, if multiple versions of the font Times New Roman are found, one in the local Library and one in the user's Library, the copy of the font in the user's Library will be the one used.

System Resource Troubleshooting

System resource issues are rare, and they are generally easy to identify. You will occasionally see an error message calling out an issue with a specific item, but you may also experience a situation where the item appears to be missing. In some cases, the system resource in question may be missing, but many times the system will simply ignore a system resource if it determines that the resource is in some way corrupted. The solution for both of these situations is to simply replace the missing or suspect item with a known working copy.

When troubleshooting system resources, you must also remember to heed the resource domain hierarchy. Using font resources as an example, you may have loaded a specific version of a font in the local Library that is required by your workflow to operate properly. In spite of this, a user may have loaded another version of the same font in her home folder. In this case, the system will load the user's font and ignore the font you installed. Therefore, this user may experience workflow problems even though it appears that she is using the correct font.

TIP ▶ If fonts are missing from within applications but appear to be properly installed, remember to check Font Book as the font may be temporarily disabled. Font Book is covered in the next section of this chapter.

Logging in with another account on the Mac is always a quick way to determine if the problem is in the user's home folder. You can also use /Applications/Utilities/System Information to list active system resources. System Information will always show the file path of the loaded system resources, so it's easy to spot resources that are loading from the user's Library.

Managing Font Resources

An excellent way to experience the system resource domain hierarchy is by managing fonts. Lion has advanced font-management technology that enables an unlimited number of fonts using nearly any font type, including bitmap, TrueType, OpenType, and all PostScript Type fonts. As mentioned previously, fonts are installed in the various Font folders located in the Library folders throughout the system. A user can manually install fonts simply by dragging them into a Fonts folder.

On the other hand, Lion includes a rather nice font-management tool, /Applications/Font Book, which will automatically install fonts for you. Font Book can also be used to organize fonts into more manageable collections, enable or disable fonts to simplify font lists, and resolve duplicate fonts.

NOTE ▶ Third-party font-management tools, such as Extensis's Suitcase Fusion or Universal Type Server, will interrupt Font Book and take over font management for the system.

To manage fonts with Font Book:

1 Open /Applications/Font Book.

The main Font Book window appears, allowing you to preview any currently installed font by clicking on it in the Font list.

2 Choose Font Book > Preferences to adjust where Font Book will install new fonts.

By default, Font Book will install fonts to the user's Library folder. If you are an administrative user, you can choose to install fonts to the local Library folder by choosing Computer from the pop-up menu. Close the Font Book Preferences dialog once you have made your selections.

NOTE ▸ Font Book will, by default, automatically validate a font before enabling it. This helps prevent font issues by making sure the font file isn't compromised. Thus, installing fonts via Font Book is favored over manual installation via the Finder.

3 From the Finder, simply double-click on the font you wish to install. Font Book will automatically open the font and show you a preview.

4 Click the Install Font button to validate and install the font to your selected default Library folder.

NOTE ▸ Some applications may need to be restarted to take advantage of recently added fonts.

5 If you, or the application you're using, have difficulties choosing fonts from a large list, you can temporarily disable fonts within Font Book by selecting the font and then

selecting the small checkbox button at the bottom of the font list. You will also have to verify your choice by clicking the Disable button when a verification dialog appears.

Disabled fonts will appear dimmed in the font list with the word Off next to their name. To enable the font, simply select it again and select the same checkbox button at the bottom of the font list.

6   Fonts that have multiple copies on your system will show a small dot next to their name in the font list. You can automatically disable fonts that are duplicated in your system with Font Book, by choosing Edit > Resolve Duplicates from the menu bar.

7   To remove a font, select it from the font list and press the Delete key. You will be presented with a summary dialog, reminding you that continuing will move the selected fonts to the Trash folder. If you are sure this is what you want to do, then click the Remove button.

TIP   Remember, you can always disable a font instead of deleting it entirely.

8   If you're having font issues, you can identify problem fonts by forcing the system to revalidate all the fonts on your system. To do this, select All Fonts from the Collection list, then select a single font in the Font list, and finally use the Command-A keyboard shortcut to select all the fonts. Choose File > Validate Fonts to start the validation process.

The Font Validation window will open and scan all the selected fonts. This window will clearly show any problem font with a status indicator (exclamation mark icon) next to the font's name. To remove a problem font, simply select the checkbox next to its name and then click the Remove Checked button.

9   If you're still having problems with Fonts, a final option in Font Book is to restore
all the system fonts back to the defaults for Lion. To do this, choose File > Restore
Standard Fonts. A dialog will appear verifying your choice. Click the Proceed button
to remove third-party fonts from the system.

Managing Hidden Items

Lion is a fully UNIX compliant operating system, and as such requires a number of files
that the average user will never touch. The root level of the Mac's system volume is lit-
tered with resources that UNIX processes require and UNIX administrators expect. Apple
made the wise choice of configuring the Finder to hide these items from the average user.
On a daily basis, the average user—and even most administrative users—does not need
to access any of these items from the graphical interface. Realistically, the only people
who even care about these normally hidden resources are going to be using Terminal to

do their work anyway. In other words, keeping these system items hidden in the Finder not only provides a tidier work environment but also prevents average users from poking around in places they don't need to go.

As a hybrid of UNIX and Mac OS technologies, Lion uses two methods to hide files and folders. The first is a UNIX tradition; simply using a period at the beginning of the item's name will hide the item in both the Finder and while using the default options to list items with ls in Terminal. The second method is a Mac OS tradition; enable an item's hidden file flag. This method, however, will only hide the item in the Finder.

> **NOTE ▶** If you aren't already comfortable with navigation in the UNIX command line available from Terminal, then it's strongly recommended that you study the command-line concepts in Appendix B, "Command-Line Essentials," before reading the remainder of this section.

Opening Hidden Items in the Finder

Should you want or need to open normally hidden items in the Finder, there are two methods. The first involves use of the Finder's Go menu to open any folder; the second involves using the open command from Terminal to open any file or folder.

Using the Go Menu

To reveal hidden folders in the Finder:

1   From the Finder, choose Go > Go to Folder from the menu bar, or you can use the Command-Shift-G keyboard shortcut.

This will reveal a dialog allowing you to enter an absolute path to any folder on the Mac. A good starting place is a user's Library folder, ~/Library; as covered previously, many system resources are found in this folder.

2   Click the Go button once you have entered the path.

The Finder will reveal the hidden folder in a window. Note the dimmed folder icon representing the normally hidden folder. To save time for when you return to the Go dialog, the previous path you entered will be there.

Using the open Command

The open command is a rather unique command that spans Terminal's command line and the graphical interface. The open command can be used to open files, folders, and URLs from Terminal to an application in the graphical interface. Folders are opened in a Finder window, the default web browser opens URLs, and files are opened by the default application for the specified file type. Again, because Terminal doesn't respect the hidden file flag, you can use the open command to open any hidden item as well.

> **NOTE** ▸ The only caveat when using the open command is that the user who executes the open command must also be logged in to the graphical interface. In other words, the same user account must be logged in to the graphical interface and Terminal to use the open command.

The following example will use the open command to open the user's current working folder from Terminal to a Finder window. The period used in the command is command-line shorthand for "this folder," thus this example literally translates to "open this folder."

MyMac:~ michelle$ open .

The next example will open the /private folder, which is normally hidden, in a Finder window:

    MyMac:~ michelle$ open /private

This next example will open a file on Michelle's desktop called Proof.pdf with the default PDF reader, most likely the Preview application:

    MyMac:~ michelle$ open Desktop/Proof.pdf

This final example will open Apple's main website in the default web browser, most likely the Safari application:

    MyMac:~ michelle$ open http://www.apple.com/

TIP ▶ Remember, you can automatically enter paths in Terminal by dragging a file or folder from the Finder to a Terminal window.

Revealing Hidden Items via Terminal

From Terminal's command line, you can easily override both types of hidden items. Again, by default, the ls command ignores the hidden file flag used by the Finder; thus it will simply show these items in the list. However, in its default mode the ls command doesn't show items whose names begin with a period. You can modify this behavior by using the –a option to list all items.

In the following Terminal example, Michelle will use the ls command with the -a option to reveal all items at the root of a system volume:

```
MyMac:~ michelle$ ls -a /
total 36669
.                                          Users
..                                         Volumes
.DS_Store                                  bin
.Spotlight-V100                            cores
.Trashes                                   dev
.com.apple.timemachine.supported           etc
.file                                      home
.fseventsd                                 mach_kernel
.hotfiles.btree                            net
.vol                                       private
Applications                               sbin
```

Developer	tmp
Library	usr
Network	var
System	

Of the nearly 30 items at the root of the system volume shown in this example, only 5 are shown in the Finder: Applications, Developer, Library, System, and Users. All of these additional items are created and used by the operating system, so they should generally be left alone. Again, for this reason they are hidden to most users by the Finder.

Hiding or "Unhiding" Items

The easiest way to hide an item is to simply name it with a period at the beginning of the filename. However, to prevent novice users from accidentally hiding their items, the Finder will not let you save a file with a period at the beginning of its name. Therefore, you must use Terminal. Simply use the mv command to rename the item, as covered in Appendix B, "Command-Line Essentials."

If you need to hide an item from the Finder, but you can't change its name to start with a period, then you can enable the hidden file flag. This is also only possible from Terminal. You can use the chflags command with the hidden option to hide any item from the Finder. Conversely, you can use the chflags command with the nohidden option to permanently reveal an item in the Finder. Finally, you can use the -O option, along with the long list option -l, to show any file system flags, verifying which items have the hidden file flag enabled.

In the following example, Michelle uses the chflags command to permanently reveal her home Library folder. She also uses the ls command before and after to show the file flags, verifying that the folder is no longer hidden after the change. In this example, the output of the ls command has been truncated to show only the results of the ~/Library folder.

```
MyMac:~ michelle$ ls -lO
total 0
...
drwx------@ 48 michelle staff hidden 1632 Aug 3 18:35 Library
...
MyMac:~ michelle$ chflags nohidden Library/
MyMac:~ michelle$ ls -lO
total 0
...
drwx------+ 48 michelle staff - 1632 Aug 3 18:35 Library
...
```

TIP ▶ You can use the chflags command to enable or disable any file flag, including the notorious locked file or folder flag, as covered in Chapter 3, "File Systems."

Using Aliases and Links

Another example of Lion being a hybrid of both UNIX and the classic Mac OS is the multiple methods used for file system pointers or shortcuts. Generally speaking, file system shortcuts are files that reference other files or folders. This allows you to have a single item appear in multiple locations or with multiple names without having to create multiple copies of the item. Both the system and users take advantage of file system shortcuts to access items in more convenient locations without having to duplicate those items.

NOTE ▶ Do not confuse the shortcuts found in the Dock or the Finder's sidebar with true file system shortcuts. Both the Dock and Finder save their references to original items as part of their configuration files, whereas file system shortcuts appear as individual files that can be located anywhere on a volume.

Lion uses three primary file system shortcut types:

▶ Aliases—These shortcuts are a holdover from the classic Mac OS but have been updated for Mac OS X duties. Aliases can be created with the Finder but are useless in Terminal. Command-line tools think that aliases are nothing more than data files and do not know how to follow their references back to the original items. Aliases, however, are more resilient than other shortcut types in that if the original item is replaced or moved, the alias will almost never lose the original item. An example of how aliases are used by the operating system is the Finder's Burn Folder feature, which allows you to organize files before you burn them to an optical disc. The Finder populates the burn folder with aliases instead of copies of the original items in order to save space.

▶ Symbolic Links—These shortcuts are part of the traditional UNIX file system and are simple pointers to the file system path of the original item. Thus, if you move the original item, the symbolic link will be broken. However, replacing the original item works because the path remains the same. You can create symbolic links with the ln command. The Finder cannot create symbolic links, but it can follow them to the original item. An example use of symbolic links in Lion is the way the system layout stores several fundamental UNIX folders in the /private folder but also makes those items available at the root of the file system using symbolic links.

▶ Hard Links—These shortcuts are also part of the traditional UNIX file system and are actual additional references to the original item. Think of a normal file as two parts; first, the bits on the physical drive that make up the file's actual content, and second, a name that points to those bits. A hard link is an additional name that points to the same bits on the physical drive. You can also use the ln command to create hard links. The Finder cannot create hard links, but it can follow them. An example use of hard links in Lion is for Time Machine backups. Time Machine uses hard links to reference items that have not changed since the previous backup, thus saving a tremendous amount of space. Finally, Mac OS X is unique in its ability to use hard links of both files and folders; again, this is to support Time Machine backups.

Creating Aliases

The Finder provides several methods for creating aliases. Simply select the item you want to create an alias for, and then choose one of the following methods:

▶ Choose File > Make Alias from the menu bar.

▶ Use the Command-L keyboard shortcut.

▶ In a Finder window, select the Action button (the small gear icon) from the toolbar and then from the pop-up menu select Make Alias.

▶ Right-click or Control-click the item, and then from the pop-up menu select Make Alias.

▶ Click and drag the original item while holding down the Option and Command keys to drop the alias in another location. This is the only method that doesn't append the word "alias" to the new alias filename.

Once you have created the alias, you can rename it or move it anywhere you like. As long as the original item remains somewhere on the original volume, even if it's replaced or its name changes, the Finder will be able to locate the alias. An alias file is easy to recognize by the small curved arrow that appears at the bottom left corner of the icon. From the Finder, you can locate the alias's target by right-clicking, or Control-clicking, on the alias and then selecting Show Original from the pop-up menu.

In the rare case that an alias is broken, most likely because the original item was copied to another volume and then deleted off the original volume, you can repair the alias in the Finder. One method is to double-click on the broken alias; the Finder will automatically prompt you to select a new original. Another option, which can also be used to redirect an existing alias, is to open the Finder's Get Info window and then in the General area click the Select New Original button. Both methods will open a browser dialog allowing you to select a new original for the alias.

Creating Symbolic Links

Because UNIX tools do not support aliases, you will need to create links if you wish to use shortcuts in Terminal. The ln command used with no additional options creates hard links, while the -s option creates symbolic links. In both cases the arguments are the original item's path and name first, followed by the new link's path and name.

> **NOTE ▸** The ln command cannot create hard links of folders, even though Lion supports this via Time Machine. In most cases a symbolic link is sufficient as a folder shortcut.

In the following example, Michelle has already created a folder named MyFolder and an alias to that folder named MyFolderAlias. She first lists the items using ls -lh to list in long format with "human readable" file sizes. She then attempts to navigate into the alias folder, but, as covered previously, the command line does not understand alias files, so it returns an error. Next, Michelle uses ln -s to create a symbolic link of MyFolder with the new link being named MyFolderSymLink. She lists items again to verify the symbolic link was created; note the "l" at the beginning of the permissions string and the arrow after the symbolic link's name pointing to the original item. Finally, she successfully navigates into the symbolic link folder.

```
MyMac:Desktop michelle$ ls -lh
total 2032
drwxr-xr-x 19 michelle staff 646B Jul 15 21:24 MyFolder
-rw-r--r--@ 1 michelle staff 507K Jul 15 22:39 MyFolderAlias
MyMac:Desktop michelle$ cd MyFolderAlias
```

```
-bash: cd: MyFolderAlias: Not a directory
MyMac:Desktop michelle$ ln -s MyFolder MyFolderSymLink
MyMac:Desktop michelle$ ls -lh
total 2040
drwxr-xr-x 19 michelle staff 646B Jul 15 21:24 MyFolder
-rw-r--r--@ 1 michelle staff 507K Jul 15 22:39 MyFolderAlias
lrwxr-xr-x 1 michelle staff 8B Jul 15 22:47 MyFolderSymLink -> MyFolder
MyMac:Desktop michelle$ cd MyFolderSymLink
MyMac:MyFolderSymLink michelle$ pwd
/Users/michelle/Desktop/MyFolderSymLink
```

Comparing File System Shortcut Types

This next example shows the differences between aliases, symbolic links, and hard links from Terminal. Michelle has already created a rather large disk image file named BigFile and an alias to that item named BigFileAlias. She starts by listing the items showing their size; note that the original file is much larger, measured in megabytes, than the alias, measured in kilobytes. She then makes two links; the first is a hard link named BigFileHardLink, and the second is a symbolic link named BigFileSymLink. Finally, she lists the items to compare their sizes once more.

```
MyMac:Desktop michelle$ ls -lh
total 200512
-rw-r--r--@ 1 michelle staff 98M Jul 15 21:07 BigFile.dmg
-rw-r--r--@ 1 michelle staff 109K Jul 15 23:03 BigFileAlias
MyMac:Desktop michelle$ ln BigFile.dmg BigFileHardLink
MyMac:Desktop michelle$ ln -s BigFile.dmg BigFileSymLink
MyMac:Desktop michelle$ ls -lh
total 400584
-rw-r--r--@ 2 michelle staff 98M Jul 15 21:07 BigFile.dmg
-rw-r--r--@ 1 michelle staff 109K Jul 15 23:03 BigFileAlias
-rw-r--r--@ 2 michelle staff 98M Jul 15 21:07 BigFileHardLink
lrwxr-xr-x 1 michelle staff 11B Jul 15 23:04 BigFileSymLink -> BigFile.dmg
```

Note in the previous example that the hard link is the exact same size as the original, indicating that they are both pointing to the same bits on the physical drive. Also note that the number between the permissions string and the owner for the original item has increased from 1 to 2. This number represents the number of links to a file, thus creating the new hard link incremented this number by one. Finally, notice how small the symbolic link is, measured in bytes, compared with the alias. The extra information in the alias is what allows the system to keep track of the original item if it should ever change locations.

NOTE ▶ Removing additional hard links will not delete the original item. Furthermore, deleting the original item will not delete the hard links; they still point to the same bits on the disk, which won't be freed until there are no links left to them. This is unlike aliases and symbolic links, where deleting the original item leaves the shortcut pointing at nothing.

Finally, the following screenshots show multiple Finder Get Info dialogs examining all four of the items created for this example. Specifically, look at what the Get Info dialog reports for the item's Kind. Both the alias and the symbolic link are reported as an Alias despite their size and technology difference. Besides the size, another clue is that the Finder cannot select a new original for the symbolic link. Also notice that the hard link is reporting the exact same information as the original item, again indicating that they share the same bits on the physical drive.

Understanding File System Metadata

Metadata is data about data. More specifically, metadata is information used to describe content. The most basic forms of file and folder metadata employed by nearly every operating system are names, paths, modification dates, and permissions. These metadata objects are not part of the item's content, yet they are necessary to describe the item in the file system. Lion uses several types of additional file system metadata for a variety of technologies that ultimately lead to a richer user experience.

Mac OS Extended Metadata

Resource forks, dating back to the original Mac OS, are the legacy metadata technology in the Macintosh operating system. To simplify the user experience, Apple created a forked file system to make complex items, such as applications, appear as a single icon. Forked file systems, like Mac OS Extended, allow multiple pieces of data to appear as a single item in the file system. In this case, a file will appear as a single item, but it is actually composed of two separate pieces, a data fork and a resource fork. This also allows the Mac OS to support standard file types in the data fork, while the extra Mac-specific information resides in the resource fork. For many years the Mac OS has relied on forked files for storing both data and associated metadata.

Lion not only continues but also expands the use of metadata, even going so far as to allow developers to take advantage of an arbitrary number of additional metadata items. This enables Apple, and other developers, to implement unique file system solutions without having to modify the existing file system. For instance, Mac OS X v10.6 introduced compressed application code, wherein the actual executable program files are all compressed to save space and then when needed automatically decompressed on the fly. To prevent previous versions of Mac OS X or older applications from improper handling of these compressed executables, Apple chose to hide the compressed bits in additional metadata locations.

The downside to legacy resource forks, and other types of additional file system metadata, is that some third-party file systems, like FAT, do not know how to properly store this additional data. The solution to this issue is addressed with the AppleDouble file format covered later in this chapter.

File Flags and Extended Attributes

Lion also uses file system flags and extended attributes to implement a variety of file system features. In general, file system flags are holdovers from the original Mac OS and are primarily used to control user access. Examples of file system flags include the locked flag covered in Chapter 3, "File Systems," and the hidden flag covered previously in this chapter.

With Mac OS X, Apple needed to expand the range of possible attributes associated with any file or folder, which is where so-called extended attributes come into play. Any process or application can add an arbitrary number of custom attributes to a file or folder. Again, this allows developers to create new forms of metadata without having to modify the existing file system. The Mac OS Extended file system will store any additional attributes as another fork associated with the file.

The Finder uses extended attributes for several general file features, including setting an item's color label, stationary pad option, hide extension option, and Spotlight comments. All of these items can be accessed from the Finder's Get Info window.

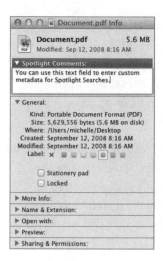

Metadata via Terminal

From Terminal's command line, you can verify that an item has additional file system metadata present using the ls command with both the long list option, -l, and the -@ option. In the following example, Michelle uses the ls command to view the file system metadata associated with an alias file and the file shown in the previous Get Info window screen shot.

```
MyMac:Desktop michelle$ ls -l@
total 1368
-rw-r--r--@ 1 cadmin staff 43316 Jul 15 15:49 AliasFile
        com.apple.FinderInfo                        32
        com.apple.ResourceFork              42950
```

```
-rw-------@ 1 michelle staff 557722 Jul 1 17:16 Document.pdf
        com.apple.FinderInfo                        32
        com.apple.metadata:kMDItemFinderComment    120
```

Note the @ symbol at the end of the permissions string, which indicates the item has additional metadata. This symbol is shown any time you perform a long listing. For the sake of simplification, using ls -l@ combines the viewing of both resource fork and extended attribute data. The indented lines below the primary listing show the additional metadata that the Finder has added. In the case of the alias file, it's clear from the file sizes that the resource fork is used to store the alias data.

Bundles and Packages

Sometimes forked files aren't the most efficient solution for hiding data, especially if you have a lot of related files that you need to hide. So instead of creating a new container technology, Apple simply modified an existing file system container, the common folder. Bundles and packages are nothing more than common folders that happen to contain related software and resources. This allows software developers to easily organize all the resources needed for a complicated product into a single bundle or package, while discouraging normal users from interfering with the resources.

Bundles and packages use the same technique of combining resources inside special folders. The difference is that the Finder treats packages as opaque objects that, by default, users cannot navigate into. For example, where a user sees only a single icon in the Finder representing an application, in reality it is a folder potentially filled with thousands of resources. The word "package" is also used to describe the archive files used by the installer application to install software—that is, installer packages. This is appropriate, though, as users cannot, by default, navigate into the contents of a legacy installer package because the Finder again displays it as a single opaque object. Starting with Mac OS X v10.5, Apple allowed the creation of fully opaque installation packages wherein the entire contents are inside a single file, further preventing users from accidentally revealing installation content.

The anatomy of an installer package is quite simple; it usually contains only a compressed archive of the software to be installed and a few configuration files used by the installer application. Other software bundles and packages, on the other hand, are often much more complex as they contain all the resources necessary for the application or software.

Software bundles or packages often include:

▶ Executable code for multiple platforms

▶ Document description files

▶ Media resources such as images and sounds

▶ User interface description files

▶ Text resources

▶ Resource forks

▶ Resources localized for specific languages

▶ Private software libraries and frameworks

▶ Plug-ins or other software to expand capability

Although the Finder default is to hide the contents of a package, you can view the contents of a package from the Finder. To access a package's contents in the Finder, simply right-click or Control-click on the item you wish to explore, and then choose Show Package Contents from the shortcut menu. (You may recall this technique is used in Chapter 1, "Installation and Configuration," to reveal the installation disk image inside the Install Mac OS X Lion application.)

Nevertheless, you should be very careful when exploring this content. Modifying the content of a bundle or package can easily leave the item unstable or unusable. If you can't resist the desire to tinker with a bundle or package, you should always do so from a copy and leave the original safely intact.

MORE INFO ▶ Tools for creating and modifying bundles and packages are included with the optional Xcode Developer Tools package, which can be found in the Mac App Store.

AppleDouble File Format

While file system metadata helps make the user's experience on Lion richer, compatibility with third-party file systems can be an issue. Only volumes formatted with the Mac OS Extended file system fully support Mac OS X–style resource forks, data forks, file flags, and extended attributes. Third-party software has been developed for Windows-based operating systems to allow them to access the extended metadata features of Mac OS Extended. More often, though, users will use the compatibility software built into Lion to help other file systems cope with these metadata items.

For most non-Mac OS volumes, Lion stores the file system metadata in a separate hidden data file. This technique is commonly referred to as AppleDouble. For example, if you copy a file containing metadata named "My Document.docx" to a FAT32 volume, Lion will automatically split the file and write it as two discrete pieces on the FAT32 volume. The file's internal data would be written with the same name as the original, but the metadata would end up in a file named ._My Document.docx that would remain hidden from the Finder. This works out pretty well for most files because Windows applications only care about the contents of the data fork. But, some files do not take well to being split up, and all the extra dot-underscore files create a bit of a mess on other file systems.

NOTE ▶ Window systems default to automatically hiding these "period-underscore" files. In fact, to acquire the prior Windows XP screenshot, showing hidden files had to be manually enabled.

NOTE ▶ Because bundles and packages are really just special folders, these items simply copy over to non–Mac OS volumes as regular folders. The Finder will continue to recognize the items as bundles or packages even when they reside on a third-party volume.

Mac OS X v10.5 introduced an improved method for handling metadata on SMB network shares from NTFS volumes that doesn't require the AppleDouble format. The native file system for modern Windows-based computers, NTFS, supports something similar to file forking known as alternative data streams. The Mac's file system will write the metadata to the alternative data stream so the file will appear as a single item on both Windows and Mac systems.

NOTE ▶ Lion will always revert to using "dot underscore" files when writing to FAT and UFS volumes or older NFS shares.

AppleDouble Files via Terminal

Historically, UNIX operating systems have not used file systems with extensive metadata. As a result, many UNIX commands do not properly support this additional metadata. These commands can manipulate the data fork just fine, but they often ignore the additional metadata, leaving files damaged and possibly unusable. Fortunately, Apple has made some modifications to the most common file management commands, thus allowing them to properly work with all Mac files and support the AppleDouble format when necessary. Metadata-friendly commands in Lion include cp, mv, and rm.

In the following example, Michelle will use the metadata-aware cp command to copy a file on her desktop called ForkedDocument.tiff to a FAT32 volume. Note that the file is a single item on her desktop, but on the FAT32 volume it's in the dual-file AppleDouble format. The metadata part is named with a preceding period-underscore. Finally, Michelle will remove the file using the metadata-aware rm command. Note that both the data and the metadata part are removed from the FAT32 volume.

```
MyMac:~ michelle$ ls -a Desktop/
.                             .localized
..                            ForkedDocument.tiff
MyMac:~ michelle$ cp Desktop/ForkedDocument.tiff /Volumes/FAT32VOLUME/
```

```
MyMac:~ michelle$ ls -a /Volumes/FAT32VOLUME/
.                                    ._.Trashes
..                                   ._ForkedDocument.tiff
.DS_Store                            .fseventsd
.Spotlight-V100                      ForkedDocument.tiff
.Trashes
MyMac:~ michelle$ rm /Volumes/FAT32VOLUME/ForkedDocument.tiff
MyMac:~ michelle$ ls -a /Volumes/FAT32VOLUME/
.                                    ._.Trashes
..                                   .DS_Store
.fseventsd                           .Spotlight-V100
.Trashes
```

Managing Launch Services

Aside from a file's name, the most fundamentally important piece of metadata about a file is its type. Identifying a file's type allows Lion to almost always choose the correct application to open when you double-click on a file. Launch Services is the technology responsible for helping Lion make the connection between a file's type and the appropriate application. When you double-click on a file from the Finder, it asks Launch Services to open the file with the appropriate application. Launch Services identifies the file based on its type and then references an application registration database to determine which application should open the file.

File Type Identification

Apple pioneered file type identification when it first introduced the Macintosh operating system. Apple designed the file identification system to use four-character file type and creator signature file attributes, which were normally hidden from the user. This was a brilliant design that separated the file's type and default application binding from the file's name.

Unfortunately, the popularity of other operating systems forced the awkward practice of adding a file type identifier to the end of a file's name, thus complicating the practice of naming files by requiring the user to identify and maintain the appropriate filename extension such as .mp3 for compressed audio files, .jpg for compressed picture files, or .doc for Microsoft Word files. Using filename extensions has become standard practice, so modern operating systems have been designed to work around this poor design choice by simply hiding the filename extension from the user. For the sake of compatibility, Apple adopted this later method of file type identification as the default for all versions of Mac OS X.

NOTE ► Lion still supports the legacy file type attribute but no longer supports the creator code attribute. Thus some files may not default to opening in the application that created them. However, you can change the default behavior, as covered later in this section.

Since the Finder hides many file type extensions by default, you can toggle file type extension visibility from the Finder's preferences by choosing Finder > Preferences from the menu bar. Then click the Advanced button and select or deselect the checkbox next to "Show all file extensions."

NOTE ► Choosing to show all file extensions in the Finder will override the individual file attribute for hiding the extension as configured from the Get Info and Inspector windows in the Finder.

Application Registration

When a user attempts to open a file of a certain type, Launch Services reads from a database of applications and the types of files each can open to determine a match. Successful file and application match information is cached, so future attempts to open an application are as quick as possible. However, after every startup or login, a background process automatically scans for new applications and updates this database. Further, both the Finder and Installer keep track of new applications as they arrive on your system and add their supported file types to the database.

The application registration system is pretty good at finding matches, so odds are if the system gives you an error message, then you probably don't have the correct application for the file. In Lion, Launch Services maps many common file types to the built-in Preview and TextEdit applications if the primary application is missing. For example, Numbers or Excel documents open in Preview and Pages and Word documents open in TextEdit.

TIP ▶ Lion's Quick Look feature can also preview many common file types even without the applications installed. This includes both iWork and Microsoft Office documents. Quick Look details are covered later in this chapter.

If Preview, or any other application, cannot properly open a specific file type, you can change the Launch Service settings to force those files to open in a more appropriate application, as outlined below. Other times, though, Launch Services may not have any idea which application to use for the file type. If you attempt to open a file type that is not stored in the Launch Services database, the computer will prompt you to find an application that supports the file. Alternately, you can use a new feature in Lion that will search the Mac App Store for a compatible application.

Change Launch Service Settings

From the Finder's Get Info window, you can override Launch Services' default application settings for any specific file type. These custom settings are saved per user, so one user's application preferences will not override another user's. They are saved to the com.apple. LaunchServices.plist preference file in each user's ~/Library/Preferences folder.

To change a user's Launch Services settings in the Finder:

1   In the Finder, select the file or multiple files you wish to change the Launch Services settings for, and then open the Get Info or Inspector window.

2   To open the Get Info window, do one of the following (performing the same tasks while holding the Option key will open an Inspector window):

▶   Choose File > Get Info from the menu bar.

▶   Use the Command-I keyboard shortcut.

▶   Choose Get Info from the Action pop-up menu (the small gear icon) in a Finder window toolbar.

▶   Choose Get Info from the Finder's shortcut menu by right-clicking or Control-clicking on an item.

3   Once you have opened a Get Info window, click the "Open with" disclosure triangle to reveal the default application selected by Launch Services.

4   To change just the selected files' default application, simply select another application from the pop-up menu.

5 To change the default application for all files of this type, click the Change All button.

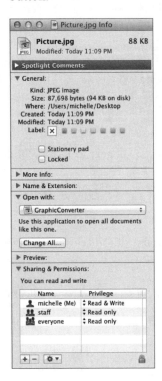

NOTE ► If you do not click the Change All button, the Launch Services settings will be saved only for the selected files. These settings will, however, stay with the selected file until changed again.

6 All Launch Services changes take place immediately.

TIP ► You can also modify Launch Services settings in the Finder by right-clicking or Control-clicking the selected files and then choosing Open With from the pop-up menu. Additionally, holding down the Option key will change the menu command to Always Open With.

Using Spotlight and Quick Look

Spotlight was a significant new feature in Mac OS X v10.4 that revolutionized the way users searched for files on their Macs. Spotlight enables you to perform nearly instantaneous searches that go wider and deeper than previous Mac desktop search technology. Spotlight has the ability to go beyond simple file system searches and actually search for relevant metadata inside application files and databases. For example, an application like Address Book stores contact information in a database that appears opaque to the file system. Nevertheless, Spotlight can return search results from Address Book along with results from other databases and the entire file system hierarchy nearly instantly.

> **NOTE ▸** In addition to the file system metadata that was covered previously in this chapter, many files also contain internal metadata used to describe the file's content. For example, many digital camera image files contain additional camera setting information embedded as metadata inside the file. Spotlight can search through both file system and internal metadata information.

Though Spotlight was pretty amazing when it debuted, Apple added a few more tricks to Spotlight over the years. These included the ability to search through the contents of shared files from other Mac clients, servers, AirDisk volumes over the network, and Time Machine backups. Lion introduced the ability for Spotlight searches to automatically return results from your default web search engine and Wikipedia.

Apple has also incorporated the ability to use advanced search operations while performing Spotlight searches from the Finder or menu bar. Advanced Spotlight search operations include:

▶ The use of multiple search criteria types in a single search

▶ The use of Boolean logic by using AND, OR, or NOT

▶ The use of exact phrases and dates by using quotation marks

▶ The use of search ranges by using greater-than and less-than symbols.

Another feature, dubbed Quick Look, augments Spotlight by allowing you to quickly preview the content of most files even if you don't have the application that created the file installed on your Mac. The combination of Spotlight and Quick Look allows you to locate and preview items with unmatched ease and speed.

Using Spotlight for Searching

You can initiate a Spotlight search any time by clicking the Spotlight icon on the far right of the menu bar or using the Command-Space bar keyboard shortcut. The Spotlight search is so fast that the results will actually change in real time as you type in your search query. In the results list, moving your mouse over an object (but not clicking) or using the arrow keys will open a Quick Look preview of the content. Clicking on an item or pressing the Return key with a result selected will open it immediately.

TIP ▶ When previewing with Quick Look from the Spotlight search, hold the Command key to reveal location information at the bottom of the Quick Look window.

Selecting Show All in Finder from the Spotlight search results menu will open a new Finder window with the results. You could also arrive at this same window by opening a new Finder window and entering your search in the Spotlight field from the Finder's toolbar, or by selecting File > Find from the menu bar, or using the Command-F keyboard shortcut. Selecting an item from the search results will show you the path to the selected item at the bottom of the Finder window. Selecting an item and then tapping the Space bar will open a Quick Look preview of the selected item.

You can refine your Spotlight search from a Finder search window by clicking the small plus buttons on the right below the search field. This will allow you to add as many specific search attributes as you need. After you add a new search attribute, click the first word in the search attribute to choose another type from the pop-up menu.

If you don't see the search attribute you're looking for, you can add literally dozens of other attributes that aren't enabled by default. To enable additional search attributes, select any attribute, and from the pop-up menu select the Other option. This will reveal a dialog that allows you to add search attributes to the pop-up menu. Two especially useful search attributes for administrators are "File visibility" and "System files," neither of which is shown by default in any Spotlight search.

TIP Take some time to explore the additional search attributes; you may be surprised at the depth of Spotlight's search capabilities. Search attributes include specifying audio file tags, digital camera metadata, authorship information, contact information, and many other metadata types.

Clicking the Save button on the right will save these search criteria as a Smart Folder. Smart Folders are like normal folders in that they can be given a unique name and placed anywhere you like, including the Finder's sidebar. Smart Folders are special because their contents will always match your search criteria no matter how the file system changes. In fact, the All My Files item in the Finder's sidebar is simply a predefined Smart Folder searching for the most recently opened documents in the user's home folder.

NOTE ▶ Smart Folders do not work from Terminal.

Using Quick Look for Previewing

Again, Quick Look allows you to preview nearly any file type without having to open any additional applications, or even having those applications installed on your Mac. This makes Quick Look the most convenient method to view the contents of any file. Quick Look previews can be accessed, or dismissed, by pressing the Space bar from any Finder view, the Time Machine restore interface, most open and save browser dialogs, the Mail application, or any other application that supports Quick Look. A new feature in Lion makes Quick Look preview windows stay open in the Finder until closed, just like traditional windows. The Quick Look close window button is in the top-left corner, again just like a traditional window. You can also quickly dismiss the Quick Look preview by pressing the Space bar again.

With the Quick Look preview window open, you can resize the window by clicking and dragging any edge of the window, or you can go full-screen by clicking the twin arrow button at the top right of the preview window. Note the Open with Application button next to the full-screen button. Use the arrow keys to navigate and preview the items adjacent to the original previewed item in the Finder. If the previewed file has multiple pages, you'll be able to scroll through the document. In some cases—Keynote presentations, for example—Quick Look will show a thumbnail preview of each slide, allowing you to scroll through the thumbnails as well. Finally, if you select multiple items to preview, the Quick Look window will allow some basic slideshow features via buttons at the top left of the window.

Quick Look technology is also used to provide the Finder with previews for files in icon view, previews in column view, and the preview section of the Get Info and Inspector windows. Finally, Quick Look also provides previews for the Finder's Cover Flow view. This view allows you to browse folder content in a similar way to browsing with iTunes or Apple's other mobile devices. Quick Look can be accessed from any Finder window by selecting its icon in the toolbar.

Quick Look Plug-ins

Quick Look is able to preview an ever-growing variety of file types using a plug-in technology. Each Quick Look plug-in is designed to preview specific types of files. Many Quick Look plug-ins are included by default, but Apple and third-party developers can create additional plug-ins to expand Quick Look's preview capabilities.

Included Quick Look plug-ins enable you to:

▶ Preview any audio or video file that can be decoded by QuickTime

▶ Preview a variety of graphics files, including many digital camera files, PDF files, EPS files, and any standard graphics file

▶ Preview a variety of productivity files, including standard text files, script files, and files created by the iWork and Microsoft Office suites

▶ Preview a variety of Internet-centric files, including mailboxes, iChat transcripts, and web archives

Quick Look plug-ins, like any other system resource, are stored inside the various Library folders. Apple's built-in Quick Look plug-ins are always found in the /System/Library/QuickLook folder and sometimes appear in the /Library/QuickLook folder. Third-party plug-ins should always be installed in either /Library/QuickLook or the ~/Library/QuickLook folder, depending on who needs access to them.

Understanding the Spotlight Service

Spotlight is able to perform wide and deep searches quickly because it works in the background to maintain highly optimized databases of indexed metadata for each local volume. When you first set up Lion, it will create these databases by indexing all the available local volumes. The system will also index new local volumes when they are first attached.

On your Mac, a background process called mds, short for metadata server, will automatically update the index databases on the fly as changes are made throughout the file system. Because these indexes are kept current, the Spotlight process need only search through the databases to return thorough results. Essentially, Spotlight preemptively searches everything for you in the background so you don't have to wait for the results when you need them.

> **NOTE** ▶ Spotlight does not create index databases on read-only volumes or write-once media such as optical discs.

NOTE ▶ Your Mac's Spotlight service will index Time Machine and AirDisk volumes directly, but it will not index shared volumes from other computers. However, Spotlight can connect to indexes on shared volumes from other Mac OS X Server computers.

You can find the Spotlight general index databases at the root level of every volume in a folder named .Spotlight-V100. A few applications maintain their own databases separate from these general index databases. One example is the built-in email application Mail. It maintains its own optimized email database in each user's folder at ~/Library/Mail/ Envelope Index. Also, the Spotlight index database for a Legacy FileVault user is stored at the root level inside his encrypted home folder for enhanced security. If you are experiencing problems with Spotlight, you can force it to rebuild the index databases by deleting them and restarting your Mac or by managing the Spotlight settings as covered later in this chapter.

Spotlight Security

In order to provide security on par with the rest of the file system, Spotlight also indexes every item's permissions. Even though Spotlight indexes every item on a volume, it will automatically filter search results to show only items that the current user has permissions to access. There is still a security concern, though, when users search through locally attached non-system volumes because they can choose to ignore ownership on these volumes. In other words, all users can search through locally attached non-system volumes, including mounted disk images, even if another user attached the device.

Spotlight Plug-ins

Spotlight is able to create indexes, and thus search, from an ever-growing variety of metadata using a plug-in technology. Each Spotlight plug-in is designed to examine specific types of files or databases. Many Spotlight plug-ins are included by default, but Apple and third-party developers can create additional plug-ins to expand Spotlight's search capabilities.

Included Spotlight plug-ins enable you to:

▶ Search via basic file metadata, including name, file size, creation date, and modification date

▶ Search via media-specific metadata from picture, music, and video files, including time code, creator information, and hardware capture information

▶   Search through the contents of a variety of file types, including text files, iLife related files and databases, Photoshop files, PDF files, iWork files, and Microsoft Office files

▶   Search through personal information like Address Book contacts and iCal calendar events

▶   Search for correspondence information like the contents of Mail emails and iChat chat transcripts

▶   Search for highly relevant information like your favorites or web browser bookmarks and history

Spotlight plug-ins, like any other system resource, are stored inside the various Library folders. Apple's built-in Spotlight plug-ins are always found in the /System/Library/Spotlight folder and sometimes appear in the /Library/Spotlight folder. Third-party plug-ins should always be installed in either the /Library/Spotlight or the ~/Library/Spotlight folder, depending on who needs access to it.

TIP ▶ You can create custom metadata for Spotlight by entering Spotlight comments in the Get Info and Inspector windows from the Finder.

Managing Spotlight Settings

From the Spotlight preferences, any user can choose to disable specific categories from appearing in Spotlight searches. A user can also prevent volumes from being indexed by specifying those volumes in the privacy list. However, by default all new volumes are automatically indexed, so a user must manually configure Spotlight to ignore a volume.

The Spotlight privacy list is a computer-level setting that remains the same across all user accounts, but it's not protected by administrative access, which means any user can change the privacy list. In this case, the Spotlight privacy list isn't any less secure than the rest of the file system, as any user can still have full access to locally connected non-system volumes because the system defaults to ignoring ownership on those volumes.

To change Spotlight settings:

1   Open the Spotlight preferences by choosing Apple menu > System Preferences, and then clicking the Spotlight icon.

The Spotlight preferences will open to the Search Results tab, allowing you to disable specific categories from the search results.

2   Simply deselect the checkboxes next to the categories you wish to ignore.

You can also drag categories to change their order in the search results. Each user has her own separate Search Results settings.

3   To prevent Spotlight from indexing specific items, click the Privacy tab to reveal the list of items for Spotlight to ignore.

To add new items, click the small plus icon at the bottom of the privacy list and choose the items from a browser dialog, or simply drag and drop items into the privacy list.

4   You can delete an item from the privacy list by selecting it and then clicking the minus icon at the bottom of the list.

All Spotlight settings are applied immediately. If you add an entire volume to the privacy list, then the system will delete the Spotlight index database from that volume. In turn, removing a volume from the privacy list will rebuild the Spotlight index database on that volume. This technique, to rebuild the Spotlight index databases by adding, then removing, a volume from the privacy list, is the most common method to resolve problematic Spotlight performance.

Using File Archives and Disk Images

Archiving and backup are both synonymous with copying data to another location for safekeeping, yet in the context of this chapter, they are different processes serving different purposes. In Lion, archiving is typically a manual process that involves creating compressed copies of selected data. Archive formats are efficient from a storage and data transfer perspective, but they generally require user interaction. On the other hand, the backup service introduced with Mac OS X v10.5, Time Machine, is an automated process that allows users to easily browse the backup history of their entire file system. As you can imagine, maintaining a history of your file system is not space efficient, but it is extremely useful.

Understanding Archive versus Disk Image

At its essence, archiving is the practice of saving copies of important information to another location or format better suited for long-term storage or network transfer. Large amounts of hard disk drive storage have become much less expensive in the last few years, but this type of storage is still not as reliable as tape or optical media in terms of longevity. This type of archival media has not kept up with the tremendous growth of hard drives, so storing archival data in a more efficient form by compressing it is still relevant. Also, no matter how robust your Internet connection is, there never seems to be enough bandwidth, so compressing items in preparation for data transfer is almost always a time-saver. Lion includes two archival technologies, archives and disk images, that allow you to combine multiple files and compress the data into a more efficient file suited for long-term storage or network data transfer.

First, the Mac's Finder will allow you to create zip archives from a selection of files or folders. This is an efficient method for archiving relatively small amounts of data quickly. The zip archive format is also widely compatible, as many operating systems include software to decompress zip archives back to their original items. However, zip archives in Lion do not offer the flexibility provided by disk images.

Disk images, created using Disk Utility, are more widely used in Lion for archival purposes because they offer many features not available from zip archives. Primarily, disk images allow you to archive the contents of an entire file system into a single file that can be compressed, encrypted, or both. Disk images can also be created as read/write so you can easily make changes to them over time. The only downside to disk images created using Disk Utility is that, by default, only Macs can access the content—other systems require third-party software to access Mac disk image content.

Creating Zip Archives

Lion's Finder allows you to quickly create a compressed zip archive from any number of selected items. By default, creating a zip archive in the Finder will not delete the original items you've selected to compress.

To create a zip archive in the Finder:

1 Select the items you wish to archive and compress in the Finder.

You can hold down the Shift key to quickly select contiguous lists of items, or hold down the Command key to quickly select noncontiguous items. It's best to put all of the items in one folder and then compress that, as opposed to selecting multiple items.

2 Choose File > Compress "Items" from the menu bar.

The word "Items" in the menu will be replaced by the name of a single item you have selected or the number of items you have selected.

If the archival process is going to take more than a few seconds, the Finder will show a progress dialog with the estimated time required to complete the erase task. You can also choose to cancel the archive by clicking the small X button on the far right.

3 When the archival process has completed, you will be left with a zip archive named either Archive.zip or Item.zip, where Item is the name of the single item you chose to archive and compress.

TIP You can also archive and compress items in the Finder by right-clicking or Control-clicking the selected files and then choosing Compress "Items" from the shortcut menu.

TIP From Terminal, you have more options when using the zip command to create compressed archives.

Once the archive process is complete, it's always interesting to compare the original items' size with the archive's size using the Get Info or Inspector windows in the Finder. In many cases, you can expect at least a 50 percent decrease in file size. On the other hand, many media formats are already quite compressed in their original form, so you may not experience very good results when compressing these types of files.

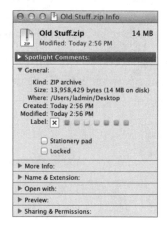

Expanding Zip Archives

Expanding a zip archive in the Finder is as simple as double-clicking on the zip archive file. The Finder will decompress the entire archive file and place the resulting files and folders in the same folder as the original zip archive. The Finder cannot list or extract individual items from a zip archive. By default, the Finder will not delete the original zip archive.

TIP From Terminal you have more options when using the unzip command to expand the contents of compressed archives.

TIP ▶ If you need more control over how zip archives are expanded, open /System/
Library/Core Services/Archive Utility.app, and then from the menu bar choose
Archive Utility > Preferences.

Understanding Disk Images

Disk images are files that contain entire virtual drives and volumes. Lion relies on disk
images for several core technologies, including software distribution, system imaging,
NetBoot, Legacy FileVault, and network Time Machine backups. Disk images are also
useful as a personal archive tool. Though Mac-created disk images work only on Mac
computers by default, they are much more flexible to use than zip archives. Disk images
provide advanced compression and encryption, but their greatest benefit is that they can
be treated like a removable volume.

To access the contents of a disk image, you simply double-click on the disk image file in
the Finder. This will mount the volume inside the disk image file as if you had just connected a normal storage device. Even if the disk image file is located on a remote file
server, you can still mount it as if it were a local drive. You can treat the mounted disk
image volume as you would any other storage device by navigating through its hierarchy
and selecting files and folders as you need them. Further, if the disk image is read/write,
you can add to the contents of the disk image by simply dragging items to the volume.

Disk Image File.dmg   Disk Image Volume

NOTE ▶ When you are done with a disk image volume, be sure to properly unmount
and eject it as you would any other removable volume.

Using /Applications/Utilities/Disk Utility to make disk images allows you to create blank
images, or images containing copies of selected folders or even entire file systems. Lion
supports disk images up to 2 terabytes. Disk images also feature a number of configuration options, including:

▶   Image format—Disk images can be read-only or read/write. They can also be a set
    size or expandable as a sparse disk image. Sparse disk images will take up only as
    much space as necessary and automatically grow as you add items to them.

▶ Compression—Read-only disk images can be compressed to save space. With a compressed disk image, any free space becomes negligible in size, and most other files average a 50 percent reduction in size.

▶ Encryption—Any disk image can be protected with a password and encrypted with strong 128-bit or 256-bit AES encryption. Choosing a higher bit rate is more secure but degrades performance. This feature is useful for securing data stored on otherwise unsecure volumes like removable drives and network shares. The encryption always happens on the local computer, so even if the disk image file is physically stored externally, as on a network file share, the data is always encrypted as it travels across the connection.

▶ File system—Disk images can contain any partition scheme or volume format that Lion supports, including optical media formats. Details regarding the differences between file system options are covered in Chapter 3, "File Systems."

Creating Empty Disk Images

To create an automatically resizing empty disk image that you can fill with content over time:

1 Open /Applications/Utilities/Disk Utility, and then choose File > New > Blank Disk Image from the menu bar. Or with nothing selected in the drives list, you can click the New Image button in the toolbar.

2 Enter a name for the disk image file, and then select a destination for the disk image file from the Where pop-up menu. Also enter a name for the volume inside the disk image.

The disk image file and volume names do not have to match but should be similar so that you can recognize their relationship.

3   Select a volume size from the Size pop-up menu, or select Custom to specify a disk image of arbitrary size.

Remember, this disk image will occupy only as much space as the files you copy inside it. Obviously if you're going to save it on an external volume of limited size, that should define your maximum size.

4   You can select a different volume format or partition scheme from the pop-up menus, but in most cases you will want to stick with the default Mac OS Extended (Journaled) and Apple Partition Map selections.

5 You can also select an encryption at this point from the pop-up menu. For most uses, 128-bit AES is secure enough and still provides good performance.

6 Choose "sparse disk image" from the Image Format pop-up menu to create an automatically resizable disk image.

7 Click the Create button to create the disk image.

8 If you have selected an encrypted disk image, you will be prompted to enter a password for the disk image. After you have selected a secure password, click the OK button to finish the disk image creation process.

After the system has created the new blank disk image, it will automatically mount it. From the Finder, you can open Get Info windows on both the disk image file and the disk image volume to verify that the volume size is much larger than the image size. As you copy files to the volume, the disk image file will grow accordingly.

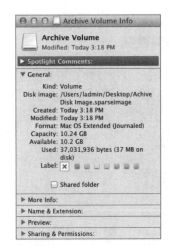

TIP You can change the format of a disk image at any time in Disk Utility by choosing Images > Convert from the menu bar. This will open a dialog allowing you to select the image you want to change and save a copy of the image with new options.

TIP From Terminal, you have more options when using the hdiutil command to manage disk images.

Creating Disk Images from Items

To create a disk image that contains copies of selected items:

1   Open /Applications/Utilities/Disk Utility.

2   At this point you can choose to create a new disk image from the contents of a folder or the contents of a volume.

   To create a disk image from the contents of a folder, choose File > New > Disk Image from Folder from the menu bar, and then select the folder you wish to copy into a new disk image from the file browser window. Once you have made your selection, click the Image button to continue.

To create a disk image from the contents of an entire volume, use the same menu option, Disk Image from Folder, and then simply choose the volume. It may be tempting to choose Disk Image from (Select a Device), but this option will copy the empty space on the volume as well, making the resulting disk image artificially large. The only time you should create an image of a device is when creating images of optical media.

NOTE ▶ Disk Utility can only make disk images of volumes that it can temporarily unmount. Thus, you cannot make a disk image of the currently running system volume.

3 Enter a name for the disk image file, and then choose a destination for the disk image file from the Where pop-up menu.

Again, the disk image file and volume names do not have to match but should be similar so that you can recognize their relationship.

NOTE ▶ Make sure you have enough free space on the destination volume where you plan to save your disk image file.

4   Choose an image format from the pop-up menu. Remember that compressed images are also read-only.

NOTE ▶ It takes nearly twice as much free space to create a compressed disk image—the system must create a noncompressed image first, and then convert the first image to a compressed image.

5   You can also choose an encryption at this point from the pop-up menu.

For most uses, 128-bit AES is secure enough and still provides good performance.

6   Click the Save button to create the disk image.

If you have selected an encrypted disk image, you will be prompted to enter a password for the disk image. After you have selected a secure password, click the OK button to start the disk image creation process.

NOTE ▶ You will have to authenticate as an administrator in order to image items for which you don't have read permissions.

Depending on the amount of data that has to be copied and the image format you chose, it can take anywhere from minutes to hours for the disk image copy process to complete. Disk Utility will open a small progress dialog that will also allow you to cancel the disk image copy by clicking the Cancel button.

Managing Time Machine

Several mature and relatively easy-to-use backup solutions are available for the Mac, so you may be wondering why the folks at Apple chose to invent a new backup architecture for Mac OS v10.5. They did a little research and discovered that, prior to Time Machine's introduction, only 4 percent of Mac users were backing up their data on a regular basis. This was an unacceptable number, so Apple decided that the only way to convince users to do so on a regular basis was to create a new backup process that would be as easy as possible and also surprisingly fun to use. Apple's solution was Time Machine.

Aside from being built into the operating system, Time Machine has two features that make it fundamentally different from any other solution currently out there. First, configuring Time Machine is so easy it's nearly automatic. The system practically begs you to set up Time Machine if you haven't done so already, and with as little as one click it's configured.

The second, more significant feature is that Time Machine is so tightly integrated with the operating system that users don't even have to exit the application they are currently using to recover data. Applications, both built in and third party, can tie directly into the Time Machine backup system. From applications supporting Time Machine, a user can activate the visually striking Time Machine interface and travel back through time to see the application's data as it was in the past. If an application doesn't yet support Time Machine, you can use the Finder while in Time Machine's interface to browse the entire file system through time.

Understanding Time Machine Backups
Time Machine can save backup archives to any locally connected Mac OS Extended volume that is not the startup volume. You are allowed to select a backup destination

volume that resides as another partition on the system disk drive, but this is an incredibly bad idea—if the system drive dies, so does your backup. New in Lion is support for an encrypted local backup destination. This option automatically reformats the backup drive as Mac OS Extended (Journaled, Encrypted). If you don't have a local volume suited for backup, you can also select a shared network volume as your backup destination. Time Machine supports network shares by creating a disk image on the share to store the backups. Time Machine currently only supports backing up to Apple Filing Protocol (AFP) network shares hosted from Mac OS X Servers or Time Capsule wireless base stations.

> **MORE INFO** ▶ You can find out more about Apple's Time Capsule wireless base station at Apple's website, www.apple.com/timecapsule.

Logistically, Time Machine uses a sophisticated background process, named `backupd`, to automatically create new backups of the entire file system every hour. This only works, though, if the backup destination is readily available. As more users go for portable Macs, it's becoming increasingly possible that a user may be away from his backup destination for quite a while. New with Time Machine in Lion is support for local snapshots. As the name implies, Time Machine will take local snapshots if the backup destination is unavailable. Even if the user is away from the backup destination, he will at least have access to restore from the local snapshots. This feature is only enabled on Mac portables with Time Machine left in the "on" state. Once the Mac can locate the backup destination again, the local snapshots will be converted to traditional backups and saved to the destination.

While Time Machine's local snapshots are a convenient new feature, they certainly aren't true backups, as they are located on the same drive they are backing up. If the system drive fails, then the local snapshots are lost as well. This is why, after not backing up to the backup destination for ten days, the system will warn the user on a regular basis to reconnect that destination. Users should be trained to ensure their Mac is connected to the Time Machine destination on a regular basis. Again, as long as the Mac can connect to the destination, Time Machine will automatically handle the backup maintenance.

Obviously, Time Machine must employ some tricks to keep backups as small as possible so that you can maintain a deep history. The initial Time Machine backup will copy almost the entire contents of your file system to the specified backup volume. In order to provide fast backups and convenient restores, Time Machine does not use a compressed archive format common to many other backup systems. Instead, Time Machine simply copies the items as is to the backup destination. As you'll see later, this allows for easy access to those items.

The space saving comes into play with each subsequent backup. Between backups, a background process, similar to the one used by the Spotlight search service, will automatically track any changes to the file system. When the next scheduled backup occurs, only the items that have changed will be copied to the backup volume. Time Machine will then combine this new content with hard link file system pointers (which occupy nearly zero disk space) to the previous backup content, and create a simulated view of the entire file system at that point in time.

Time Machine also saves space by ignoring files that do not need to be backed up, as they can be re-created after a restoration. Generally speaking, Time Machine ignores temporary files, Spotlight indexes, items in the Trash, and anything that can be considered a cache. Of particular note, Time Machine will not back up system log files, which you could need for later troubleshooting. Software developers can also tell Time Machine to ignore specific application data that does not need to be backed up.

> **MORE INFO ▶** Specifically, Time Machine always ignores files as defined by a configuration file that lives at /System/Library/CoreServices/backupd.bundle/Contents/Resources/StdExclusions.plist. You may find it beneficial to modify this file to suit your own backup needs.

Eventually, so as not to waste space on your backup volume with historical data that has outlived its usefulness, Time Machine will start "aging out" backups. Time Machine will only keep hourly backups for a day, daily backups for a week, and weekly backups until your backup volume is full. After your backup volume is full, Time Machine will start deleting the oldest items first. However, Time Machine will always keep at least one copy of every item that is still also on your current file system.

> **NOTE ▶** Do not confuse Time Machine with snapshot technology common on other operating systems. While snapshots do create multiple instances of a file system through time, they do not provide you with a backup, as they don't actually copy data to another storage device. In other words, if a drive containing file system snapshots dies, those snapshots are just as lost as the current data on the dead drive.

Configuring Time Machine

Despite the rather complex process going on behind the scenes to make Time Machine possible, configuration couldn't be easier. In fact, Time Machine is enabled by default and simply waiting for you to pick a backup destination. If you haven't configured a Time Machine backup destination, the system will automatically scan the network for a Time

Machine network share or wait for you to attach an external drive. If the system locates either, you will be prompted to select it as your backup destination. If you select your backup destination with this method, after you click the Use as Backup Disk button, Time Machine is fully configured. It's just that easy.

On the other hand, you can choose to manually configure Time Machine settings to better suit your needs:

1   Open the Time Machine preferences by choosing Apple menu > System Preferences, and then click the Time Machine icon.

> **TIP** ▶ You can also access the Time Machine preferences by clicking on Time Machine's icon in the Dock.

2   Enable Time Machine by sliding the switch to the On position, and then click the Choose Backup Disk button.

This will reveal a dialog allowing you to select a backup destination. Once you have selected an appropriate volume, click the Use Backup Disk button.

TIP ► If Time Machine ever "loses" its backup volume, simply select it again from this interface.

Depending on the Time Machine destination you chose, you may be presented with an additional dialog:

► If you selected a locally connected external drive and the encryption option, you will need to specify a password to protect the encryption. Enter a strong password twice, followed by a password hint, and then click the Encrypt Disk button to continue. This password will be saved to the local Mac's System keychain so backups can occur unattended.

NOTE ► Selecting the option to encrypt the Time Machine backup drive will erase the destination drive's contents.

NOTE ► If you forget the password used to encrypt the Time Machine backup drive, its contents will be lost forever. Not even Apple can recover the data.

▶ ·If you selected a network share or Time Capsule as the destination, you will need to specify an authentication that allows you to access the share. Enter the appropriate account information and then click the Connect button to set the network backup destination. This authentication information will be saved to the local Mac's System keychain so backups can occur unattended.

At this point Time Machine will wait two minutes, allowing you to make further configuration changes, before it starts the first backup.

NOTE ▶ If the top of the Time Machine schedule reads "Time Machine keeps:" it means local snapshots are turned off. On the other hand, if the schedule reads "Time Machine keeps local snapshots as space permits, and:" local snapshots are enabled.

3   Click the Options button to reveal a dialog allowing you to adjust a few Time Machine settings.

MORE INFO ▶ The feature at the bottom of the Time Machine options dialog, allowing you to adjust the automatic locking of documents, is related to the Auto Save feature covered in Chapter 5, "Applications and Processes."

4   The most important configuration choice you can make with Time Machine is to exclude items from the backup. Excluding items will obviously reduce the amount of space required to maintain your backups. It's not uncommon for users to leave only the /Users folder as the single item to back up; after all, that's where all the important user items reside.

You can drag and drop items into the list field, or you can click the small plus button at the bottom of the list to reveal a file browser, allowing you to select specific folders or volumes to exclude.

NOTE ▶ If you're going to save space by excluding system items, simply add the /System folder to the exclude list and you will be prompted to exclude all system files or just the /System folder. It's best to exclude all system files.

NOTE ▶ If you do not perform a full backup of your system volume, then you will not be able to perform a full restoration of it. Instead, you will have to install Lion first, and then restore the remainder using Migration Assistant, as covered later in this chapter.

5   Click the Save button when you are ready to commence with the backup.

The two-minute timer will reset every time you make a Time Machine configuration change. Once you are done, simply wait two minutes, and the initial Time Machine backup will begin.

Depending on the amount of data that has to be backed up, it can take from minutes to hours for the initial backup to complete. Time Machine will open a small progress dialog that will also allow you to cancel the backup by clicking the small "X" button to the right of the progress bar. The Time Machine preferences have a similar progress bar.

Subsequent backups will occur automatically in the background. Revisiting the Time Machine preferences will show you the time and date of the oldest, last, and next backup. You can also verify the last backup and force an immediate backup from the Time Machine menu extra (or icon) near the clock in the menu bar.

TIP ▸ If you only want Time Machine to back up when you say so, then simply turn it off in the Time Machine preferences and use the Time Machine menu extra to initiate manual backups. You can also postpone backups by disconnecting from the backup volume, though this works only for locally attached backup volumes.

TIP ▸ Advanced Time Machine management and automation can be accomplished with the tmutil command. As always, you can find out more about the tmutil command by reading its man page from Terminal.

Restore from Time Machine

Using Time Machine to restore data is what many will consider the best part because of the dynamic interface Apple has created to "look through time." Opening the Time Machine application or using the Time Machine menu extra will take you into the Time Machine history browser. Few applications currently support the Time Machine interface, so in most cases you will be presented with a historical view in the Finder.

TIP ▸ For quick access to Time Machine, you can also drag its icon to the Dock. From the Time Machine icon in the Dock, you can right-click or Control-click to reveal a shortcut menu allowing you to adjust Time Machine preferences, start a backup immediately, or browse another Time Machine backup.

The Finder windows will let you browse as usual, with one significant addition. You can use the navigation arrows on the bottom right, or the navigation timeline on the right side, to view Finder contents as they change through time. New in Lion is support for local Time Machine snapshots. If this feature is enabled, the local non-backed-up snapshots will show as purple tick marks in the navigation timeline. Normal snapshots, which are backed up to the Time Machine destination, will show as white tick marks in this timeline.

To aid in your search through time, the Spotlight search field remains active, and you can quickly preview any item using the Finder's Quick Look feature. Once you have found the item you were looking for, simply click the Restore button at the bottom-right corner and the Finder will return to "the present" with your recovered file intact where it once was.

NOTE ▶ Legacy FileVault users cannot access their home folder backup via the standard Time Machine interface. They can, however, use the following three methods to restore their home folder from a Time Machine backup.

NOTE ▶ If you use an encrypted drive or network share for your Time Machine destination, and you are trying to restore to a different Mac, you will have to enter a password to access the backup data.

Restoring with Migration Assistant

You can also restore a complete user home folder or other non-system data from a Time Machine archive using the Migration Assistant. You can use this technique if you choose not to perform full system backups, if your system is already running and you want to migrate specific information from a backup. First, make sure the Time Machine backup volume is available to the destination Mac, then open /Applications/Utilities/Migration Assistant. When the Migration Assistant opens, simply choose to restore from a Time Machine backup. The remainder of the Migration Assistant process is similar to the standard migration process covered in Chapter 1, "Installation and Configuration," for system items, or Chapter 2, "User Accounts," for user home folders.

NOTE ▶ Legacy FileVault user accounts can only be fully restored by using the Migration Assistant during the Lion initial system setup.

Restoring an Entire System

You can restore an entire system volume when started up from Lion Restore. This technique assumes you did not exclude any items from your system volume; thus, you have backed up the entire system volume. When started up from Lion Restore, as covered in Chapter 1, "Installation and Configuration," choose Restore From Time Machine backup from the Mac OS X Utilities window. This will open the Time Machine System Restore Assistant. The assistant will first scan for local and network Time Machine backup volumes. Once you have selected the Time Machine volume, you can restore the entire system from any backup instance on that volume to your new system drive.

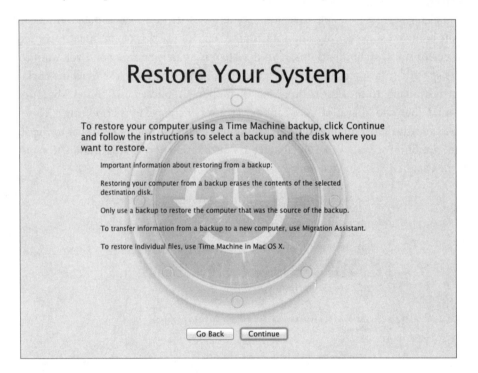

Manually Restoring from Time Machine

If you are experiencing problems using one of the Time Machine restoration interfaces, you can always browse the backup from the Finder. Time Machine's backup technology uses file system features that are part of standard Mac OS Extended volumes, so no special software is needed to browse through backup contents.

NOTE ▶ You should not directly modify the contents of a Time Machine backup, as doing so could damage the backup hierarchy. The default file system permissions will not give you write access to these items.

NOTE ▶ Legacy FileVault home folders will remain inside an encrypted disk image in the Time Machine backup. Thus you will need the user's password to access the secure home folder contents.

NOTE ▶ If your Time Machine configuration supports local snapshots, those snapshots are cached locally to a hidden /Volumes/MobileBackups folder. While you can navigate here and look around, the items in this location aren't permanent, as they will eventually be copied to the backup destination and then erased on the local drive to save space.

If you're accessing a locally attached drive for Time Machine, then the backups are located on the root of your backup volume in a folder named Backups.backupdb. Once inside the backup database folder, you will see folders with the name of each computer that is backed up to that volume. Inside each computer folder you will see folders named with a date and time indicating each backup. Finally, inside each dated folder you will see folders representing each volume that was backed up.

If you're accessing Time Machine over a network, you will need to manually connect to the Time Machine share first. Connecting to shares is covered in Chapter 7, "Network Services." Once connected, you will need to locate the Time Machine backup disk images. They will be at the root of the Time Machine share and named with the computer's name followed by the .sparsebundle extension. Double-click to mount the Time Machine backup disk image volume, which will be named "Backup of" followed by the computer's name. Inside this volume you will find the same Backups.backupdb folder and contents that you would find on a directly connected Time Machine backup.

Time Machine Caveats

Though Time Machine is supported by Apple, it is not without flaws. Time Machine's backup architecture does not lend itself well to large files that change often. For example, many database files appear as large, single files to the file system. While the database application may be able to change just a few bytes of the large file as a user edits the database, Time Machine will not recognize this, and it will have to create another copy of the entire database file during the next backup. This will obviously fill your backup volume much quicker than if the database had been stored as many smaller files.

This leads to the next Time Machine issue: running out of backup space. Once Time Machine fills up the backup volume, it will begin deleting older items to make room for newer ones. Therefore, the depth of your backup history will vary based not only on the size of your backup volume, but also on how often you change your files and how Time Machine recognizes those changes. Because you cannot change how Time Machine chooses to delete older items, you may discover that items you thought would still be on the backup volume have already been deleted.

TIP By default, Time Machine will let you know if it needs to delete older items to make space for new backups.

One final issue is that Time Machine can only back up Legacy FileVault accounts when the user is logged out of the system. The solution to this problem is to simply stop using Legacy FileVault in favor of Lion's FileVault2, as covered in Chapter 3, "File Systems."

What You've Learned

- ▶ Lion's file system is laid out to enhance ease of use and administration.
- ▶ System resources are stored in various Library folders throughout the system, and these folders provide different levels of access.
- ▶ Font Book is the primary tool for managing font resources.
- ▶ You can reveal and manage hidden items from Terminal.
- ▶ Lion provides aliases and links as methods to provide file system shortcuts.
- ▶ You can override Launch Services to open files in your preferred applications.
- ▶ Lion uses extensive metadata to provide robust file system searches with Spotlight.
- ▶ Time Machine backup, along with other archival tools like disk images, provides ample means to secure your data from human or hardware failure.

References

You can check for new and updated Knowledge Base documents at www.apple.com/support.

Font Management

▶ HT2435, "Mac OS X: Font locations and their purposes"

Spotlight

▶ TA23187, "Mac OS X 10.4: Where does Spotlight search?"

▶ HT2409, "Spotlight: How to re-index folders or volumes"

Time Machine

▶ HT3275, "Time Machine: Troubleshooting backup issues"

▶ TS2986, "Mac OS X v10.6, OS X Lion: Cannot install Mac OS X v10.6 or later on a volume used by Time Machine for backups"

▶ Add another bullet with text:

▶ HT4878, "OS X Lion: About Time Machine's 'local snapshots' on portable Macs"

URLs

Apple's Time Capsule wireless base station: www.apple.com/timecapsule

Review Quiz

1. What are the four default top-level folders visible in the Finder?

2. What are six common system resources? What purpose does each resource serve? Where are they located in the file hierarchy?

3. What are the four system resource domains? What purpose does each domain serve?

4. Why does the Finder hide certain folders at the root of the system volume?

5. What two methods can be used to hide items from the Finder?

6. What is file system metadata? What are some examples of file system metadata?

7. What are some of the common file flags used by Lion?

8. What does Lion use bundles or packages for?

9. How does the system identify which application to open when a user double-clicks on a file?

10. What are some privacy and security concerns with the Spotlight service?

11. What are the differences between zip archives and disk images?

12. How does the Spotlight search service use metadata?

13. Where does Spotlight store its metadata index databases? How about the Spotlight plug-ins?

14. What backup destinations does Time Machine support?

15. How does Time Machine maintain a backup history of the file system?

16. What types of files are omitted from Time Machine backups?

17. Why is Time Machine inefficient at backing up large databases?

18. Why might a previously backed-up item no longer be available in Time Machine?

Answers

1. The four default top-level folders visible in the Finder are Applications, containing applications all local users have access to; Library, containing system resources all local users have access to; System, containing necessary system resources; and finally, Users, containing all the local user home folders.

2. Six common system resources are extensions, which attach themselves to the system kernel to provide hardware and peripheral driver support; frameworks, which are shared code libraries that provide additional software resources for both applications and system processes; fonts; preference files, which contain application and system configuration information; LaunchAgents and LaunchDaemons, used by launchd to provide services that automatically start when they are needed or at system startup; and finally, logs, which are text files that contain error and progress entries from nearly any application or system service.

3. The four system resource domains are User, containing applications and system resources specific to each user account; Local, containing applications and system resources available to all users on the local Mac; Network (optional), containing applications and system resources available to any Mac that has an automated network share; and finally, System, containing applications and system resources required to provide basic system functionality.

4. The Finder hides traditional UNIX resources from average users because they don't need to have access to those items. If users do need access to these UNIX items, they can access them from the Terminal.

5. The Finder will not show items with periods at the beginning of their filename or items with the hidden file flag enabled.

6. Metadata is information stored outside of a file or folder. It provides additional information about files and folders. Examples include file flags, extended file attributes, and permissions.

7. Common file flags include the locked flag, which locks files from changes, and the hidden flag, which hides the item in the Finder.

8. Bundles and packages are used to combine complex items into individual folders. Packages have the additional advantage of appearing as a single item in the Finder. This allows software developers to combine resources into a single item and prevents users from messing with those resources.

9. Files are identified primarily by their filename extension. Launch Services maintains a database of known applications and which file types they can open. When you double-click on a file in the Finder, Launch Services tries to find an appropriate match. You can override the default application selection in the Finder.

10. Though Spotlight indexes file and folder permissions, it will allow other users to search the contents of locally attached non-system volumes when ownership is ignored on those volumes.

11. Zip archives are created with the Finder from a specific selection of items. Zip archives are compatible with many operating systems. On the other hand, disk images are made using Disk Utility and allow you to create highly flexible archive volumes that can contain nearly anything.

12. The Spotlight search service creates index databases of file system metadata so that it can perform normally time-intensive searches nearly instantly.

13. Spotlight metadata index databases are stored at the root of every volume in a /.Spotlight-V100 folder. However, a Legacy FileVault user's database is stored in his encrypted home folder. Also, the Mail application maintains its own database in each user's home folder at ~/Library/Mail/V2/MailData/Envelope Index. Spotlight plug-ins can be located in any Library in a folder named Spotlight.

14. Time Machine can back up to any Mac OS Extended volume, or network shares hosted from Time Capsule or a Mac OS X Server.

15. Time Machine starts with a full copy of the file system; then it records any changes to the file system, and only copies the changes. It creates a simulation of the full file system using hard links for files that have not changed.

16. Time Machine always ignores temporary files, Spotlight indexes, items in the Trash, and anything else that can be considered a cache. Time Machine will also ignore any files an application has defined as exempt, or any files you have defined as exempt in the Time Machine preferences.

17. Time Machine is inefficient at backing up large databases because it must back up the entire database file every time any change, no matter how small, is made to the database.

18. A previously backed-up item will not be available if your backup volume has become full and Time Machine has had to start deleting older items to make room for newer items.

5

Time

Goals

This chapter takes approximately 3 hours to complete.

Understand and support the various application types

Monitor and control processes and applications

Locate and manage application preferences

Chapter 5

Applications and Processes

People use computers because they want to run applications, not operating systems. Most users don't care about the technologies underneath as long as the applications they want run smoothly. This is why, despite the Mac's growing popularity, non-Mac users are apprehensive about switching. It cannot be ignored that there are many applications that run only on Windows-based computers.

Yet many Mac-only applications tempt non-Mac users because they represent the best solutions available. For several years now, Apple has held a strong lead on media creation applications with the iLife and Pro production suites. Third-party developers have stepped up their game in the last few years as well, as OS X Lion provides a robust development platform with many unique features. For hundreds of examples, look no further than the Mac App Store.

In this chapter you will explore the application environments available to Lion, and you will learn how to monitor and control applications and processes. You will also learn proper application configuration and troubleshooting techniques.

Understanding Applications and Processes

A process is any instance of executable code that is currently activated and addressed in system memory. In other words, a process is anything that is currently "running" or "open" on a Mac. Lion handles processes very efficiently, so although an idle process will likely consume zero processor resources, it's still considered an active process because it has dedicated address space in system memory. The four general process types are applications, commands, daemons, and agents.

Applications are a specific category of process that is generally identified as something the user opened in the graphical interface. *Commands* are also normally opened by the user but are only available at the command-line interface. The key similarity between most applications and commands is that they are running in the user's space. In other words, most applications and commands are started, stopped, and limited to accessing resources available only to the user.

Processes that run on behalf of the system fall into another category, *daemons*, also referred to as background processes because they rarely have any user interface. Daemons usually launch during system startup and remain active the entire time the Mac is up and running; as such, most daemons run with root or systemwide access to all resources. These background daemons are responsible for most of the automatic system features like detecting network changes and maintaining the Spotlight search metadata index.

Agents are technically also daemons, or background processes. The primary difference is that agents only run when a user is logged in to the system. Agents are always started automatically for the user by the system. While applications and commands can also be opened automatically, they are not controlled by the system the way agents are. Most important, all three of these process types are considered part of the user's space because they are executed with the same access privileges the user has.

Lion Process Features

Lion is a desirable platform for running applications and other processes because it combines a rock-solid UNIX foundation with an advanced graphical user interface. Users will most likely recognize the graphical interface elements right away, but it's the underlying foundation that keeps things running so smoothly. Specifically, a few fundamental features of Lion are responsible for providing a high level of performance and reliability.

Lion Process Performance Features

▶ Preemptive multitasking—This gives Lion the ability to balance computing resources without letting any single process take over. It allows the system to run dozens of processes without significantly slowing down user applications.

▶ Symmetric multiprocessing—Whenever possible the system will use all available computing resources to provide the best performance. This is a key feature since every currently shipping Mac includes at least two processor cores. Mac OS X v10.6 introduced two new unique multiprocessing features, Grand Central Dispatch and OpenCL, which provide for even greater performance than previous versions of Mac OS X. Grand Central Dispatch makes it much easier for application developers to take full advantage of not just multiprocessor systems but also multicore processors. OpenCL takes this even further by allowing applications to use your Mac's powerful graphics processor to accelerate general computing tasks.

▶ Simultaneous 32-bit and 64-bit support—Lion supports both 32-bit and 64-bit modes simultaneously. A process running in 64-bit mode has the ability to individually access more than 4 GB of system memory, can perform higher-precision computational functions much faster, and can take advantage of Intel's updated x86-64 architecture for improved performance and security. All Lion-compatible Macs feature 64 bit–capable processors and can take advantage of 64-bit system features. With the previous version, Mac OS X v10.6, Apple updated nearly all included software to take advantage of 64-bit resources, including the core of Mac OS X, the system kernel.

Lion Memory Management Features

▶ Protected memory—Similar to how the file system prevents users from meddling with items they shouldn't, processes are also kept separate and secure in system memory. The system manages all memory allocation so processes are not allowed to interfere with each other's system memory space. In other words, an ill-behaved or crashed application will not normally affect any other process on the system.

▶ Dynamic memory allocation—The operating system will automatically manage system memory for processes at their request. Though real system memory is clearly limited by hardware, the system will dynamically allocate both real and virtual memory when needed. Thus, the only memory limitations in Lion are the size of installed RAM and the amount of free space you have available on your system volume.

Lion Process Security Features

▶ Security architecture—At both the command line and graphical interface, processes are not allowed to access resources unless they are authorized. Again, access restrictions at the file system are responsible for much of the security here. However, system privileges are allowed when needed. The most obvious example of this is the Installer application, which requires administrative authorization to install software that affects more than one user. The security architecture built into Lion is one of the primary reasons Macs remain relatively free of malware.

▶ Code signing—Mac OS X v10.5 introduced support for secure signed application and process code. Signed applications and processes include a digital signature, which is used by the system to verify the authenticity and integrity of the software code and resources. Code is verified not only on disk but also as it is running. Therefore, even if some part of the application's or process's code is inappropriately changed while it's active, the system can automatically quit it. Code signing is also used for application verification by the keychain, the personal application firewall, Parental Controls preferences, application sandboxing, and Managed Client settings. Further, all applications on the Mac App Store must be signed.

▶ Application quarantine—Mac OS X v10.5 also introduced an application quarantine service that displays a warning when you attempt to open an application downloaded from an external source. This gives you the chance to verify your intent to open a new application or cancel if you have any suspicions about the safety of an item. Apple further enhanced this feature in Mac OS X v10.6 by starting to maintain a list of known malicious software. If you attempt to open any software on this list, the system will present a warning dialog suggesting that the item should be moved to the Trash.

MORE INFO ▶ The list of malicious software can be updated by Software Update and is located on your Mac at /System/Library/CoreServices/CoreTypes.bundle/Contents/ Resources/XProtect.plist.

▶ Application sandboxing—A significant new security feature in Lion is support for full application and process sandboxing. As the name implies, applications and pro- cesses in Lion can "play" inside a protected environment that has little or no access to other parts of the system. Prior to application sandboxing, an application could be restricted by file system permissions, but this still meant it could access all the user's items. However, with application sandboxing, applications are granted access only to the items they need through a sophisticated arrangement of rules. Apple's developer requirements govern the majority of sandbox rules, but one of these rules is user- initiated. If a user opens a specific document, the user is implying her intent to allow that application to access that file; thus the application is granted access to that file outside of the sandbox.

▶ It's important to note that sandboxing is an optional feature. Despite this, Apple has already sandboxed any application or process built in to Lion that could benefit from this feature. Further, starting in fall of 2011, all applications available from the Mac App Store must use application sandboxing.

Application Environments

Lion supports a wide range of application environments. Application developers create their products based on support for these environments. Several are specific to Mac OS X, while others add support for popular UNIX-based tools. Most important, though, average users do not need to concern themselves about which environment their application is using—the system will provide the appropriate resources automatically. The five primary application environments in Lion are Cocoa, Carbon, Java, BSD, and X11.

MORE INFO ▶ To learn more about Lion system architecture and application environments, see Apple's development resources, http://developer.apple.com/ technologies/mac.

Cocoa

Cocoa is the application environment most specific to Lion, as Cocoa-based applications run only on iOS and Mac OS X. Cocoa is primarily based on the Objective-C object- oriented programming language. Often, developers must use the Cocoa environment if they want to take advantage of the latest Mac features. As an example, only Cocoa applications can both have a graphical interface and take advantage of 64-bit services. For this reason, most of the built-in system software and new third-party software is developed for the Cocoa environment.

> **MORE INFO** ▶ To learn more about the Cocoa application environment, refer to Apple's own development resources, http://developer.apple.com/technologies/mac/cocoa.html.

Carbon

The Carbon application environment is a streamlined and significantly updated version of the previous Mac OS 9 environment. Developers can update their legacy Mac applications, often with little work, to run natively in Mac OS X. Carbon is based on the industry-standard C and C++ programming languages. On the surface, it's hard for a user to identify any differences between Carbon and Cocoa applications. As Mac OS X advanced, Apple further blurred the lines between Cocoa and Carbon by allowing applications to use a mix of both environments. However, Apple drew the line in Mac OS X v10.6 by adding full 64-bit support for Cocoa graphical applications but not for Carbon graphical applications. Apple has made it clear that going forward, new development for Lion should be exclusively in Cocoa.

> **MORE INFO** ▶ To learn more about Carbon, see Apple's development resources, http://developer.apple.com/carbon.

Java

Java is an application environment developed by Sun Microsystems with the goal of creating non-platform-specific applications. This means a developer can create software code once and it can run on many environments. While Lion does support the Java application runtime, it does not by default include the Java application runtime installation. The first time you run a Java applet or application in Lion, the Software Update mechanism engages to automatically download Java for OS X Lion from Apple's servers.

As with any Apple Software Update, administrative user access is required to install the Java runtime. Thus, if you know that your users require access to Java applications, you may want to manually download and install Java for OS X Lion as part of your standard Lion configuration.

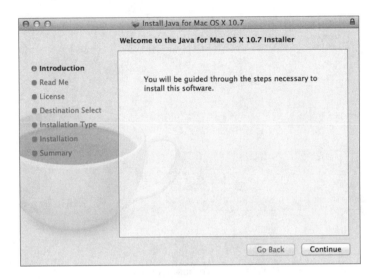

MORE INFO ▶ To manually download Java for OS X Lion, see Knowledge Base article DL1421, "Java for OS X Lion."

With Java for OS X Lion installed, the system supports both 32- and 64-bit Java SE 6 version 1.6.x. Many Java applications are delivered via a web download from a small Java Web Start (.jnlp) file. Double-clicking on a .jnlp file opens /System/Library/CoreServices/ Java Web Start, which downloads the remainder of the Java application to ~/Library/ Caches/Java/cache folder. Once the download is complete, the Java application runs in its own environment alongside your other Mac applications. When you open a Java application the second time, the Java Web Start application automatically converts the small .jnlp file to a stand-alone Java application. You can further adjust Java applications by opening the /Utilities/Java Preferences application.

MORE INFO ▶ To learn more about Java on Mac OS X, see Apple's development resources, http://developer.apple.com/java.

MORE INFO ▶ JavaScript, another technology, is used almost exclusively by web browsers and is fundamentally quite different than the Java application runtime. The included web browser in Lion, Safari, provides robust support for JavaScript.

BSD

Since the introduction of Mac OS X v10.5, the system has been both POSIX- and UNIX 03-compliant. Thus, Lion is compatible with most UNIX software. Mac OS X's system foundation, named Darwin, is based on the open source Free Berkeley Software Distribution (FreeBSD) UNIX command-line interface. The command line is most often accessed via the /Applications/Utilities/Terminal application. Various command-line utilities are covered throughout this guide, but Appendix B, "Command-Line Essentials," serves as an introduction to this environment.

> **MORE INFO** ▶ To learn more about Darwin, see Apple's open source development resources, http://developer.apple.com/opensource/.

X11

X11 is an extension of the BSD environment that provides a common graphical applications platform for UNIX workstations. Apple's implementation of X11 is based on the popular open source XFree86 project. You can access X11 applications by simply double-clicking on their executable binary file or by opening the X11 interface located at /Applications/Utilities/X11.

> **MORE INFO** ▶ To learn more, visit Apple's X11 resource website, http://developer.apple.com/opensource/tools/X11.html.

Classic and Rosetta

Previous versions of Mac OS X supported applications created for Mac OS 9 and PowerPC processors. The Classic compatibility environment, which enables users to run software created for Mac OS 9, is not supported on Mac OS X as of v10.5 or later. The Rosetta compatibility environment, which enables users to run software created for PowerPC processors, is not supported on Mac OS X as of Lion or later.

Open Source Software

By now you may have noticed that quite a bit of Lion is based on something called open source software. Generally speaking, open source is a method of software creation based on the free distribution and contribution of software source code. In other words, it's software whose code is available at no cost to anyone for general use or further modification. Interested individuals are expected and usually encouraged to provide improvements to open source software by adding to the software's code. It's expected that over time this community involvement will yield software products of exceptional quality, often free of cost.

Apple is deeply involved with many open source projects; this includes not just borrowing from open source but also contributing to existing projects and creating entirely new open source projects as well. In fact, the core of Lion, Darwin, is an entirely open source operating system that includes more than 200 individual open source projects. Keep in mind, though, that Apple maintains proprietary closed software solutions as part of Lion as well. Apple charges for these proprietary parts of Lion, but this is what allows Apple to employ hundreds of talented developers to create exceptional software.

> **MORE INFO** ▶ To learn more about Apple's open source involvement, visit http://developer.apple.com/opensource/.

The astounding growth of open source software in the last decade has not only produced some great software but also led to the rise of an entirely new operating system, Linux. With the growing popularity of Linux, high-quality open source applications have taken off as well. Because of Lion's open source and UNIX heritage, you can also take advantage of many of these open source applications on your Mac. Some open source applications run in the command line, others through X11, and some have even been converted to full-fledged Mac applications. Take some time to explore these free open source solutions for your Mac, as they may be suitable replacements for commercially purchased software.

> **MORE INFO** ▶ The MacPorts project hosts over 5,900 open source software titles for Mac OS X at www.macports.org.

64-bit versus 32-bit Mode

As covered previously, in Lion nearly all of the operating system and included applications support both 32-bit and 64-bit modes. In fact, only two of the main built-in applications are still limited to 32-bit mode: DVD Player and Grapher.

While moving most of the applications to support 64-bit mode will generally improve performance, this advancement is not without drawbacks. Namely, applications that run in 64-bit mode can't take advantage of any 32-bit code. This means any application that uses plug-in technology may suffer from compatibility issues with third-party plug-ins that have not been updated to support 64-bit mode.

Examples of plug-in software affected by this issue include:

▶ Printer drivers that add additional interfaces for the printer dialog

▶ Screen savers

▶ Audio device drivers known as Audio Units

▶ Spotlight metadata import plug-ins

▶ Dashboard widgets that require plug-in code, though most widgets don't use extra code, so they should work without issues

▶ Safari plug-ins

In short, applications running in 64-bit mode will not load 32-bit plug-ins. If you need to use a third-party 32-bit plug-in with a 64-bit capable application, then you will have to force the application to run in 32-bit mode on most Macs. This can be accomplished from the Finder's Get Info or Inspector windows by simply selecting the "Open in 32-bit mode" checkbox. Obviously, forcing 32-bit mode may make the application run slower, but this is required to use nonupdated plug-ins.

One system application will automatically switch modes for you, System Preferences. When a user tries to open a third-party 32-bit System Preferences plug-in, often called a System Preferences pane, it will prompt him to restart System Preferences. If the user selects the default OK button, then System Preferences will restart in 32-bit mode and load the selected pane.

NOTE ▶ The process that handles Dashboard will automatically run both 64-bit and 32-bit widgets. Dashboard is detailed in the "Managing Dashboard" section later in this chapter.

NOTE ▶ With the exception of Dashboard and System Preferences, third-party plug-ins that tie into a system resource or background process must support 64-bit mode in order to work with Lion.

Installing and Updating Applications

A variety of methods exist for installing software in Lion. Traditional installation methods fall into one of two categories; drag-and-drop installations or installation packages. Both methods are easy enough for an average user to complete, but they assume the user knows where to get the software from in the first place. With traditional installation methods, acquiring the software is often much more difficult than actually installing it. Taking a page from the iOS playbook, Apple has solved this issue as well with the Mac App Store included in Lion. It gives users a single easy-to-use interface for locating, downloading, and installing software via the Internet. In this section you will explore both the traditional installation methods and the Mac App Store.

Traditional Installation Methods

Again, traditional installation methods are generally either of the drag-and-drop variety or of the installation package variety. Software developers can choose any method they wish to deploy their wares. Often the distinction between the two traditional methods is the complexity of the software being deployed. If a software developer creates a product that only requires a folder of a few items or even one single item, it's often deployed as a drag-and-drop installation. However, if a software developer creates a product that requires a more complex set of items that must be installed in multiple specific locations throughout the system, it's often deployed as an installation package.

Understanding Drag-and-Drop Installations

Apple heralded the era of drag-and-drop in computing, so it should come as no surprise that many software installations in Lion are of the simple drag-and-drop variety. In general, Lion doesn't care where an application or process resides. So long as the application itself doesn't have a specific location requirement, applications can run from any location on the Mac. That said, as covered in previous chapters, some locations are more appropriate and secure than others.

Specifically, Lion includes the /Applications folder as the default location for applications available to all users. Only administrative users can make changes to the /Applications folder. If users want to install their own drag-and-drop applications, they can create their own ~/Applications folder. However, a user can place an application anywhere she pleases inside her own home folder. Again, many drag-and-drop applications work from any location on the system.

Also, it's important to recognize that because of the default security and permissions model in Lion, any application a standard user is allowed to install and open cannot interfere with other users on the system. Poorly written or malicious software could potentially harm items in the user's home folder, but as long as the user is not allowed to authenticate as an administrator, it is extremely difficult for the software to cause damage to the system or other users. Keep in mind, the same is true for a user's intentional actions as well. A user could, by his own hand, cause similar damage. In short, allowing nonadministrative users the ability to install software is no more dangerous than allowing them to use the computer in the first place.

Installing Drag-and-Drop Items

Drag-and-drop software deployed via optical disc, or any other physical drive, is often ready to copy to wherever the user wishes to install it. On the other hand, software downloaded from the Internet will almost always be deployed in some kind of archive format. As covered in Chapter 4, "Data Management," zip files and disk images are the most common archive formats for Lion.

In Lion the Safari browser will, by default, automatically unarchive zip files to the ~/Downloads folder. The user could technically leave the application in the ~/Downloads folder and continue to open it from there, but she should be trained to move the new application to a more appropriate location in her home folder. An example of this type of installation is SubEthaEdit by the Coding Monkeys, available at www.codingmonkeys.de/subethaedit/.

In Lion the Safari browser will not, however, automatically mount a downloaded disk image. As covered in Chapter 3, "File Systems," you must double-click on a disk image to make its contents available to the Finder. Once the disk image volume is mounted, again the user could technically leave the application inside the disk image and open it from there, but he should be trained to move the new application to another location. This is especially true of disk images because if the user logs out or restarts the computer, the disk image will unmount. For many novice users, this would result in their "losing" the application. Fortunately, many developers will use a helpful Finder window background graphic that should encourage the user to copy the software to a more appropriate location. An example of this type of installation is Firefox by the Mozilla Project, available at www.mozilla.com.

NOTE ▶ As covered previously in this chapter, the first time software downloaded from the Internet is opened, the user will be prompted with the quarantine security dialog. If an administrator account accepts the quarantine dialog, by clicking the Open button, it will never appear again for any user. Normal user accounts, on the other hand, can still open an application that presents the quarantine dialog, but they cannot permanently disable it.

Similar to a drag-and-drop install is the double-click install. Instead of the user dragging the item into place, she double-clicks on the item, and the system prompts her with an offer to copy the item into place. In most cases when a double-click install is required, moving the item into a specific location is necessary for the item to work properly. The user can still drag and drop the item into the appropriate location, often in a Library folder, if desired. Items the system will install for you when double-clicked include fonts, preference panes, screen savers, and widgets. An example of this type of installation is Perian by the Perian Project, available at http://perian.org.

Understanding Installation Packages

Installation packages are the default deployment mechanism for most Apple software and third-party software that requires the installation of items in multiple locations. Installation packages are deployed via user interaction with the Installer application. When a user opens an installation package, he is presented with the Installer application. This application has the user walk through a few simple screens to configure and initiate the installation process.

Most significantly, installation packages often require administrative user authentication, as they are frequently used to install items that can affect other users and the operating system. Chapter 1, "Installation and Configuration," details the use and troubleshooting of installation packages for Apple software updates. The same techniques apply to third-party installation packages deployed via the Installer application.

BrotherPrinter
Drivers.pkg

That said, on occasion you will find third-party installers that do not use Apple's Installer application. These installations are easily identified because the installation assets are themselves an application using the .app filename extension. Apple's native installation assets come only in the form of installation packages using the .pkg or .mpkg filename extensions. If you have problems with a third-party installer, you must contact the developer for any issues regarding installation, as it has elected to use a proprietary installation mechanism.

Updating Installed Software

Similar to installation, there are a variety of methods for keeping installed software up-to-date:

▶ Apple software—Apple software is updated via the Apple Software Update mechanism, as covered in Chapter 1, "Installation and Configuration."

▶ Mac App Store third-party software—Any third-party software installed via the Mac App Store can be updated from the Mac App Store's Update interface, as covered in the "Installation via the Mac App Store" section later in this chapter.

▶ Automatically updating third-party software—Automatic update mechanisms for third-party software vary widely. Prior to the Mac App Store, no unified method for providing third-party software updates existed. Thus, software developers often implemented their own automatic update methods. Unfortunately, this means there is no standard method to determine if an application has automatic update capability. You can start by looking in common locations including the application menu (the menu that appears with the application's name), the application's preferences window, or the application's Help menu. If the third-party item installed a preference pane, it's highly likely any automatic update mechanism will be found within. Finally, it's important to note that nearly all automatic update mechanisms require administrative user authentication.

▶ Manually update third-party software—In some cases the only update mechanism for third-party software is to simply install a newer version. Keep in mind, only administrative users can replace or update software in the /Applications folder. Further, many package installations require administrative user authentication.

Installation via the Mac App Store

Chances are you are already familiar with the Mac App Store, as it's the primary distribution method for upgrade installations of Lion. However, if you purchased a Mac with Lion preinstalled, you may not have used the Mac App Store yet. Even if you have used it, you may not be familiar with all its features. This section will provide an introduction to the Mac App Store from a support perspective.

Understanding the Mac App Store

Introduced in Mac OS X v10.6.6, the Mac App Store is the premier location for Mac-compatible software, and it's increasingly the only location for new Apple software. The Mac App Store combines all the steps of acquiring new software into a single interface. These steps, covered in greater detail later in this section, include browsing and searching for new software, downloading and installing software, managing an account for purchasing software, updating installed software, and managing purchased software.

Aside from having Mac OS X v10.6.6 or later, there are a few requirements for installing software via the Mac App Store:

▶ An Internet connection—Obviously you must have an Internet connection to access content from the Mac App Store. A fast broadband connection is recommended, but slower connections are adequate as long as you have the time.

▶ An Apple ID—Identification with Apple is required to install anything from the Mac App Store, free or otherwise. If you intend to purchase items, you must also associate a valid credit card with your Apple ID. All Apple ID account management can be handled via the Mac App Store as covered in the "Mac App Store Account Management" section later in this chapter.

▶ Authorization as an administrative user—You do not have to be logged in to the Mac with an administrator account to open the Mac App Store. However, to install applications via the Mac App Store, you must authenticate as an administrative user. This is because the Mac App Store installs new applications in the /Applications folder, the contents of which are only modifiable by the system or administrative users.

MORE INFO ▶ The Mac App Store has its own support site with even more details than are covered in this book. You can find the site at www.apple.com/support/mac/app-store/.

Limit Access to or Disable the Mac App Store

Some items on the Mac App Store, specifically games, may contain content not suitable for children. Because software on the Mac App Store is rated with a system similar to that for motion pictures, you can limit a user's access to specific ratings. Further, if your organization prevents users from installing their own applications or users are not allowed administrative access, then you may want to disable access to the Mac App Store altogether. If you wish to limit access or completely disable the Mac App Store for a user, you can do so via parental controls.

NOTE ▶ Do not attempt to throw away the Mac App Store. Even if you do temporarily remove the Mac App Store with this method, you may need access to it later.

To limit access or disable the Mac App Store:

1 Open the Parental Controls preferences and authenticate as an administrative user to unlock its settings.

2 Select the user from the accounts list you wish to manage with parental controls, and then click the Enable Parental Controls button.

This will reveal the parental controls for the selected user in the pane to the right of the user list. The Apps tab should be selected by default; if not, select the Apps tab now.

3 Select the Limit Applications checkbox. This will enable you to further limit Mac App Store selections.

4 Click the Allow App Store Apps pop-up menu to reveal the list of restrictions.

The ratings restrictions are based on ages 4, 9, 7, 12, and 17. The Don't Allow choice will completely disable the user's ability to use the Mac App Store.

5   At this point you should also check the list of already installed applications, Allowed Apps.

You may find that the default selection is too limiting for this user account. On the other hand, you may want to explore the remaining sections of the Parental Controls preferences to further restrict this user.

6   Once you have made your selections, close the Parental Controls preferences.

MORE INFO ▸ Parental controls are further covered in Chapter 2, "User Accounts."

Mac App Store Browse, Search, and Install

Even if you don't have an Apple ID, you can easily browse and search the Mac App Store. To get started, open the Mac App Store in the Dock, or choose App Store from the Apple menu. When the Mac App Store opens, you will be greeted with the Featured view.

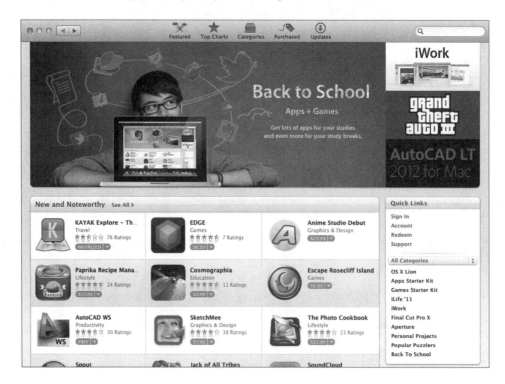

The main area of the Featured view allows you to browse new, popular, and staff favorite items. To the right of the Featured view you'll find Quick Links, which link to specific categories and Mac App Store management features. Across the top of the Mac App Store window is a toolbar. Note the arrow buttons in the top-left corner that allow you to navigate back and forward much like a web browser's history. If you're still browsing for new applications, you can click Top Charts to see the most downloaded items or Categories to browse for a specific type of application.

TIP The buttons in the Mac App Store toolbar correspond to keyboard shortcuts Command-1 through Command-5. For example, use the Command-2 keyboard shortcut to quickly navigate to the Top Charts page.

The most direct route is the Spotlight search in the top right of the window. Simply start typing part of the name of an application, and the search will immediately return a list of matching items.

Selecting one from the list will return a search results page, giving you a more detailed view of the matching items. Click on an application's icon or name to view the details page.

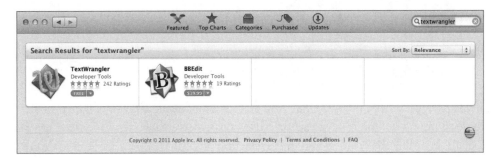

Once you're at an application's details page, you can read more about the application, view application screenshots, and at the bottom browse or write your own customer ratings and reviews. To the far right you'll also see developer and application information including version, download size, and system requirements.

Directly under the application's icon, you'll see the application's price. Some applications on the Mac App Store are free and you can download those items without entering payment information. Paid items obviously require that you enter valid credit card or PayPal information. To download and install an item, click the price button. The button will change to either Install App for a free application or Buy App for a paid application. Click either to start the installation process.

If you have yet to sign in to the Mac App Store with an Apple ID, you will be prompted to do so now. If you don't have an Apple ID yet, you can create one in the Mac App Store. Details regarding the creation and management of accounts in the Mac App Store are covered in the next section. If, however, you already have an Apple ID, enter it to continue the installation process. Also, if you have opened the Mac App Store as a standard user, you will be asked to authenticate as an administrative user to complete the installation.

Once your Apple ID is validated, the selected application will download and install directly to what appears to be the Launchpad. In reality the application is being installed to the /Applications folder. Thus, if you prefer to use the Finder, you can also open the application from this folder.

Any item your Apple ID has purchased will always be available to update or reinstall from the Mac App Store. You can find out more about this in the "Updating and Managing Purchases in the Mac App Store" section later in this chapter.

Mac App Store Account Management

Again, an Apple ID is required to purchase anything from the Mac App Store. If you have purchased items from Apple previously using iTunes or the iOS App Store, then you can use the same Apple ID you used for those previous purchases. If you have not purchased anything from Apple via an online store, you can add purchasing information to an existing Apple ID or create a new Apple ID. The only requirement to creating a new Apple ID is a unique email address, which will be used for contact and verification.

You can begin any account management process by clicking the Sign In link under the Quick Links area to the right or by selecting Store > Sign In from the menu bar.

This will present the Mac App Store authentication dialog. If you already have an Apple ID, enter it now. If you don't have an Apple ID, or you wish to create a new one just for purchases, click the Create Apple ID button now.

NOTE ▶ Apple IDs created previously with .Mac or MobileMe can be used for the Mac App Store. Further, these account types can be identified by both @mac.com and @me.com domains.

Depending on the state of your Apple ID, one of the following situations will occur:

▶ Your Apple ID is ready to install items—If your Apple ID has been used to purchase items from Apple previously, it may be ready to go for the Mac App Store. If this is the case, you will not be presented with any further screens. When you are signed in, the first line of the Quick Links items says Welcome, followed by your first name. You can also verify the signed-in Apple ID by selecting the Store menu. Note that you can sign out from the Store menu as well.

▶ Your Apple ID information needs to be verified or updated—If this is the case, you will be prompted to review your account. You will first need to agree to the App Store terms and conditions, and then you will need to verify your Apple ID security details. Finally, you must enter a valid credit card and billing address for purchasing items. When using an existing Apple ID, you must always enter credit card information even if you plan to only install free items. If you need to create an Apple ID that can only install free items, then you must create a new Apple ID in the Mac App Store. Once you have completed updating your account, you will have to sign in to the Mac App Store again to purchase or install any items.

▶ **You're creating a new Apple ID**—If you don't have an Apple ID, or you wish to create a new one just for making purchases, you can do so almost entirely from the Mac App Store. After you click the Create Apple ID Now button, you will first need to agree to the App Store terms and conditions. Next you will need to provide an email address that will become the new Apple ID. Next you must provide a payment method. If you want to create an Apple ID that can only install free items, then you can choose None as a payment method. However, to make the None choice appear, you must first start the Apple ID creation process by attempting to install a free application. Thus, you may need to cancel the current Apple ID creation process and restart it to get the None choice. Finally, when creating a new Apple ID, you will have to verify the email address specified. The App Store system will send an email verification; click the link inside the email to open a web page allowing you to authenticate and verify the account. Once you have verified it, you will have to sign in to the Mac App Store again to purchase or install any items.

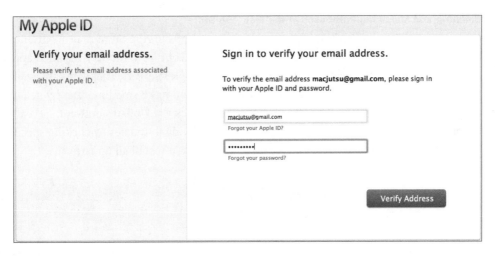

Any time you wish to make changes to your Apple ID, you can do so from within the Mac App Store by clicking the Account link in the Quick Links section or by selecting Store > View My Account from the menu bar. From the Account Information page, you can change your Apple ID, payment information, and country or region setting. Also, this screen is the only location to create or change your nickname. Your App Store nickname is used to hide your personal identification in any reviews you may have posted in the App Store.

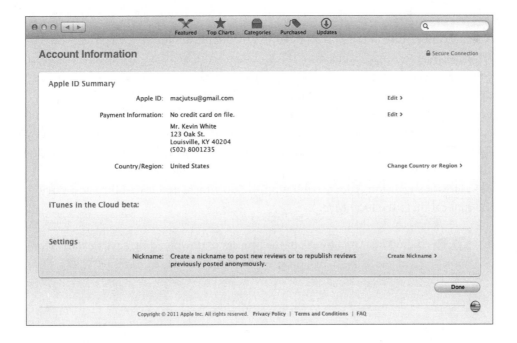

Updating and Managing Purchases in the Mac App Store

Updating applications you originally installed from the Mac App Store is also extremely easy. Every time you open the Mac App Store, it scans your local Mac for installed applications and compares the results to what's current on Apple's servers. If updates are available, you may notice in the toolbar that the Updates icon has a small number by it. This represents applications that have updates available. Click the Updates button to reveal the list of available updates. You can choose to install individual updates by clicking specific Update buttons, or you can click the Update All button to install all updates.

A significant feature of the Mac App Store is that applications are "owned" by your Apple ID. According to Apple, "Apps from the Mac App Store may be used on any Macs that you own or control for your personal use." This means that if you personally use multiple Macs, you can install items from the Mac App Store on all of them. This is possible because Apple keeps track of the items purchased or installed by your Apple ID. To install an application you already own on a new Mac, open the Mac App Store, sign in with your Apple ID, and then click the Purchased button in the toolbar. The Purchased page shows all the items owned by the signed-in Apple ID, both installed and not installed on the Mac. Obviously, clicking the Install button will download and install the latest version of the application to the local Mac.

> **TIP** ▶ If the Mac App Store is in the process of downloading a particularly large item, you can check the item's, progress from the Purchased page.

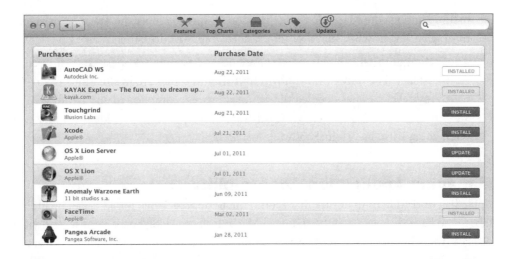

Removing Installed Software

In many cases removing installed software is much easier than installing it in the first place. One thing that often surprises veteran support people who are new to the Mac is that there's no default Apple software removal mechanism. This is because the vast majority of Mac software can simply be thrown in the Trash. That being said, it's never recommended to remove any part of the Lion system software.

Software removal methods include:

▶ Mac App Store software—While it's true that applications installed via the Mac App Store can be dragged to the Trash, you can also remove these applications from Launchpad. To engage Launchpad, double-click on its icon in the /Applications folder or from a Multi-Touch trackpad use the "pinch with thumb and three fingers" gesture. In Launchpad, hold down the Option key and a small "x" button will appear next to Mac App Store installed applications. Click one of the buttons and the system will remove that application.

▶ Drag and drop to the Trash—Yes, it's true, most applications are "removed enough" if you simply move the primary application icon into the Trash. If the software item is a type of resource, like a preference pane or font, just locate the item in one of the Library folders and drag it to the Trash. This method may leave some residual support files, but by removing the primary application or resource file you have rendered the software inoperable. This method works for applications installed using a traditional method and via the Mac App Store. Just don't forget to empty the Trash before continuing with your work, and a system restart wouldn't hurt either.

▶ Application uninstaller—Only in very rare occasions will third-party software require an uninstaller. The only times you will find an uninstaller are in situations where the software's developer has deemed the removal process complicated enough to warrant an uninstaller. If this is the case, the software developer must provide the uninstaller, often along with the original software installer.

Managing Application Accessibility

Apple has worked hard to ensure that Lion remains approachable for all users, including those who have trouble using the standard Mac interface via keyboard, mouse, and video display. Apple has built an extensive accessibility architecture into Lion called Universal Access. Universal Access enables assistive interaction features for Apple and many third-party applications.

You can enable these features from the Universal Access preferences by choosing Apple menu > System Preferences, then clicking the Universal Access icon. General preferences include showing the Universal Access menu item and enabling access for assistive devices like electronic Braille interfaces. The remaining Universal Access preferences are presented in four separate tabs representing different assistance features:

▶ Seeing—The accessibility features in this section are designed to assist those who have difficulty viewing the screen or who are unable to view the screen at all. Options include enabling dynamic screen zooming and adjusting display settings to enhance clarity. The VoiceOver spoken-word interface, covered next in this section, is also enabled here.

▶ Hearing—The accessibility features in this section are designed to assist those who have difficulty hearing or who cannot hear sound. The primary option here is to enable screen flashing as an alternative to the alert sound.

▶ Keyboard—The accessibility features in this section are designed to assist those who have difficulty using a keyboard. Options include enabling sticky keys to assist with using keyboard combinations and slow keys to help with initial or repeated keystrokes.

▶ Mouse & Trackpad—The accessibility features in this section are designed to assist those who have difficulty using or who cannot use a mouse or trackpad. Options include increasing the cursor size so it's easier to see and enabling mouse keys that allow you to use the keyboard arrow keys in place of a mouse or trackpad.

MORE INFO ▶ To learn more, visit Apple's Accessibility resource website, www.apple. com/accessibility.

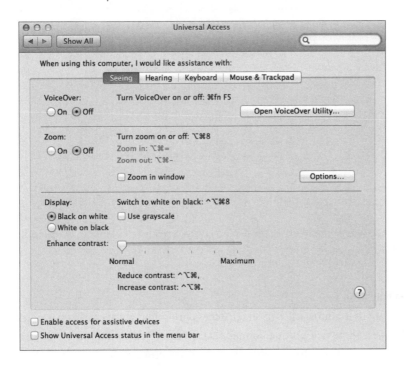

Using VoiceOver

VoiceOver is an interface mode that enables you to navigate the Mac OS X user interface using only keyboard control and spoken English descriptions of what's happening onscreen. You enable VoiceOver from the Seeing section of the Universal Access preferences. The first time you enable VoiceOver, it will automatically launch an interactive tour of the VoiceOver interface. This spoken tour teaches the user how to use the various VoiceOver keyboard shortcuts. Learning these shortcuts is necessary to use VoiceOver. A highly customizable interface, VoiceOver allows the user to adjust almost every interaction parameter by opening the /Applications/Utilities/VoiceOver Utility application.

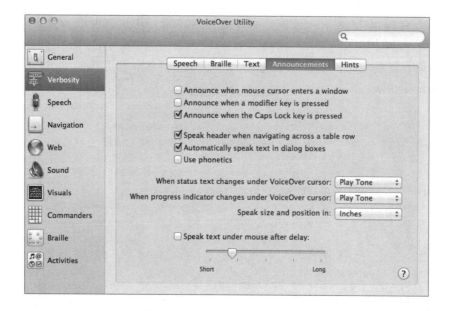

MORE INFO ▶ To learn more, visit Apple's VoiceOver resource website, www.apple. com/accessibility/voiceover.

Managing Accessibility Preferences

It is important to note that almost all Universal Access preferences are saved on a per-user basis. Thus, each user will have a unique com.apple.universalaccess.plist located in her ~/Library/Preferences folder. In other words, each user has unique accessibility preferences that are active only when that user's account is logged in to the Mac. The one exception is that an administrative user can enable the VoiceOver feature for use by all accounts at the login window. This preference is available in the Accounts preferences by clicking the Login Options button.

The VoiceOver system includes a portable preferences feature that helps a user move his VoiceOver settings between multiple Macs. From the /Applications/Utilities/VoiceOver Utility application, the user can define an external storage device as a location to save his VoiceOver settings. This will place a VoiceOver folder at the root of the external volume that contains all the user's VoiceOver preferences. As he moves to a new Mac, he need only attach the external storage device, and if VoiceOver is enabled, it will automatically detect his preferences.

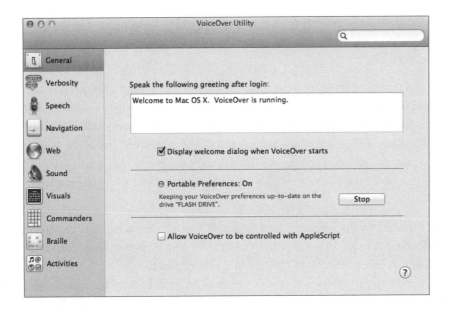

Using Auto Save, Versions, and Resume

Perhaps the most significant change in Lion is how users manage their documents. For over 30 years most applications have relied on users to remember to save their work. It's true that for many years some applications have featured optional auto save features. In fact, many of Apple's own applications have always provided an environment where users don't have to remember to save. Examples include Aperture, iPhoto, and iTunes. However, with Lion Apple has introduced a sophisticated automatic document management model that can be used by applications. Not only will the system automatically save for the user, it will also automatically maintain a history of versions for the user's documents as well.

In this section you will learn how the new Auto Save and Versions features work together. These two features also work hand in hand with another new Lion feature, Resume, to maintain a current state of the user's work environment even if he logs out or restarts the computer.

Understanding Auto Save and Versions

The goal with Lion was to incorporate many of the iOS features and workflows. A primary tenet of iOS application design is that the user never has to remember to save her work. However, Mac users are accustomed to having more control over their documents.

Further, Mac computers in general have more storage and computing resources than iOS devices. Thus, with Lion Apple took the Auto Save concept and extended it with support for document versions.

For applications that support Auto Save, once the user saves the first time, he is never again bothered by dialogs asking if the application should save changes. In addition, if the user wishes to use the document in another application or share it with another user, he doesn't have to remember to save the latest version of the document. From the user's point of view, the document seen in the Finder is always the same as the document seen in the application—the location where the document was first saved will always be the latest version.

In addition, applications that support Auto Save also support Versions. This provides an environment where the system automatically maintains a history of changes for any document. The user can easily return a document to a previous state with just a few clicks. Or she can navigate to an earlier version of a document and quickly copy specific elements to the latest version of the document.

The user can access a document's version history using an interface very similar to Time Machine's Restore interface. However, from a technical perspective, the document version histories are saved in a hidden folder, /.DocumentRevisions-V100, at the root of the drive containing the original document file. Again, the most recent version of a document is always automatically saved to its original location and can be copied or shared with other applications or users immediately after a change is made. Finally, in order to avoid unintentional changes, older documents are automatically locked, but as you'll see later, the user can easily manage this behavior as well.

Applications that support Lion's Auto Save and Versions are easily identified by the content of the File menu in the application. Applications that have not been updated still retain the traditional File > Save and File > Save As menu options. Applications updated for Lion still feature File > Save for saving a document the first time, but this changes to

File > Save a Version once a document has been created or is opened. Updated applications can also be identified by a File > Duplicate menu option. Most Apple-designed applications already support Auto Save and Versions, including TextEdit, Preview, Pages, Numbers, and Keynote.

Using Auto Save

Saving the first time in an application that supports Auto Save is much like using a traditional application. Users may not be prepared for what comes next, though. The irony is that many users may find it difficult to move to this new method even though it requires less work. Simply, most users have grown accustomed to the traditional save methods and will have to "unlearn" them. Thus, training may be required for users to get the most out of Lion's Auto Save and Versions.

TIP TextEdit is a great application for testing Auto Save and Versions techniques.

If you start by creating a new document, the first time you save the document, you will be prompted to choose a location and name for the new file.

TIP When you open an existing document, you'll never have to save even the first time because the document already has a storage location.

After you have picked a location for the file, you'll never have to save it again. The mere act of making a significant change or closing the document window or attempting to access the document from another application will automatically trigger the application to save. As you make changes to the document, you may notice the word "Edited" in the document title bar. This is also a visual cue to let the user know the system is automatically saving changes. You can test this by making some changes to the document, and then immediately using Quick Look to preview the document by selecting it in the Finder and pressing the Space bar. The Quick Look preview will be identical to the open document in the application.

If you need to save another copy of a document, you do so by using the Duplicate option. With the document open, select File > Duplicate from the menu bar or select the document name in the title bar to reveal a pop-up menu allowing you to select Duplicate. If you have recently edited the document, you will need to select Edit in the title bar. Once the application has duplicated a copy, you can then save the copy as you would a new document.

TIP ▶ There is no default keyboard shortcut for the Duplicate command, but you can set a custom keyboard shortcut for the Duplicate menu item from the Keyboard preferences.

Using Versions

With Versions in Lion, applications always maintain a history of your changes. Any time an application automatically saves, a new document version will also be saved. If the user, perhaps out of habit, attempts to manually save the file with the Command-S keyboard shortcut, he is essentially telling the system to save a version. This can also be accomplished by selecting Save > Save a Version from the menu bar.

If you have yet to trigger an auto save, you can easily revert to the previously saved state by selecting File > Revert to Saved from the menu bar or by selecting the document name in the title bar to reveal a pop-up menu allowing you to select Revert to Last Saved Version.

If a deeper history of versions is available, you will be prompted to navigate to either an older version or just the last saved version.

Obviously, selecting the Last Saved Version button will revert the document to the most recently saved version. However, clicking the Older Version button will reveal the versions history browser interface. You can also access this interface by selecting the document name in the title bar to reveal a pop-up menu allowing you to select Browse All Versions.

NOTE ▶ A document's versions history is maintained in a hidden folder on the Mac used to make the edits. If you share a document by creating or sending a copy of the document, other users will not have access to the document's version history.

NOTE ▶ Version history will not be maintained on files being edited from a shared network volume. If you wish to maintain version history, you must copy the shared file to a local drive.

If you've ever used Time Machine, the versions browser interface should look pretty familiar. To the left you'll see the current version of the document, and to the right you can see previous versions. Navigate by either clicking on a previous version's title bar or using the timeline to the right.

If you would like to restore a previous version in its entirety, click the Restore button. However, if you just want a specific section of a previous version copied to the latest version, simply make a selection inside the previous document, and then copy and paste to the current document. When you are done making targeted edits, click the Done button to return to the standard application interface.

> **TIP** In the versions browser, you can copy and paste using the Command-C and Command-V keyboard shortcuts, or by using the secondary click to reveal a pop-up menu.

> **TIP** To delete a previous document version, in the versions browser select the document name in the title bar to reveal a pop-up menu allowing you to select Delete This Version.

> **TIP** If you have Time Machine enabled, as covered in Chapter 4, "Data Management," an application's version history can go much deeper by showing you versions in the Time Machine backup.

Using Locked Documents

Applications that support Auto Save and Versions also provide easy access to document locking. Locking a document prevents users, or more appropriately their applications, from accidentally auto saving changes. Users can choose to manually lock or unlock documents within supported applications. However, as a safety mechanism, Lion automatically locks documents after two weeks of inactivity. You can modify this behavior in the Time Machine preferences by clicking the Options button. This is a bit of a strange location for managing this setting, as it does not require Time Machine to be configured, nor does it affect the backup process.

As long as you are the owner of a document, you can manually lock it to prevent further changes. To manually lock a document in an application that supports Auto Save and Versions, select the document name in the title bar to reveal a pop-up menu allowing you to select Lock.

You'll note that locked documents are clearly marked in the title bar with the word "Locked" and a small lock icon. As long as you are the owner of a document, you can manually unlock it to enable changes. To unlock a document, select Locked in the title bar to reveal a pop-up menu allowing you to select Unlock.

If you aren't the owner of a locked document, you will not be allowed to unlock it; thus you will not be allowed to edit it. You can, however, treat a locked document as a template by duplicating the document and then editing the duplicate copy. Attempting to edit a locked document will reveal a prompt that allows the user to duplicate the document. You can also duplicate a locked document by selecting File > Duplicate from the menu bar or by selecting the word Locked in the title bar to reveal a pop-up menu allowing you to select Duplicate. Again, once the application has duplicated a copy, you can then save the copy as you would a new document.

NOTE ▶ Duplicating a locked document in the Finder will simply result in another locked copy of the document. In Lion, only applications that support Auto Save and Versions can create an unlocked duplicate of a locked file. You can find out more about file locks in Chapter 3, "File Systems."

Understanding Application Resume

An ancillary Lion feature to Auto Save and Versions is Resume. This feature allows supported applications to maintain their current state even if the application is quit. When a user quits an application, not only are any open documents automatically saved, the state of the application is saved as well. Upon application restart, everything returns to how it was when the user quit the application. This includes automatically saving and restoring documents and windows open in the application, the view and scrolling position of each window, and even the last user selection in the application.

NOTE ▶ Applications that support Resume can also be automatically quit by the system when it's determined that the system resources, specifically memory, are running low. The system will only quit applications that are sitting idle for the user.

Resume is, by default, enabled in Lion. You can however, prevent this behavior in two ways. First, you can temporarily disable an option on user logout that will prevent applications from automatically reopening when the user logs back into the system. This option will reengage any time the user logs out of the system.

The second option is a permanent change for the user that will prevent applications from restoring their state when they are reopened. You can find this setting in the General preferences. Deselect the "Restore windows when quitting and re-opening apps" checkbox to effectively disable Resume for the user.

Monitoring Applications and Processes

Lion provides several methods for identifying and managing applications and processes. You can use the Finder or System Information to identify application and command information, including what processor architectures the item supports. The Activity Monitor application and the ps and top commands are used for viewing and managing all processes as they are running on your Mac.

Application Identification

To quickly locate basic application information from the Finder:

1 In the Finder, select the application you wish to identify, and then open the Get Info or Inspector window.

   There are several ways to open the Get Info window: choose File > Get Info from the menu bar; press Command-I; choose Get Info from the Action pop-up menu in a Finder window toolbar; or right-click or Control-click an item and choose Get Info from the shortcut menu.

2 Once you have opened a Get Info window, click the General disclosure triangle to reveal general application information.

   This will reveal that the selected application is one of three types:

   Application (Intel). Designed for Mac OS X on Intel-based Macs.

   Application (Universal). Designed for Mac OS X on both PowerPC- and Intel-based Macs. It has both types of code embedded in it, so it will run natively on whichever platform it is opened from.

Application. Designed for Mac OS X on PowerPC-based Macs, these applications will not open in Lion as indicated by the prohibitory sign on top of the application icon.

NOTE ▶ Classic applications, though identifiable from the Get Info dialog, are not compatible with Lion.

If you want to quickly gather information about all the applications on your Mac, try the /Applications/Utilities/System Information application. Upon opening, System Information scans the contents of all available Application folders. This includes /Applications, /Applications/Utilities, ~/Applications, /System/Library/CoreServices, and any other Applications folders at the root of any mounted volumes. Select Applications from the Contents list to see which applications System Information found. Selecting an application from the list reveals its name, version number, modification date, application type, and whether it was purchased from the Mac App Store. Note that applications installed as part of Lion will not show as being purchased from the Mac App Store.

Application Name	Version	Last Modified	Kind	64–Bit (Intel)	App Store ▼
1Password	3.7.1	8/1/11 9:40 PM	Intel	Yes	No
1PasswordAgent	3.7.1	8/1/11 9:40 PM	Intel	Yes	No
2. Create Binder Package		2/22/10 8:33 AM	Universal	Yes	No
50onPaletteServer	1.0.3	6/16/11 6:07 PM	Intel	Yes	No
Accessibility Inspector	3.0	7/21/11 11:46 AM	Intel	Yes	No
Accessibility Verifier	1.3	7/21/11 11:46 AM	Intel	Yes	No
Activity Monitor	10.7	6/23/11 3:35 AM	Intel	Yes	No
AddPrinter	7.0	6/19/11 12:09 AM	Intel	No	No
Address Book	6.0	6/16/11 7:34 PM	Intel	Yes	No
AddressBookLDAPSyncAgent	2.1	6/16/11 7:34 PM	Intel	Yes	No
AddressBookManager	2.1	6/16/11 7:34 PM	Intel	Yes	No
AddressBookMobileMeSharingAgent	2.1	6/16/11 7:34 PM	Intel	Yes	No
AddressBookSourceSync	1.0	6/16/11 7:34 PM	Intel	Yes	No
AddressBookSync	2.1	6/16/11 7:34 PM	Intel	Yes	No
AddressBookUrlForwarder	1.0	6/16/11 7:33 PM	Intel	Yes	No
AdSheet		7/21/11 11:46 AM	Intel	No	No
AdSheet~ipad		7/21/11 11:46 AM	Intel	No	No
AirPort Base Station Agent	1.5.5	6/13/11 7:29 PM	Intel	Yes	No
AirPort Utility	5.5.3	5/24/11 12:48 PM	Intel	Yes	No
AirPortDevicesUIAgent	1.0	6/16/11 5:59 PM	Intel	Yes	No

Address Book:

Version: 6.0
Last Modified: 6/16/11 7:34 PM
Kind: Intel
64–Bit (Intel): Yes
App Store: No
Location: /Applications/Address Book.app

MyMac ▸ Software ▸ Applications ▸ Address Book

Monitoring Processes via Activity Monitor

The primary application in Lion for monitoring processes as they are running is Activity Monitor. This extremely useful tool shows you the vital signs of any currently running process and the system as a whole. If an application has stopped responding or has become noticeably slow, check Activity Monitor. Also check here if the overall system is running noticeably slower. Activity Monitor will help you identify an application or background process that is using a significant percentage of system memory or processor resources.

To view your Mac's currently running processes with Activity Monitor:

1 Open /Applications/Utilities/Activity Monitor.

Process Identification (PID). Each process has a unique identifier that is chosen based on the order in which it was opened since system startup.

Process Name. This is the name of the running process chosen by the user who created it.

User. Each process is opened on behalf of a particular user. Thus, each application has file system access based on the assigned user account.

% CPU. This number is the percentage of total CPU usage the process is consuming. Note that the maximum percentage possible is 100 percent times the number of processor cores.

Threads. Each process is further broken down into the number of thread operations. Multithreading helps increase a process's responsiveness by enabling it to perform multiple simultaneous tasks. Multithreading also increases performance as each thread of a single process can run on a separate processor core.

Real Mem. This represents the amount of physical memory that the process is currently occupying.

Kind. This shows what processor architecture the application is currently using: Intel (64 bit) or Intel.

2   Click a column title to sort the process list by that column.

Click the column title again to toggle between ascending and descending sorts. You can also adjust the number of statistics shown in the columns and the update frequency from the View menu.

3   By default, Activity Monitor will only show processes running for the currently logged-in user. To view all active processes, choose All Processes from the Show pop-up menu.

Use the Spotlight search filter in the upper-right corner of the Activity Monitor window to quickly pare down the list of running processes.

By viewing all processes and then re-sorting the list by either % CPU or Real Mem, you can determine whether any process is using excessive resources.

4   To further inspect a process, double-click its name in the Activity Monitor list. This reveals a window showing detailed process information.

5   Finally, to inspect overall system information, click through the tabs at the bottom of
the Activity Monitor window.

These monitoring features are invaluable for troubleshooting, as they show you real-
time system statistics.

> **TIP** ▶ Take time to explore all the features available from the Activity Monitor
> menu options. For an even more detailed process inspector, check out the /Developer/
> Applications/Instruments application installed as part of the optional Xcode
> Developer Tools package that can be found on the Mac App Store.

Monitoring Processes via Command Line

Two primary commands exist for viewing active processes from the command-line interface, top and ps.

> **NOTE** ▶ If you aren't already comfortable with navigation in the UNIX command
> line available from Terminal, then it's strongly recommended that you study the com-
> mand-line concepts in Appendix B, "Command-Line Essentials," before reading the
> remainder of the section.

top

The top command is so named because it's typically used to show the top processes that are taking up the most processor resources. However, by default in Lion, top lists commands in reverse order based on their process ID number. To have top sort by processor usage, include the -u option. The top command takes over the Terminal window when you open it. To return to the command prompt, press the Q key. The following code shows the default output of the top command. Notice the similarities to Activity Monitor.

```
Processes: 51 total, 2 running, 49 sleeping, 216 threads          16:56:52
Load Avg: 0.12, 0.07, 0.13   CPU usage: 1.46% user, 2.43% sys, 96.9% idle
SharedLibs: 10M resident, 6936K data, 0B linkedit.
MemRegions: 5649 total, 185M resident, 12M private, 140M shared.
PhysMem: 330M wired, 387M active, 440M inactive, 1158M used, 890M free.
VM: 119G vsize, 1041M framework vsize, 72392(0) pageins, 0(0) pageouts.
Networks: packets: 208547/32M in, 544054/595M out.
Disks: 26496/931M read, 19094/513M written.


PID  COMMAND      %CPU TIME     #TH  #WQ  #POR #MRE RPRVT  RSHRD  RSIZE  VPRVT
751  top          3.3  00:02.69 1/1  0    24   34   844K   264K   1416K  17M
741  mdworker     0.0  00:00.04 3    1    48   84   1360K  11M    3288K  23M
737  bash         0.0  00:00.01 1    0    17   25   348K   856K   1008K  17M
736  login        0.0  00:00.01 1    0    22   54   436K   312K   1572K  10M
...
```

ps

Short for "process status," the ps command lists active processes, but it does not take over the Terminal window as the top command does. Sometimes you have so many active processes that the top command simply can't show them all on your monitor, and this is where the ps command comes in handy. The syntax is ps, followed by any listing options you specify. The most useful options are -ax (to show all processes), -c (to only show the process name instead of the absolute path to the process), and -u followed by a user's short name (to list only processes belonging to that user). In the following example, Michelle first uses the ps command with the -c and -u options to shorten the process name and list active processes belonging to her user account. She then uses the ps command with only the -ax options to view all active processes with full pathnames. The results were too long to print, so they have been cut off at process six in this example.

```
MyMac:~ michelle$ ps -cu michelle
UID PID TTY TIME CMD
502 922 ?? 0:00.05 launchd
502 1113 ?? 0:00.65 sshd
502 1205 ?? 0:00.35 Spotlight
502 1206 ?? 0:00.17 UserEventAgent
502 1208 ?? 0:00.13 Dock
502 1210 ?? 0:00.76 SystemUIServer
...
MyMac:~ michelle$ ps -ax
PID TTY TIME CMD
1 ?? 0:03.65 /sbin/launchd
9 ?? 0:00.86 /usr/libexec/kextd
10 ?? 0:05.01 /usr/sbin/DirectoryService
...
```

Application Troubleshooting

Application issues are as diverse as the applications themselves. Just as each application is designed to provide unique features, problems often manifest in unique ways as well. Fortunately, you can take several general troubleshooting steps when diagnosing and resolving an application issue. The actions in the following list are in order from the least invasive and time-consuming to the most invasive and time-consuming. Actions are also generally presented by the likelihood of their success in resolving the issue, from most to least likely.

> **NOTE ▶** Some software is just incompatible with Lion. Apple maintains a list of software known to be incompatible at Knowledge Base article HT3258, "Mac OS X v10.6, OS X Lion: About incompatible software."

General application troubleshooting methods include:

▶ Restart the application—Often, restarting an application will resolve the issue, or at least resolve application responsiveness. In some cases, the application may become unresponsive and you may have to forcibly quit it to restart it, as detailed later in this section.

▶ Try another known working document—This is an excellent method to determine if a document has become corrupted and is the cause of the problem. If you discover that the problem's source is a corrupted document file, usually the best solution is to restore the document from an earlier backup. Lion includes a sophisticated and yet easy-to-use backup system called Time Machine. Time Machine is covered in Chapter 4, "Data Management."

▶ Try another application—Many common document types can be opened by multiple Mac applications. Try opening the troublesome document in another application. If this works, save a new "clean" version of the document from the alternate application.

▶ Try another user account—Use this method to determine if a user-specific resource file is the cause of the problem. If the application problem doesn't appear when using another account, you should search for corrupted application caches, preferences, and resource files in the suspect user's Library folder. Creating a temporary account to test and then delete is quite easy, as covered in Chapter 2, "User Accounts."

▶ Check diagnostic reports and log files—This is the last information-gathering step to take before you start replacing items. Few applications keep detailed log files; however, every time an application crashes, the Lion diagnostic reporting feature saves a diagnostic report of the crash information. Diagnostic reports are detailed later in this chapter.

▶ Delete cache files—To increase performance, many applications create cache folders in the /Library/Caches, ~/Library/Caches, and ~/Library/Saved Application State folders. A specific application's cache folder almost always matches the application's name. While not the most likely application resource to cause problems, cache folders can be easily deleted without affecting the user's information. Once you delete an application's cache folder, the application will create a new one the next time you open it. One cache type that can't be removed easily from the Finder is the various font caches. However, the system font cashes are cleared during a Safe Boot, as covered in Chapter 9, "System Startup."

TIP ▶ The ~/Library folder is hidden by default in Lion. The easiest method to reveal this folder in the Finder is to hold the Option key and select Go > Library from the menu bar.

▶ Replace preference files—Corrupted preference files are the most likely of all application resources to cause problems, as they change often and are required for the application to function properly. Application preference troubleshooting is detailed later in this chapter.

▶ Replace application resources—Although corrupted application resources can certainly cause problems, they are the least likely source of problems, since application resources are rarely changed. Application resource troubleshooting is also detailed later in this chapter.

Forcibly Quit via Graphical Interface

It's pretty easy to tell when an application becomes unresponsive—it stops reacting to your mouse clicks, and the cursor often changes to a spinning beach ball for more than a minute. Hence, the term "beach-balling" has become slang for a frozen Mac application. Because the forward-most application controls the menu bar, it may seem as if the application has locked you out of the Mac entirely. But moving the cursor from the frozen application window to another application window or the desktop usually returns the cursor to normal—and you can then click another application or the desktop to regain control of your Mac.

Lion provides no less than three methods for forcibly quitting applications from the graphical interface:

▶ From the Force Quit Applications dialog—Choose Apple menu > Force Quit or use the Option-Command-Escape keyboard combination to open the Force Quit Applications dialog. A frozen application will appear in red text with "(not responding)" next to it. To forcibly quit, select any application and click the Force Quit button. Note that you can only restart the Finder from this dialog.

▶ From the Dock—Control-click, right-click, or click and hold the application's icon in the Dock to display the Dock's application shortcut menu. If the Dock has recognized that the application is frozen, simply choose Force Quit from this menu. Otherwise, hold down the Option key to change the Quit menu command to Force Quit.

▶ From Activity Monitor—Open /Applications/Utilities/Activity Monitor and select the application you wish to quit from the process list. Next, click the Quit Process button in Activity Monitor's toolbar, and then click the Force Quit button. Activity Monitor is the only built-in graphical application that will also allow administrative users to quit or forcibly quit any other user processes or background system process.

Forcibly Quit via Command Line

Two primary commands exist for viewing and forcibly quitting processes from the command-line interface, kill and killall.

The intent of the kill command is clear by its name. This command is used to forcibly quit processes. The syntax is kill, followed by the process identification number (PID) of the process you wish to forcibly quit. As covered previously, you can identify a process's PID from the Activity Monitor application or the top and ps commands.

In the following example, Michelle attempts to use the kill command to kill the opendirectoryd process, which happens to be process 11 and is always owned by the system. Initially she isn't allowed to do so because the process belongs to the system, so, being an administrative user, she uses the sudo command to execute the kill command as the root user. Michelle uses ps -axc to verify the opendirectoryd process before and after the kill command. Notice that the opendirectoryd process has a new PID after the kill command, indicating that it has been restarted by the system. The full output of the ps command has been truncated for this example.

```
MyMac:~ michelle$ ps -axc

...

11 ??           0:00.99 opendirectoryd

...

MyMac:~ michelle$ kill 11

-bash: kill: (11) - Operation not permitted

MyMac:~ michelle$ sudo kill 11

Password:

MyMac:~ michelle$$ ps -axc

...

705 ??          0:00.13 opendirectoryd

...
```

The killall command was invented to kill all the instances of a named process. This is especially useful when a process spawns multiple instances of itself, as is the case with some network service processes. In the previous example, Michelle had to locate the PID of the opendirectoryd process to forcibly quit it with the kill command. She could have accomplished this same task with the killall command without having to know the PID. She would, however, have to enter the exact spelling of the running process. In this case Michelle would simply enter:

```
LeoClient:~ michelle$ sudo killall opendirectoryd
```

Diagnostic Reports

To help diagnose persistent issues, Lion's diagnostic reporting feature springs into action any time an application quits unexpectedly, commonly known as a *crash*, or stops functioning and you have to forcibly quit it, commonly known as a *hang*. This process displays a warning dialog to the user, letting her know a problem has occurred. More important, this process records log files that detail the circumstances surrounding the application's crash or hang. If you click the Report button when the warning dialog appears, then you can see the diagnostic report and optionally add comments to send to Apple.

TIP ▶ You can disable the automatic sending of diagnostic reports to Apple from the Security & Privacy preferences.

Even if you don't send the report to Apple, you can revisit diagnostic reports again, as they are always saved to the system volume. If the application crashed, a diagnostic report log with the name of the application followed by .crash is saved in the user's ~/Library/Logs/DiagnosticReports folder. However, if the application hung, a diagnostic report log with the name of the application followed by .hung is saved in the local /Library/Logs/DiagnosticReports folder. The easiest way to view these reports is to open the /Applications/Utilities/Console application, and then click the Show Log List button in the toolbar. The diagnostic reports will be chronologically listed in the Diagnostic Information section.

These diagnostic report logs include highly technical information that most will not understand, but they also include key pieces of information that may help the average troubleshooter diagnose the issue. For example, diagnostic reports often indicate which files were being used by the application at the time. One of the reported files could be the source of the problem due to corruption.

Preference Troubleshooting

Applications primarily access two types of often-changing files during their use: the documents that the application is responsible for viewing or editing, and the preference files that contain all the application's settings. From an administration perspective, preference files are often more important, as they may contain important settings that are required for an application to work properly. For instance, an application's serial number or registration information is often stored in a preference file.

Preference files can be found in any Library folder, but most application preferences end up in the user's Library, specifically in the ~/Library/Preferences folder. This is because the local Library should only be used for system preferences. More important, it enables each user to have his own application settings that do not interfere with other users' application settings. By this logic, it's clear that if you're troubleshooting a system process, then you should look for its preferences in the /Library folder.

> **TIP** The ~/Library folder is hidden by default in Lion. The easiest method to reveal this folder in the Finder is to hold the Option key, then select Go > Library from the menu bar.

Most application and system preference files are saved as property list files. The naming scheme for a property list file is usually in the form of a reverse domain name, followed by the program name, ending with the file type .plist. For example, the Finder's preference file is named com.apple.finder.plist. This naming scheme may seem strange at first, but it helps avoid confusion by identifying the software's maker along with the application. In this folder you may also notice items with the file type .plist.lockfile. These lock files are the result of a new behavior in Lion that maintains a persistent lock on the preference files, preventing other applications from improperly tampering with an applications preference file.

Application preference files are one of the most common application resources to cause problems. Because these files can contain both internal application configuration information and user-configured preferences, even if you haven't changed any preferences, odds are the application is constantly storing new information in this file. It is the only file required by most applications that is regularly being rewritten, so it's a potential target for corruption.

Apple has worked hard to make its own applications and the user preference system wary of corrupt preference files. Many applications, including third-party applications, that use Apple's preference model will simply recognize the corrupt preference file, ignore it, and create a new one. On the other hand, many third-party applications use their own proprietary preference models that are not as resilient. If this is the case, corrupted preferences typically result in an application that crashes frequently or during startup.

Resolving Corrupted Preferences

The most convenient method of isolating a corrupted preference in this case is to rename the suspect preference file. If any part of the preference filename is different than expected, the application will ignore it and create a new preference file. In the Finder, add an identifier to the end of the suspect preference filename—something like .bad. Alternately you could simply put a tilde (~) at the beginning of the preference file, which will cause the Finder to put it at the beginning of the file listing when sorted alphabetically. Any lock files associated with a preference file can be largely ignored when troubleshooting as they don't contain any data and are simply the result of Lion's preference locking mechanism.

Restarting the application or process creates a new preference file based on the code's defaults. If this resolves the issue and doesn't remove any irreplaceable settings, go ahead and trash the old preference file; if not, you should move on to resource troubleshooting. If you eventually resolve the problem elsewhere, you can then restore the previous settings by deleting the newer preference file and removing the filename identifier you added to the original preference file. The benefit is that you don't lose any of the settings or custom configuration from the previous preference file.

Viewing and Editing Preferences

One of the primary advantages of using the property list file format is that it can generally be understood by humans. During your troubleshooting, you may find it advantageous to verify settings by directly viewing the contents of the configuration property list file. Many applications and processes keep additional settings items in these files that may not have a graphical interface for configuration.

> **NOTE ▶** A few third-party applications do not store their preference files as property lists. Thus, they will likely sport a different naming convention, and you will probably not be able to view or edit the file's contents.

The content of a property list file is formatted either as plain-text Extensible Markup Language (XML) or binary. The XML format is relatively human-readable with normal text interspersed alongside special text tags that define the data structure for the information. Thus, you can view and attempt to decipher the XML code of plain-text-formatted property list files using any text-reading application. Binary-encoded files are only readable using special tools designed to convert the binary code into human-readable format. Fortunately, Lion includes a Quick Look plug-in that will allow you to easily view the contents of either type of property list file by simply hitting the Space bar while you have the file selected in the Finder.

If you determine that you need to edit a property list file, the most complete graphical application for doing so is Xcode. The Xcode application can decode binary property list files, and it enables you to view and edit any property list in an easy-to-read hierarchical format. Again, Xcode is an optional install with Lion and can be found on the Mac App Store.

Resource Troubleshooting

Although rare, corrupted application software and associated nonpreference resources can be a source of application problems. These types of files rarely, if ever, change after the initial application installation, so the likelihood that such a resource is the cause of a problem is low. However, keep in mind that many applications use *other* resources from the local and user Library folders, such as fonts, plug-ins, and keychains, as well as items in the Application Support folder. The hard part is locating the suspect resource; once you have, the fix is to simply remove or replace the corrupted resource and restart the application.

> **NOTE ▸** Applications running in 64-bit mode will not load plug-in resources that only support 32-bit mode. This compatibility issue is covered in the "64-bit versus 32-bit Mode" section previously in this chapter.

Remember that corrupted resources in the user's home folder Library will affect only that user, while corrupted resources in the local Library affect all users. Use this fact to narrow your search when looking for a corrupted resource. Further, application and diagnostic report logs, covered earlier in this section, may tell you which resources the application was attempting to access when it crashed. Obviously, those resources should be your primary suspects.

TIP ▶ The ~/Library folder is hidden by default in Lion. The easiest method to reveal this folder in the Finder is to hold the Option key, then select Go > Library from the menu bar.

If the application exhibits problems with only one user, attempt to locate the specific resource at the root of the problem in the user's Library folder. Start with the usual suspects; if you find a resource that you think could be causing the problem, move that resource out of the user's Library folder and restart the application.

NOTE ▶ Some older applications have a habit of storing their resources in the user's Documents folder, so you may have to check there as well.

If you've determined that the application issue is persistent across all user accounts, start by reinstalling or upgrading to the latest version of the application. You will probably find that there is a newer version of the application available that likely includes bug fixes. At the very least, by reinstalling you will replace any potentially corrupted files that are part of the standard application. If you continue to experience problems after reinstalling the application, search through the local Library resources to find and remove or replace the corrupted resource.

NOTE ▶ If you are discovering a large number of corrupted files, this probably indicates a much more serious file system or storage hardware issue. Troubleshooting these items is covered in Chapter 3, "File Systems."

Managing Dashboard

Mac OS X v10.4 introduced Dashboard as a new interface concept that provides instant access to narrowly focused, but usually very attractive, mini-applications called widgets. When Dashboard is activated, your chosen mini-applications will instantly spring to life and appear "on top" of the Mac's normal interface. A simple click on the Mac's normal interface will dismiss Dashboard just as quickly. The convenience of using these mini-applications from Dashboard caught on quickly, and within a few months of its introduction hundreds of new third-party widgets were available.

Apple has been adding new tricks to Dashboard with every revision, including the ability for any user to quickly make new widgets from any website using Safari's File > Open in Dashboard menu option. Apple also completely reworked the widget runtime architecture to run more efficiently and securely than before. To help increase the number of third-party widgets, Apple formalized the widget creation process by introducing a full widget development environment called Dashcode. Dashcode is installed as part of the optional Xcode package on the Mac App Store. With Mac OS X v10.6, the Dashboard process made the move to 64-bit mode for improved performance, and finally with Lion, Dashboard has been given a new home with its own space in Mission Control.

Adding More Widgets

By default, Dashboard is activated by clicking the Dashboard icon in the Dock, pressing the F12 key on older Macs, pressing the F4 key on current Macs, or using the multifinger swiping gesture to the right on a Multi-Touch device. If you don't like the default shortcuts, you can adjust the Dashboard key from the Mission Control preferences, or adjust the Dashboard device gestures from the Mouse and Trackpad preferences. Further, you can activate Hot Corner for Dashboard from the Desktop & Screen Saver preferences.

Built-in Apple widgets are located in /Library/Widgets, while third-party widgets are typically installed in ~/Library/Widgets in the user's home folder. Most users will use the automatic widget install mechanisms in Lion to add new widgets to their Dashboard.

To easily locate, test, and install a new widget:

1 Open Dashboard using one of the methods outlined previously. The default method on all Macs is to click on the Dashboard icon in the Dock.

2 Once in Dashboard, click the small plus button at the bottom corner of the screen to reveal the widget bar.

The widget bar allows you to add currently installed widgets to your Dashboard area by simply clicking on the widget's icon.

3 With the widget bar open, click the Manage Widgets button or the Widgets icon in the bottom-right corner of the screen.

This will open the widget manager, which allows you to disable installed widgets or download new widgets from Apple's website.

4   From the widget manager, click the More Widgets button, and it will automatically open the default web browser and take you to Apple's online widget repository.

At this point you can browse and download any additional widgets that strike your fancy. Alternately, you can acquire widgets using any method you like, including from other websites or via file sharing.

TIP You can also create your own custom widgets from web pages in Safari by selecting File > Open in Dashboard from the menu bar.

5   If you downloaded the widget with Safari, it will automatically prompt for installation. However, if you acquired the widget through other means, you will have to double-click on the widget file in the Finder to start the widget installer.

6   When the Widget Installer dialog appears, click the Install button to open the widget in Dashboard for installation.

Dashboard will open the new widget in a test environment.

7   Thoroughly explore the widget and, if you like it, click the Keep button to complete the installation process.

The widget will be installed in the currently logged-in user's home folder and in the ~/Library/Widgets folder, and will always be available to that user in Dashboard from the widget bar.

Manually Manage Widgets

You can also manually install widgets by simply dragging them into one of the Widgets folders. This is necessary if you want to install a widget for all users of the system. Similar to other system resources, widgets installed in the user's home folder will only be available to that user, and widgets installed in the local Library folder will be available to all local users. If you manually install a widget, thus bypassing the automatic widget installer, users will still have to manually add that widget to Dashboard from the widget bar.

To remove a widget, locate it in either the local or user Library Widgets folder and drag it to the Trash. If the widget is still active in Dashboard after you have removed it from the Widgets folder, log the user out and then back in again to restart the Dashboard process.

Understanding Widget Architecture

The widget runtime architecture was reworked for Mac OS X v10.5 to provide a more effi-cient and secure Dashboard environment. When a user logs in, the launchd process starts the Dock process. The first time a user attempts to access Dashboard, the Dock process starts the DashboardClient process. The DashboardClient process is responsible for running the Dashboard environment, including all widgets.

The DashboardClient process maintains two general Dashboard preference files in the ~/Library/Preferences folder: com.apple.dashboard.client.plist and com.apple.dashboard.plist. Each open widget also maintains its own preference file in the user Preferences folder named widget-com.*widgetmaker*.widget.*widgetname*.plist, where *widgetmaker* is the name of the software developer who created the widget, and *widgetname* is the name of the widget.

The DashboardClient process has the same access privileges as the user. So generally, widgets are as secure as any other normal application. Nevertheless, it is possible for someone to create and distribute widgets that have a negative effect. Widgets are basically miniature specialized web browsers, so just about any data transfer or software that can run from a web browser can also be run by a widget. Dashboard is only as safe as the widgets a user chooses to run. If you are at all suspicious of a third-party widget, simply avoid using it.

> **TIP** ▶ Although an administrator can't prevent a user from downloading third-party widgets, she can limit a user's ability to use third-party widgets with the Parental Controls preferences, as covered in Chapter 2, "User Accounts."

Troubleshooting Widgets

If a widget appears to stop working or becomes unresponsive, your first step should be to attempt to reset it. From Dashboard, click once on the widget, then press Command-R to reset the widget. Widgets use a swirling animation to indicate that they have reset.

If the widget is still having problems, or you're having trouble using all the widgets, restart the DashboardClient process associated with the user account. You can forcibly quit the DashboardClient process by using /Applications/Utilities/Activity Monitor. More information about forcibly quitting processes is available in the "Forcibly Quit" sections earlier in this chapter. After you quit the DashboardClient process, reactivate Dashboard and the DashboardClient process, and all open widgets will reopen. Another method is to restart all user processes by logging the user out and then back in again.

If restarting the widget and the DashboardClient process doesn't work, you may have a corrupted widget or widget preference file. Widgets are similar to other applications in that they are susceptible to errors from corrupted files. Start by removing the specific widget preference file, and then restart the DashboardClient process. If you're having trouble with a third-party widget, download a new copy and replace the widget itself. Finally, you can reset the entire Dashboard system by removing all Dashboard and widget preference files and then logging the user out and back in again.

What You've Learned

▶ Lion supports a variety of new and old applications on both 32-bit and 64-bit Intel-based Mac systems.

▶ The Mac App Store provides an easy-to-use interface allowing you to find, download, install, and update Mac applications.

▶ Lion introduces Auto Save and Versions, an entirely new document management model that's both easier to use and more powerful.

▶ Lion includes application accessibility interfaces via Universal Access and VoiceOver.

▶ You can use Activity Monitor to monitor applications and processes.

▶ Application troubleshooting involves locating the problem source by taking steps from the least invasive and time-consuming action to the most invasive and time-consuming action.

▶ Dashboard provides instantaneous access to useful mini-applications called widgets.

References

You can check for new and updated Knowledge Base documents at www.apple.com/support.

Application Accessibility

HT1343, "Mac OS X keyboard shortcuts"

HT3786, "VoiceOver command differences between Mac OS X v10.6 and Mac OS X v10.5"

Application Troubleshooting

DL1421, "Java for OS X Lion"

TS3938, "OS X Lion: Application icon has a prohibitory sign, or 'PowerPC applications are no longer supported' appears"

HT3258, "Mac OS X v10.6, OS X Lion: About incompatible software"

TS3624, "Troubleshooting the Mac App Store"

HT4753, "OS X Lion: About Auto Save and Versions"

HT1342, "Mac OS X: Reading system memory usage in Activity Monitor"

HT1199, "Mac OS X: How to troubleshoot a software issue"

HT3662, "About file quarantine in Mac OS X v10.5 and v10.6"

HT4774, "OS X Lion: Diagnostic & Usage"

Dashboard

HT2254, "Mac OS X 10.4.2 or later: Installing and removing Dashboard widgets"

TS1549, "Mac OS X 10.5: Dashboard widgets issues with Parental Controls and Fast User Switching enabled"

URLs

Lion architectural overview: http://developer.apple.com/technologies/mac

Cocoa application environment: http://developer.apple.com/technologies/mac/cocoa.html

Carbon application environment: http://developer.apple.com/carbon/

Apple's Java implementation: http://developer.apple.com/java/

Apple's open source software initiatives: http://developer.apple.com/opensource/

Apple's X11 implementation: http://developer.apple.com/opensource/tools/X11.html

MacPorts project open source collection: www.macports.org/

Mac App Store support website: www.apple.com/support/mac/app-store/

Apple's Accessibility resource: www.apple.com/accessibility/

Apple's VoiceOver resource: www.apple.com/accessibility/voiceover/

Apple's online widget site: www.apple.com/downloads/dashboard/

Review Quiz

1. What is protected memory? What is 64-bit memory addressing?

2. What are the five application environments supported by Lion? Which one requires an additional download and installation?

3. What are the advantages of code signing?

4. What are the requirements for purchasing applications via the Mac App Store?

5. What system preference enables the accessibility features in Lion? What accessibility features are available in Lion?

6. What is Auto Save? How can you identify an application that supports Auto Save?

7. How deep is the version history of a file when shared via email?

8. How can you identify the type of a particular application?

9. How can you identify which applications are installed on your Mac?

10. What steps should you use when troubleshooting application issues?

11. What three ways can you forcibly quit an application from the graphical interface?

12. What does the diagnostic reporting feature do?

13. Where are application preferences stored? What format is often used for preference files?

14. What process or processes are responsible for Dashboard widgets?

Answers

1. The system keeps applications from interfering with one another by segregating their memory usage using protected memory. Macs with 64-bit-capable processors allow processes to run in 64-bit mode, which allows them to individually access more than 4 GB of memory.

2. The five application environments supported by Lion are Cocoa, the native application environment for Mac OS X; Carbon, which is based on Mac OS 9 but still

provides native performance; BSD, which is Lion's command-line interface (CLI) and is based on Berkeley Software Distribution (BSD) UNIX; X11, which is a popular UNIX windowing environment; and Java, which works as a cross-platform application solution. Lion does not include the Java application runtime, so it must be downloaded and installed after Lion's initial installation.

3.   Code-signed items include a digital signature that the system can use to verify the authenticity and integrity of the application or process and its resources.

4.   The requirements to purchase items from the Mac App Store are Mac OS X v10.6.6 or later, an Apple ID, an Internet connection, and authorization as a local administrator.

5.   Lion's accessibility features are available from the Universal Access preferences. Universal Access includes options to assist users who have difficulty seeing, hearing, using the keyboard, or using the mouse and trackpad.

6.   Auto Save is a new feature in Lion that allows applications to automatically save changes to users' documents. Once the user saves a document the first time, he never has to think about saving changes again. Applications that support Auto Save feature a Duplicate function in the File menu as opposed to a Save As function.

7.   Documents sent via email or otherwise copied to a shared location do not retain any version history.

8.   You can identify an application's type with the Get Info or Inspector window in the Finder or with System Profiler.

9.   You can use the System Profiler application to easily scan all the appropriate application locations and return a list of installed applications.

10.   General application troubleshooting steps include restarting the application, trying another known working document, trying another user account, checking log files, deleting cache files, replacing preference files, and replacing application resources.

11.   The three ways to forcibly quit an application from the graphical interface are from the Force Quit Application dialog accessed from the Apple menu, from the Dock's application shortcut menu accessed by Control-clicking or right-clicking on the application's icon, or from the /Applications/Utilities/Activity Monitor application.

12.   The diagnostic reporting feature automatically springs into action any time an application crashes or hangs. This process creates a diagnostic report log that can be viewed immediately, reported to Apple via the Internet, or viewed later in the /Applications/Utilities/Console application.

13. Application preferences are almost always stored in the user's Library folder in the ~/Library/Preferences folder. Most application preferences are property lists, which are XML-formatted files that use the ".plist" filename extension.

14. The Dock process starts the DashboardClient process on behalf of the currently logged-in user. All open widgets run inside the DashboardClient process.

6

Time   This chapter takes approximately 3 hours to complete.

Goals   Understand fundamental TCP/IP network concepts

Configure OS X Lion networking

Manage multiple network locations and interfaces

Identify and resolve network connectivity issues

Chapter **6**

Network Configuration

The capability to share information between computers across a network has always been important. During the early years of personal computer development, vendors designed their own proprietary local network systems. Apple was no exception with its implementation of AppleTalk and LocalTalk network standards for file sharing and network printing. Yet although these vendor-specific technologies were suitable for private networks, they didn't allow for direct communication between dissimilar networks. Special hardware or software had to be put in place to translate from one vendor's network to another.

Around the same time, researchers were working at the behest of various U.S. organizations to create a wide area network (WAN) standard for military and governmental use. From this research was born the Internet protocol suite known as TCP/IP. The marriage of the Transmission Control Protocol (TCP) and the Internet Protocol (IP) became the universal language that allows computers to communicate on the Internet. This standard became so pervasive that nearly every network today, from small local networks all the way up to the largest long-distance network on Earth, the Internet, is based on the TCP/IP suite.

It should come as no surprise, then, that Lion includes a robust TCP/IP implementation. In fact, the first computer systems to popularize the use of TCP/IP were UNIX systems. Thus, much of the TCP/IP software built into every version of Mac OS X is based on open source UNIX software that was established long before Lion ever existed as a product from Apple.

In this chapter, you will configure network settings and troubleshoot network connectivity issues using Lion. Before that, though, you must have a fundamental understanding of core network concepts, to which the first part of this chapter is devoted.

Understanding Network Concepts

Properly configuring and troubleshooting networking on any operating system requires a basic understanding of fundamental network concepts. Due to the widespread adoption of standardized network technology, the following network overview applies to nearly any operating system, Lion included. Basic network terminology is covered first, followed by an overview of the processes involved in actual data delivery across a network.

Network Terminology

It's best to explore networking from a layered perspective. In fact, there is an established seven-layer model used to describe network technologies, the Open Systems Interconnection Reference Model (known as the OSI model). Exploring networking using the OSI model goes well beyond the scope of this text. Consequently, networking concepts will be presented in a more simplistic abstraction of three basic elements:

▶   Network interface—The network interface is the medium through which network data flows. Network interfaces can be physical or virtual. The most common physical network interfaces for computers are Ethernet and 802.11 wireless Ethernet, which is known most commonly as Wi-Fi. Virtual network interfaces are also available that can be used to increase the functionality of the physical interface: for example, a virtual private network (VPN) that uses the existing physical network interface to provide a secure connection without the need for a dedicated physical interface.

▶   Network protocol—A protocol defines a set of standard rules used for data representation, signaling, authentication, or error detection across network interfaces. Primarily, protocols are designed to ensure that all data is communicated properly and completely. Specific protocols have a narrow focus, so often multiple protocols are combined or layered to provide a complete network solution. For example, the combined TCP/IP protocol suite provides only for the addressing and end-to-end transport of data across the Internet; dozens of other protocols are required for something as simple as checking your email or browsing a website.

▶ Network service—In the context of the Network preferences, the term *network service* describes a configuration assigned to a network interface. For example, in Network preferences, you will see listed the Wi-Fi service, which represents the connection settings for the Wi-Fi network interface. A fundamental feature of Lion is the ability to support multiple network services, or connections, per each individual network interface.

▶ A different definition of the term *network service* is used in Chapter 7, "Network Services," wherein a network service is information provided on the network by a server for use by clients. Common examples in Chapter 7 include file sharing services, messaging services, and collaboration services. Often a specific set of protocols is used to define how the particular service works.

MORE INFO ▶ For more details on the OSI model for describing computer networks, refer to this Wikipedia entry: http://en.wikipedia.org/wiki/OSI_model.

Simplifying computer network technology to only three distinct elements does not provide a detailed abstraction, but it still shows clearly how each is related. When a network interface, service, or protocol is created, it is often put through a review process before it's deemed a network standard. Standards committees are formed with members from multiple network organizations and vendors to ensure that new network standards remain interoperable with existing network standards. Most networking technologies in use today have been ratified by some standards body, so you may often come across an interface, protocol, or service labeled as a "standard."

Media Access Control (MAC) Address

The Media Access Control (MAC) address is used to uniquely identify a physical network interface on a local network. Each physical network interface has at least one MAC address associated with it.

NOTE ▶ The Intel-based Xserve has two MAC addresses per Ethernet interface to provide functionality for lights-out management.

Because the most common network interface is Ethernet, people often refer to MAC addresses as Ethernet addresses. Still, nearly every other network interface type also uses some type of MAC address for unique identification. This includes, but isn't limited to, Wi-Fi, Bluetooth, FireWire, and Fibre Channel.

A MAC address is usually a 48-bit number represented by six groups of two-digit hexadecimal numbers each separated by colons. For example, a typical MAC address would look something like this: 00:1C:B3:D7:2F:99. The first three number groups are the Organizationally Unique Identifier (OUI), and the last three number groups identify the network device itself. In other words, you can use the first three number groups of a MAC address to identify who made the network device.

MORE INFO ▶ The Institute of Electrical and Electronics Engineers (IEEE) maintains a searchable database of publicly listed OUIs at its website: http://standards.ieee.org/regauth/oui/index.shtml.

Internet Protocol (IP) Address

Communicating with computers on both local and remote networks requires an Internet Protocol (IP) address. IP addresses, unlike MAC addresses, are not permanently tied to a network interface. Instead, they are assigned to the network interface based on the local network it's connected to. This means if you have a portable computer, every new network you connect to will probably require a new IP address. If necessary, you can assign multiple IP addresses to each network interface, but this approach is often only used for computers that are providing network services.

There are currently two standards for IP addresses: IPv4 and IPv6. IPv4 was the first widely used IP addressing scheme and is the most common today. An IPv4 address is a 32-bit number represented by four groups of three-digit numbers, also known as octets, separated by periods. Each octet has a value between 0 and 255. For example, a typical IPv4 address would look something like this: 10.1.45.186.

With IPv4, a little over 4 billion unique addresses exist. This may seem like a lot, but considering how many new network-ready gadgets come out and the number of people who want to own multiple network-ready gadgets, this number isn't really big enough. For the time being, the available IPv4 addresses are extended by using network routers that can share a single real IPv4 address to a range of reusable private network addresses. This is how most home networks are configured, but it is only a temporary solution for what's to come next.

The successor to IPv4 is IPv6, but because IPv4 is so entrenched in the backbone of the Internet, the transition to IPv6 has been slow. The main advantage to IPv6 is a much larger address space—so large, in fact, every person on Earth could have roughly 1.2 x 1019 copies of the entire IPv4 address range. This may appear to be a ridiculous number of IP addresses, but the design goal of IPv6 was to eliminate the need for private addressing and allow for easier address reassignment and changing to a new network. An IPv6 address is a 128-bit number that is presented in eight groups of four-digit hexadecimal numbers separated by colons. Hexadecimal numbers use a base-16 digit system, so after the number 9 you use the letters A through F. For example, a typical IPv6 address would look something like this: 2C01:0EF9:0000:0000:0000:0000:142D:57AB. Large strings of zeros in an IPv6 address can be abbreviated using a double colon, resulting in an address more like this: 2C01:0EF9::142D:57AB.

Subnet Mask

The computer uses the subnet mask to determine the IPv4 address range of the local network. Networks based on the IPv6 protocol do not require subnet masks. A subnet mask is similar to an IPv4 address in that it's a 32-bit number arranged in four groups of octets. The computer applies the subnet mask to its own IP address to determine the local network's address range. The nonzero bits in a subnet mask (typically 255) correspond to the portion of the IP address that determines which network the address is on. The zero bits correspond to the portion of the IP address that differs between hosts on the same network. For example, assuming your computer has an IP address of 10.1.5.3 and a commonly used subnet mask of 255.255.255.0, the local network is defined as hosts that have IP addresses ranging from 10.1.5.1 to 10.1.5.254.

> **MORE INFO** ▶ Another way of writing the subnet mask is known as CIDR notation. This is written as the IP address, a slash, and then the number of 1 bits in the subnet mask. The previous subnet example would be 10.1.5.3/24. You can find out more about CIDR notation from Wikipedia: http://en.wikipedia.org/wiki/Classless_Inter-Domain_Routing.

Whenever the computer attempts to communicate with another network device, it applies the subnet mask to the destination IP address of the other device to determine if it's on the local network as well. If so, the computer will attempt to directly access the other network device. If not, the other device is clearly on another network, and the computer will send all communications bound for that other device to the router address.

Router Address

Routers are network devices that manage connections between separate networks; as their name implies, they route network traffic between the networks they bridge. Routing tables are maintained by routers to determine where network traffic goes. Even if a router is presented with traffic destined for a network that the router is unaware of, it will still route the traffic to another router that it thinks is closer to the final destination. Thus, routers literally are the brains of the Internet.

In order to be able to reach computers beyond the local network, your computer needs to be configured with the IP address of the router that connects the local network with another network or, more commonly in residential situations, an Internet service provider. Typically the router's address is at the beginning of the local address range, and it's always in the same subnet. Using the previous example, assuming your computer has an IP address of 10.1.5.3 and a commonly used subnet mask of 255.255.255.0, the local network IP address range would be 10.1.5.0 to 10.1.5.255 and the router address would most likely be 10.1.5.1.

Transmission Control Protocol (TCP)

TCP is the primary protocol used to facilitate end-to-end data connectivity between two IP devices. TCP is the preferred transport mechanism for many Internet services because it guarantees reliable and in-order delivery of data. In other words, IP provides network addressing and data routing, and TCP ensures that the data arrives at its destination complete. The combination of these two protocols encompasses the TCP/IP suite, commonly known as the Internet protocol suite.

The TCP/IP protocol suite chops continuous data streams into many individual packets of information before they are sent across the network. This is because IP networks use packet-switching technology to route and transmit data. Almost all digital networking technologies are packet-based because this provides efficient transport for network connections that aren't always reliable. Remember, the TCP/IP protocol was originally designed with the military in mind, so packet-based network technology is ideal because it's designed to work around communications link failure. This is why sophisticated routing hardware was originally developed for TCP/IP networks, so data could be literally rerouted and re-sent should a network link go down.

A lesser-used protocol known as User Datagram Protocol (UDP) is also attached to the TCP/IP suite. UDP is a simpler protocol that does not guarantee the reliability or ordering of data sent across networks. This may seem like a poor choice for networking, but in some cases UDP is preferred because it provides better performance than TCP. Examples of network services that use UDP include Domain Name System (DNS), media streaming, voice over IP (VoIP), and online gaming. These services have been designed to tolerate lost or out-of-order data so they can benefit from UDP's increased performance.

MORE INFO ▸ For more information regarding the Internet protocol suite, refer to this Wikipedia entry: http://en.wikipedia.org/wiki/internet_protocol_suite.

Understanding Networks in Action

Manually assigning an IP address, a subnet mask, and a router address is technically all that is needed to configure a computer to use TCP/IP-based networking on both local area networks (LANs) and wide area networks (WANs). Yet two other network services are almost always involved in basic network functionality: Dynamic Host Configuration Protocol (DHCP) and DNS. These two services, combined with TCP/IP, characterize core network functionality that provides the foundation for nearly any network service.

Local Area Network (LAN) Traffic

Most LANs use some form of wired or wireless connection. Once the network interface has been established, TCP/IP networking must be configured, either manually or via DHCP. Once both these steps are complete, network communication can begin.

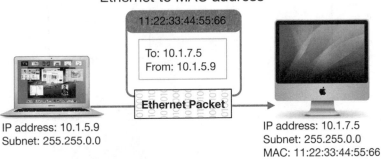

TCP/IP packets are encased inside Ethernet frames to travel across the local network. The TCP/IP packet includes the originating IP and destination IP addresses along with the data to be sent. The network device applies the subnet mask setting to determine if the destination IP address is on the local network. If so, it will consult its Address Resolution

Protocol (ARP) table to see if it knows the MAC address corresponding to the destination IP address. Each network host maintains and continuously updates an ARP table of known MAC addresses that correspond to IP addresses on the local network. If the MAC address is not listed yet, it broadcasts an ARP request to the local network asking the destination device to reply with its MAC address, and adds the reply to its ARP table for next time. Once the MAC address is determined, an outgoing Ethernet frame, encasing the TCP/IP packet, will be sent using the destination MAC address.

The other network device will likely return some information as well using the same technique of transferring TCP/IP packets inside of MAC-addressed Ethernet frames. This goes on and on for thousands of packets every second to complete a data stream. For standard Ethernet the maximum frame size is only 1,500 bytes (that's roughly 1.5 kilobytes or 0.0015 megabytes), so you can imagine how many Ethernet frames are necessary to transmit even a small file.

Wide Area Network (WAN) Traffic

Sending data over a WAN differs only in that data is sent through one or more network routers to reach its intended destination. WANs exist in all shapes and sizes, from a small WAN perhaps used to connect separate LANs in a large building all the way up to the biggest and most popular WAN, the Internet.

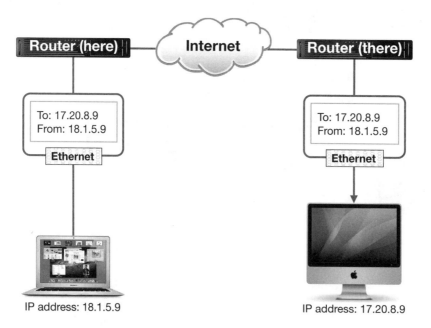

Initially, transferring data across a WAN is similar to transferring data on a LAN. After all, the first stop for the data destined for the WAN is at the network router on the local network. The network device will prepare the packets as before by encasing the TCP/IP packets inside Ethernet frames. Once again, the subnet mask will be applied to the destination IP address to determine if the address is on the local network. In this case, the network device determines that the destination is not on the local network, so it sends the data to the router. Because the router is on the local network, the transmission between the local network client and the router is identical to standard LAN traffic.

Once the router receives the Ethernet-encased TCP/IP packets, it will examine the destination IP address and use a routing table to determine the next closest destination for this packet. This almost always involves sending the packet to another router closer to the destination. In fact, only the last router in the path will send the data to the destination network device.

Network routers also often perform some sort of hardware interface conversion, as WAN network links are rarely standard copper Ethernet connections. The router will strip the Ethernet container away from the original TCP/IP packet and then rewrap it in another container that is appropriate for the WAN connection. Obviously, the final router will have to prepare the TCP/IP packet for the last leg of the journey on the destination device's local network by rewrapping it in an Ethernet frame addressed to the destination's MAC address.

In most cases, network data will be transferred back and forth several times to establish a complete connection. Remember, these packet sizes are very small. The default packet size for Internet traffic is also 1,500 bytes with a maximum packet size of 65,535 bytes for most TCP/IP connections. Network routers are highly optimized devices that can easily handle thousands of data packets every second, so for small amounts of data many WAN connections "feel" as fast as LAN connections. Conversely, a lot of latency is introduced from all the different routers and network connections involved in transferring data across a WAN, so often sending large amounts of data across a WAN is much slower than across a LAN. Thus, many a user's favorite time-wasting computer practice was born: waiting for an Internet download or upload.

Domain Name System (DNS)

Most people are bad at remembering strings of seemingly arbitrary numbers used to define addresses, so additional technology is often implemented to help users find addresses. Even the simplest cell phones feature a contact list so users don't have to remember phone numbers. For TCP/IP networks, DNS makes network addressing much more approachable to normal humans.

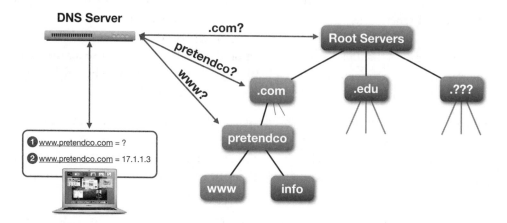

In essence, DNS is a worldwide network of domain servers with the task of maintaining human-friendly host names used to easily locate specific network IP addresses. If you've spent any time at all on the Internet, you're already familiar with the DNS naming convention: For example, Apple's main website is located at www.apple.com. Any network device can have a host name, but only those network devices providing a service that needs to be easily located need to have host name entries on a DNS server. Devices providing shared services, such as printers and server computers, are the most common devices to have DNS entries.

The hierarchical DNS naming convention relates directly to the hierarchical structure of the DNS domain architecture. As you know, DNS names are broken into labels separated by periods. Each label represents a different level, or domain, of the DNS hierarchy. The top of the DNS hierarchy is the "root" or "." domain. The names that are part of the root domain are the familiar abbreviations at the end of nearly every Internet resource. Common examples are .com, .edu, .gov, and others, including various country codes. These top-level domains (TLDs) are hosted by a consortium of commercial and governmental organizations.

Below the TLDs, individual organizations or users host or rent their own DNS domains. For example, Apple hosts several DNS servers that are known by the TLD servers in order to maintain the apple.com domain. Apple can host an unlimited number of host names inside the apple.com domain. Apple can create unlimited domain names by preceding apple.com with any text. Examples include www.apple.com, training.apple.com, and developer.apple.com.

When a local network device needs to resolve a DNS name into the corresponding IP address, it sends the name query to the IP address of a DNS server. The IP address for a DNS server is usually configured along with the other TCP/IP address information for the network device. The DNS server will search its local and cached name records first. If the requested name isn't found locally, the server will query other domain servers in the DNS hierarchy. This process may take a while, so DNS servers will temporarily cache any names they have recently resolved to provide a quicker response for future requests. Querying a DNS server to resolve an IP address given a known host name is called a forward lookup, whereas querying a DNS server to resolve a host name from a known IP address is called a reverse lookup. When initially configured, network clients will query the DNS server with a reverse lookup of its own IP address to determine if the network client has its own DNS name.

> **MORE INFO** ▶ For more information regarding DNS, refer to this Wikipedia entry: http://en.wikipedia.org/wiki/Domain_Name_System.

> **MORE INFO** ▶ Bonjour is a name discovery service that uses a name space similar to DNS. Bonjour is covered in Chapter 7, "Network Services."

Dynamic Host Configuration Protocol (DHCP)

Although not required to provide network functionality, DHCP is used by nearly all network clients to automatically acquire preliminary TCP/IP configuration. In some situations, an administrative user may still choose to manually enter TCP/IP networking configuration information. This is often the case with network devices that are providing network services. However, manually configuring multitudes of network clients is tedious work that is prone to human error. Thus, even on rigorously managed networks, DHCP is still widely used to configure network clients.

> **NOTE** ▶ DHCP is specifically designed to assign IPv4 addressing, as IPv6 addressing is handled automatically via other mechanisms.

> **NOTE** ▶ A precursor to DHCP is Bootstrap Protocol (BOOTP). DHCP is backward compatible with BOOTP but provides greater functionality and reliability.

DNS Server

Server responds if
address available

Server responds if
address available

Client requests
IP address

Client requests
IP address

IP address:
10.0.0.210

IP address:
10.0.0.211

A DHCP server is required to provide the service. On many networks, the network routers provide the DHCP service, but in some cases a dedicated server can be used for this purpose. When a network device becomes active on the network, it first negotiates a link with the hardware interface, and then sends out a broadcast to the local network requesting DHCP information. Because the new network client doesn't yet have an IP address, it uses the network interface's MAC address for identification. If a DHCP server that is listening has available addresses, it will send back a reply to the client with TCP/IP configuration information. At a minimum, this information includes IP address, subnet mask, router, and a DHCP lease time that defines how long the client can retain the address before it's given away. Ancillary DHCP information can include DNS information, directory service information, and NetBoot information.

If the DHCP server has run out of available network addresses, or there is no DHCP service available, as is the case with small ad hoc networks, the client will automatically generate a self-assigned link-local address. Link-local addresses are always in the IP address range of 169.254.xxx.xxx with a subnet mask of 255.255.0.0. The network client will automatically generate a random link-local address and then check the local network to make sure no other network device is using that address. Once a unique link-local address is established, the network client will only be able to establish connections with other network devices on the local network.

MORE INFO ▶ For more information regarding DHCP, refer to this Wikipedia entry: http://en.wikipedia.org/wiki/Dhcp.

Configuring Basic Network Settings

Initial networking configuration is handled by Setup Assistant, which runs the first time you start up a new Mac or a fresh Lion system installation. Setup Assistant makes it easy for even a novice user to configure network settings. Yet even if you choose to not set up networking during the initial system setup process, the Mac will automatically enable any active network interface, including connecting to unrestricted wireless networks, and attempt to configure TCP/IP via DHCP. Consequently, for many users Lion does not require any initial network configuration at all.

If network changes are required after initial setup, you can still use Network Setup Assistant to help guide you through the network configuration process. You can access Network Setup Assistant by clicking the "Assist me" button at the bottom of the Network preferences.

Although this assistant is helpful for novice users, you should be familiar with all network configuration options so you're prepared for any potential network situation or trouble-shooting issue. With a previous version, Mac OS X v10.5, Apple introduced a consolidation of previously separate network configuration windows into a new, unified Network preferences. Thus, all network settings can be found in the Network preferences. You'll note that the Network preferences are locked, indicating that only administrative users have access to these settings and that DHCP is enabled by default for Ethernet and Wi-Fi interfaces.

NOTE ▸ In the screen shot above, note that DHCP is also providing configuration for the DNS server. It's important to recognize that if there is no DNS server IP address configured, your Mac will not be able to resolve DNS host names.

As a convenience, many network settings are also available outside the Network preferences as menu items near the top-right corner of the screen. These network menu items also give nonadministrative users access to the most commonly needed network settings. An example of this is the frequently used Wi-Fi status menu, which allows you to select from the wireless networks within range of your Mac.

Using Network Locations

Similar to how applications are designed to save information to any number of individual documents, Lion allows you to save network settings to any number of individual network configurations known as network locations. A network location contains all network interface, service, and protocol settings, allowing you to configure as many unique network locations as you need for different situations. For example, you could create one network location for home and a different one for work. Each location would contain all the appropriate settings for that location's network situation.

A network location can contain any number of active network service interfaces. This allows you to define a single location with multiple network connections. The system will automatically prioritize multiple service interfaces based on a service order that you set. Details about using multiple network service interfaces are covered in the "Using Multiple Simultaneous Interfaces" section later in this chapter.

It is not necessary to add new network locations to change network settings, but it is more convenient as you can easily switch back to the previous network location should you make a mistake. Thus, creating additional network locations is an essential network troubleshooting technique. Also, because Lion always requires one active network location, if you ever want to temporarily turn off networking, you will have to create a new location with all the network service interfaces disabled.

Configuring Network Locations

The default network location on Lion is called Automatic. Despite this, this first location is no more automatic than any other network location you create. The initial location is simply called Automatic to indicate that it will attempt to automatically initialize any network service interface to establish a TCP/IP connection via DHCP, but all network locations regardless of their name attempt this as well.

To configure network locations:

1 Open the Network preferences by choosing Apple menu > System Preferences, then clicking the Network icon.

You may have to click the lock icon in the bottom-left corner and authenticate as an administrative user to unlock the Network preferences.

2 Choose Edit Locations from the Location pop-up menu.

This will reveal the interface for editing network locations.

3 To add a new location with default settings, click the small plus button at the bottom of the locations list, and then enter a new name for the location.

Or, you can duplicate an existing location by selecting its name from the locations list and clicking the gear icon at the bottom of the list, and then choosing Duplicate Location from the pop-up menu.

Finally, double-clicking on a location name will allow you to rename any location.

4   When you are finished making location changes, click the Done button to return to the Network preferences.

The Network preferences will automatically load the newly created location but won't apply the location settings to the system.

If you want to work with another location, simply choose it from the Locations pop-up menu, and the Network preferences will load it but won't apply it to the system.

5   Once you have completed all the necessary network location changes, click the Apply button at the bottom-right corner of the Network preferences to activate the currently selected network location.

TIP ▶ If you make a mistake at any time using Network preferences, click the Revert button in the bottom-right corner to return to the current active network configuration.

You may have noticed that the Network preferences are different from all the other system preferences in that you must click the Apply button to activate the new settings. This allows you to easily prepare new network locations and services without disrupting the current network configuration.

Changing Network Locations

Though you can certainly choose and apply a different network location from the Network preferences, only administrative users have this ability, as normal users do not have access to the Network preferences. Conversely, all users who can log in to the Lion graphical user interface can quickly and easily change the network location by choosing Apple menu > Locations > *location name* from the menu bar. This will apply the selected network location. Keep in mind that changing locations may interrupt network connections. Once a network location is selected, it will remain active until another location is selected. Even as other users log in to the Mac, or the Mac is restarted, the selected network location will remain active.

Using Network Service Interfaces

Mac hardware has a long history of providing built-in network connectivity. Apple started including Ethernet on Macs as early as 1991 and was the first manufacturer to have wireless as a built-in option when it introduced the iBook in 1999. Mac models have varied over the years as network technologies have grown increasingly faster and more affordable. You can identify the hardware network service interfaces available to your Mac from the /Applications/Utilities/System Information or /Applications/Utilities/Network Utility applications. Detecting network information and troubleshooting with Network Utility will be covered later in this chapter. Virtual network interface services, like those used for virtual private networks (VPNs) or link aggregation, will also be covered later in this chapter.

Lion includes built-in support for the following hardware network interfaces:

▶ Bluetooth—This relatively low-speed wireless interface has become popular as a short-range connectivity standard. Every recent Mac that includes Wi-Fi support also includes Bluetooth. Lion supports Bluetooth as a network bridge to some cellular network phones and hotspots, like iPhones, that can provide Internet connectivity via the cellular phone network.

▶ Ethernet—Ethernet is the family of IEEE 802.3 standards that define most modern wired LANs. Every Mac since 1997 has included standard built-in Ethernet connectivity, with some models even featuring multiple Ethernet ports. The lone exception to this rule is the current MacBook Air, which requires an optional Apple USB Ethernet Adapter.

▶ External (analog) modem—Although no currently shipping Mac includes an analog modem, it's available via an optional Apple External USB Modem and is still supported by Lion. For many years the analog modem was the standard method for home users to connect to the Internet. With the proliferation of high-speed and wireless Internet connections, analog modems are usually only necessary from the most remote of locations or to provide fax services.

▶ FireWire—FireWire is Apple's marketing name for the IEEE 1394 connection standard. Though not a common network standard, Lion includes software that allows you to create small ad hoc networks using daisy-chained FireWire cables. FireWire is standard on many Mac models.

▶ USB—While not technically a network connectivity standard, Lion supports a variety of USB adapters that provide cellular phone–based Internet access. Again, the iPhone is an example of such a device.

▶ Wi-Fi—Previously referred to by the Apple marketing name AirPort, Wi-Fi is the more common name for the family of IEEE 802.11 wireless standards, which have become the default implementation for most wireless LANs. The AirPort name is still used in reference to Apple's family of Wi-Fi network base stations, AirPort Express and AirPort Extreme. Every desktop and portable Mac since 2006 has included standard built-in Wi-Fi connectivity. Wi-Fi remains an option for the Mac Pro as well.

Using Multiple Simultaneous Interfaces

Lion supports a multilink networking architecture, which means that Lion supports multiple simultaneous network service interfaces. For example, you can have both an active wired Ethernet connection and an active Wi-Fi, or wireless Ethernet, connection at the same time. However, the first active service in the list is referred to as the primary network service interface, as it is used for all WAN connectivity, Internet connectivity, and DNS host name resolution.

Typically, having multiple active network service interfaces means you will also have multiple active IP addresses. To handle multiple IP addresses, Lion also features IP network multihoming. In fact, Lion supports multiple IP addresses for each physical network interface. Thus, the network service list can contain multiple instances of the same physical network interface. Again, a "network service" in this context is a single configuration of a physical network interface.

In other words, you can configure as many separate network service interfaces with as many unique IP addresses as you need. This may seem like overkill for most Mac clients, but remember OS X Lion and OS X Lion Server share the same underlying architecture. For some servers, multilink multihoming networking is a requirement, but Mac clients can also benefit from this technology. You may have a work environment where you have one insecure network for general Internet traffic and another network for secure internal transactions. With Lion, you can be on both of these networks at the same time.

When multiple IP addresses are available, the system can communicate via any of those network service interfaces but will attempt to pick the most appropriate route for every network connection. As described earlier, a network client will use the subnet mask to determine if an outgoing transmission is on the LAN. Lion takes this a step further by examining all active LANs when determining a destination for outgoing transmission. Because a LAN connection is always faster than a WAN connection, Lion will always route outgoing transmissions to the most appropriate LAN.

Any network connections that are not destined for a LAN that your Mac is connected to will be sent to the router address of the primary active network service interface, which is the topmost service listed in Network preferences. Again, this means the primary active network service interface is responsible for all WAN connections, Internet connections, and DNS host name resolution. Any active network service interface with a valid TCP/IP setting will be considered, but the primary active network service interface is automatically selected based on the network service order. You can manually configure the network service order, as outlined in the next section of this chapter.

Using the previous example where you have a Mac active on both wired Ethernet and Wi-Fi, the default network service order prioritizes wired Ethernet over Wi-Fi because wired is almost always faster. Thus, in this example, even though you have two active valid network service interfaces, the primary active network service interface will be the wired Ethernet connection.

> **NOTE ▸** Lion features automatic source routing. This means incoming connections to your Mac over a specific network service interface will always be responded to on the same interface, regardless of the service order.

Configuring Network Service Interfaces

Every time you open the Network preferences, the system identifies all available network service interfaces. Even if a physical network interface is not connected or properly configured, it will create a configuration for that interface, which will show up in the network services list. In the Network preferences, each network interface is tied to one or more network services.

A quick glance at the network services list clearly shows the status of all network interfaces and their configured services. Network services with a red indicator are not connected, a yellow indicator shows services that are connected but not properly configured, and a green indicator shows connected and configured network services. The active service at the top of this list is the primary network service interface as defined by the network service order. This list updates dynamically as new services become active or as active services become disconnected, so it's always the first place you should check when attempting to troubleshoot a network issue.

To manage network interfaces and their configured services:

1 Open and unlock the Network preferences.

   Choose the network location you wish to edit from the Locations pop-up menu, or configure a new network location, as detailed previously in this chapter.

2 To configure a particular network service, simply select it from the network services list.

Remember, each network service has its own settings separate from the other services. The configuration area to the right of the list will change to reflect primary options available to the selected service. Clicking the Advanced button in the bottom-right corner of the Network preferences will reveal all the network protocol options available to the selected network service. Network protocol configuration will be covered later in this chapter.

3 To make a service inactive, select it from the services list, click the gear icon at the bottom of the list, and then choose Make Service Inactive from the pop-up menu.

An inactive service will never activate even if connected and properly configured. You can also delete an existing network service by selecting its name from the services list and then clicking the minus button at the bottom of the list.

Deactivating or deleting a network service from this list is the only way to disable a hardware network interface in Lion.

4 To create another configurable instance of a network interface, click the small plus button at the bottom of the network services list.

This reveals a dialog that allows you to choose a new interface instance from the Interface pop-up menu and then assign it a unique service name to identify it in the services list. Click the Create button to continue. Or you can duplicate an existing network service by selecting its name from the services list, clicking the gear icon at the bottom of the list, then choosing Duplicate Service from the pop-up menu. Using this menu, you can also rename an existing network service.

Creating additional instances of a network service allows you to assign multiple IP addresses to a single network interface.

5   To change the network service order, click the gear icon at the bottom of the network services list, and then choose Set Service Order from the pop-up menu.

This reveals a dialog that allows you to click and drag network services into your preferred order for selection as the primary network interface. Click the OK button when you have finished reordering.

6   Once you have completed all the necessary network interface and service changes, click the Apply button at the bottom-right corner of the Network preferences to activate the currently selected network location.

TIP ▶ If you make a mistake at any time using the Network preferences, click the Revert button in the bottom-right corner to return to the currently active network configuration.

Using Virtual Network Services

A virtual network service is a logical network within a hardware network interface. Think of a virtual network service as providing another unique network interface by carving out a section of an established network connection.

Some virtual network services are used to increase security by encrypting data before it travels across an IP network, and others are used to segregate or aggregate network traffic across LAN connections. Lion includes the necessary client software that will allow you to connect to many common virtual network services and establish a virtual network service interface.

If necessary, you can define multiple separate virtual network service interfaces for each network location. Virtual network service interfaces are not always tied to a specific physical network interface, as the system will attempt to seek out the most appropriate route when there are multiple active connections. Likewise, any virtual network service interface that is not destined for a LAN connection will always be routed to the primary active network service interface.

> **NOTE ▸** Third-party virtualization tools, like Parallels Desktop and VMware Fusion, also use virtual network interfaces to provide networking for multiple simultaneous operating systems.

Lion includes built-in support for the following virtual network services:

- ▸ Point-to-Point Protocol over Ethernet (PPPoE)—Used by some service providers for directly connecting your Mac to a modem providing a high-speed Digital Subscriber Line (DSL) Internet connection.

- ▸ Virtual private network (VPN)—By far the most commonly used virtual network service, VPNs are primarily used to create secure virtual connections to private LANs over the Internet.

- ▸ Virtual local area network (VLAN)—Lion's VLAN implementation allows you to define separate independent LAN services on a single physical network interface.

- ▸ Link aggregation—Allows you to define a single virtual LAN service using multiple physical network interfaces.

- ▸ 6 to 4—Creates a VPN of sorts to transfer IPv6 packets across an IPv4 network. There is no enhanced security when using a 6 to 4 connection, but your Mac will appear to be directly connected to a remote IPv6 LAN. The differences between IPv4 and IPv6 were covered earlier in this chapter.

Configuring PPPoE

PPPoE is a connection protocol that encapsulates PPP packets inside standard Ethernet packets. This protocol is primarily used by high-speed DSL providers. You may or may not need to use PPPoE for your DSL connection.

To manage PPPoE connections:

1   Open and unlock the Network preferences.

Choose the network location you wish to edit from the Locations pop-up menu, or configure a new network location, as detailed previously in this chapter.

2   Click the small plus button at the bottom of the services list to add a PPPoE virtual network interface.

This will reveal a dialog allowing you to add a new network interface and service.

3   Choose PPPoE from the Interface pop-up menu.

PPPoE is tied to a specific Ethernet interface, so you must choose the specific interface that will be used for the PPPoE connection from the Ethernet pop-up menu. Finally, enter a descriptive name and click the Create button to make a new PPPoE virtual network interface and service.

4   Select the PPPoE service from the network services list to configure PPPoE settings.

Basic PPPoE configuration settings will appear to the right of the services list. At a minimum you will need to enter the account name and password given by the service provider. You should also probably check the "Remember this password" checkbox to save the PPPoE authentication information to the system keychain so other users don't have to remember it.

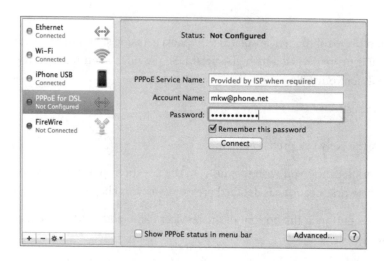

5   To configure advanced PPPoE settings, click the Advanced button in the bottom-right corner of the Network preferences. This reveals the advanced settings dialog. Click the PPP tab to view PPP-specific settings.

Because PPPoE is based on PPP, they share similar advanced configuration options. Probably the most significant settings are to optionally connect automatically when needed and to not disconnect when switching to another user account. Click the OK button when you have made all your selections.

6   Once you have completed all PPPoE settings, click the Apply button at the bottom-right corner of the Network preferences to save and activate the changes.

7   You can make accessing PPPoE connectivity options much easier by clicking the "Show PPPoE status in menu bar" checkbox. The PPPoE menu bar item allows you to easily connect, disconnect, and monitor PPPoE connections.

As you can see, PPPoE connections are not always on, the way other high-speed services are. Lion supports automatically connecting PPPoE when needed, but you can also manually connect and disconnect the PPPoE link from the PPPoE menu bar item or by clicking the Connect button in the Network preferences. Once the connection is established, the PPP process automatically configures TCP/IP and DNS settings. You can also manually configure these settings, as outlined later in this chapter. PPPoE services are automatically placed above all other services in the network service order, so as soon as the PPPoE service is connected and completely configured, it will be the primary network interface for all Internet traffic. Rearranging the network service order was covered previously in this chapter.

Configuring VPN

A VPN is an encrypted tunnel from your client to the network routing device providing the VPN service. Once it is established, your Mac will appear to have a direct connection to the LAN that the VPN device is sharing. So even if you're on a wireless Internet connection thousands of miles away from your LAN, a VPN connection provides a virtual network interface as if your computer were directly attached to that LAN. Lion supports three common VPN protocols: the Layer 2 Tunneling Protocol over Internet Protocol Security (L2TP over IPSec), Point-to-Point Tunneling Protocol (PPTP), and Cisco's version of IPSec.

> **NOTE ▶** Some VPN services require a third-party VPN client. Third-party VPN clients usually include a custom interface for managing the connection. Although you may see the virtual network interface provided by the third-party VPN client appear in the Network preferences, it's usually not configurable from there.

To manage VPN connections:

1 Open and unlock the Network preferences.

Choose the network location you wish to edit from the Locations pop-up menu, or configure a new network location, as detailed previously in this chapter.

2 To add a VPN interface, click the small plus button at the bottom of the services list.

This reveals a dialog that allows you to add a new network interface and service.

3   Choose VPN from the Interface pop-up menu.

You must choose the appropriate VPN protocol from the VPN Type pop-up menu. Again, Lion supports the L2TP over IPsec, PPTP, and Cisco IPSec VPN protocols. All three have similar configuration options, but for the purposes of this chapter L2TP will be used because it has a few more authentication and advanced options.

Finally, if you're going to have more than one type of VPN protocol, you may want to enter a descriptive name for the service. Otherwise, you can leave the service name as is because you can define multiple VPN configurations per VPN protocol. Click the Create button to make the new VPN virtual network interface and service.

4   To begin configuring VPN settings, select the VPN service from the network services list, and basic VPN configuration settings will appear to the right of the services list.

5   If you plan to have only one VPN configuration, leave the Configuration pop-up menu as is and continue to the next step. Multiple configurations are only needed if you will be switching between multiple VPN servers.

If you do want to set multiple VPN configurations, choose Add Configuration from the Configuration pop-up menu. This reveals a dialog where you can name and create a new VPN configuration. You can also delete and rename your configuration from this pop-up menu.

Continue editing VPN configurations. When finished, you will have to enter the settings for each VPN configuration, as outlined in the following steps.

6   To configure VPN settings, first enter the VPN server address and if you use user-based authentication, an account name. You must also define authentication methods by clicking the Authentication Settings button.

This will reveal a dialog allowing you to specify user and computer authentication settings. The VPN administrator should provide you with the appropriate authentication settings. Supplying a password here will add it to the system keychain. If the field is left blank, the user will be prompted for the password when connecting. Once you have made your selections, click the OK button to save the authentication settings.

7   To configure advanced VPN settings, click the Advanced button in the bottom-right corner of the Network preferences. In the advanced settings dialog that opens, click the Options tab to view general VPN options.

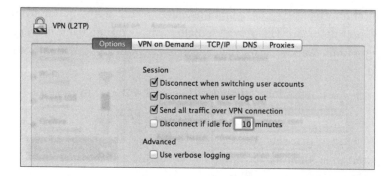

The most important optional setting is to send all traffic over the VPN connection. By default, active VPN connections will not act as the primary network interface, so the system will route traffic to the VPN only if the destination IP address is part of the LAN that the VPN service is providing or the VPN server supplies special routing information. Selecting the "Send all traffic over VPN connection" checkbox will force the VPN connection to act as the primary network interface.

8 If you are using certificate-based VPN authentication, then you can enable automatic VPN connections by clicking the VPN on Demand tab. The options on this tab allow you to assign domains that, when accessed, will automatically activate specific VPN configurations.

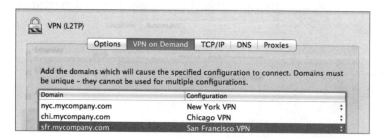

Click the small plus button at the bottom of the list to add a domain and an associated VPN configuration. Double-click on a domain name to change it, and click once on the VPN configuration name to choose an alternate configuration from the pop-up menu. When you have finished, click the OK button to save the VPN on Demand settings.

NOTE ▶ The built-in Cisco IPSec client does not feature any advanced options or VPN on demand settings.

9 Once you have completed all VPN settings, click the Apply button at the bottom-right corner of the Network preferences to save and activate the changes.

10 You can make accessing VPN connectivity options much easier by clicking the "Show VPN status in menu bar" checkbox. The VPN menu bar item allows you to easily select VPN configurations and connect, disconnect, and monitor VPN connections.

TIP VPN connections can be complicated and take a while to configure properly, so you can save time and prevent mistakes by using network configuration files. Click the gear icon at the bottom of the services list and use the Import and Export configuration menu options to use network configuration files.

TIP When troubleshooting VPN connections, it's useful to view the connection log info in /var/log/system.log. You can view the system log from the /Application/ Utilities/Console application.

VPN connections are not typically always-on connections. As you saw in the instructions, Lion supports automatic VPN connections with the VPN on Demand feature, but many users may still manually enable VPN connections when necessary. You can manually connect and disconnect the VPN link from the VPN menu bar item or by clicking the Connect button in the Network preferences. VPNs are usually implemented in situations where user authentication is required, so for many, initiating a VPN connection will prompt an authentication dialog.

Once the connection is authenticated and established, the VPN process will automatically configure TCP/IP and DNS settings using the PPP protocol. You can also manually configure these protocol settings, as outlined later in this chapter. VPN interfaces are, by default, set at the bottom of the network service order, so they will not automatically become the primary network interface when activated. This behavior is overridden when the optional "Send all traffic over VPN connection" checkbox is enabled, as covered in the instructions. You can also manually reorder the network service order, as explained previously in this chapter.

Configuring VLANs

VLANs are used to define separate independent logical LANs on a single network interface. In other words, your Mac could have a single Ethernet connection that allows it to simultaneously connect to multiple separate LANs. VLANs are configured in software, which gives network administrators much greater control over how network traffic is allocated and routed. VLAN services require special network infrastructure, but Lion includes the appropriate network client software to support VLANs. Lion supports the standard protocol used for VLAN configuration: the IEEE 802.1Q specification.

To manage VLANs:

1   Open and unlock the Network preferences.

Choose the network location you wish to edit from the Locations pop-up menu, or configure a new network location, as detailed previously in this chapter.

2   To add a VLAN interface, click the gear icon at the bottom of the services list and choose Manage Virtual Interfaces from the pop-up menu.

This will reveal a dialog allowing you to add a new virtual network interface and services. Click the small plus button at the bottom of the virtual interface list and then choose New VLAN from the pop-up menu.

3 The dialog will transition to the VLAN creation dialog.

Enter a recognizable name for the new VLAN, and select a tag as indicated by the network administrator. VLANs are tied to a specific wired Ethernet interface, so if you have multiple interfaces, you must specify one from the Interface pop-up menu. When you have finished configuring the VLAN, click the Create button to continue.

4 The dialog will transition back to the virtual interface dialog.

Here you can edit any virtual interface by double-clicking on its name. You can also delete a virtual interface by selecting it from the list and clicking the minus button at the bottom of the list.

When you have finished managing virtual interfaces, click the Done button.

5 Once you have completed all VLAN settings, click the Apply button at the bottom-right corner of the Network preferences to save and activate the changes.

If properly configured, the VLAN interface should activate a few moments after you click the Apply button. The VLAN interface will act like any other Ethernet interface and automatically attempt to configure using DHCP-supplied TCP/IP and DNS settings, but you can also manually configure these settings, as outlined later in this chapter. New virtual network interfaces are, by default, set at the bottom of the network service order, so they will not automatically become the primary network interface when activated. You can manually reorder the network service order as covered previously in this chapter.

Configuring Link Aggregation

Link aggregation, also known as interface bonding, allows you to define a single LAN interface using multiple separate hardware network interfaces. The advantage here is that you greatly increase network performance by using multiple physical connections. Link aggregation also increases network reliability by introducing connection redundancy, so if a network interface goes down there is at least one other interface to fall back on. Link aggregation services also require special network infrastructure, but again, Lion includes the appropriate network client software to support link aggregation. Lion supports the standard protocol used for link aggregation: the IEEE 802.3ad specification.

To manage link aggregation:

1   Open and unlock the Network preferences.

Choose the network location you wish to edit from the Locations pop-up menu, or configure a new network location, as detailed previously in this chapter.

2   To add a new aggregate virtual interface, click the gear icon at the bottom of the services list and choose Manage Virtual Interfaces from the pop-up menu.

This will reveal a dialog allowing you to add a new virtual network interface and service. Click the small plus button at the bottom of the virtual interface list and then choose New Link Aggregate from the pop-up menu.

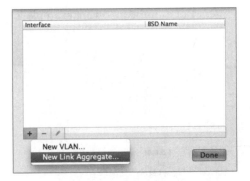

3 The dialog will transition to the link aggregate creation dialog.

Enter a recognizable name for the new aggregate interface, and select the check-boxes next to the Ethernet interfaces you want to bond together. Once bonded, these Ethernet interfaces cannot be used for another service. When you have finished configuring the aggregate interface, click the Create button to continue.

4 The dialog will transition back to the virtual interface dialog.

Here you can edit any virtual interface by double-clicking its name. You can also delete a virtual interface by selecting it from the list and clicking the minus button at the bottom of the list.

When you have finished managing virtual interfaces, click the Done button.

5 Once you have completed all link aggregation settings, click the Apply button at the bottom-right corner of the Network preferences to save and activate the changes.

If properly configured, the link aggregate interface should activate a few moments after you click the Apply button. You can check the status of the link aggregate interface by clicking the Advanced button in the bottom-right corner of the Network preferences, and then clicking the Bond Status tab. The Development Bond in the following example is obviously not properly configured.

The link aggregate interface will act like any other Ethernet interface and automatically attempt to configure using DHCP-supplied TCP/IP and DNS settings, but you can also manually configure these settings, as outlined later in this chapter. New virtual network interfaces are, by default, set at the bottom of the network service order, so they will not automatically become the primary network interface when activated. You can manually reorder the network service order, as explained earlier in this chapter.

Using Network Protocols

Each hardware or virtual network interface provides connectivity for a number of standard networking protocols. The Network preferences show primary protocol settings whenever you select a service from the services list, but many protocol configuration options are only available by clicking the Advanced button. The remainder of this section covers how to configure each built-in networking protocol supported by Lion.

NOTE ► AppleTalk is not supported on Mac OS X v10.6 or later.

Lion includes built-in support for the following network protocols:

► TCP/IP configured via DHCP—As explained previously in this chapter, TCP/IP is the primary network protocol for LANs and WANs, and DHCP is a popular network service that will automatically configure TCP/IP clients.

► TCP/IP configured manually—If you do not have DHCP service on your local network or if you want to ensure that the TCP/IP settings never change, you can manually configure TCP/IP settings.

► DNS—As covered previously, DNS provides host names for IP network devices. DNS settings are often configured alongside TCP/IP settings either by DHCP or manual configuration. Lion supports multiple DNS servers and search domains.

▶ Wireless Ethernet (Wi-Fi) protocol options—The wireless nature of Wi-Fi often requires additional configuration to facilitate network selection and authentication.

▶ Authenticated Ethernet via 802.1X—The 802.1X protocol is used to secure Ethernet networks (both wired and Wi-Fi) by allowing only properly authenticated network clients to join the LAN.

▶ Network Basic Input/Output System (NetBIOS) and Windows Internet Naming Service (WINS)—NetBIOS and WINS are protocols most often used by older Windows-based computers to provide network identification and service discovery.

▶ IP proxies—Proxy servers act as intermediaries between a network client and a requested service and are used to enhance performance or provide an additional layer of security.

▶ Ethernet hardware options—Lion supports both automatic and manual Ethernet hardware configuration.

▶ Cellular network connections—This isn't so much a specific network protocol as it is a general type of connection that uses a variety of protocols. Lion supports several methods for acquiring Internet access through cellular networks. This includes Bluetooth dial-up networking (DUN), Bluetooth personal area network (PAN), and USB cellular network adapters. The iPhone is an example of a device that can provide Internet access via a cellular phone network.

▶ External (analog) modem with PPP—For many years this was the only method for accomplishing any sort of digital computer-based communication. Lion still supports this, though the rarity of analog modems in the age of broadband Internet has put an end to coverage of analog modem configuration in this book.

▶ Point-to-Point Protocol (PPP)—PPP is an older protocol originally intended for use with analog modems. Again, Lion still supports PPP for analog modems, but it also supports PP for Bluetooth DUN, and PPPoE connectivity.

Manually Configuring TCP/IP and DNS

Many network situations do not require any manual intervention to configure TCP/IP and DNS, as the DHCP or PPP service will automatically acquire these settings. The default configuration for all Ethernet and Wi-Fi services is to automatically engage the DHCP process as soon as the interface port becomes active. To verify TCP/IP and DNS settings for hardware or virtual Ethernet services when using the DHCP service, simply select the service from the Network preferences.

> **NOTE** ▶ IPv6 addressing information is automatically detected as well if available. However, automatic IPv6 configuration is not provided by standard DHCP or PPP services.

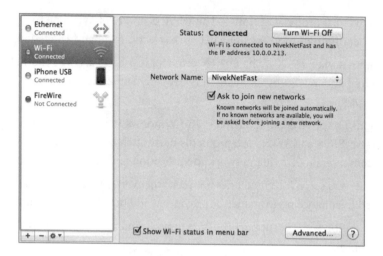

NOTE ▶ Automatically configured DNS settings will show as gray text. This indicates that you can override these settings by manually entering DNS information, as covered later in this section.

Service interfaces that may require a manual connection process, like Wi-Fi, analog modems, VPN, and PPPoE interfaces, will automatically engage the DHCP or PPP process to acquire TCP/IP and DNS settings. To verify TCP/IP and DNS settings when using these interfaces, select the service from the services list, and then click the Advanced button in the bottom-right corner of the Network preferences. This will open the advanced settings dialog, where you can click the TCP/IP or DNS tabs to view their respective settings. You can also verify network settings of any other interface this way.

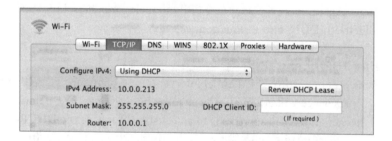

NOTE ▶ In some DHCP configurations, a DHCP client ID must be set. You can access this setting by clicking the Advanced button and then selecting the TCP/IP tab, as covered by steps 1 through 3 below.

Despite the convenience of automatic TCP/IP and DNS configuration, there may be times where manual configuration is required. For example, the network server providing the DHCP service will require a manual configuration. In fact, most network devices that provide services, like servers or printers, use manually entered network configuration information so they don't run the risk of changing to a different TCP/IP address should DHCP reset.

To manually configure TCP/IP and DNS settings:

1   Open and unlock the Network preferences.

Choose the network location you want to edit from the Locations pop-up menu, or configure a new network location, as detailed previously in this chapter.

2   Select the network service you wish to configure from the network services list.

If you selected an Ethernet interface, at this point you could configure TCP/IP settings from the general information area to the right of the services list, but for the purposes of this chapter you need to click the Advanced button in the bottom-right corner of the Network preferences to open the advanced settings dialog.

3   Click the TCP/IP tab at the top to view the TCP/IP settings.

4   If you want to keep using DHCP but manually assign the IP address, choose "Using DHCP with manual address" from the Configure IPv4 pop-up menu.

You will only have to manually enter an IPv4 address for the Mac, as the rest of the TCP/IP settings will remain as populated by DHCP. When you have entered the appropriate IP address, click the OK button to dismiss the advanced network options dialog, and then click the Apply button in the bottom-right corner of the Network preferences to save and activate the changes.

You can disregard the rest of these steps because the DHCP service will continue to manage the rest of the TCP/IP and DNS settings.

5 If you want to manually enter all TCP/IP settings, choose Manually from the Configure IPv4 pop-up menu.

At a minimum you will have to manually enter the IP address, the subnet mask (for this you can also use CIDR notation), and the router address. The user interface will cache the TCP/IP settings from the DHCP service, so you may only have to enter a new IPv4 address.

6 If you have to manually set up IPv6 settings as well, choose Manually from the Configure IPv6 pop-up menu.

At a minimum you will have to manually enter the IPv6 address, router address, and prefix length. The user interface will cache any automatic IPv6 settings, so you may only have to enter a new IPv6 address.

7 To configure DNS, click the DNS tab at the top to view the DNS settings. Again, the user interface will cache the DNS settings from the DHCP service, so you may not have to enter any DNS settings at all.

NOTE ▶ If the IP address of a DNS server is not specified, then the Mac will not be able to resolve DNS host names.

If configuring manually, you should configure at least one DNS server. Click the plus button at the bottom of the DNS server list to add a new server, and then enter the server's IP address. Entering a search domain is optional. Click the plus button at the bottom of the Search Domains list, and then enter the domain name.

If you configure multiple DNS servers or search domains, the system will attempt to access those resources in the order in which they appear in the list. To edit an address, double-click on its entry in the list, or you can delete an entry by selecting it and clicking the minus button at the bottom of the list.

8   When you have entered all the appropriate IP and DNS settings, click the OK button to dismiss the advanced network options dialog, and then click the Apply button in the bottom-right corner of the Network preferences to save and activate the changes.

Whenever you manually configure TCP/IP or DNS settings, you should always test network connectivity to verify that you properly entered all information. Using standard applications to access network and Internet resources is one basic test, but you could also test more thoroughly using the included network diagnostic utilities. Using network diagnostic tools built into Lion is covered later in this chapter.

Basic Wi-Fi Configuration

Apple made basic wireless Ethernet (Wi-Fi) network management a breeze with automatic Wi-Fi network discovery and the Wi-Fi status menu. By default, if you start up or wake your Mac, and it cannot establish a valid network connection, the system will automatically scan for new local Wi-Fi networks. If the Mac discovers an open wireless network that doesn't require authentication, it will automatically connect to that network. However, if wireless networks requiring authentication are found or multiple new networks are found, the system will then prompt the user to join a Wi-Fi network.

If the Mac doesn't automatically prompt you for Wi-Fi configuration, then you can manually select a wireless network from the Wi-Fi status menu. When you select this menu, the Wi-Fi background process will automatically scan for any advertised networks that are within range for you to choose from. Aside from Wi-Fi network names, the most important indicator this menu shows is the relative strength of any Wi-Fi network, as indicated by the number of black bars to gray bars. The more black bars displayed, the higher the relative strength of the Wi-Fi signal.

> **MORE INFO** ▶ The Wi-Fi menu is capable of several tricks, including helping you quickly identify network issues, as outlined in Knowledge Base article HT3821, "Mac OS X 10.6 Snow Leopard: The AirPort status menu (AirPort Menu Extra) FAQ."

If you select an open wireless network, the Mac will immediately connect, but if you select a secure wireless network, as indicated by the small lock icon, you will have to enter the network password. When you select a secure network, in most cases the system will automatically negotiate the authentication type, and for many networks you need only enter a common shared Wi-Fi password. By default, if you join a Wi-Fi network as an administrative user, the system will automatically remember secure networks by saving the passwords to the system keychain. This will later allow the Mac to automatically connect to the Wi-Fi network so all users can access the wireless network without needing to re-enter the password.

If you join and authenticate to a wireless network that uses WAP or WAP2 Enterprise, it's implied that the authentication is handled via 802.1X. Thus, joining this type of network will automatically create an 802.1X service configuration. As you can see in the following screenshot, when 802.1X is used you must enter both a username and password to authenticate the connection. You may also be prompted with a certificate verification dialog that requires administrative authentication to bypass. Again, the system will save this information to the system keychain by default.

MORE INFO ▶ Additional configuration of 802.1X is covered in the "Using 802.1X" section later in this chapter.

In some cases, to increase security, wireless networks may not advertise their availability. You can connect to these hidden wireless networks (also called closed networks) as long as you know their network name (or Service Set Identifier, aka SSID) by choosing Join Other Network from the Wi-Fi status menu. This will reveal a dialog where you can enter all the appropriate information to join the hidden wireless network.

Lastly, if you are unable to connect to a standard wireless network, you can create an ad hoc wireless network using your Mac's Wi-Fi connection to share files wirelessly with other computers. Choose Create Network from the Wi-Fi status menu and then enter the wireless network information that will be used to connect to your ad hoc network.

NOTE ▸ It is a security risk to leave an ad hoc network enabled on your Mac. To disable the ad hoc network, turn off the Wi-Fi hardware or choose another wireless network from the Wi-Fi status menu.

NOTE ▸ Do not confuse the creation of an ad hoc Wi-Fi network with Lion's new AirDrop Wi-Fi sharing feature. Creating a Wi-Fi network has permanence, and it can be used by other non-Lion systems, while AirDrop allows for only temporary connections between Lion systems. You can find out more about AirDrop in Chapter 7, "Network Services."

Advanced Wi-Fi Configuration

Some administrators may find the need to restrict some of the wireless features. You may want to require that the Mac connect only to specific secure wireless networks, or that the Mac always connect to one particular network. In these situations, you will access the advanced Wi-Fi configuration options in the Network preferences.

To manage advanced Wi-Fi options and connections:

1 Open and unlock the Network preferences.

Choose the network location you wish to edit from the Locations pop-up menu, or configure a new network location, as detailed previously in this chapter.

2 Select the Wi-Fi service from the services list.

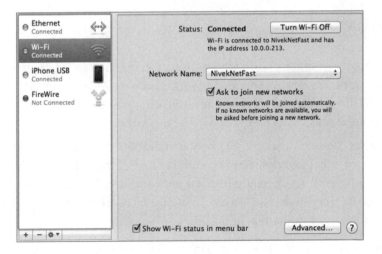

At this point you can configure basic Wi-Fi settings in a manner similar to how you would do it from the Wi-Fi status menu, including the ability to join or create another wireless network, from the Network Name pop-up menu.

3   You can also prevent nonadministrative users from accessing Wi-Fi settings by disabling the following:

▶   Deselecting the "Ask to join new networks" checkbox will prevent the user from being prompted when the Mac can't find a preconfigured wireless network but there are other networks in the area.

▶   Deselecting the "Show Wi-Fi status in menu bar" checkbox will disable the Wi-Fi status menu; however, this won't prevent a user from choosing a wireless network if the Mac presents a wireless discovery dialog.

4   Click the Advanced button in the bottom-right corner of the Network preferences to reveal the advanced settings dialog. If the Wi-Fi tab at the top is not selected, then click it to view the advanced Wi-Fi settings.

From the top half of the advanced Wi-Fi settings pane, you can create a list of preferred wireless networks. By default, wireless networks that were added previously will appear here as well. If you disable user access to Wi-Fi settings as described in step 3, the system will connect only to the preferred wireless networks in this list.

To add a new wireless network, click the plus button at the bottom of the preferred network list, and then either join a wireless network in range or manually enter the information for a hidden or not-currently-in-range network. To edit a network, simply double-click on its entry in the list, or you can delete a network by selecting it and clicking the minus button at the bottom of the list.

5   At the bottom of the advanced Wi-Fi settings pane you have several settings that allow for more specific Wi-Fi administration options. Thus, if you choose to leave the

Wi-Fi status menu available to regular users, you can restrict certain settings to only administrative users.

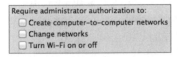

6 When you have entered the appropriate Wi-Fi settings, click the OK button to dismiss the advanced settings dialog, and then click the Apply button in the bottom-right corner of the Network preferences to save and activate the changes.

Using 802.1X

The 802.1X protocol is used to secure both wired and wireless (Wi-Fi) Ethernet networks by only allowing properly authenticated network clients to join the LAN. Networks using 802.1X will not allow any traffic until the network client properly authenticates to the network.

To facilitate 802.1X authentication, Lion provides two methods for automatic configuration:

▶ User-selected Wi-Fi network with WPA or WPA2 Enterprise authentication—As covered previously, if a Wi-Fi network is selected that uses WPA or WPA2 Enterprise authentication, the system will automatically configure 802.1X. You can verify the 802.1X configuration by selecting Wi-Fi in the Network preferences, though you cannot modify the connection details in any way.

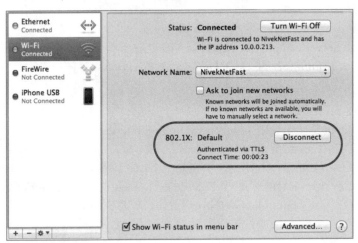

▶ Administrator-provided 802.1X configuration profile—The 802.1X architecture often relies on shared secrets or certificates to validate client connections; thus a network administrator must securely deploy these items to client computers. In Lion, the only mechanism for non-Wi-Fi or managed 802.1X configuration is via a configuration profile. This profile can be deployed by simply double-clicking a local copy of a configuration profile, or by having the Mac managed by a Mobile Device Management (MDM) solution. From the local Mac, however, you can verify the 802.1X configuration by selecting the 802.1X tab among the advanced configuration panes of the Network preferences.

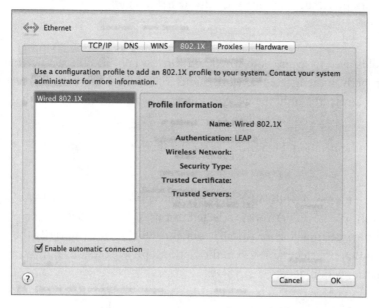

MORE INFO ▶ Lion Server can provide MDM services through Profile Manager, as covered in *Apple Pro Training Series: OS X Lion Server Essentials*.

Configuring NetBIOS and WINS

Network Basic Input/Output System (NetBIOS) and Windows Internet Naming Service (WINS) run on top of TCP/IP to provide network identification and service discovery. NetBIOS and WINS are used primarily by legacy Windows-based systems to provide identification and service discovery on LANs, while WINS is used to identify and locate NetBIOS network devices on WANs. You can think of WINS as a form of DNS for NetBIOS network clients.

Modern Windows networks now use Dynamic DNS as a solution for network client discovery, but Lion still supports NetBIOS and WINS to support legacy network configurations. Further, these discovery protocols are mainly used to provide naming for the Server Message Block (SMB) protocol commonly used to share files and printers. In other words, the NetBIOS name is there to provide support for SMB sharing services hosted from your Mac, as covered in Chapter 7, "Network Services."

NOTE ▸ Lion supports NetBIOS and WINS on any active network interface except for VPN connections.

Lion automatically configures your computer's NetBIOS name based on your Mac's sharing name, and for many networks this should be sufficient. If your Mac is on a larger legacy Windows network and you want to share resources from your Mac with other network clients, you may want to manually select the NetBIOS workgroup. NetBIOS workgroups are used to make navigation easier on large networks by grouping devices into smaller collections. You may have to manually configure the WINS service to provide faster NetBIOS resolution.

NOTE ▸ It's not required to configure NetBIOS and WINS in order to connect to Windows resources. For certain legacy Windows clients, however, it may help when attempting to connect to those resources.

To manually configure NetBIOS and WINS settings:

1 Open and unlock the Network preferences.

Choose the network location you wish to edit from the Locations pop-up menu, or configure a new network location, as detailed previously in this chapter.

2 Select the network service you wish to configure from the network services list, and then click the Advanced button in the bottom-right corner of the Network references.

3 In the advanced settings dialog that opens, click the WINS tab at the top to view the NetBIOS and WINS settings.

4   To manually configure NetBIOS, enter a unique name, and then choose a workgroup from the pop-up menu.

It may take a while for the NetBIOS workgroup list to refresh, thus preventing you from selecting it via the pop-up menu. If you already know the name of the workgroup you want the Mac to be in, you can manually enter the workgroup name.

NOTE ▸ NetBIOS names and workgroup names are in all capital letters and cannot contain any special characters or spaces.

5   To enable WINS, enter at least one WINS server IP address. Click the plus button at the bottom of the WINS server list to add a new server, and then enter the server's IP address.

If you configure multiple WINS servers, the system will attempt to access those resources in the order in which they appear in the list. To edit a server address, double-click its entry in the list, or you can delete a server by selecting it and clicking the minus button at the bottom of the list.

6   When you have entered all the appropriate NetBIOS and WINS settings, click the OK button to dismiss the advanced network options dialog, and then click the Apply button in the bottom-right corner of the Network preferences to save and activate the changes.

Configuring IP Proxies

Proxy servers act as intermediaries between a network client and a requested service. Proxy servers are often used to enhance the performance of slow WAN or Internet connections by caching recently requested data so future connections appear faster to local network clients.

Primarily, though, proxy servers are implemented so network administrators can limit network connections to unauthorized servers or resources. Administrators can manage lists of approved resources, having the proxy servers allow access only to those resources.

Lion supports proxy services for File Transfer Protocol (FTP), web protocols (HTTP and HTTPS), streaming (RTSP), SOCKS, and Gopher. For proxy configuration, Lion supports manual configurations, automatic proxy configuration using local or network-hosted proxy auto-config (PAC) files, and full auto proxy discovery via the Web Proxy Autodiscovery Protocol (WPAD).

NOTE ▶ It's highly likely that you will have to acquire specific proxy configuration instructions from a network administrator.

To configure proxy settings:

1 Open and unlock the Network preferences.

Choose the network location you wish to edit from the Locations pop-up menu, or configure a new network location, as detailed previously in this chapter.

2 Select the network service you wish to configure from the network services list, and then click the Advanced button in the bottom-right corner of the Network preferences.

This will reveal the advanced settings dialog.

3 Click the Proxies tab at the top to view the proxy settings.

4 At this point you will perform one of three routines based on your network's proxy implementation:

▶ If your proxy service supports the Web Proxy Autodiscovery Protocol (WPAD), then simply enable the Auto Proxy Discovery checkbox.

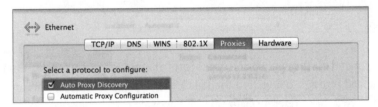

▶ If you have access to a proxy auto-config (PAC) file, enable the Automatic Proxy Configuration checkbox at the bottom of the proxy protocols list. You must then specify a PAX proxy configuration file. To specify a local file, click the Choose File button and then select the file using the file browser dialog. To specify a network-hosted file, enter the full network path to the file in the URL field.

▶ To manually configure proxy settings, select the checkboxes next to each protocol you wish to send through the proxy servers. Select each protocol individually to enter the proxy connection information provided by the network administrator. At the bottom you can also elect to bypass the proxy for specific additional hosts and domains.

5 When you have entered all the appropriate proxy information, click the OK button to dismiss the advanced settings dialog, and then click the Apply button in the bottom-right corner of the Network preferences to save and activate the changes.

Manually Configuring Ethernet Hardware

Ethernet connections are designed to establish connection settings automatically. Yet Lion allows you to manually configure Ethernet options from the Network preferences should the automatic selections prove problematic. The most common case for this is when you have an environment with fast gigabit Ethernet switches and old or substandard wired infrastructure. In this case it's common for the Mac to attempt to automatically establish a gigabit connection but ultimately fail because the wired infrastructure doesn't support the high speeds. The most common symptom is that even with the Ethernet switch showing that the Mac has an active connection, Network preferences on the Mac show Ethernet as disconnected.

To manually configure Ethernet settings:

1   Open and unlock the Network preferences.

Choose the network location you wish to edit from the Locations pop-up menu, or configure a new network location, as detailed previously in this chapter.

2   Select the Ethernet service you wish to configure from the network services list, and then click the Advanced button in the bottom-right corner of the Network preferences.

This will reveal the advanced settings dialog.

3   Click the Hardware tab at the top to view the current automatically configured Ethernet hardware settings.

4   To manually configure Ethernet options, choose Manually from the Configure pop-up menu. The system will cache the current automatically configured Ethernet settings so you will not have to change all the settings.

The system will prepopulate the Speed, Duplex, and MTU Ethernet options based on your Mac's network hardwire. Make your custom selections from these pop-up menus.

5   When you have selected all the appropriate Ethernet hardware settings, click the OK button to dismiss the advanced settings dialog, and then click the Apply button in the bottom-right corner of the Network preferences to save and activate the changes.

Using Cellular Internet Connections

Internet access via cellular networks is nothing new, but in the last few years this type of connectivity has seen a huge growth in popularity. With most major carriers offering ever-faster near-broadband speeds and expanded geographical coverage, many are relying on cellular networks as their primary Internet access. As such, a variety of devices and methods are available for providing cellular Internet access for your Mac computer.

NOTE ► The capabilities and configuration of cellular devices vary greatly. Check with your cellular device vendor regarding how to enable Internet access for your specific device.

Lion supports use of cellular Internet connections via:

► Bluetooth dial-up networking (DUN) with PPP—Older cellular phones allow for Internet connectivity via dial-up networking (DUN) with a PPP connection channeled through Bluetooth wireless. Configuring a Bluetooth DUN connection is similar to configuring an analog modem, as these connections also use PPP as a control and transport mechanism for the TCP/IP connection. Only one extra step is required: pairing your Mac to the cellular phone providing the Internet access via Bluetooth. If you have already paired your Bluetooth-enabled mobile phone to your Mac, then all you have to do is enter the rest of the connection information as if you were configuring an analog modem. Again, your cellular service provider usually provides the configuration information. Otherwise, follow the instructions presented in Chapter 8, "Peripherals and Printing," to pair your Mac to a Bluetooth-enabled cellular phone.

▶ Bluetooth personal area network (PAN)—Modern cellular devices allow for Internet connectivity by acting as a small router providing a personal area network (PAN) available via Bluetooth wireless. For example, an iPhone can provide Internet access via Bluetooth PAN. As with Bluetooth DUN, you must first pair your Mac with the mobile device as covered in Chapter 8, "Peripherals and Printing." Once paired, configuration should be automatic as the Mac should configure TCP/IP using DHCP hosted from the cellular device. You will have to initiate the connection by clicking the Connect button in Network preferences or by choosing the device and "Connect to Network" in the Bluetooth status menu.

▶ USB cellular network adapters—Again, USB is not technically a network connectivity standard, but Lion supports a variety of USB adapters that provide cellular phone–based Internet access. The iPhone is an example of such a device, and in typical Apple fashion all configuration on the Mac is automatic. Simply plug an iPhone in via the USB adapter cable, and then on the iPhone turn on the Personal Hotspot feature. Conversely, third-party cellular Internet devices vary, and many require the installation and configuration of third-party drivers.

▶ Wi-Fi personal area network—In a move to simplify the connection and configuration of cellular Internet devices, many can act as a small Wi-Fi router. Thus, any device that supports Wi-Fi can connect to the cellular device without any special software. On the Mac, simply select the Wi-Fi network the cellular device is hosting and

provide authentication if necessary. Inspecting the Wi-Fi connection in Network preferences reveals that the cellular Internet device appears identical to a traditional Wi-Fi
router. Again, an iPhone can provide cellular Internet access via Wi-Fi.

Troubleshooting Network Configuration

The most important thing to remember about troubleshooting network issues is that it is
often not the computer's fault. There are many other points of failure to consider when
dealing with LAN and Internet connection issues. So the second most important thing
to remember about troubleshooting network issues is to isolate the cause of the problem
before attempting generic resolutions.

To help isolate network issues, you can categorize them into three general areas:

▶ Local issues—These are usually related to either improperly configured network settings or disconnected network connections.

▶ Network issues—These are by far the hardest to nail down, as there could be literally
hundreds of points of failure involved. It always helps to be familiar with the physical
topology of your network. Start by checking the devices that provide network access
closest to your Mac. Something as simple as a bad Ethernet port on a network switch
can cause problems. As you move on to investigating devices farther away from your
Mac, you will find that it's often easiest to start your investigation using the network
diagnostic utilities included with Lion.

▶ Service issues—These issues are related to the actual network device or service you
are trying to access. For example, the devices providing DHCP or DNS services
could be temporarily down or improperly configured. It's often easy to determine if
the problem is with the service alone by testing other network services. If the other
network services work, you're probably not dealing with network or local issues.
Again, Lion provides some useful diagnostic tools for testing service availability.
Troubleshooting network services is also covered in Chapter 7, "Network Services."

You will be using three main tools for diagnosing network issues in Lion: the Network
preferences, Network Diagnostics Assistant, and Network Utility.

Troubleshooting via Network Preferences

The first diagnostic tool you should always check is the Network preferences. Network preferences features a dynamically updating list that will show you the current status of any network interface. If a network connection is not working, you will find out about it here first.

Network status indicators include:

▶ Green status—The connection is active and configured with TCP/IP settings. This, however, does not guarantee that the service is using the proper TCP/IP settings. For instance, in the previous screenshot of the Network preferences, you'll note that the Ethernet service appears with a green status, indicating proper TCP/IP settings.

▶ Yellow status—The connection is active but the TCP/IP settings are not properly configured. For example, if you look at the previous screenshot, the Wi-Fi service is using a link-local TCP/IP configuration, indicating this interface is not receiving proper configuration from the DHCP service. If you are still experiencing problems with this service, double-check the network settings. If the settings appear sound, move on to the other diagnostic utilities.

▶ Red status—This status usually indicates either improperly configured network settings or disconnected network interfaces. If this is an always-on interface, check for proper physical connectivity. If this is a virtual or PPP connection, double-check the settings and attempt to reconnect.

TIP ▶ Remember that the network service interface order plays a huge part in how the Mac routes network traffic. Specifically, the primary network service is the one that will be used to reach the Internet and primary DNS resolution. Become familiar with how the Mac uses multiple network connections, as covered earlier in this chapter.

Using Network Diagnostics Assistant

Lion includes Network Diagnostics Assistant to help you troubleshoot common network issues. Some networking applications will automatically open this assistant when they encounter a network issue. You can also open it manually by clicking the Assist Me button at the bottom of the Network preferences, and then clicking the Diagnostics button.

Network Diagnostics Assistant will ask you a few simple questions about your network setup, and then, based on your answers, it will run a battery of tests to determine where the problem might be occurring. Test results are displayed using colored indicators on the left side of the window. If there are problems, the assistant makes suggestions for resolution. In the following example, the modem connection has failed and Network Diagnostics Assistant is suggesting that you double-check your modem settings.

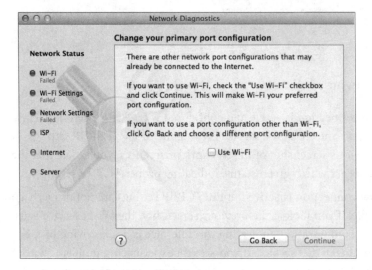

Using Network Utility

The Network preferences and Network Diagnostics Assistant are good places to start troubleshooting network issues, but the most powerful application in Lion for diagnosing network issues is /Applications/Utilities/Network Utility. Network Utility provides an array of popular network identification and diagnostic tools. In fact, most of the tools in Network Utility are based on UNIX command-line network utilities that have been used by network administrators for years.

Network Utility is broken up into the following sections:

▶   Info—Allows you to inspect details regarding hardware network interfaces.

▶   Netstat—Shows routing information and network statistics.

▶   Ping—This fundamental network troubleshooting tool lets you test network connectivity and latency.

- ► Lookup—Lets you test DNS resolution.
- ► Traceroute—Helps you analyze how your network connections are routed to their destination.
- ► Whois—Lets you query whois database servers and find the owner of a DNS domain name or IP address of registered hosts.
- ► Finger—Enables you to gather information based on a user account name from a network service.
- ► Port Scan—A handy tool for determining if a network device has services available.

Network Utility can also be opened when your Mac is started from Lion Recovery as covered in Chapter 1, "Installation and Configuration." Any time the Mac is started from Lion Recovery, you can open Network Utility by choosing it from the Utilities menu. However, when running from a Lion Recovery system, you do not have access to the Network preferences. This means that the Mac will automatically activate built-in wired Ethernet connections and attempt to acquire configuration via DHCP. Alternately, the Wi-Fi status menu is available, allowing you to temporarily connect to wireless networks.

Network Utility: Interface Information

When you open Network Utility, you will first see the Info section. This section lets you view the detailed status of any hardware network interface. Even if you've opened Network Utility to use another section, always take a few moments to verify that the network interface is properly activated.

Start by selecting the specific interface you're having issues with from the pop-up menu. You'll notice the selections here do not necessarily match the service names given in the Network preferences. Instead, this menu shows the interfaces using their interface type and UNIX-given names. When working properly, the en0 interface should be the first internal Ethernet port, and in most cases the en1 interface is the Wi-Fi interface. If you have a Mac with two internal Ethernet ports, the second internal port will be en1 and the Wi-Fi interface will be bumped to en2. The FireWire interface will be labeled as fw0.

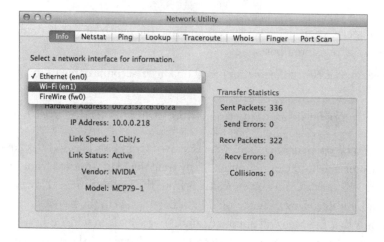

Once you have selected an interface, you can view general interface information to the left and transfer statistics to the right. The primary pieces of information you're looking for here are Link Status, Link Speed, and IP Address(es). Only active hardware network interfaces will show as such, and the link speed will indicate if the interface is establishing a proper connection. Obviously, a proper IP address is required to establish a TCP/IP connection. You can also identify the selected interface's MAC address, which is used to identify this particular interface on the LAN.

As a final validation of the selected network interface, you can view recent transfer statistics. If you open other network applications to stir up some network traffic, you will be able to verify that packets are being sent and received from this interface. If you are seeing activity here but still experiencing problems, the issue is most likely due to a network or service problem and not the actual network interface. Or, if this interface is experiencing transfer errors, a local network hardware connectivity issue may be the root of your problem.

To resolve hardware network interface issues, always start by checking the physical connection. With wired networks, try different network ports or cabling to rule out physical connection issues. With wireless networks, double-check the Wi-Fi settings and the configuration of any wireless base stations. On rare occasions, you may find that the Mac's network hardware is somehow no longer working properly, in which case you should take your Mac to an Apple Authorized Service Provider.

Network Utility: Ping

If you have determined that your network settings are properly configured and the hardware network interface appears to be working correctly, but you are still experiencing network issues, your next step is to test network connectivity using the ping tool. The ping tool is the most fundamental network test to determine if your Mac can successfully send and receive data to another network device. Your Mac will send a ping data packet to the destination IP address, and the other device should return the ping packet to indicate connectivity.

To use ping:

1   Open /Applications/Utilities/Network Utility, and then click the Ping tab at the top.

2   Enter the IP address or host name of a network device to test connectivity to that device.

Start by entering an IP address to a device on the LAN that should always be accessible, like the network router.

Remember, using a domain name assumes that your Mac is properly communicating with a DNS server, which might not be the case if you're troubleshooting connectivity issues.

3   Click the Ping button to initiate the ping process.

If the ping is successful, it should return the amount of time it took for the ping to travel to the network device and back. This is typically within milliseconds; experiencing ping times any longer than a full second is unusual.

4   Once you have established successful pings to local devices, you can branch out to WAN or Internet addresses.

Using the ping tool, you may find that everything works except for the one service you were looking for that prompted you to start troubleshooting the network.

NOTE ▸ Some network administrators view excessive pinging as a threat, so many configure their firewalls to block pings or network devices to not respond to any network pings.

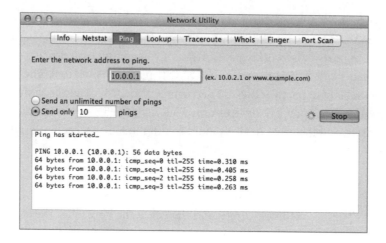

Network Utility: Lookup

If you are able to successfully ping other network devices by their IP address, but attempting to connect to another device by its host name doesn't work, then you are experiencing issues related to DNS. The network lookup process will allow you to test name resolution against your DNS server.

To use lookup:

1   Open /Applications/Utilities/Network Utility, and then click the Lookup tab at the top.

2   Enter the IP address or host name of a network device to test DNS resolution.

Start by entering the host name of a device or service in your local domain. If you can resolve local host names but not Internet host names, this indicates that your local DNS server is resolving local names but it's not properly connecting to the worldwide DNS network.

If you don't have a local domain, you can use any Internet host name.

3   Click the Lookup button to initiate the network lookup process.

A successful forward lookup will return the IP address of the host name you entered. A successful reverse lookup will return the host name of the IP address you entered.

4   If you are unable to successfully return any lookups, this means that your Mac is not connecting to the DNS server. You can verify this by pinging the DNS server IP address to test for basic connectivity.

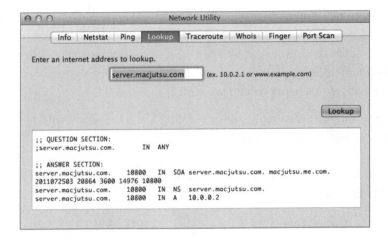

NOTE ► The Network Utility lookup feature is not designed to test Bonjour resolution; thus it cannot resolve ".local" names.

Network Utility: Traceroute

If you are able to connect to some network resources but not others, you should use the network traceroute utility to determine where the connection is breaking down. Remember that WAN and Internet connections require the data to travel through many network routers to find their destination. The traceroute tool will examine every network hop between routers using the ping tool to determine where connections fail or slow down.

To use traceroute:

1   Open /Applications/Utilities/Network Utility, and then click the Traceroute tab at the top.

2   Enter the IP address or host name of a network device to trace the connectivity to that device.

   Start by entering an IP address to a device on the LAN that should always be accessible, like the network router.

   Remember, using a domain name assumes that your Mac is properly communicating with a DNS server, which might not be the case if you're troubleshooting connectivity issues.

3   Click the Trace button to initiate the traceroute process.

If traceroute is successful, it should return with the list of routers required to complete the connection and the amount of time it took for the ping to travel to each network router. Note that it sends three probes at each distance, so three times will be listed for each hop. Again, the delay is typically measured within milliseconds; experiencing delay times of any longer than a full second is unusual.

NOTE ▸ If traceroute doesn't get a reply from any router along the way, it will show an asterisk instead of listing the router address.

4 Once you have established successful routes to local devices, you can branch out to WAN or Internet addresses.

Using the traceroute tool, you may find that a specific network router is the cause of the problem.

NOTE ▸ Some network administrators view excessive pinging as a threat, so many configure their firewalls to block pings or set up network devices to not respond to any network pings.

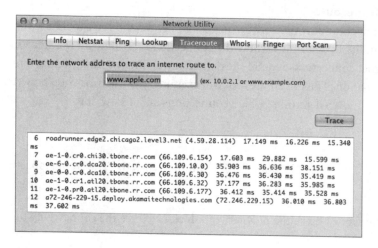

What You've Learned

▸ The Internet protocol suite, TCP/IP, provides the basis for nearly all local area and wide area networks. DHCP provides automatic configuration for TCP/IP networks, and DNS provides local and worldwide TCP/IP host naming.

▶ Lion supports a wide array of hardware network interfaces, virtual network interfaces, and network protocols, all managed via the Network preferences.

▶ Lion includes a variety of network troubleshooting tools, among them the Network preferences, Network Diagnostics Assistant, and Network Utility.

References

You can check for new and updated Knowledge Base documents at www.apple.com/support.

General Network

TS1629, "'Well-known' TCP and UDP ports used by Apple software products"

HT3152, "Apple USB Modem: Frequently asked questions (FAQ)"

TA20531, "Mac OS X: Frequently Asked Questions (FAQ) for PPP Modem Connections"

TA20530, "Mac OS X: DSL/PPPoE Frequently Asked Questions (FAQ)"

HT3821, "Mac OS X 10.6 Snow Leopard: The AirPort status menu (AirPort Menu Extra) FAQ"

Network Troubleshooting

HT1714, "Mac OS X: Connect to the Internet, troubleshoot your Internet connection, and set up a small network"

HT4628, "Troubleshooting Wi-Fi issues"

TS1843, "Mac OS: Troubleshooting 'A connection failure has occurred', 'The specified server could not be found' or Similar Messages"

TS3798, "Internet connection does not work with an IP address space of 169.254.xxx.xxx from ISP, router, or manual configuration"

TS2756, "iPhone: Troubleshooting Personal Hotspot"

URLs

Wikipedia entry about the OSI reference model: http://en.wikipedia.org/wiki/OSI_model

IEEE's searchable database of OUIs used for MAC addresses: http://standards.ieee.org/regauth/oui/index.shtml

Wikipedia entry for CIDR notation:
http://en.wikipedia.org/wiki/Classless_Inter-Domain_Routing

Wikipedia entry about the Internet protocol suite:
http://en.wikipedia.org/wiki/Internet_protocol_suite

Wikipedia entry about DNS: http://en.wikipedia.org/wiki/Domain_Name_System

Wikipedia entry about DHCP: http://en.wikipedia.org/wiki/Dhcp

Review Quiz

1. What do the terms *interface, protocol,* and *service* mean in relation to computer networks?

2. What is the purpose of Internet Protocol (IP) addresses and subnet masks? What is their format?

3. How does the IP use the MAC address to send messages between computers on a local area network (LAN)?

4. How does the IP transfer messages between computers over a wide area network (WAN)?

5. How is the Domain Name Service (DNS) used to facilitate network naming?

6. How do network devices acquire and use link-local TCP/IP addresses?

7. What interfaces and protocols are supported by default in Lion?

8. How does network service order affect network connectivity?

9. In the Network preferences, how can you tell which interface is currently being used for network activities?

10. What functionality does Lion support with the AppleTalk protocol?

11. What are four common issues that can interrupt network services on a Mac computer?

12. How can you identify the MAC addresses for all of the Mac's network interfaces?

Answers

1. An *interface* is any channel through which network data can flow. Hardware network interfaces are defined by physical network connections, while virtual network interfaces are logical network connections that ride on top of hardware network connections. A *protocol* is a set of rules used to describe a specific type of network

communication. Protocols are necessary for separate network devices to communicate properly. Finally, a network *service* (as it pertains to the Network preferences) is the collection of settings that define a network connection.

2. The Internet Protocol (IP) address identifies the location of a specific network device. IP addresses are the primary identification used by the Internet protocol suite TCP/IP for both local area and wide area networks. Subnet masks are used by network devices to identify their local network range and to determine if outgoing data is destined for a network device on the LAN. Most common IP addresses and subnet masks share the same IPv4 formatting. An IPv4 address is a 32-bit number represented in four groups of three-digit numbers, known as octets, separated by periods. Each octet has a value between 0 and 255.

3. If a network device needs to send data to another network device on the same LAN, it addresses the outgoing packets based on the destination device's MAC address.

4. A network client uses the subnet mask to determine if the destination IP address is on the LAN. If the destination IP address is not on the LAN, then it's assumed the destination address is on another network, and the client sends the data to the IP address of the local network router. The network router then sends the data, via a WAN connection, on to another router that it thinks is closer to the destination. This continues across WAN connections from router to router until the data reaches its destination.

5. The DNS service is used to translate host names to IP addresses via forward lookups and translate IP addresses to host names via reverse lookups. DNS is architected as a hierarchy of worldwide domain servers. Local DNS servers provide name resolution and possibly host names for local clients. These local DNS servers connect to DNS servers higher in the DNS hierarchy to resolve both unknown host names and host local domain names.

6. If DHCP is specified as the configuration for a TCP/IP connection and no DHCP service is available, the device will automatically select a random IP address in the 169.254.xxx.xxx range. It will check the local network to ensure that no other network device is using the randomly generated IP address before it applies the IP address. In most cases, though, this addressing is not normal, and it's often indicative of a problem with DHCP services.

7. Lion supports the following network interfaces and protocols:

   Wired Ethernet IEEE 802.3 family of hardware network interface standards

   Wireless (Wi-Fi) IEEE 802.11 family of hardware network interface standards

FireWire IEEE 1394 hardware network interface

Analog modem hardware network interface

Bluetooth wireless hardware network interface

USB connectivity via cellular network adapters

Virtual private network (VPN) virtual network interface via the Point-to-Point Tunneling Protocol (PPTP)

VPN virtual network interface via the Layer 2 Tunneling Protocol (L2TP) over Internet Protocol security (IPsec)

Point-to-Point Protocol over Ethernet (PPPoE) virtual network interface

6 to 4 virtual network interface

Virtual local area network (VLAN) virtual network interface via the IEEE 802.1Q standard

Link Aggregation virtual network interface via the IEEE 802.3ad standard

Transmission Control Protocol/Internet Protocol (TCP/IP), also known as the Internet protocol suite

Dynamic Host Configuration Protocol (DHCP)

Domain Name Service (DNS) protocol

Network Basic Input/Output System (NetBIOS) and Windows Internet Naming Service (WINS) protocols

Authenticated Ethernet via the 802.1X protocol

Point-to-Point Protocol (PPP)

8. The network service order list is used to determine the primary network service interface if there is more than one active service. All network traffic that isn't better handled via local connection to an active network service interface is sent to the primary network service interface. Thus, all Internet traffic is sent through the primary network service interface. Further, all DNS resolution is handled via the primary network service interface.

9. In the Network preferences, all network service interfaces with a green status indicator are being used for network activities. However, again, all network traffic that isn't better handled via a local connection will be sent to the primary network service interface. The primary network service interface is the topmost active interface in the listing.

10. Lion does not support AppleTalk.

11. Four common issues that interrupt network services on Macs are:

    A disconnected network cable will cause the hardware network interface to become inactive.

    A nonfunctioning network interface port will cause the hardware network interface to become inactive.

    A DHCP service issue will prevent proper TCP/IP configuration.

    A DNS service issue will prevent host name resolution.

12. You can identify all the MAC addresses for the Mac's network interfaces from the Info pane of Network Utility.

7

Time This chapter takes approximately 5 hours to complete.

Goals Connect to common network services using built-in Lion network applications

Browse and access network file services using the Finder

Configure Lion computers to provide network file sharing and web sharing services

Use remote control tools to access other network hosts

Provide and protect network sharing and host services

Access network directory service information

Troubleshoot network shared service issues

Chapter **7**
Network Services

Modern operating systems provide a wide range of network and Internet service options, but all of them share the basic network architecture of client software, which accesses services, and server software, which provides services. OS X Lion includes support for many popular network protocols, allowing you to connect and access a wide variety of network services.

On the other hand, one of Apple's best-kept secrets is that OS X Lion and OS X Lion Server are nearly identical operating systems. Many of the core technologies that make Lion a stable and secure client operating system also make it a great server operating system. In fact, Lion can provide many of the same network services as Lion Server. Although Lion Server supports several additional advanced network services and administration tools, the two systems share the same software for providing many network services.

The majority of this network service functionality is a result of Lion's UNIX foundation, which includes extensive use of open source software. Because of this diverse foundation, your Mac should integrate with any other modern operating system for both accessing and providing network services.

In this chapter, you will focus on using Lion as both a network client and a shared resource for a variety of network and Internet services. First, you will be introduced to the key network service applications built into Lion. You will then learn how Lion can both access and provide sharing via popular file and web sharing services. Next, you will discover how to access and enable a variety of network and host sharing services. You will also learn techniques for securing and troubleshooting these services. Finally, you will be introduced to the client side of Lion's directory services architecture, where you will learn how to manage and troubleshoot network identification and authorization technologies.

> **NOTE** ▶ This chapter assumes you have fundamental knowledge of Lion-related network topics such as the Internet Protocol (IP) and the Domain Name Service (DNS). These topics are covered in Chapter 6, "Network Configuration."

Understanding Network Services

From an architectural standpoint, network services are defined by client software (designed to access the service) and server software (designed to provide the service). The network service communication between the client and server software is facilitated by commonly known network protocols or standards. By adhering to such standards, software developers can create unique yet compatible network client and server software. This allows you to choose the software tool that best fits your needs. For instance, you can use the built-in Lion Mail client created by Apple to access mail services provided by software created by Sun Microsystems or Microsoft.

Network Services Software

Some client software takes the form of dedicated applications, as is the case with many Internet services like email and web browsing. Other client software is integrated into the operating system—file and print services, for example. In either case, when you establish a network service connection, settings for that service are saved on the local computer to preference files. These client preferences often include resource locations and authentication information.

On the other side of this relationship is the server software. Properly setting up server software is usually a much more complicated affair. Server administrators may spend months designing, configuring, and administering the software that provides network services. Server-side settings include configuration options, protocol settings, and account information.

Clients connect to servers

Applications access services

Requires mutual configuration

- File
- Web
- Mail
- Chat
- Collaboration
- Directory services
- Profile management

Network Services Communication

Network clients and servers, sometimes of different makes, communicate using commonly known network protocols or network standards. The distinction is that a protocol becomes a standard once it is widely adopted and ratified by a standards committee. Part of what defines a specific network protocol is which TCP or UDP ports are used for communications.

A primary feature of both the TCP and UDP transport mechanisms is the ability to handle multiple simultaneous connections and service protocols. This is accomplished by assigning each communication service to a specific port number or port range. Both TCP and UDP connection ports are defined between 0 and 65,535. For instance, the standard TCP port for web traffic is port 80. When troubleshooting a network service, you must know the port numbers or ranges for that service. Apple maintains a list of commonly used network services and their associated TCP or UDP ports at Knowledge Base document TS1629, "'Well Known' TCP and UDP ports used by Apple software products."

> **NOTE ▶** This book assumes the default port numbers and port ranges for each network service. Network administrators may choose to use a different port number than the default for testing, to "hide" a service, or to bypass router restrictions.

Network Services Identification

At a minimum, accessing a network service requires you to know the service's network location and often requires some way to prove your identity to the service provider. For some network services, you will have to manually identify the service's location with an

Internet Protocol (IP) address or Domain Name Service (DNS) host name. Others feature dynamic service discovery that allows you to easily locate a network service by simply browsing from a list of available services. Details regarding dynamic network service discovery are covered in the next section of this chapter.

Once you have selected a network service to connect to, often you must prove your identity to that service provider. This process is called authentication. Successful authentication to a network service is usually the last step to establishing a connection to that service. Once a connection is established, security technologies are normally in place to ensure that you're allowed to access only certain resources. This process is called authorization. Both of these fundamental network service concepts, authentication and authorization, will be covered throughout this chapter.

Dynamic Network Service Discovery

Requiring users to manually enter network addresses to access a network service simply isn't very user-friendly. What if you were to join a new network where you don't know the exact names of all the available resources? Or what if the shared resource you need is hosted from another client computer that doesn't have a DNS host name or the same IP address every time? To address these issues, Lion supports dynamic network service discovery protocols.

Dynamic network service discovery protocols allow you to browse local area and wide area network resources without having to know specific service addresses. In a nutshell, network devices that are providing a service advertise the availability of their services on the network, and clients that are looking for those services get this information to provide the user with a list of available network services. As available network resources change, or as you move your client to different networks, the service discovery protocols will dynamically update the list of available services.

Lion makes ample use of dynamic network service discovery throughout. For example, dynamic network service discovery allows you to browse for available network file shares with the Finder, or locate new network printers from the Print & Scan preferences. Other network applications built into Lion use service discovery to locate a variety of shared resources, including iChat, Image Capture, iPhoto, iTunes, Safari, and the Lion Server Admin Tools. Third-party network applications also take advantage of dynamic network service discovery.

It is important to remember the discovery protocol is only used to help you and the system locate available services. Once the discovery protocol provides your computer with a list of available services, its job is done. When you connect to a discovered service, the Mac will establish a connection to the service using the service's protocol. For example, Bonjour's service discovery protocol can provide the Mac with a list of available file services, but when you select a file server from this list, the Mac will establish a connection to the server using the AFP protocol.

Lion provides built-in support for the following dynamic network service discovery protocols:

▶ Bonjour's multicast DNS on UDP port 5353—Bonjour is Apple's implementation of Zero Configuration Networking, or Zeroconf, a collection of standards drafts that provide automatic local network configuration, naming, and service discovery. Bonjour is the primary set of dynamic network service discovery protocols used by Mac OS X native services and applications. Bonjour is preferred because it is based on TCP/IP standards, and so integrates well with other TCP/IP-based network services. Mac OS X v10.5 added support for Wide-Area Bonjour, allowing you to browse WAN resources as well as LAN resources. While local Bonjour requires no configuration, Wide-Area Bonjour requires that your Mac be configured to use a DNS server and search domain that supports the protocol. Configuring DNS is covered in Chapter 6, "Network Configuration."

   MORE INFO ▶ You can find out more about Zeroconf at www.zeroconf.org.

▶ Server Message Block (SMB) on UDP ports 137 and 138—Originally designed by Microsoft, SMB has become the most common network service for sharing files and printers. Most modern operating systems provide support for SMB. Apple's implementation of SMB also supports browsing through the legacy Network Basic Input/ Output System (NetBIOS) and Windows Internet Naming Service (WINS) protocols. Details regarding configuration of NetBIOS and WINS are also covered in Chapter 6, "Network Configuration."

   NOTE ▶ On Mac OS X v10.5 and later, you can no longer disable Bonjour or SMB network discovery protocols from the graphical interface.

   NOTE ▶ Mac OS X v10.6 and later no longer support the AppleTalk network browsing protocol.

Host Network Identification

If you want to provide network services from your Mac or otherwise identify your Mac from another computer, you must configure it so that other network hosts can easily reach it. Even if you aren't providing file sharing services from your Mac clients, if you plan to use any network administration tools, then you must have some way of identifying your Mac clients from across the network.

At a minimum your Mac can be reached by its IP address, but IP addresses are hard to remember and can change if your Mac is using DHCP. Thus, it is much more convenient for you and other network clients to locate your Mac using a network name and discovery service.

Lion network identification methods include:

▶   IP address(es)—The primary network identifier for your Mac, an IP address can always be used to establish a network connection.

▶   DNS host name—All Macs have a host name configured via one of two methods. Traditionally, these names are hosted on a DNS server configured by administration at the DNS server. The Mac will attempt to resolve its host name by performing a DNS reverse lookup on its primary IP address. However, many network clients don't have properly configured DNS host names because of the administrative overhead required to create and update client DNS entries. As such, if the Mac can't resolve a host name from the DNS server, it will instead use the Bonjour name.

▶   Computer name—This name is used by other Apple systems to identify your Mac. The computer name is part of Apple's Bonjour implementation and is set in the Sharing preferences. The computer name is also used by Lion's new AirDrop peer-to-peer file sharing technology.

▶   Bonjour name—As covered previously, Bonjour is Mac OS X's primary dynamic network discovery protocol; in addition, Bonjour provides a convenient naming system for use on a local network. The Bonjour name is usually similar to the computer name but differs in that it conforms to DNS naming standards and ends with .local. This allows the Bonjour name to be supported by more network devices than the standard computer name, which is generally recognized only by Apple systems. This name is also set in the Sharing preferences.

▶   NetBIOS/WINS name—This is used for the legacy Windows dynamic network discovery protocols as part of the SMB service. This name is set by either the Sharing or Network preferences.

Identifier	Example	Set by	Used by
IP address	10.1.17.2	Network preferences	Any network host
DNS host name	client17.pretendco.com	Defined by DNS server	Any network host
Computer name	Client 17	Sharing preferences	Mac systems (Bonjour or AirDrop)
Bonjour name	Client-17.local	Sharing preferences	Any Bonjour host
NetBIOS name	CLIENT17	Network preferences	Any SMB host

Configuring Network Identification

You may be unable to control your Mac's IP address or DNS host name; the network administrator usually controls these. But as long as the Mac has properly configured TCP/IP settings as outlined in Chapter 6, "Network Configuration," your configuration is complete for these two identifiers. If your Mac has multiple IP addresses or DNS host names properly configured, it will also accept connections from those.

For dynamic network discovery protocols, though, your Mac will use network identification that can be set locally by an administrator. By default, your Mac will automatically choose a name based either on its DNS name or on the name of the user created with the Setup Assistant. However, at any time an administrative user can change the Mac's network identifier from the Sharing preferences. Simply enter a name in the Computer Name field, and the system will set the name for each available discovery protocol.

For example, if you enter the computer name "My Mac", the Bonjour name will be set for "My-Mac.local" and the NetBIOS/WINS name will be set for "MY_MAC". If the name you chose is already taken by another local device, the Mac will automatically append a number on the end of the name. NetBIOS/WINS may require additional configuration if your network uses multiple domains or workgroups, as covered in Chapter 6, "Network Configuration."

The local Bonjour service needs no additional configuration, but if you want to set a custom Bonjour name, click the Edit button below the Computer Name field to reveal the Local Hostname field. From this interface you can also register your Mac's identification for Wide-Area Bonjour. To do so, select the "Use dynamic global hostname" checkbox to reveal the Wide-Area Bonjour settings.

Using Network Applications

Because of the widespread adoption of TCP/IP for nearly all LAN, WAN, and Internet communications, there really isn't any difference between how you access a "standard network service" and an "Internet service." With few exceptions, nearly all network services work the same way across a LAN as they do across the Internet. The primary difference between the two is scope of service. Services like email and instant messaging can certainly work on a local level, but these services are also designed to communicate across separate networks and between servers. Lion includes a range of client applications designed to access different network services.

New in Lion are the Mail, Contacts, & Calendars preferences, which provide a single unified interface for configuring network service accounts to be used in Mail, iCal, Address Book, and iChat. In other words, entering a single network service account in the Mail, Contacts, & Calendars preferences will configure all four primary network service applications in Lion. These applications can be configured to use network service accounts for Microsoft Exchange, MobileMe, Gmail, Yahoo, AOL, and other common network service protocols.

Lion can also accept a configuration profile for automatic configuration of network service accounts settings. A network administrator would provide a configuration profile containing all the necessary settings to properly configure Lion's network applications for a specific network service account. These settings can be deployed by simply double-clicking a local copy of a configuration profile or by having the Mac managed by a Mobile Device Management (MDM) solution.

MORE INFO ▸ OS X Lion Server can provide MDM services through Profile Manager, as covered in Chapter 4, "Managing Accounts," of *Apple Pro Training Series: OS X Lion Server Essentials*.

Although this book focuses on the network client software built into Lion, many excellent third-party network clients are available for the Mac. In fact, when troubleshooting a network access problem, using an alternative network client is an excellent way to determine if the issue is specific to your primary client software.

Safari 5.1 for Web Browsing

Lion includes Apple's Safari 5.1 web browser. Safari is an efficient and robust browser that supports most websites. Apple has even made Safari available for the Windows operating system. However, you may find that some websites do not render properly or work correctly with Safari. If you are unable to access certain websites with Safari, try a third-party web browser. Several are available for the Mac, including Firefox, OmniWeb, and Opera.

By far the most popular and ubiquitous network service, web communication is handled via the Hypertext Transfer Protocol (HTTP) using TCP port 80. Secure web communication, known by the acronym HTTPS, encrypts HTTP over a Secure Sockets Layer (SSL) connection and by default uses TCP port 443. Generally, little additional network configuration is required to use web services, as you only need to provide the web browser with the Uniform Resource Locator (URL) or web address of the resource you desire to connect to. The only exception is if you have to configure web proxies, as described in Chapter 6, "Network Configuration."

MORE INFO ▶ You can find out more about Safari and download it for Windows from Apple's website, www.apple.com/safari.

Mail 5 for Email and Exchange

Lion includes an entirely new email client, Mail 5, for handling email communications along with mail-based notes and task lists. Mail supports all standard email protocols and their encrypted counterparts, along with a variety of authentication standards. Mail also includes support for Microsoft Exchange Server 2007 and Exchange Server 2010 via Exchange Web Services.

NOTE ▶ Mail in Lion requires Microsoft Exchange Server 2007 Service Pack 1 Update Rollup 4 or Exchange Server 2010, with Exchange Web Services enabled.

With this many service options, properly configuring mail service settings can be quite daunting. Ideally Mail is configured automatically via the Mail, Contacts, & Calendars preferences or via a configuration profile. However, Mail also includes its own Account Setup Assistant to walk you through the process of configuring mail account settings. The assistant will even attempt to automatically determine the appropriate mail protocol security and authentication mail protocol settings. This includes support for the Autodiscovery feature of Microsoft Exchange Server 2007 or Exchange Server 2010. Further, when you set up Mail to use Exchange, the system will automatically configure Address Book and iCal to use Exchange as well.

In summary, Mail 5 supports the following email services:

▶ Standard mailbox access protocols—The standard protocol used between mail clients and mail servers for receiving mail is either Post Office Protocol (POP) on TCP port 110 or Internet Message Access Protocol (IMAP) on TCP port 143. Both protocols can also be encrypted with an SSL connection. By default, encrypted POP uses TCP port 995 and encrypted IMAP uses TCP port 993. Finally, Apple's MobileMe service defaults to secure IMAP.

▶ Standard mail sending protocols—The standard protocol used for sending mail from clients to servers and from server to server is Simple Mail Transfer Protocol (SMTP) on TCP port 25. Again, SMTP can be encrypted with an SSL connection on ports 25, 465, or 587. The ports used for secure SMTP vary based on mail server function and administrator preference. Finally, Apple's MobileMe service defaults to secure SMTP.

▶ Microsoft Exchange Server 2007 or Exchange Server 2010—Although popular, this does not use mail standards for client communication. Instead, the Mail application relies on the Exchange Web Services (EWS) protocol for client communication. EWS, as its name implies, uses the standard ports for web traffic: TCP port 80 for standard transport and TCP port 443 for secure transport. Further, though the Exchange server itself uses SMTP for sending mail to other servers, the Mail client again uses the EWS protocol to send the outgoing mail message to the Exchange server.

iCal 5 for Calendaring

Lion includes iCal 5 for handling calendar information. While iCal can certainly work on its own for managing your nonshared calendar information on your Mac, it also integrates with a variety of network synchronized and shared calendar services. Again, ideally iCal is configured automatically via the Mail, Contacts, & Calendars preferences or via a configuration profile. However, iCal also features an easy-to-use Setup Assistant for configuring specific calendar network service accounts.

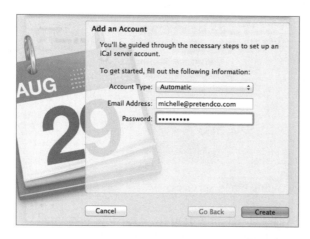

iCal 5 supports the following network calendar services:

▶ Local synchronized calendars—Calendars that are managed locally can be synchronized via the Internet to MobileMe, Yahoo, and Google calendar services. All three of these services use the encrypted HTTPS protocol over TCP port 443.

▶ Calendar web publishing and subscription— iCal allows you to share your calendar information by publishing iCalendar files to WebDAV-enabled web servers. Web-based Distributed Authoring and Versioning (WebDAV) is an extension to the HTTP protocol, so it runs over TCP port 80 or TCP port 443 if encrypted. You can also subscribe to iCalendar files hosted on WebDAV servers. Configuration is fairly easy, as accessing a shared calendar is identical to accessing a webpage. Simply provide iCal with the URL of the iCalendar file. Although calendar publishing allows you to easily share calendars one way over the web, it doesn't provide a true collaborative calendaring environment.

MORE INFO ▶ Apple hosts dozens of iCal-compatible calendars at www.apple.com/downloads/macosx/calendars.

▶ Calendar email invitation—iCal, again using iCalendar files, is integrated with Mail to automatically send and receive calendar invitations as email attachments. In this case the transport mechanism is whatever your primary mail account is configured to use. While this method isn't a calendaring standard, most popular mail and calendar clients can use this method.

▶ CalDAV collaborative calendaring—iCal supports an emerging calendar collaboration standard known as CalDAV. As the name implies, this standard uses WebDAV as a transport mechanism on TCP port 8008 or 8443 for encrypted, but CalDAV adds the administrative processes required to facilitate calendar and scheduling collaboration. Lion Server's iCal service is based on CalDAV. Furthermore, CalDAV is being developed as an open standard so any vendor can create software that provides or connects to CalDAV services.

▶ Exchange 2007 or Exchange 2010 collaborative calendaring—With the latest version of iCal, Apple included support for this popular calendar service. Again, Lion's Exchange integration relies on EWS, which uses TCP port 80 for standard transport and TCP port 443 for secure transport.

Address Book 6 for Contacts

Lion includes Address Book 6 for handling contact information. Similar to iCal, while Address Book can certainly work on its own for managing nonshared contact information on your Mac, it also integrates with a variety of network synchronized and shared contact services. Again, ideally Address Book is configured automatically via the Mail, Contacts, & Calendars preferences or via a configuration profile. However, Address Book also features an easy-to-use Setup Assistant for configuring specific address or directory network service accounts.

Address Book 6 supports the following network contact services:

▶ Local synchronized contacts—Contacts that are managed locally can be synchronized via the Internet to MobileMe, Yahoo, and Google contact services. All three of these services use the encrypted HTTPS protocol over TCP port 443.

▶ Directory service contacts—Address Book can search against contact databases via the standard for network directory services, the Lightweight Directory Access Protocol (LDAP). Address Book can be configured for LDAP services either directly from the Setup Assistant or via integration with Lion's systemwide directory service, as covered later in this chapter.

▶ CardDAV contact sharing—Address Book supports an emerging calendar collaboration standard known as CardDAV. Again, as the name implies, this standard uses WebDAV as a transport mechanism on TCP port 8800 or 8843 for encrypted, but CardDAV adds the administrative processes required to facilitate contact sharing. Lion Server's Address Book service is based on CardDAV. Furthermore, CardDAV is being developed as an open standard so any vendor can create software that provides or connects to CardDAV services.

NOTE ▶ Apple's selection of TCP ports 8800 and 8843 for CardDAV is not based on any assigned standard. Some implementations of CardDAV may use the standard ports for HTTP(S) and TCP ports 80 and 443 for encrypted.

▶ Exchange 2007 or Exchange 2010 contact sharing—With the latest version of Address Book, Apple included support for this popular contact sharing service. Again, Lion's

Exchange integration relies on Exchange Web Services (EWS), which uses TCP port 80 for standard transport and TCP port 443 for secure transport.

iChat 6 for Instant Messaging

Instant messaging has grown well beyond text chatting with iChat 6, included with Lion. The latest iChat supports ten-way audio conferencing, four-way video conferencing, peer-to-peer file sharing, remote screen sharing, and high-resolution iChat Theater for sharing video from supported applications. Again, ideally iChat is configured automatically via the Mail, Contacts, & Calendars preferences or via a configuration profile. However, iChat also features an easy-to-use Setup Assistant for configuring specific chat network service accounts.

NOTE ▶ iChat's advanced features, such as video conferencing, screen sharing, and iChat Theater , are not supported by many third-party chat clients. When you select a chat participant, iChat will automatically determine the client software's messaging capabilities and allow you to use only supported features.

iChat 6 supports three categories of chat services:

▶ Messaging services that are open to the public—iChat supports MobileMe, AOL Instant Messenger, Google Talk, and Yahoo chat accounts. Assuming you have already registered for an account through one of these service providers, configuring iChat simply involves entering your account name and password. Once again, MobileMe accounts will be configured automatically based on the MobileMe preferences.

▶ Privately hosted messaging services—iChat supports open source Jabber servers, including Mac OS X Server's iChat service. If your Mac is connected to a directory server that is hosting Jabber account information, iChat will be automatically configured based on those settings. Otherwise, you will have to manually enter Jabber server and account information. Jabber servers are based on the eXtensible Messaging and Presence Protocol (XMPP), which uses TCP port 5222 or 5223 for encrypted.

▶ Ad hoc messaging—iChat will use the Bonjour network discovery protocol to automatically find other iChat users. No configuration is necessary to access Bonjour messaging. Bonjour details were covered earlier in the "Dynamic Network Service Discovery" section of this chapter.

iChat supports a wide variety of messaging features and instant messaging protocols—which means it uses far too many TCP and UDP ports to list here. However, Knowledge Base document HT1507, "Using iChat with a firewall or NAT router," lists all the possible ports iChat may attempt to use.

Using File Sharing Services

Lion supports a variety of network protocols to facilitate the sharing of files across a network connection. In this section you will explore both sides of file sharing services, client and server. For most users, Macs function exclusively as clients to established file servers. Yet any Mac can also act as a server to provide access to shared resources. Further, Lion introduces AirDrop, which is the easiest way yet to share files between Mac systems.

Understanding File Sharing Services

Many protocols exist for transferring files across networks and the Internet, but the most efficient are those designed specifically to share file systems. Network file servers can make entire file systems available to your client computer across the network. The key distinction is that client software built into Lion's Finder can mount a network file service much as it would mount a locally connected storage volume. Once a network file service is mounted to the Mac, you will be able to read, write, and manipulate files and folders as if you were accessing a local file system. Additionally, access privileges to network file services are defined by the same ownership and permissions architecture used by local file systems. Details regarding file systems, ownership, and permissions are covered in Chapter 3, "File Systems."

Lion provides built-in support for these network file service protocols:

▶ Apple Filing Protocol (AFP) version 3 on TCP port 548 or encrypted over SSH on TCP port 22—This is Apple's native network file service. The current version of AFP supports all the features of Apple's native file system, Mac OS Extended.

▶ Server Message Block (SMB) on TCP ports 139 and 445—This network file service is mainly used by Windows systems, but many other platforms have adopted support for this protocol. SMB also supports many of the advanced file system features used by Lion. Further, new in Lion is support for Distributed File Service (DFS) referrals. DFS allows windows administrators to distribute SMB services across multiple servers.

▶ Network File System (NFS) version 4, which may use a variety of TCP or UDP ports—Used primarily by UNIX systems, it supports many advanced file system features used by Lion.

▶ Web-based Distributed Authoring and Versioning (WebDAV) on TCP port 80 (HTTP) or encrypted on TCP port 443 (HTTPS)—This protocol is an extension to the common HTTP service and provides basic read/write file services.

▶ File Transfer Protocol (FTP) on TCP ports 20 and 21 or encrypted on TCP port 989 and 990 (FTPS)—This protocol is in many ways the lowest common denominator of file systems. FTP is supported by nearly every computing platform, but it provides only the most basic file system functionality. Further, the Finder supports only read capability for FTP or FTPS volumes.

NOTE ▶ Don't confuse FTPS with another similar protocol, SFTP. The distinction is that FTPS uses SSL encryption on TCP port 990 and SFTP uses SSH encryption on TCP port 22. The Finder does not support FTPS. However, both are supported in the Terminal.

NOTE ▶ From the Terminal you can access a full FTP/FTPS client with the ftp command. Additionally, you will find several third-party FTP/FTPS clients on Apple's Macintosh Products Guide.

The Finder provides two methods for connecting to a network file system: automatically discovering shared resources by browsing to them in the Finder's Network folder or manually connecting by entering the address of the server providing the file service.

Browsing File Services

You can browse for dynamically discovered file services from two locations in the Finder. The first location is the Shared list located in the Finder's sidebar. If enabled in the Finder preferences, the Shared list is ideal for quickly discovering computers providing file services on a small network. The Shared list will show only the first eight discovered computers providing services. If additional servers are discovered, the last item in the Shared list, All Items, is a link to the Finder's Network folder.

TIP ▶ The sidebar also appears in any application's Open dialog with exactly the same items as are available from the Finder.

TIP ▶ The Finder's Shared list will show servers that you are currently connected to even if they didn't originally appear in the Shared list.

TIP ▶ The Finder will also let you browse to screen sharing (VNC) hosts via Bonjour, as covered later in this chapter.

The Finder's Network folder is a special place in Lion. The Network folder is not a standard folder at all; it's an amalgamation of all dynamically discovered network file services and all currently mounted file systems, including manually mounted file systems. Obviously, the Network folder is constantly changing based on information gathered from the two dynamic network service discovery protocols supported by Lion—Bonjour and SMB/NetBIOS/WINS—so you can only browse AFP or SMB file services from the Network folder.

On smaller networks there may only be one level of network services. Conversely, if you have a larger network that features multiple service discovery domains, they will appear as subfolders inside the Network folder. Each subfolder will be named by the domain it represents. Items inside the domain subfolders represent shared resources configured for that specific network area.

NOTE ▸ From the Terminal, the Network folder will show only file systems that were mounted by Lion's automatic network file mounting system.

To browse and connect to an AFP or SMB file service:

1   From the Finder's Sidebar, select the computer you wish to connect to from the Shared list, or select a computer from the Finder's Network folder. In the Finder, the quickest routes to the Network folder are to either choose Go > Network from the menu bar or use the Shift-Command-K keyboard shortcut.

Selecting a computer from either the Shared list or the Network folder will yield similar results.

2   The moment you select a computer providing services, the Mac will attempt to automatically authenticate using one of three methods:

▶   If you are using Kerberos authentication, the Mac will attempt to authenticate to the selected computer using your Kerberos credentials. Kerberos is covered later in this chapter.

▶   If you are using non-Kerberos authentication but you connected to the selected computer previously and chose to save the authentication information to your keychain, the Mac will attempt to use the saved authentication information.

▶   The Mac will attempt to authenticate as a guest user. Keep in mind that guest access is an option on file servers that many administrators disable.

If the Mac succeeds in authenticating to the selected computer, the Finder will show you the account name it connected with and also list the shared volumes available to this account.

3   If the Mac was unable to automatically connect to the selected computer, or you need to authenticate with a different account, click the Connect As button to open an authentication dialog. You can authenticate to a share using one of three methods:

▶   Choosing the Connect as Guest radio button will indicate that you wish to connect anonymously to the file service.

▶ Choosing the Registered User radio button allows you to authenticate using a local or network account known by the computer providing the shared volume. Optionally, you can select the checkbox that will save this authentication information to your login keychain.

▶ Choosing the Using an Apple ID radio button allows you to authenticate to an AFP shared volume using an Apple ID. In order for this option to appear, both the local Mac and the computer hosting the shared volume must be running OS X Lion or a newer system. Further, the local account on your Mac must be tied to an Apple ID as covered in Chapter 2, "User Accounts."

Click the Connect button, and the Mac will authenticate and show you a new list of shared volumes available to the account.

4   Each available shared volume will appear as a folder. Click once on a shared volume to connect and mount its file system.

5   Once the Mac has mounted the network file volume, it can appear in several locations from the Finder or any application's open dialog, including the Computer location, the desktop, and the sidebar's Shared list, depending on configuration.

By default, connected network volumes will not show up on the desktop. You can change this behavior from the General tab of the Finder Preferences dialog.

TIP ▶ Again, the sidebar also appears in any application's Open dialog with exactly the same items as are available from the Finder.

TIP ▶ From the Terminal, mounted network volumes will appear in the /Volumes folder along with all the other mounted file systems.

Manually Connecting File Services

To manually connect to a file service, you must specify a network identifier (URL) for the file server providing the service. You may also have to enter authentication information and choose or enter the name of a specific shared resource path. When connecting to an AFP or SMB service, you can authenticate first and then choose a shared volume. Conversely, when connecting to an NFS, WebDAV (HTTP), or FTP service, you can specify the shared volume or full path as part of the server address and then authenticate if required.

Manually Connect to AFP or SMB

To manually connect an AFP or SMB file service:

1   From the Finder, choose Go > Connect to Server from the menu bar, or use the Command-K keyboard shortcut.

    This will open the Finder's Connect to Server dialog.

2   In the Server Address field, enter afp:// or smb:// followed by the server's IP address, DNS host name, computer name, or Bonjour name.

    Click the Connect button to continue.

    TIP ▶ If you don't specify a protocol, the Connect to Server dialog will default to the AFP protocol.

    TIP ▶ Optionally, after the server address, you can enter another slash and then the name of a specific shared volume. This will allow you to skip step 4.

TIP ▶ When connecting to DFS via SMB, make sure to follow the guidelines as outlined in Knowledge Base article HT4794, "OS X Lion: Guidelines for connecting to a DFS namespace via SMB."

3   A dialog will appear requiring you to enter authentication information.

You can authenticate to a share using one of three methods:

▶   Choosing the Connect as Guest radio button will indicate that you wish to connect anonymously to the file service.

▶   Choosing the Registered User radio button allows you to authenticate using a local or network account known by the computer providing the shared volume. Optionally, you can select the checkbox that will save this authentication information to your login keychain.

▶   Choosing the Apple ID radio button allows you to authenticate to an AFP shared volume using an Apple ID. In order for this option to appear, both the local Mac and the computer hosting the shared volume must be running OS X Lion or newer system. Further, the local account on your Mac must be tied to an Apple ID as covered in Chapter 2, "User Accounts."

Click the Connect button, and the Mac will authenticate and show you a new list of shared volumes available to the account.

NOTE ▶ If you are using Kerberos or you have previously saved your authentication information to a keychain, the computer will automatically authenticate for you and will not present the authentication dialog. Kerberos is covered later in this chapter.

4 You will be presented with the list of shared volumes that your account is allowed to access.

Select the volume or volumes you wish to mount. Hold down the Command key to select multiple volumes from the list. Click the OK button to mount the selected shared volumes.

Manually Connect to NFS, WebDAV, or FTP

To manually connect an NFS, WebDAV, or FTP file service:

1 From the Finder, choose Go > Connect to Server from the menu bar, or use the Command-K keyboard shortcut.

The Finder's Connect to Server dialog opens.

2 In the Server Address field, enter one of the following:

▶ nfs:// followed by the server address, another slash, and then the absolute file path of the shared volume.

▶ http:// for WebDAV (or https:// for WebDAV encrypted via SSL), followed by the server address. Each WebDAV site only has one mountable volume, but you can optionally enter another slash and then specify a folder inside the WebDAV volume. If you are connecting to a Lion Server, the default folder for all WebDAV shares is /webdav.

▶ ftp:// (or ftps:// for FTP encrypted via SSL) followed by the server address. FTP servers also have only one mountable root volume, but you can optionally enter another slash and then specify a folder inside the FTP volume.

Click the Connect button to continue.

TIP ▶ Clicking the Browse button in the Connect to Server dialog will bring you to the Finder's Network folder, allowing you to browse for a server, as covered in the previous section of this chapter.

3 Depending on the protocol settings, you may be presented with an authentication dialog.

NFS connections will never display an authentication dialog. The NFS protocol u ses the local user that you're already logged in as for authorization purposes or Kerberos.

If you are presented with an authentication dialog, enter the appropriate authentication information here. Optionally, you can select the checkbox that will save this authentication information to your login keychain.

Click the OK button to mount the shared volume.

Again, once the Mac has mounted the network file volume, it can appear in several locations from the Finder, including the Computer location, the desktop, and the sidebar's Shared list, depending on configuration. However, mounted network volumes will *always* appear at the Computer location in the Finder, accessible by choosing Go > Computer from the menu bar or by pressing Shift-Command-C. Again, you can also set Finder preferences to show mounted network volumes on the desktop and in the sidebar's Shared list, as covered in the previous section. Finally, from the Terminal, mounted network volumes will appear where all other mounted volumes appear: in the /Volumes folder.

TIP Again, the sidebar also appears in any application's Open dialog with exactly the same items as are available from the Finder.

Manually entering server information every time you connect to a server is a hassle. Two features in the Connect to Server dialog make this process efficient for your users. The Connect to Server dialog maintains a history of your past server connections. You can access this history by clicking the small clock icon to the right of the Server Address field. Also, you can create a list of favorite servers in the Connect to Server dialog by clicking the plus button to the right of the Server Address field.

Managing Connected Volumes

It is important to recognize that the Mac treats mounted network volumes similarly to locally attached volumes, so you must remember to always properly unmount and eject network volumes when you are done with them. Mounted network volumes are unmounted and ejected from the Finder using the same techniques you would use on a locally connected volume. Unmounting and ejecting mounted volumes is covered in Chapter 3, "File Systems." One difference is that the Eject button appears multiple times in the Finder wherever the server name or the shared volumes appear.

In practice, though, it's difficult for users to remember they have network volumes mounted, as there is no locally attached hardware device to remind them. Further, laptop users will often roam out of wireless network range without even thinking about what network volumes they may have mounted. If a network change or problem disconnects the Mac from a mounted network volume, the Mac will spend several minutes attempting to reconnect to the server hosting the volume. If after several minutes the Mac cannot reconnect to the server, the user will see an error dialog allowing him to fully disconnect from the server.

Automatically Connecting Network Volumes

On a positive note, because the Finder treats mounted network volumes as similar to other file system items, you can save time and make life easier for you and your users by creating automatic connections to network volumes. One method is to have a network volume mount automatically when a user logs in by adding the network volume to the user's login items. Managing login items is covered in Chapter 2, "User Accounts."

Alternately, you can create easy-to-use shortcuts to often-used network volumes. One method involves creating Dock shortcuts by dragging network volumes or their enclosed items to the right side of the Dock. You can also create aliases on the user's desktop that link to often-used network volumes or even specific items inside a network volume. Creating aliases is covered in Chapter 4, "Data Management." Either method you use will automatically connect to the network volume when the user selects the item.

> **TIP** You cannot drag and drop from the Finder's sidebar or the Network browser to the login items or the Dock. Instead, select the network volume from the desktop or the Computer location in the Finder. You can access the Computer location in the Finder by selecting Go > Computer from the menu bar.

TIP ▸ Remember that by using Kerberos authentication or by saving authentication information to the keychain, you can bypass authentication dialogs as well.

Understanding AirDrop

In addition to traditional file sharing services, Lion features a new peer-to-peer Wi-Fi file sharing service dubbed AirDrop. Although AirDrop is only available on newer Mac models, it's the easiest method to share files between Macs in close proximity. Also, while AirDrop does use Wi-Fi networking, it uses radio frequencies outside the Mac's normal network connection; thus it does not travel across your established network. In fact, you don't need a network at all to use AirDrop, as it creates a closed network between local Macs.

The most significant feature of AirDrop is that it requires no setup or configuration. Users who want to share items need only navigate to the AirDrop window in the Finder, and the system will present an interface allowing those users to easily share files. AirDrop handles all the details of peer-to-peer file sharing, including discovery, easy authentication, and secure file transfer, using TLS encryption.

AirDrop does have a few significant caveats. First, it only works between computers within the Macs' local Wi-Fi range. This range varies based on many factors, but it's generally limited to within 150 feet in an open space or less than 50 feet in a space with heavy interference. Also, AirDrop was specifically designed to provide direct file sharing for selected items, as opposed to traditional file sharing, which allows the user to browse another computer's file system. Finally, AirDrop is not supported on older Macs or Macs lacking Wi-Fi support. You can verify if a Mac supports AirDrop in the Finder by selecting the Go menu. If an AirDrop menu option appears, then the Mac supports AirDrop.

MORE INFO ▶ A list of Macs that support AirDrop can be found in Knowledge Base article HT4783, "OS X Lion: Can I use AirDrop with my computer?"

Using AirDrop

To quickly share files between Macs that support AirDrop:

1 From the Finder's sidebar, choose the AirDrop icon, or choose Go > AirDrop to Server from the menu bar, or use the Shift-Command-R keyboard shortcut.

The AirDrop window opens.

Any time you select the AirDrop window, the system will automatically scan for other AirDrop Macs within local Wi-Fi range. For another Mac to show up in within your AirDrop range, it must also have the AirDrop window selected in the Finder. Note the animated sweeping AirDrop icon in the Finder's sidebar, indicating that AirDrop is active for this Mac.

NOTE ▸ If the Mac's Wi-Fi interface is turned off, click the Turn Wi-Fi On button to enable AirDrop.

The icons that appear in AirDrop are based on the Mac's currently logged-in user account. The names that appear in AirDrop will default to the Mac's computer name set in the Sharing preferences, as covered earlier in this chapter. If the currently logged-in user has an Apple ID associated with her account, and you have that Apple ID in your Address Book, the name that appears in AirDrop will be the user's human name from the associated Address Book entry.

2   Once AirDrop has found the other Mac you wish to transfer an item to, drag a file or folder from another Finder window to the icon representing the other Mac.

3   A pop-up will appear to verify that you want to transfer the item. Click Send to initiate the AirDrop connection.

Once you click the Send button, the pop-up will show that AirDrop has sent a request to the other Mac and is waiting for the other user to accept the item.

4   From the other Mac, a pop-up will appear, allowing the user to accept the incoming item.

If the Save button is clicked, the item will be transferred to the user's Downloads folder. Clicking the Save and Open button will save to the same location, and then automatically open the item. Clicking the Decline button will cancel the transfer and notify the other user in the AirDrop window.

Providing Network File Services

Lion has built-in support for providing access via popular file sharing services—AFP and SMB—along with web sharing services via HTTP. When you enable any network service, always confirm proper configuration by testing access to the service from another computer, as covered previously in this chapter.

> **MORE INFO ▸** Lion includes support for providing NFS and FTP services, though not via the graphical interface. From the Terminal, you can find out more about providing NFS services by reading the nfsd manual page, and for FTP services, by steps outlined in Knowledge Base article HT4704, "Lion Server: Enabling the FTP service." Although this title references Lion Server, the same techniques work with Lion clients as well.

Lion's network file sharing services are, for the most part, enabled and managed entirely from the Sharing preferences (choose Apple menu > System Preferences and click the Sharing preferences icon). Three primary steps are required to properly configure your Mac so other computers can access its shared file resources: setting your Mac's network identification as covered previously in this chapter, enabling the network file service, and defining access to file system resources.

> **NOTE ▸** Users will not be able to access services on a Mac in sleep mode. You can disable your Mac's automatic sleep activation or enable automatic waking for network access from the Energy Saver preferences. Mac OS X v10.6 introduced automatic wake on both wired and wireless networks if your network hardware supports it. You can find out more from Knowledge Base article HT3774, "Mac OS X v10.6: About Wake on Demand."

Enabling File Sharing

If your Mac's network identification is set up correctly, it's easy to enable AFP and SMB file sharing services with the default access settings.

To enable network file sharing:

1   Choose Apple menu > System Preferences, then click the Sharing icon.

2   Click the lock icon in the bottom-left corner and authenticate as an administrative user to unlock Sharing preferences.

3   Select the File Sharing checkbox to enable the AFP network file service.

This is the only service that will be enabled by default when you select the File Sharing checkbox. The launchd control process will now listen for AFP service requests on TCP port 548 and automatically start the AppleFileServer process as necessary to handle any requests.

MORE INFO ▶ Details regarding the launchd control process are covered in Chapter 9, "System Startup."

4   To enable the SMB network file service, make sure File Sharing is selected in the Service list, and then click Options.

Select the "Share files and folders using SMB" checkbox. The launchd control process will now listen for SMB service requests on TCP ports 139 and 445 and automatically start the smbd process as necessary to handle any requests.

TIP ▶ From this dialog, you can also choose to disable the AFP service if you intend to provide only SMB services. You can also view the number of connected AFP clients.

5   The SMB service stores passwords in a different format than the standard Lion account password. Therefore, you will have to select the checkbox next to each account for which you wish to grant SMB access and reenter the password for that account.

6   Once you have made your selections, click the Done button and then close the Sharing preferences.

Now that you have enabled a network file sharing service, if the Mac is up and running the service is actively listening for connections. Deactivating a service closes any current connections, and they remain deactivated until you re-enable the service.

NOTE ▶ Deselecting the File Sharing checkbox deactivates all network file services.

NOTE ▶ Deactivating a File Sharing service disconnects any currently active AFP and SMB connections. Only the AFP service will remind you of this and allow you to warn currently connected users that the service will soon be unavailable.

The AFP service is limited to ten simultaneous connections. All other services remain limited only by your Mac's resources. For more simultaneous connections, look at OS X Lion Server, as it does not have this restriction.

While modern Macs are able to handle many simultaneous connections and multiple services, it's not a good idea to leave these services running all the time because they can be a security risk. This is especially true for portable Macs that often connect to public wireless networks, or any time you enable Guest access.

It's important to always be aware of exactly which files and folders you are allowing others to access. Next you will cover the default access configuration and how to change access settings to better fit your needs.

Understanding File Sharing Authorization

Enabling a network file sharing service enables other users on the network to connect to your computer; however, they will still need to supply a user name and password to make any changes to your files or to access files beyond your Public folder.

By default, both the AFP and the SMB services allow others to authenticate to your Mac anonymously or as a guest user. Still, both protocols also allow sharing, standard, and administrative users to authenticate to your Mac with their user account information. If you only want to grant known user accounts the ability to access network file sharing resources on your Mac, you can easily disable guest access from the Users & Groups preferences. (Configuring user accounts was covered in Chapter 2, "User Accounts.")

Once a user has been authenticated, the authorization services take over to control which files, folders, or volumes the user account is allowed to access on your Mac. File sharing access is controlled by these three authorization settings:

▶ Default shared items—AFP and SMB network file services will automatically grant default access to connect and mount specific folders or volumes based on the account type. The default shared items are covered in the next section.

▶ Custom shared items—For AFP and SMB, you can define custom folders or volumes as shared items, sometimes called share points, on your Mac. Making a folder or volume a shared item defines it as a location that other users can connect to and mount on their network client.

▶ File system permissions—Once users have mounted a shared item from your Mac, they will have access to files and folders inside the mounted file system based on your Mac's file system permissions settings.

Understanding Default File Sharing Access

To keep things simple, Lion uses a predefined set of file sharing access rules for AFP and SMB services. You don't have to define a single shared item or configure any file system permissions settings to provide file sharing services on Lion. You can simply enable file sharing, and users will be able to access their items based on the default file sharing access settings. These default settings are based on user account types as defined in the Users & Groups preferences:

▶ Guest user—The guest user, if enabled, is normally only allowed access to other standard and administrative users' Public folders.

▶ Sharing user—By default, sharing users have the same access as the guest user. This allows you to disable anonymous access but still restrict certain users to Public folder access only.

▶ Standard user—Because standard users have local home folders, they will be allowed full access to their home folder contents as if they were using the Mac locally. Standard users also have access to all users' Public folders.

▶ Administrative user—Having full control over the Mac, administrative users can access every locally mounted volume on the shared Mac, including attached external drives and inserted optical media. Administrative users can also mount their home folder and all users' Public folders.

NOTE ▶ The exception to all these file sharing rules applies to any Legacy FileVault user. Nothing in these user's home folders can be shared because of the Legacy FileVault encryption. However, these users will be able to connect to their home folder via file sharing, but they will have to take the additional step of authenticating and mounting their Legacy FileVault home folder disk image.

These default access settings will fulfill many users' file sharing needs, but for those Macs that are used as full-time network file sharing resources, the defaults are often not good enough. In the next section, you will learn how to override these defaults and configure custom file sharing access.

Customize File Sharing Access

Earlier versions of Mac OS X provided flexibility for configuring custom file sharing access by allowing you to edit file system permissions settings from the Finder's Get Info window. However, you could not enable additional shared folders or volumes using the built-in interface tools. Mac OS X v10.5 introduced revamped Sharing preferences that allow you to configure custom shared folders and volumes and easily edit permissions for shared items. You can use the Finder's Get Info window to set ownership and permissions, but you can also use the Get Info window to configure custom shared folders and volumes.

Before you begin configuring custom file sharing access, you should be aware of a few file sharing access rules. First, administrative users will always be allowed to remotely mount any volume, and both standard and administrative users will always be allowed to remotely mount their home folders. Second, as you create new standard and administrative users, their Public folders will be automatically set as a shared item. But you can easily disable the shared setting for each Public folder separately from the Sharing preferences or the Finder's Get Info window.

Ultimately, all file sharing access is controlled by Lion's file system permissions settings. When you enable a folder or volume as a shared item, the file permissions settings dictate which users can access the shared item. For example, the Public folders' Everyone permission setting is what grants all users, including guest and sharing-only users, local and file sharing access to the Public folder's contents. So, if you want to properly configure custom file sharing access, you must be familiar with the file system permissions architecture, as detailed in Chapter 3, "File Systems."

Custom File Sharing via Finder

To configure custom file sharing settings from the Finder:

1 If you're setting up a new shared item, prepare the folder or volume to be shared. If you're sharing a new folder, create and name the folder with the Finder. If you're sharing a volume, be sure the volume is properly mounted and formatted as Mac OS Extended (Journaled), as outlined in Chapter 3, "File Systems."

2 In the Finder, select the folder or volume for which you wish to configure the sharing settings, and then open the Get Info window (choose File > Get Info or press Command-I). You may have to click the General disclosure triangle to reveal the general information section.

3 Select the "Shared folder" checkbox to share the selected folder or volume.

Deselecting this checkbox will stop sharing of the item.

NOTE ▶ If you are not an administrative user, you'll have to authenticate with an administrative user account to enable or disable a shared item.

4 Click the Sharing & Permissions disclosure triangle.

You'll see the item's ownership and permissions settings. Click the small lock icon in the bottom-right corner of the Get Info window and authenticate as an administrative user to unlock the Sharing & Permissions section.

5 From the Sharing & Permissions area, you can configure custom file sharing access settings for any number of users or groups.

Only users or groups with read access will be able to mount the shared item. Always test newly shared items using multiple account types to ensure you have configured appropriate access settings.

Custom File Sharing via the Sharing Preferences

To configure custom file sharing settings from the Sharing preferences:

1   If you're setting up a new item to be shared, prepare the folder or volume to be shared.

2   Open the Sharing preferences and authenticate as an administrative user to unlock their settings.

3   Select File Sharing from the Service list to access the network file sharing settings. The shared folders list will show currently shared items, including the Public folders, which are shared by default.

4   To share a new folder or volume, click the small plus icon at the bottom of the shared folders list.

A file browser dialog appears. Select the folder or volume you wish to share, then click the Add button to start sharing that item.

To stop sharing an item, select it from the Shared Folders list and click the small minus button at the bottom of the list.

5   Select a shared item to reveal its access settings in the Users list. The users list is identical to the Sharing & Permissions area in the Finder's Get Info window.

Again, only users or groups with read access will be able to mount the shared item, and you should always thoroughly test newly shared items to ensure you have configured appropriate access settings.

Configure Web Sharing

Lion also includes the Apache 2.2 web server to allow users to share web pages and files from their own systems. Apple has preconfigured web sharing so that it can be enabled with literally a single click.

To enable basic web sharing:

1   Open the Sharing preferences by choosing Apple menu > System Preferences and clicking the Sharing icon.

2   Click the lock icon in the bottom-left corner and authenticate as an administrative user.

3   Select the Web Sharing checkbox to enable the Apache 2.2 web service.

The launchd control process now starts the httpd background process, which listens for web service requests on TCP port 80.

With the web sharing service enabled, other users can browse websites hosted from your Mac. This service is preconfigured with a main computer website and, optionally, individual websites for each user who has a local home folder.

Configuring the Computer Website

With web sharing enabled, you can browse to your Mac's primary computer website by entering http://<yourmac>/, where <yourmac> is your Mac's IP address, DNS host name, or Bonjour name. For example, if your Mac's IP address was 192.168.1.200 and its sharing name was My Mac, then you could enter http://192.168.1.200/ or http://my-mac.local/. If you navigate to this website with the default configuration, you will see the Apache 2.2 test page, which simply proclaims, "It works!"

Configuring a custom website for your Mac is as simple as replacing the contents of your Mac's computer website folder (located at /Library/WebServer/Documents/). You can navigate to this folder in the Finder or simply click the Open Computer Website button in the Sharing preferences. To use your own custom website, replace this folder's contents with the website resources you created.

You can use any website creation tool that you like, such as iWeb or Pages, but you must keep in mind a few rules. First, the main page of your website must be named index. html. Second, you must ensure that file system permissions settings for your website files allow read access to the web server, which accesses them as a system user named _www. The easiest way to accomplish this is to grant Everyone read access to the website items. Finally, if you want to use advanced website features such as server-side scripts or secure transfers, you have to manually enable these services from the Apache 2.2 configuration files.

> **MORE INFO** ▶ The Apache 2.2 web server has capabilities that go well beyond basic web sharing. With Web Sharing enabled, you can find out more by accessing the built-in locally hosted documentation at http://localhost/manual/, or visit the Apache web server project page at http://httpd.apache.org.

Configuring Personal User Websites

Lion's web sharing service can also be configured to allow individual websites for each user with a local home folder on your Mac. For a user to host a website from within his home folder, you must enable the Sites folder on a per-user basis. To do so, you must log in as that user and then open the Sharing preferences. With the Web Sharing service selected and enabled, click the Create Personal Web Folder button. Notice that the button changes from Create to Open once the system has created the user's personal website folder.

Once enabled, each user's personal website is located inside the Sites folder within her home folder. To configure a custom website for the user, replace this folder's contents with the website resources you created. Again, you can use any website creation tools you like, and you must also follow the same website rules listed in the previous section.

You can browse to personal user websites by entering http://<yourmac>/~<username>/, where <yourmac> is your Mac's IP address, DNS host name, or Bonjour name, and <username> is the short name of the user account. For example, if your computer, with the sharing name of My Mac, has two user accounts with the short names of mike and debbie, then you could enter http://My-Mac.local/~mike/ or http://My-Mac. local/~debbie/. If you navigate to this website with the default configuration, you will see the default user test page.

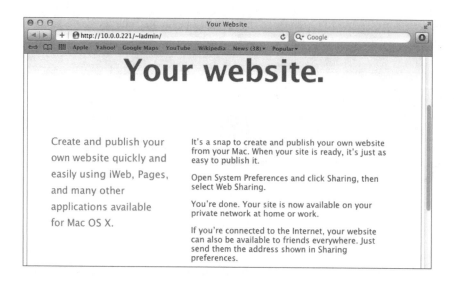

Using Host Sharing Services

In addition to the file and web sharing services covered in the previous section, Lion includes an assortment of non-file-sharing network services, which you'll now see how to manage. These "host sharing" services vary in implementation and purpose, but they all allow users to remotely access resources on the Mac providing the service. They are also all easily enabled and managed from the Sharing preferences.

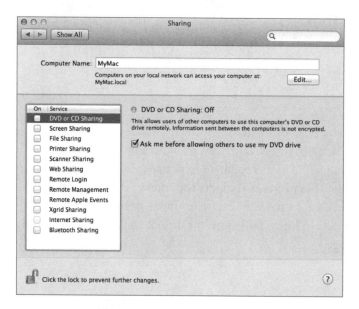

NOTE ► Users will not be able to access services on a Mac in sleep mode. You can disable your Mac's automatic sleep activation or enable automatic waking for network access from the Energy Saver preferences. Mac OS X v10.6 introduced automatic wake on both wired and wireless networks if your network hardware supports it. You can find out more from Knowledge Base article HT3774, "Mac OS X v10.6: About Wake on Demand."

It's important to recognize the security risk involved in providing a service that allows other users to control processes on your Mac. Obviously, if you're providing a service that allows remote control and execution of software, it's certainly possible for an attacker to cause trouble. Thus, it's paramount that when you enable these types of services, you choose strong security settings. Using strong passwords is a good start, but you can also configure limited access to these services from the Sharing preferences.

Lion's network host sharing services include:

► DVD or CD Sharing (Remote Disk)—This service, also known as Remote Disk, allows you to share your Mac's optical drive via the network. It's primarily designed to let you install software for MacBook Air or the Mini, which lack a built-in optical drive. Do not confuse Remote Disk with the standard file sharing services covered previously in this chapter. This service differs in several key respects; it shares only what is in the optical drive, you cannot configure user-specific access, and it can only be accessed via Bonjour. By enabling this service, the launchd control process starts the ODSAgent background process, which listens for Remote Disk requests on a very high randomly selected TCP port. This service can be accessed only by other Macs from the Finder's sidebar or the Migration Assistant application.

MORE INFO ► Several Apple Knowledge Base articles contain more information about Remote Disk, including HT1131, HT1777, and HT2129.

► Screen Sharing—Allows remote control of your Mac. Using this service is covered later in this chapter.

► Printer Sharing— Allows network access to printers that are directly attached to your Mac. Using this service is covered in Chapter 8, "Peripherals and Printing."

► Scanner Sharing—Allows network access to document scanners that are directly attached to your Mac. This service only works with other Macs on a local network (Bonjour) via the Image Capture application. This service is also enabled only on a per-user basis, and available only when the user is logged in. By enabling this service, the launchd control process listens for scanner sharing requests on a very high randomly selected TCP port and starts the Image Capture Extension background process as needed to handle any requests. The only additional configuration is that you can, from the Sharing preferences, enable specific scanners if you have more than one attached.

▶ Remote Login—Allows remote control of your Mac's command line via Secure Shell (SSH). Using this service is covered later in this chapter.

▶ Remote Management—Augments the screen sharing service to allow remote administration of your Mac via the Apple Remote Desktop 3.5 (ARD) application. Using this service is covered later in this chapter.

▶ Remote Apple Events—Allows applications and AppleScripts on another Mac to communicate with applications and services on your Mac. This service is most often used to facilitate automated AppleScript workflows between applications running on separate Macs. By enabling this service, the launchd control process listens for remote Apple Events requests on TCP and UDP port 3130 and starts the AEServer background process as needed to handle any requests. By default, all nonguest user accounts will be allowed to access the service, but this can be limited to specific users from the Sharing preferences.

▶ Xgrid Sharing—Allows you to join an Xgrid system, which is Apple's distributed computing solution that allows you to turn a collection of networked Macs into a supercomputer. The Xgrid software built into Mac OS X only allows your Mac to become an agent of the Xgrid system. An Xgrid agent performs tasks at the behest of an Xgrid controller, which can only be a Mac OS X server. Further, though Xgrid is the easiest distributed computing solution to date, it is not designed for the casual user. You cannot just send any application process through the Xgrid system. At the very least, issuing jobs to Xgrid requires familiarity with the command line or the use of software designed to take advantage of the Xgrid service. By enabling this service, the launchd control process starts the xgridagentd background process, which contacts the Xgrid controller on TCP port 4111 and waits for any available jobs. Finally, to join an Xgrid system, you must configure a password on your Mac to authenticate it to the Xgrid controller.

MORE INFO ▶ You can find out more about Xgrid at http://developer.apple.com/ hardwaredrivers/hpc/xgrid_intro.html.

▶ Internet Sharing—This allows your Mac to "reshare" a single network or Internet connection to any other network interface. For example, if your Mac had Internet access via a cellular network USB adapter, you could enable Internet Sharing for the Mac's

Wi-Fi and turn it into a wireless access point for the other computers. When you enable the Internet Sharing service, the launchd process starts several background processes. The natd process performs the Network Address Translation (NAT) service that allows multiple network clients to share a single network or Internet connection. The bootpd process provides the DHCP automatic network configuration service for the network devices connected via your Mac. When a network device connects to your Mac's shared network connection, it will automatically obtain an IP address, usually in the 10.0.2.X range. Finally, the named process provides DNS resolution for network devices connected via your Mac.

▶ Bluetooth Sharing—Allows access to your Mac via Bluetooth short-range wireless. Using this service is covered in Chapter 8, "Peripherals and Printing."

Understanding Screen Sharing

Providing remote phone support can be arduous. Inexperienced users don't know how to properly communicate the issues they are experiencing or even what they are seeing on the screen. Further, attempting to describe the steps involved in performing troubleshooting or administrative tasks to an inexperienced user over the phone is at best time consuming and at worst a painful experience for both parties.

When it comes to troubleshooting or administration, nothing beats actually seeing the computer's screen and controlling its mouse and keyboard. Lion includes built-in software that allows you to view and control the graphical interface via three methods; system screen sharing, iChat screen sharing, and Apple Remote Desktop 3.5 (ARD) remote management.

Both system screen sharing and iChat screen sharing are included with the standard system software, and their use is covered in the following sections of this chapter. However, the standard installation of Lion includes only the client-side software for ARD 3.5, as the administrative side of ARD used to control other Macs is a separate purchase. Yet, screen sharing is a subset of ARD, so when you enable ARD remote management, you are also enabling screen sharing. This may seem a bit confusing if you look at the Sharing preferences interface, which will disable the screen sharing checkbox when remote management is enabled. Rest assured, though, enabling remote management will also enable screen sharing. Thus, you can save yourself a step by initially configuring remote management, which allows for both ARD and screen sharing access. Configuring ARD remote management is also covered later in this chapter, as it can still be used to provide basic screen sharing.

All Apple screen sharing is based on a modified version of the Virtual Network Computing (VNC) protocol. The primary modification is the use of optional encryption for both viewing and controlling traffic. Another change is the ability to copy and paste between Macs using screen sharing. Further, Lion has introduced two new screen sharing features. The first allows you to quickly copy files to another Mac via screen sharing. The second allows you to access a virtual desktop on another Mac via screen sharing. In other words, on Lion systems screen sharing allows you to have your own virtual login on another Mac, completely separate from the login currently being used by the local user. This feature is similar to fast user switching, covered in Chapter 2, "User Accounts," except the second user is entirely remote via screen sharing and potentially using the computer at the same time as the local user.

> **NOTE** ▶ VNC is a cross-platform standard for remote control, so if configured properly, Lion's screen sharing technology integrates well with other third-party VNC-based systems. Thus, your Mac can control (or be controlled by) any other VNC-based software regardless of operating system.

> **NOTE** ▶ Lion's screen sharing is backward compatible with Mac OS X v10.5 or later screen sharing. Further, Lion computers can control previous Mac OS X systems that have ARD remote management or other VNC software enabled.

Using System Screen Sharing

This service, as its name implies, allows users to remotely view and control a Mac's graphical interface via a network connection. Obviously, in order to access a Mac remotely via screen sharing, the remote Mac must first have screen sharing enabled.

Enabling the Screen Sharing Service

To enable screen sharing:

1 Open the Sharing preferences by choosing Apple menu > System Preferences, then clicking the Sharing icon.

2 Click the lock icon in the bottom-left corner and authenticate as an administrative user to unlock the Sharing preferences.

> **NOTE** ▶ The screen sharing service is part of the ARD remote management service. Thus, if Remote Management is enabled, the Screen Sharing checkbox will be inaccessible.

3 Select the Screen Sharing checkbox in the Service list to enable screen sharing.

The launchd control process starts the AppleVNCServer background process, which listens for screen sharing service requests on TCP and UDP port 5900. By default, only administrative user accounts will be allowed to access the service.

4   Optionally, to adjust screen sharing access, select the "All users" radio button, or use the plus and minus buttons at the bottom of the users list.

When adding accounts, a dialog appears allowing you to select the specific users or groups for whom you wish to grant screen sharing access. You can select existing users or groups, or create a new Sharing user account by clicking the New Person button or selecting a contact from your Address Book.

5   Optionally, to allow a wider range of operating systems to access your Mac's screen sharing service, click the Computer Settings button. Enable guest and VNC screen sharing access in the resulting dialog.

When attempting to access your Mac's screen sharing, the currently logged-in user must authorize the session. By default, only local authorized users and groups are allowed to use screen sharing. Select the top checkbox to allow anyone (from another Mac) to ask permission to share the screen.

Standard third-party VNC viewers cannot authenticate using the secure methods employed by screen sharing, so you must set a specific password for VNC access. Remember that all standard VNC traffic is unencrypted. Further standard VNC viewers cannot use screen sharing's copy and paste, file copy, or virtual desktop features.

Control Another Computer via Screen Sharing

The process to connect to and control another computer for screen sharing is similar to how you connect to a shared file system. From the Finder, you can connect to another computer for screen sharing either by browsing to the computer from the Shared list or Network folder or by manually entering its network address in the Connect to Server dialog. The latter method will also allow you to connect to and control any host providing standard VNC services.

NOTE ▶ Browsing for screen sharing computers works only for Bonjour-compatible clients.

To control the graphical interface of another computer with screen sharing, ARD 3 remote management, or VNC enabled:

1   From the Finder, initiate a connection to the computer you wish to control using one of two methods:

▶   Browse to and select the computer from the Finder sidebar's Shared list, or select the computer from the Finder's Network folder. Then click the Share Screen button to continue.

▶ In the Finder's Connect to Server dialog, enter vnc:// followed by the computer's IP address, DNS host name, or Bonjour name. Then click the Connect button to continue.

The Mac will automatically open the /System/Library/CoreServices/Screen Sharing application and initiate a connection to the specified host.

2   You are presented with a dialog where you must enter the authentication information. Optionally, you can select the checkbox that will save this information to your login keychain. Click the Connect button to continue.

NOTE ▶ If you are using Kerberos or you have previously saved your authentication information to a keychain, the computer will automatically authenticate for you and will not present the authentication dialog.

3   Depending on the remote computer's system and the user you authenticated with, one of three situations will occur:

▶ If the remote computer is not a Mac running Lion, then you will instantly connect to the current screen of the remote computer.

▶ If the remote computer is a Mac running Lion and no one is logged in, or if you authenticated as the currently logged-in user, you will instantly connect to the current screen of the remote Mac.

▶   If the remote computer is a Mac running Lion and you authenticated using a different user than the one currently using the Mac, you will be presented with a dialog allowing you to choose between the currently logged-in user and a virtual desktop for your user account. If you select the top choice, the remote user will be prompted with a dialog to either allow or deny you access. The remote user's choice will dictate if you can connect. If, however, you select the bottom choice, you will instantly be connected to a new virtual screen that will log in to your account. The other user will not know that you are remotely using the computer.

4   Once connected to the remote computer, a new window opens, titled with the controlled computer's name, showing a live view of the controlled computer's screen(s).

Any time this window is active, all keyboard entries and mouse movements will be sent to the controlled computer. For example, using the Command-Q keyboard shortcut will quit the active application on the computer being controlled. Thus, in order to quit the Screen Sharing application, you have to click the close (X) button at the top-left corner of the window.

5   Optionally, select View > Show Toolbar to reveal additional screen sharing features, including the ability to take a screen shot of the remote Mac and copy and paste between your Mac and the remote Mac.

6   Optionally, if the remote computer is a Mac running Lion, you can drag and drop files from your Finder to the Mac's remote desktop. Doing so will open a File Transfers dialog allowing you to verify the transfer progress or cancel the file transfer.

NOTE ▶ If Remote Management is enabled, you will not be allowed to drag and drop files via screen sharing.

While using the Screen Sharing application, be sure to check out the preference options by choosing Screen Sharing > Preferences from the menu bar. Use these preferences to adjust screen size, encryption, and quality settings. If you are experiencing slow performance, adjust these settings for fastest performance. Keep in mind that some network connections, such as crowded wireless or dial-up connections, are so slow that these preferences won't matter much and you will simply have to wait for the screen to redraw.

Using iChat Screen Sharing

The included iChat instant messaging application can be used to initiate screen sharing, and as an added bonus will simultaneously provide voice chat services between the administrator Mac and the controlled Mac. iChat screen sharing also makes it much easier to locate other Macs to control, as iChat will automatically resolve the location of remote computers based on your active chats or available buddies. Further, iChat also supports reverse screen sharing—the administrator Mac can push its screen to display on another Mac for demonstration purposes.

> **NOTE** ▶ iChat does not require either Mac to have screen sharing enabled in the Sharing preferences because iChat includes a quick and easy authorization process to initiate each screen sharing session.

> **NOTE** ▶ iChat's screen sharing is only compatible with other Macs running Mac OS X v10.5 or later. When you select chat participants, iChat will automatically determine if their computer is using a compatible version of iChat.

To initiate an iChat screen sharing session:

1   From iChat, select an available chat user from a buddy list, and then click the Screen Sharing button at the bottom of the buddy list.

   This opens a pop-up menu where you can choose "Share My Screen with <chatuser>" or "Ask to Share <chatuser>'s Screen," where <chatuser> is the name of the user whose computer you are asking to control.

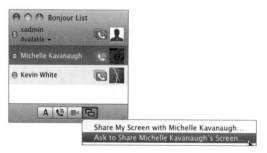

2   The user on the other computer will see an authorization dialog where he can choose to accept or decline your request to share screens.

3   If the other user clicks the Accept button, the screen sharing session will begin. The following screen capture shows the screen sharing "controller's" point of view. The other user will see the same screen without the small My Computer window in the bottom-left corner.

Further, if both computers support voice chat, iChat will automatically start a voice chat session between the two computers. You may need to configure Audio/Video settings in the iChat preferences for this feature to work properly.

Both users will have simultaneous control of the Mac being shared, including the ability to end the screen sharing session at any time from the Screen Sharing menu item on the right side of the menu bar.

NOTE ▶ Even as an administrative user, you cannot force other users to share screens using iChat; they have the sole power to allow or deny your request.

Understanding Remote Login

Lion includes support for command-line remote login via the Secure Shell (SSH) protocol, which by default runs on TCP port 22. Apple's implementation of remote login is based on the popular OpenSSH project and defaults to the more secure SSH version 2 standard. OpenSSH provides a robust and secure environment for remotely accessing the command line of another network host.

With graphical interface screen sharing so readily accessible in Lion, you may wonder why the ability to remotely log in to the command line is still relevant. After all, if you need to remotely access another Mac's command line, you can always use screen sharing to open and control the Terminal application on the remote Mac. Well, aside from screen sharing being a bandwidth hog, there are many uses for remote login and SSH that remote screen sharing does not provide.

For starters, using remote login is much more efficient than screen sharing because only text is transmitted. Often, remote login is so fast that it's indistinguishable from using the Terminal's command line on a local computer. As an administrative user, you can remotely log in to a Mac and resolve an issue from the Terminal without the user even knowing you were there. Even if the Mac is sitting idle at the login window, you can still remotely log in to its command line and take care of business.

Aside from providing a secure network connection for remote login, the SSH protocol can also provide secure connections for any other network protocol. You can use SSH to create an encrypted tunnel between two SSH-enabled network devices and then pipe any other TCP- or UDP-based network protocol through the SSH connection. Further, SSH remote login allows you to securely transfer files using Secure File Transfer Protocol (SFTP) or the secure copy command scp.

Finally, because SSH is a network standard, it's compatible across many platforms. In other words, your Mac can securely log in remotely via the Terminal to any compatible network host with SSH enabled. Conversely, any systems with a command-line prompt and SSH client software can securely log in remotely to your Mac.

MORE INFO ▶ As with any Terminal command, you can learn more about SSH by reading the ssh manual page.

Using Remote Login (SSH)

This service, as its name implies, allows users to remotely log in to your Mac's command line via an SSH network connection. Obviously, in order to access a Mac via remote login, the remote Mac must first have the remote login service enabled.

> **NOTE** ▶ If you aren't already comfortable with navigation in the UNIX command line, then it's strongly recommended that you study the command-line concepts in Appendix B, "Command-Line Essentials," before reading the remainder of the section.

Enabling the Remote Login (SSH) Service

To enable the Remote Login service:

1   Open the Sharing preferences and authenticate as an administrative user to unlock the preferences.

2   Select the Remote Login checkbox in the Service list to enable the SSH Remote Login service.

The launchd control process listens for remote login service requests on TCP 22 and starts the sshd background process as needed to handle any requests. By default, all standard and administrative user accounts will be allowed to access the service.

3   Optionally, to limit remote login access, select "Only these users" and click the plus icon. In the resulting dialog, select the standard users, administrative users, or groups for whom you wish to grant access.

TIP ▶ Enabling the Remote Login service also enables the SFTP service, a secure version of the FTP protocol, and allows for use of the remote secure copy command, scp.

Remotely Access a Host via SSH

The primary interface for SSH is the Terminal's ssh command. The syntax for initiating a remote login connection is ssh followed by the name of the user you will be logging in as, then the @ symbol, and then the address or host name of the computer you wish to log in to. If you're logging in to a computer for the first time using SSH with standard password authentication, you'll be prompted to trust the authenticity of the remote host. If a network administrator has given you a public key file for authentication, you won't have to enter a user password.

TIP ▶ From the Terminal, you can also browse for ssh hosts by choosing Shell > New Remote Connection from the menu.

In the following example, Michelle starts off in the Terminal on a Mac named "client." She issues the ssh command to connect to the "server.pretendco.com" Mac using the user name "sadmin." She has never established an SSH connection between these two computers, so she is asked if she wants to trust the authenticity of the "server" computer. In most cases, the answer to this question is "yes." Michelle then enters the sadmin user's password, but note that it is never shown onscreen.

Notice how the command prompt changes to show that Michelle is using the "server" computer. Using the command line remotely via SSH is nearly indistinguishable from using it locally. Michelle issues the who command on "server" to see who is currently using that computer. You can see that a user has logged in to the graphical interface, "console," also using the sadmin account, and you can see Michelle's SSH connection, "ttys000." Finally, in this example, Michelle logs out and closes the SSH connection by issuing the exit command.

client:~ michelle$ ssh sadmin@server.pretendco.com

The authenticity of host 'server.pretendco.com (10.0.1.200)' can't be established.

RSA key fingerprint is bd:34:8c:1e:c6:bf:9a:46:e9:2a:b1:cc:81:7c:a3:02.

Are you sure you want to continue connecting (yes/no)? yes

Warning: Permanently added 'server.pretendco.com,10.0.1.200' (RSA) to the list of known hosts.

Password:

Last login: Sat Oct 6 18:19:09 2009

server:~ sadmin$ who

sadmin console Oct 2 11:57

sadmin ttys000 Oct 6 22:13 (client.pretendco.com)

server:~ sadmin$ exit

logout

Connection to server.pretendco.com closed.

client:~ michelle$

TIP ▶ The OpenSSH software includes a secure copy command, scp, and a secure FTP client, sftp. These commands can be used to securely transfer files to and from a Mac with remote login enabled.

Enable ARD Remote Management

Remote Management is client-side software that allows the Apple Remote Desktop 3.5 (ARD) administration tool to access your Mac. ARD is the ultimate remote management tool for Mac OS X computers. In addition to screen sharing, ARD allows administrators to remotely gather system information and usage statistics, change settings, add or remove files and software, send UNIX commands, and perform nearly any other management task you can think of. The real power of ARD is that you can execute all these tasks simultaneously on dozens of Macs with just a few clicks. Again, if you plan to use ARD in the future, but you want to enable screen sharing for now, you can enable remote management in one step and take advantage of both remote control features.

MORE INFO ▶ The ARD 3.5 administration software provides advanced functionality that goes well beyond simple screen sharing. You can find out more about ARD at www.apple.com/remotedesktop.

To enable ARD remote management:

1 Open the Sharing preferences and authenticate as an administrative user to unlock the preferences.

2   Select the Remote Management checkbox in the Service list to enable both screen
sharing and the ARD client-side services.

The launchd control process starts the ARDAgent background process, which listens for
incoming administration requests on UDP port 3283, and also starts AppleVNCServer,
which listens for screen sharing requests on TCP port 5900.

NOTE ▸ The screen sharing service is part of the ARD remote management service. Thus, if Remote Management is selected, the Screen Sharing checkbox will be
inaccessible.

3   If this is the first time you have enabled remote management, you'll see a dialog
that allows you to select the ARD options you wish to allow for all nonguest local
users. You can individually select options, or you can hold down the Option key and
then select any checkbox to enable all options. Click OK once you have made your
selections.

4   Optionally, to further limit ARD access, select "Only these users" and click the plus icon.

Then select a standard or administrative local user for whom you wish to grant ARD access. When you're done, another dialog appears, from which you select the ARD options this user can access.

 You can edit a user's ARD options at any time by double-clicking that user's name in the user access list.

5   Additional optional ARD computer options are available by clicking the Computer Settings button.

This opens a dialog that allows you to enable guest and VNC screen sharing access (covered earlier in this chapter) and the Remote Management menu bar item that allows users to request help from administrators, and add any additional information to help identify this particular Mac.

Securing Network Services

From a network services standpoint, your Mac is already very secure because, by default, there are only a few essential services running that respond to external requests. Even once you start providing individual shared services, your Mac is designed to respond only to those services that are enabled. Further, services that could cause trouble if compromised, like file or screen sharing, can be configured to have limited access authorization, as covered previously in this chapter. Still, users can open third-party applications or background services that could leave a Mac vulnerable to a network attack.

> **TIP** ▶ To maintain a high level of network security, you should leave sharing services disabled unless absolutely necessary. If you do enable sharing services, be sure to limit authorization access as best you can.

Understanding the Personal Application Firewall

The most common method to secure network services is to configure a firewall, which will block unauthorized network service access. Most networks use a firewall to limit inbound traffic from an Internet connection. In fact, most personal routers, like AirPort base stations, are by design also network firewalls. While network-level firewalls will block unauthorized Internet traffic into your network, they will not block traffic that originated from inside your network to your Mac. Also, if your Mac is mobile and is often joining new networks, odds are that every new network you join will have different firewall rules.

Thus, to prevent unauthorized network services from allowing incoming connections to your specific Mac, you can enable the built-in personal application firewall. A personal firewall will block unauthorized connections to your Mac no matter where they originated. The Lion firewall also features a single-click configuration that provides a high level of network service security, which will work for most users.

A standard firewall uses rules based on service port numbers. As you've learned previously in this lesson, each service defaults to a standard port or set of ports. However, some network services, like iChat, use a wide range of dynamic ports. If we were to manually configure a traditional firewall, we would have to make dozens of rules for every potential port that the user may need.

To resolve this issue, Lion's firewall uses an adaptive technology that allows connections based on applications and service needs, without you having to know the specific ports they use. For example, you can authorize iChat to accept any incoming connection without configuring all of the individual TCP and UDP ports used by the iChat application.

TIP ▶ A more traditional port-based firewall, ipfw, is still in place in Lion and can be configured from the Terminal or the ipfw configuration files if that's your preferred method.

The personal application firewall also leverages another built-in feature, code signing, to ensure that allowed applications and services aren't changed without your knowledge. Further, code signing allows Apple and third-party developers to provide a guarantee that their software hasn't been tampered with. This level of verifiable trust allows you to configure the firewall in default mode with a single click, which will automatically allow signed applications and services to receive incoming connections.

Finally, because the personal application firewall is fully dynamic, it will open only the necessary ports when the application or service is running. Again, using iChat as an example, the personal application firewall will allow only incoming connections to the required ports if the iChat application is running. If the application quits because the user logs out, the firewall will close the associated ports. Having the required ports open only when an application or service needs them provides an extra layer of security not found with traditional firewalls.

Configure the Personal Application Firewall

To enable and configure the Lion personal application firewall:

1   Open the Security & Privacy preferences by choosing Apple menu > System Preferences, then clicking the Security & Privacy icon.

2   Click the lock icon in the bottom-left corner and authenticate as an administrative user to unlock the Security & Privacy preferences.

3   Select the Firewall tab at the top, and then click the Start button to turn on the Lion personal application firewall using the default rules.

    Once enabled, the Start button changes to a Stop button, allowing you to disable the firewall.

The default configuration is to allow incoming traffic for established connections (connections that were initiated from your Mac and are expecting a return) and for any signed software or enabled service. This level of security is adequate for most users.

TIP Firewall logging is always enabled and can be viewed from the Console application. The firewall log is located at /private/var/log/appfirewall.log.

4 If you want to customize the firewall, any additional firewall configuration is revealed by clicking the Advanced button.

From the Advanced dialog, you can see which services are currently being allowed. Without any additional configuration, sharing services enabled from the Sharing preferences will automatically appear in the list of allowed services.

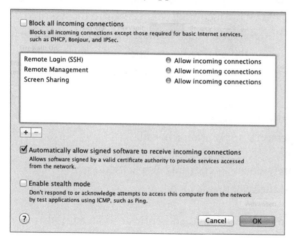

5 Optionally, for a bit more control, you can manually set which applications and services the firewall allows by deselecting the checkbox to automatically allow signed software.

With this firewall choice, as you open new network applications for the first time or update existing network applications, you will see a dialog where you can allow or deny the new network application. This dialog will appear outside the Security & Privacy preferences any time a new network application requests incoming access.

6   If you are manually setting network application and service firewall access, you can always return to the Advanced firewall dialog to review the list of items, and either delete items from the list or even specifically disallow certain items.

7   Optionally, for a bit more security, you can select the "Enable stealth mode" checkbox to prevent response or acknowledgement of a failed attempt to the requesting host.

With this enabled, your Mac will not respond to any unauthorized network connections, including network diagnostic protocols like ping, traceroute, and port scan. In other words, your computer will simply ignore the request instead of returning a response of failure to the requesting host.

However, your Mac will still respond to other services that are allowed. This includes, by default, Bonjour, which will dutifully announce your Mac presence, thus preventing your Mac from being truly hidden on the network.

8   Optionally, when the utmost security is needed, you can select the "Block all incoming connections" checkbox. Notice that selecting this option automatically selects stealth mode as well.

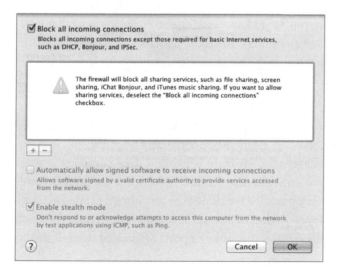

With this enabled, your Mac will not respond to any incoming network connections except for those required for basic network services or established connections, such as those needed to browse the web or check email. Obviously, this will prevent any shared service or application hosted on your Mac from working remotely.

Troubleshooting Network Services

To effectively troubleshoot a network issue, you must isolate the issue into one of three categories: local, network, or service. Most issues involving failure to access network services will probably fall under the service category. This means that you should probably focus most of your efforts toward troubleshooting the specific service that you're having issues with.

However, before digging too deep into troubleshooting the specific network service, quickly check for general network issues. First, check to see if other network services are working. Opening a web browser and navigating to a few different local and Internet websites is always a good general network connectivity test. To be thorough, also test other network services, or test from other computers on the same network. If you're experiencing problems connecting to a file server but you can connect to web servers, chances are your TCP/IP configuration is fine, and you should concentrate on the specifics of the file server. If you're only experiencing problems with one particular service, you probably don't have local or network issues and you should focus your efforts on troubleshooting just that service.

Conversely, if other network clients or services aren't working either, your issue is likely related to local or network issues. Double-check local network settings to ensure proper configuration from both the Network preferences and Network Utility. If you find that other computers aren't working, you might have a widespread network issue that goes beyond troubleshooting the client computers. For more information, general network troubleshooting was detailed in Chapter 6, "Network Configuration."

Using Network Port Scan

Once you decide to focus on troubleshooting a problematic network service, one of your most important diagnostic tools will be the network port scan utility. Part of the Network Utility application, port scan will scan for any open network service ports on the specified network address. As covered earlier in this chapter, network service protocols are tied to specific TCP and UDP network ports. Network devices providing a service must leave the appropriate network ports open in order to accept incoming connections from other network clients. A port scan will reveal if the required ports are indeed open. If the ports aren't open, that device is either not providing the expected service or is configured to provide the service in a nonstandard method. Either way, this indicates that the issue lies with the device providing the service, not your Mac.

NOTE ► Network administrators view repeated network pings and broad port scans as a threat. Thus, some network devices are configured to not respond even when working properly. In general, you should avoid excessive network pinging and scanning an unnecessarily broad range of ports when testing others' servers.

To use network port scan:

1   Open /Applications/Utilities/Network Utility and click the Ping tab at the top.

    Before performing a port scan, check for basic network connectivity by attempting to ping the device that is supposed to be providing the service. Enter the device's network address or host name and click the Ping button.

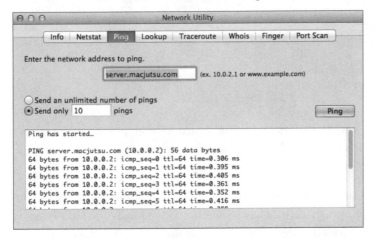

    If the ping is successful, it should return with the amount of time it took for the ping to travel to the network device and then return. Assuming you have network connectivity to the other device, continue to the next step.

2   Click the Port Scan tab at the top of the Network Utility window.

    Again, enter the network address or host name of the device that is supposed to be providing the service.

3 If you're only troubleshooting a specific service, limit the port scan to just that service's default ports, by selecting the appropriate checkbox and entering a beginning and ending port range.

There are 65,535 available TCP and UDP network ports, so a full port scan is unnecessary and can take some time. Even if you don't know the specific port, most common ports are between 0 and 1024.

4 Click the Scan button to initiate the port scan process.

Depending on the scan range you chose, it may take several minutes to complete the scan. Any open ports that were discovered will be listed along with the associated network protocol if known.

NOTE ▶ There are some inaccuracies with the protocol reporting of the port scan feature. For example, port 106 (listed as 3com-tsmux) is actually the Lion Password Server, and port 625 (listed as dec_dlm) is actually the directory service proxy. This is because these ports are registered by the IANA (iana.org) for the reported protocols. However, Apple is using these numbers for its own purposes.

Troubleshooting Network Applications

Aside from general network service troubleshooting, there are a few application-specific troubleshooting techniques you can try. First, double-check any application-specific configuration and preference settings. It takes only a few moments, and you may find that users have inadvertently caused the problem by changing a setting they shouldn't have.

Be aware of these specifics when troubleshooting network applications:

▶ Safari—Safari is a good web browser, but it's not perfect. There are certain webpages that Safari just can't get right. The only resolution is to try a different web browser. Several third-party browsers are available for the Mac, including popular alternatives like Firefox, Chrome, OmniWeb, and Opera.

▶ Mail—Improper mail account configuration settings are the most common cause of Mail application issues. Fortunately, the Mail application includes a built-in account diagnostic tool called the Mail Connection Doctor that will attempt to establish a connection with all configured incoming and outgoing mail servers. To open the Mail Connection Doctor, choose Window > Connection Doctor within the Mail application. If a problem is found, a suggested resolution will be offered, but for a more detailed diagnostic view, click the Show Detail button to reveal the progress log, and then click the Check Again button to rerun the tests.

TIP Apple also provides an online mail Setup Assistant database that may help you identify mail client configuration issues, www.apple.com/support/macosx/mailassistant.

▶ iChat—iChat also suffers from occasional improper account configuration, but it's a less frequent occurrence than with the Mail application. More often, iChat experiences connectivity issues when attempting advanced messaging features like voice and video conferencing. As such, iChat also features a Connection Doctor that will let you view conference statistics, chat capabilities, and the iChat error log. To open the iChat Connection Doctor, within the iChat application choose Video > Connection Doctor. If you have experienced recent errors, the Connection Doctor will open to the error log, but you can view other information from the Show pop-up menu.

Specific Network File Sharing Issues

There are a few known Lion file service issues that you should be aware of. They aren't software bugs in the sense that something is broken and requires a fix. These issues represent compatibility and design choices that are intentional but may still cause you problems.

As covered in Chapter 4, "Data Management," Mac files use separate metadata stores. The NFS and WebDAV file sharing protocols do not support metadata of this type. Thus, when files are written to a mounted NFS or WebDAV volume, Lion will automatically split these files into two separate files. With this practice, commonly known as AppleDouble, the data will retain the original name, but the metadata will be saved with a period and underscore before the original name. The Finder will recognize these split files and show only a single file to the user. However, users on other operating systems will see two separate files and may have trouble accessing the appropriate file.

You may encounter another issue when trying to access an AFP network volume from a Windows file server. Windows servers prior to 2008 include Services for Macintosh (SFM), which provides only the legacy AFP 2 file service. Lion is still compatible with AFP 2 but is optimized for AFP 3.1. There are many known performance issues with AFP 2, so you should avoid it at all costs. Ideally, you should use a Mac OS X Server to provide AFP services for your network. However, if you must keep the Windows file server, you can add AFP 3.1 support by installing Group Logic's ExtremeZ-IP (www.grouplogic.com). Also remember that Lion clients include a robust SMB client that will natively connect to your Windows server with a high degree of reliability and performance.

> **MORE INFO ▶** Lion only supports legacy AFP if you follow the instructions in Knowledge Base article HT4700, "OS X Lion: Connecting to legacy AFP services."

Troubleshooting Shared Services

If you're providing a shared service from your Mac, and others are having trouble reaching it, you must first consider how established the service is to determine where to focus your efforts. So, if your Mac has been reliably providing a shared service for a while, but now a single client computer has trouble accessing the service, troubleshoot the client computer before troubleshooting your shared Mac.

Otherwise, if multiple clients cannot access your shared Mac, you may indeed have an issue with the sharing service. After ruling out other potential local client and network issues, you can safely assume that the problem lies with the Mac providing shared services. If so, shared network service issues fall into two general categories: service communication or service access.

Service communication issues are manifested by an inability to establish a connection to the shared service. Keep in mind that if you are presented with an authentication dialog, the client and server are establishing a proper connection, and you should troubleshoot the issue as a service access issue. However, if you are unable to authenticate, or you can authenticate but you're not authorized to access the service, then you are experiencing a service access issue.

Network Service Communication Issues

If you are unable to establish a connection to the shared service, this may signal a network service communication issue.

To troubleshoot service communication issues:

▶ Double-check the shared Mac's network configuration—From the Network preferences, make sure the Mac's network interfaces are active and configured with the appropriate TCP/IP settings. You can also use Network Utility to verify the network configuration. If a DNS server is providing a host name for your shared Mac, use the Lookup tool in Network Utility to verify the host name.

▶ Double-check the Mac's sharing service configuration—From the Sharing preferences, verify the Mac's sharing name and ensure that the appropriate services are enabled and configured.

▶ Double-check the Mac's firewall configuration—From the Security & Privacy preferences, first temporarily stop the firewall to see if disabling it makes a difference. If you are able to establish a connection, adjust the list of allowed services and applications before you restart the firewall.

▶ Check for basic network connectivity to the shared Mac—First, turn off the firewall's stealth mode, and then, from another Mac, use Network Utility's ping tool to check for basic connectivity to the shared Mac. If you can't ping the shared Mac, you're probably having a network-level issue that goes beyond service troubleshooting.

▶ Check for network service port connectivity to the shared Mac—First, turn off the firewall's stealth mode, and then, from another Mac, use Network Utility's port scan tool to verify whether the expected network service ports are accessible. If the shared Mac is configured properly, the appropriate network service ports should register as open. If network routers exist between the network clients and the shared Mac, consider the possibility that a network administrator has decided to block access to those ports.

Network Service Access Issues

Failure to authenticate or be granted authorization to a shared service is considered a network service access issue. The following list provides methods for troubleshooting these access issues. However, if your services rely upon a network directory service as well, you should also consider the directory service troubleshooting methodology covered later in the "Troubleshooting Directory Services" section of this chapter.

▶ Verify the local user account settings—When using local user accounts, make sure the correct authentication information is being used. You may find that the user is not using the right information, and you may have to reset the account password. (Troubleshooting user account issues was covered in Chapter 2, "User Accounts.") Also, keep in mind that some services do not allow the use of guest and sharing-only user accounts. Further, the VNC-compatible and Xgrid services use password information that is not directly linked to a user account.

▶ Double-check directory service settings—If you use a network directory service in your environment, verify that the Mac is properly communicating with the directory service by checking its status in the Directory Utility application. Even if you're only trying to use local accounts, any directory service issues can cause authentication problems. Also, keep in mind that some services, like ARD remote management, do not by default allow you to authenticate with accounts hosted from network directories.

▶ Double-check shared service access settings—Several authenticated sharing services allow you to configure access lists. Use the Sharing preferences to verify that the appropriate user accounts are allowed to access the shared service.

▶ Verify file system ownership and permissions—If you're able to authenticate or connect to file and web sharing services, but you're unable to access files and folders, then file system permissions are probably getting in the way. In this case the Finder may display a message indicating that you cannot complete your action because of insufficient permissions to access the item. Use the Finder's Get Info window to inspect the file and folder permissions of the inaccessible items. Sometimes the easiest resolution is to simply create a new permission setting just for the user who is experiencing access issues. Lion's adoption of file system ACLs allows you to make as many permission rules as you want. Also, remember that any files accessed by the web sharing service should be readable by Everyone. Detailed information about file system permissions, including troubleshooting access issues, is covered in Chapter 3, "File Systems."

Understanding Directory Services

Directory services is a generic term used to describe the technologies that are used to locate network and resource information. Apple's implementation of directory services is branded as Open Directory (OD). It's responsible for providing Lion with fundamental network and resource information. The OD background process daemon, appropriately named opendirectoryd, is started during system startup and is always running as a background system process.

The primary directory service function is to act as the authority for resource information. Directory services can provide information about a variety of resources, but the most common resource type is account information. OD resolves all account identification requests and through secondary processes coordinates account authentication and authorization services. The primary focus of the remainder of this chapter is managing and troubleshooting directory services on Lion, aka OD, as it relates to account identification, authentication, and authorization.

Directory Service Resources

The "directory" in directory services and Open Directory (OD) refers to the fact that they provide a directory of information similar in many ways to an online phone book. The most commonly accessed directory resource is account information. With Lion, all account information, including user and group information, is stored in a directory. OD, or more specifically, the opendirectoryd daemon, handles all directory interaction for Lion, making it the single source for providing account information to every application, command, or background service.

Common directory resources used by Lion include:

▶ User accounts—The primary resource used to identify a human user to the computer. Detailed information regarding user accounts is covered in Chapter 2, "User Accounts."

▶ User groups—A collection of user accounts used to provide greater control over management and security settings. Detailed information regarding group accounts is also covered in Chapter 2.

▶ Computer accounts—This is information used to identify a specific computer for purposes of authentication and client management settings.

▶ Computer groups—A collection of computer accounts used to facilitate efficient client management settings for many computers.

▶ Network file mounts—Information used by Mac OS X's automatic network file mounting system. Automatic mounts are covered in *Apple Pro Training Series: OS X Lion Server Essentials.*

▶ Client management settings—Information used to automatically apply specific user and computer preferences based on administrator-controlled settings. Directory-based client management settings are covered in *Apple Training Series: Mac OS X Server Essentials v10.6.*

Directory Service Types

Through OD, Lion is able to easily access multiple directory services simultaneously. This allows Lion to integrate into a mixed directory environment with little difficulty and few compromises. As a result, Lion has become very popular among administrators who manage large networks with complicated directory service infrastructures.

Directory types supported by Lion include:

▶ Local—OD maintains a local directory database with a series of XML-encoded files located in the /var/db/dslocal/nodes/Default/ folder. Any locally stored resource information, including local user account information, is saved to this directory. The local directory is consulted first for any requested resource information.

▶ Network Information Systems (NIS)—This is a legacy protocol used by some UNIX systems to access network directory information. NIS is still supported by Lion but disabled by default. If support is enabled, NIS will always be consulted second for any requested resource information.

▶ Lightweight Directory Access Protocol version 3 (LDAPv3)—LDAPv3 has emerged as one of the most popular network directory standards. In fact, Lion Server's built-in directory service, appropriately dubbed Open Directory Server, uses the LDAPv3 protocol. Configuring Lion to connect, or bind, to an LDAPv3 service is covered in the "Configuring Network Directory Services" section later in this chapter.

▶ Active Directory (AD)—This is Microsoft's implementation of the LDAPv3 protocol. Though it's based on LDAPv3, Microsoft made so many changes to meet its design goals that AD is considered a unique network directory protocol unto itself. Configuring Lion to connect, or bind, to an AD service is also covered in the "Configuring Network Directory Services" section.

TIP ▶ Third-party developers can create their own Open Directory plug-ins to provide additional access to network directory services.

Advantages of Network Directory Services

Implementing network directory services is certainly more complicated than simply using the default local directory service. However, the administrative benefits of using resource and account information hosted on a network directory far outweigh the extra time spent setting it up.

Advantages of using network directory services are:

▶ User accounts are no longer tied to individual Macs—Users with a network or mobile account can log in to any Mac connected to the network directory service. Because the directory service maintains the account information, their entire user environment can be accessed from any Mac they can log in to.

▶ The same user account information can be used for multiple network services—Devices providing network services can connect to the network directory service. You can use the same user name and password for any network service even if those services are hosted on multiple separate servers.

▶ You can use Kerberos to provide secure single-sign-on authentication—Kerberos also happens to be the most secure popular authentication service to date. Details regarding Kerberos are covered in the "Managing Network Authentication" section later in this chapter.

▶ You can define user and computer settings from a centralized location—In addition to providing a single location for all account attributes, you can manage application and system settings from a single location. In other words, you can save client configuration information to a centralized network directory service, and any Mac connected, or bound, to the directory service will be automatically configured with those settings.

User Account Types

Until now, this text has covered only locally hosted directories, which contain resources and account information available to only a single Mac system. Even so, OD gives Lion the ability to access resource and account information hosted by network-based directory services. Thus, Lion can simultaneously access accounts located in both local and network directories.

Lion account location types include:

▶ Local account—Account information and the home folder are stored on the local Mac and available only to that Mac. Obviously, this account type can be created only on a local Mac.

▶ Network account—Account information and the home folder are stored on a network server that is providing a shared directory to any connected, or bound, network client. The Mac must be connected to the network directory in order for you to access a network account.

▶ Mobile account—Account information is stored on a network server providing a shared directory, but the account information can also be cached to the Mac's local directory. Every time you log in using a mobile account, the account information will be cached to the Mac's local directory. As long as the cached information remains on the Mac, you'll still be able to access the mobile account if the Mac isn't connected to the network directory. Mobile account home folders default to the local Mac, but the contents can also sync with a home folder on a network share.

Configuring Network Directory Services

The process of connecting Lion to a network directory service is called *directory binding*. The term *bind* is used to describe this connection because, unlike other types of network connections that come and go, the connection between a client and a network directory service is designed to be persistent.

Once you bind Lion to a network directory service, it will allow all services to request information from those network directories. Whenever directory service information is requested, the Mac will attempt to communicate with the network directories to which it's bound. Most important, you will be able to log in and authenticate to the Mac with user accounts hosted on the network directory.

Lion Directory Binding Methods

There are several methods for binding your Mac to a network directory service:

▸ Manually via the Users & Groups preferences—This manual method allows you very little control over the directory binding process. Using this method, you can bind your Mac to both Mac OS X Server providing OD services and Microsoft Active Directory services. This method is covered in the following sections of this chapter.

▸ Manually via the Directory Access application—This manual method allows for completely customizable configuration of the directory binding process. Using this method, you can bind your Mac to any LDAPv3 directory service (including OD services), Microsoft AD services, or any additional network directory via third-party directory service plug-ins. This method is also briefly covered in the following sections of this chapter.

NOTE ▸ Previous versions of Mac OS X offered other semi-automatic methods of binding to OD services, such as via Setup Assistant or an automated email. Lion and Lion Server no longer support these methods for directory service binding.

▸ Automatically via a configuration profile—Lion supports automatic configuration of directory service settings via configuration profiles. This profile can be deployed by simply double-clicking a local copy of a configuration profile or by having the Mac managed by a Mobile Device Management (MDM) solution. From the local Mac, you can, however, verify the directory service configuration from the User & Groups preferences or the Directory Access application, as covered later in this chapter.

MORE INFO ▸ OS X Lion Server can provide MDM services through Profile Manager, as covered in *Apple Pro Training Series: OS X Lion Server Essentials.*

Manually Configure Open Directory Binding

To configure binding for Open Directory (OD) services:

1 Open the Users & Groups preferences by choosing Apple menu > System Preferences, then clicking the Users & Groups icon.

2   Click the lock icon in the bottom-left corner and authenticate as an administrative user to unlock the Users & Groups preferences.

3   Click the Login Options button at the bottom of the user list and then click the Join button to the right.

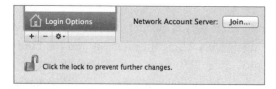

This will open a dialog allowing you to configure a directory service bind.

4   To bind your Mac to an OD server, enter the IP address or DNS host name of a server providing OD services in the server field, or you can click the pop-up menu button to select a local OD server via Bonjour.

Depending on the server configuration, this may be the only dialog you see. If the dialog doesn't automatically change, simply click the OK button to bind your Mac to the OD server. Skip to step 8.

5   If the OD server provides SSL certificates, as is the default on Lion Server, then you can choose to trust and install those certificates. Clicking the Trust button will install the OD-created certificates to the system keychain. After installation you can verify the certificates using /Applications/Utilities/Keychain Access as covered in Chapter 2, "User Accounts."

6 If the OD server does not have SSL enabled, as is the default on Lion Server, then you will be presented with a warning dialog explaining that the server isn't currently using SSL to encrypt the connection. For many, this will not be an issue, and it's acceptable to click the Continue button. However, you should consult with the server administrator to verify that this is the case.

7 If the OD server requires authentication to bind, the dialog will change to require authentication information. Optionally, you can pick a different name for your computer ID, or stick with the default based on your Mac's sharing name. Enter the authentication information provided by the server administrator and click the OK button to bind your Mac to the OD server.

8 Once the directory service bind is complete, if your Mac is successfully communicating with the OD service, you will see a green status indicator next to the server name.

Manually Configure Active Directory Binding

To configure binding for Microsoft Active Directory (AD) services:

1 Open the Users & Groups preferences by choosing Apple menu > System Preferences, then clicking the Users & Groups icon.

2   Click the lock icon in the bottom-left corner and authenticate as an administrative user to unlock the Users & Groups preferences.

3   Click the Login Options button at the bottom of the user list and then click the Join button to the right.

This will open a dialog allowing you to configure a directory service bind.

4   To bind your Mac to AD, enter the AD domain name in the server field.

The dialog will automatically change once it recognizes the AD domain.

5   Optionally, you can pick a different name for your computer ID, or simply stick with the default based on your Mac's sharing name.

6   Enter the authentication information provided by the server administrator and click the OK button to bind your Mac to the AD domain.

Depending on your AD implementation, it may take several minutes to bind your Mac to the AD domain.

7   Once the AD bind is complete, if your Mac is successfully communicating with the AD service, you will see a green status indicator next to the domain name.

MORE INFO ▶ Attempting to fully integrate Mac OS X into an AD system may require additional configuration. Find out more from Apple's AD integration technical white paper: www.seminars.apple.com/contactme/pdf/ L334436B_ActiveDirect_WP.pdf.

Advanced Directory Service Configuration

As mentioned previously, Lion's OD infrastructure allows for more complex directory service configurations, including the ability to simultaneously bind to multiple network directory services. The Users & Groups preferences allows for initial setup of multiple network directory services as long as they are either OD- or AD-based. After you have set up your initial network directory service in the Users & Groups preferences, click the Edit button to reveal the list of currently bound network directory servers.

This dialog shows the current state of all bound network directory services. The dialog will also allow you to bind your Mac to additional network directory servers or delete existing bindings. Simply click the plus button at the bottom of the list to initiate another network directory service bind. Again, follow the steps outlined previously to bind your Mac to an additional OD or AD service.

However, for more advanced configuration, you will need to use the Directory Utility application. You can open the Directory Utility from either the previously mentioned network directory service list dialog, or from the Finder by opening /System/Library/ CoreServices/Directory Utility.app. This application requires administrative access, but once authenticated will allow you to change many more directory service settings. The initial view allows you to configure various directory service settings by double-clicking on the service.

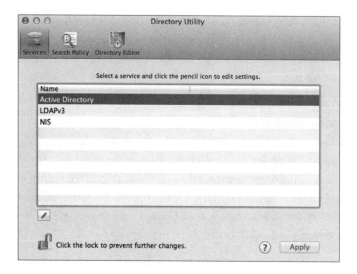

From Directory Utility, you can also manage the directory service search policy by clicking the Search Policy button in the toolbar. If your Mac has access to multiple directory services, the system will search for account information in local directories first, followed by network directories. If multiple network directory services are available, the system will search for account information based on this service order. If a similarly named account exists in multiple directories, the first account located is the one that's used. To change the search order, simply click and drag the server entries in this list.

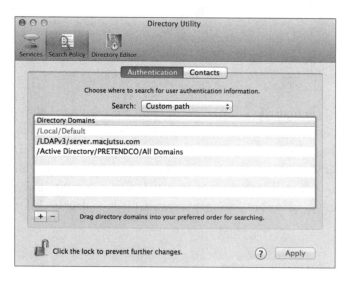

MORE INFO ▶ Directory services is a complicated topic that can extend well beyond the scope of this reference guide. For more information, check out *Apple Training Series: Mac OS X Directory Services v10.6.*

Managing Network Authentication

The concept of authentication has been covered previously, but to reiterate, authentication is the process of proving your identity to the computer. More specifically, you are proving to the computer that you should be allowed to access an account because you know a secret about the account that only the account's holder should know. Lion supports elaborate authentication systems that require special hardware to validate your identity, but alphanumeric passwords are still the most commonly used authentication secret.

Understanding Authentication and Authorization

Authorization is closely tied to authentication, but they are not the same thing. Authentication is only used to prove your account identity to the system, but authorization defines which items or services the account is allowed to access. In other words, authentication is who you are, and authorization is what you can do.

Authentication and authorization are used throughout Lion to ensure a safe computing environment. Open Directory (OD) coordinates authentication for Lion, but each service handles authorization differently. For example, Chapter 2, "User Accounts," showed how each user account type has different levels of access to the system. The login window uses the OD service to identify and authenticate the user, but Lion's system authorization services dictate which applications and services the user is authorized to access. A large part of Chapter 3, "File Systems," covered how access to files and folders is granted. Again, OD provides identification and authorization services, but the file system permissions determine which files and folders the user is authorized to access.

Understanding Network Authentication

Authentication systems vary as widely as the services they help secure. Often legacy technologies use authentication techniques that are considered rudimentary and unsecured in today's world of Internet thieves and spyware. Local account authentication tends to be more relaxed, but as you come to rely more on network and Internet services, the need to provide strong authentication becomes paramount. In general, you can categorize an authentication service into one of four groups:

▶ Basic or clear-text password—In this simplest form of authentication, passwords are passed between client and service in standard text. Obviously, this provides no network security, as passwords could be easily recovered using common network diagnostic tools. The few services that still rely on basic password authentication do so to support the widest possible audience. Lion avoids using this type of encryption whenever possible, and so should you.

▶ Encrypted password—Many variations of this type of authentication exist, but they all involve sending password information between client and service in an encrypted format. This is a more secure technique than clear text, but it still involves passing secrets across the network, so a determined individual could possibly uncover your password. The likelihood of a nefarious person decrypting your password depends on the strength of encryption being used. Lion uses encrypted passwords for local accounts, as do some generic LDAP directory services. In fact, most network services now rely on encrypted passwords if they don't already rely on the type of authentication described next here.

▶ Kerberos—This advanced authentication system provides highly secure, single-sign-on authentication. Both Apple's OD and Microsoft's Active Directory (AD) rely on Kerberos to provide authentication for a variety of network and Internet services. Details on Kerberos follow.

Understanding Kerberos Authentication

Kerberos is a secure authentication service that's popular with many universities and corporations. Both Apple and Microsoft have implemented Kerberos as their primary authentication mechanism for network directory services. Originally developed by the Massachusetts Institute of Technology (MIT), Kerberos provides ticket-based single-sign-on authentication services.

Single sign-on means that you have to enter your account password only once per session, often at the login window. As long as you remain logged in to the Mac or connected to the Kerberos system, it will use your previous credentials to satisfy the authentication for any other network service that supports Kerberos. A network service that supports Kerberos authentication is often called a *Kerberized* service. Many primary network applications and services included with Lion are Kerberized, including Mail, iChat, iCal, Address Book, screen sharing, SSH, AFP, SMB, NFS, and even FTP.

Kerberos was designed with the idea that you can't trust network traffic to be secure. So, Kerberos ensures that account passwords are never transmitted across the network. This system also provides mutual authentication, where both the client and server can verify each other's identity. Kerberos provides these features by generating tickets that are used to validate the authenticity of each Kerberos participant.

The only downside to ticket-based authentication is its relative complexity when compared with other techniques. Kerberos authentication requires a special trusted service known as the Key Distribution Center (KDC). In the case of OD and AD, the server providing directory services is often also the primary KDC. Starting with the introduction of Mac OS X v10.5, every Mac could also provide local KDC services. However, to keep things simple, this chapter will focus on the authentication relationship between a Lion client and a centralized KDC tied to a network directory service.

An example of the basic Kerberos authentication process:

1   Enter your user name and password at the login window.

The login window, via OD, negotiates a connection to the KDC. The KDC issues you an encrypted ticket-granting ticket (TGT). The TGT is encrypted in such a way that it can be unlocked and used only if you entered the correct password.

Think of the TGT as a "day pass" that can be used to access other services. TGTs are usually good for several hours, but if they expire before you log out, the Kerberos system will automatically generate a new one for you.

2   Upon attempting to connect to a Kerberized network service, such as an AFP network volume or an email service, OD will use the TGT to request a service ticket from the KDC.

If the KDC trusts your TGT and trusts the service you're attempting to connect to, it issues you a ticket for that service.

3   OD uses the service ticket to authenticate your account to the requested network service. Assuming your service ticket is good, the Kerberized service will trust your identity and allow the connection.

Notice that you only had to enter your user name and password once at the login window; after that, steps 2 and 3 are repeated for each different Kerberized service you connect to. Further, at no point did your password ever travel across the network, nor did the requested network service have to communicate with the KDC to verify your authenticity.

> **MORE INFO** ▶ The information presented here is merely an introduction to the Kerberos authentication system. For more, please visit MIT's Kerberos website at http://web.mit.edu/Kerberos.

Finally, it is important to not confuse Kerberos's single-sign-on ability with the keychain system's ability to save authentication information locally. Even though both services are used to automatically authenticate network services, they are quite different in architecture and scope. Kerberos can be used only to authenticate Kerberized services and is often managed on a networkwide scale. The keychain system can be used to save a wide variety of authentication information, but saved keychain information is accessible only to the local Mac. The keychain system is covered in detail in Chapter 2, "User Accounts."

Verifying Kerberos Authentication

Kerberos is so well integrated in Lion that it is possible to extensively use Kerberos without once having to manage its configuration. Assuming you have bound your Mac to an OD or AD service, Kerberos is already configured for you. The system configures the Kerberos settings automatically during the binding process. Users probably won't even know that they are using Kerberos because the login window and OD will automatically handle all future authentications.

Despite this level of integration, you should be aware of methods for testing and verifying Kerberos authentication. As covered previously, initial Kerberos authentication typically takes place during login. However, it's important to understand that you can test Kerberos authentication at any point, even if the user account you're testing isn't logged into the Mac. In other words, you can log in to a Mac using a known working account, like a local administrator, and then use the Kerberos tools to verify authentication to a different user's account.

Using the Kerberos Ticket Viewer Application

Basic Kerberos functionality can be tested from the Kerberos Ticket Viewer application:

1   Log in to the Mac using any working account you have access to.

    If the account you're trying to verify doesn't work, log in using another working account, possibly a local account that doesn't rely on Kerberos.

2   Open the Kerberos Ticket Viewer application using one of the following methods:

    ▶   Open /Applications/Utilities/Keychain Access.app and then select Keychain Access > Ticket Viewer from the menu.

    ▶   Open /System/Library/CoreServices/Ticket Viewer.app.

3   If you were able to log in with the user account you wish to test, it may already appear in the Ticket Viewer Kerberos user identities list.

    ▶   If no user identities appear, skip to step 4.

    ▶   If a user identity is present, and the date and time when the TGT expires is listed, then Kerberos authentication should be working.

4   If the Ticket Viewer application opens with no Kerberos user identities listed, click the Add Identity button.

In the dialog that appears, enter the user's fully qualified Kerberos identity. This usually includes the user's name, followed by the @ symbol, followed by the Kerberos realm in all capital letters. Finally, enter the user's password, and then click the Continue button.

5   If authentication was successful, then the user's identity in the list will show the date and time when the TGT expires.

If authentication failed, then you will receive an error message that should help you identify the problem. In the following example, the client's time is not correct; therefore Kerberos authentication fails.

6   Optionally, from Ticket Viewer, you can change the user's network password. To do so, click the Change Password button in the toolbar. A dialog will appear, allowing you to enter the current (old) password and then the new password twice. Click the Continue button to change the user's network password.

MORE INFO ▶ Details regarding password changes are covered in Chapter 2, "User Accounts."

7   Finally, if you are using a test account with Kerberos, for the sake of security, you should click the Remove Identity button in the toolbar to deauthenticate the user.

Using the Kerberos Commands

The Ticket Viewer application is convenient for verifying Kerberos TGTs, but as covered previously, the TGT is only the first part of Kerberos authentication. Again, if you want to connect to a Kerberized service, you must also acquire service tickets. Unfortunately, the Ticket Viewer application doesn't show service tickets. To view service tickets, you must use the Kerberos command-line utilities. These Kerberos commands, however, are very easy to use. They also allow you to test Kerberos regardless of the user you're currently logged in with.

The command to acquire a Kerberos TGT is simply kinit followed by the user's Kerberos identity. You will, of course, be prompted to enter the user's password to acquire the TGT. To list any Kerberos tickets for the current user, simply enter klist. Finally, to deauthenticate from Kerberos, enter kdestroy to destroy all the currently held tickets.

In the following example, Michelle has already authenticated via Kerberos with the spuser account, and in the Finder she has connected to an AFP share point. She enters klist to verify the TGT and service tickets. As you can see, the second ticket is an AFP service ticket, indicating that Kerberos authentication for that service is working as well.

```
MyMac:~ michelle$ klist
Kerberos 5 ticket cache: 'API:Initial default ccache'
Default principal: netuser@SERVER.MACJUTSU.COM

Valid Starting     Expires          Service Principal
08/30/09 21:43:07  08/31/09 07:43:04  krbtgt/SERVER.MACJUTSU.COM@SERVER.MACJUTSU.COM
renew until 09/06/09 21:43:04
08/30/09 21:43:12  08/31/09 07:43:04  afpserver/server.macjutsu.com@SERVER.MACJUTSU.COM
    renew until 09/06/09 21:43:04
```

Troubleshooting Directory Services

Directory services and authentication services are tightly linked to each other. Also, Open Directory (OD) is responsible for both of these services in Lion, so they share similar troubleshooting techniques. Almost all common OD issues are initially discovered because of a single symptom: A user is unable to access or authenticate to his or her account. Other symptoms might indicate an issue with OD, but an inability to authenticate is often the first and most significant issue a user will experience. After all, if the Mac has OD issues, then the user probably won't even make it past the login window.

> **NOTE ▶** Again, before digging too deep into troubleshooting a specific network service, take a few moments to check for general network service issues as outlined earlier in this chapter.

Common troubleshooting techniques specific to directory services and authentication services include:

▶ Attempt to authenticate with another user account—Remember, Lion supports multiple directory services, so first test another user account hosted from the same directory. Also, keep in mind that if a similarly named account exists in multiple directories, the first account OD locates is the one that's used. Otherwise, if the other account works properly, the problem lies only with the account record. Yet if you are unable to authenticate from multiple accounts, you are experiencing a problem with the directory service as a whole.

▶ Verify network directory service connectivity and configuration—As covered previously, the network directory listing in the Users & Groups preferences shows you the current status of bound network directory services. If a service isn't responding properly, you can reset the network directory service configuration by unbinding and then rebinding to the service using the plus and minus buttons at the bottom of the network directory list.

▶ Verify Kerberos authentication and configuration—As explained earlier, the Kerberos application will show you currently connected Kerberos accounts and tickets. First attempt a quick fix by destroying all current tickets and then reauthenticating. If multiple Kerberos KDCs or accounts are available, make sure the appropriate account is being used. Finally, Kerberos is a time-sensitive protocol, so verify that your Mac and the server(s) all have the correct date and time set. Ideally, all Kerberos participants will be configured to use the Network Time Protocol (NTP) to ensure clock synchronization.

▶ Check directory service log files—If none of these techniques work, fall back on information collected by the OD log files. OD generates very thorough log information that can help pinpoint directory service and authentication service issues. From the /Application/Utilities/Console application, inspect system.log, as it contains relevant network and authentication information. You should also inspect the directory service specific log file located in /var/log/opendirectoryd.log, which contains general usage and error messages.

▶ Reset the account password—This approach often requires that you have administrative access to the directory server hosting the account. Not only will this technique resolve any potential human errors, it will also reset the account's authentication information, which may have become compromised.

What You've Learned

▶ Lion includes built-in support for accessing and sharing a wide variety of network services, including Internet, network file, and remote control services.

▶ Your Mac is accessible to other network clients via static network identifiers like its IP address(es) and DNS host name, or dynamic network service identifiers like Bonjour, and SMB, NetBIOS, and WINS.

▶ The Finder allows you to connect to and mount network file systems by either manually entering a server address or browsing the network for servers via dynamic network discovery services.

▶ Lion includes a new easy-to-use peer-to-peer Wi-Fi sharing service dubbed AirDrop.

▶ Lion can provide AFP and SMB file sharing services.

▶ Lion also includes the Apache 2.2 web server, which is preconfigured to share a single computer website and individual websites for each user.

▶ Lion can provide several types of client sharing services that allow others to remotely control or execute software on your Mac.

▶ Lion allows you to protect other network services by enabling adaptive firewall filtering.

▶ Lion includes Open Directory (OD) for resolving network and directory resource information. OD supports several network directory services, including LDAP services and Microsoft's Active Directory service.

▶ OD also coordinates account authentication via a variety of authentication protocols, including the popular Kerberos authentication system.

References

Check for new and updated Knowledge Base documents at www.apple.com/support.

General Network Services

TS1629, "'Well known' TCP and UDP ports used by Apple software products"

HT2250, "Bonjour: Frequently asked questions (FAQ)"

HT4700, "OS X Lion: Connecting to legacy AFP services"

HT4794, "OS X Lion: Guidelines for connecting to a DFS namespace via SMB"

Network Applications

HT2008, "iChat: Frequently asked questions (FAQ)"

HT1507, "Using iChat with a firewall or NAT router"

HT3748, "Mac OS X v10.6: Using Microsoft Exchange 2007 (EWS) accounts in Mail"

Providing Network Services

HT4783, "OS X Lion: Can I use AirDrop with my computer?"

HT1810, "Mac OS X v10.5, 10.6: About the Application Firewall"

HT1344, "Choosing a password for networks that use Wired Equivalent Privacy (WEP)"

HT2370, "Apple Remote Desktop: Configuring remotely via command line (kickstart)"

HT1777, "MacBook Air: How to use Remote Disc to share DVDs or CDs on a Mac- or Windows-based computer"

HT3774, "Mac OS X v10.6: About Wake on Demand"

HT4704, "Lion Server: Enabling the FTP service"

URLs

Official Zeroconf dynamic network discovery service website: www.zeroconf.org

Apple's product guide: http://guide.apple.com

Apple's Safari 4 web browser: www.apple.com/safari

Apple's iCal shared calendars website: www.apple.com/downloads/macosx/calendars

With Web Sharing enabled, your Mac's locally hosted Apache 2.2 documentation: http://localhost/manual

Official Apache web server software resource website: http://httpd.apache.org

Apple's Xgrid distributed computing solution resource website: http://developer.apple.com/hardwaredrivers/hpc/xgrid_intro.html

Apple Remote Desktop network client management software: www.apple.com/remotedesktop

Apple's Online Mail Setup Assistant: www.apple.com/support/macosx/mailassistant

Group Logic's ExtremeZ-IP AFP server for Windows: www.grouplogic.com

Apple's Mac OS X Server Getting Started v10.6 guide: http://images.apple.com/server/macosx/docs/Getting_Started_v10.6.pdf

Apple's Active Directory integration technical white paper: www.seminars.apple.com/contactme/pdf/L334436B_ActiveDirect_WP.pdf

Official Kerberos authentication resource website: http://web.mit.edu/Kerberos

Review Quiz

1. What is the relationship between clients and servers as it relates to network service access?

2. What is the relationship between a network service and a network port?

3. What two dynamic network service discovery protocols are supported by Lion?

4. How does Lion use dynamic network service discovery protocols to access network services?

5. What five network file services can you connect to from the Finder's Connect to Server dialog?

6. How are items inside the Finder's Network folder populated?

7. What is AirDrop, and how do you know if a specific Mac supports it?

8. How do you provide Lion file sharing services so other computers can access them?

9. What password issues may arise related to a client Mac providing the SMB service?

10. What shared items are accessible to an administrative user who connects via AFP or SMB? What about a standard user?

11. What items are shared by default by all users?

12. What client sharing services can Lion provide?

13. What is the security risk of enabling client sharing services?

14. How does Lion's built-in firewall work? What advanced firewall settings are available?

15. What are some known issues that arise when connecting to network file services?

16. What are three common troubleshooting techniques for issues involving failure to connect to network services?

17. What is a directory as it relates to directory services?

18. What are six common types of resources that Lion can access from a directory service?

19. What are the primary differences between local, network, and mobile accounts?

20. What are four advantages of using network directory services to store account information?

21. What four directory service types can be used in Lion?

22. What is authentication? What is authorization?

23. What are three common authentication methods?

24. What is a Kerberos ticket? What is a Key Distribution Center (KDC)?

25. How do Kerberos and the keychain system differ for managing authentication services?

26. What are five common directory services and authentication services troubleshooting techniques?

Answers

1. Client software is used to access network services provided by server software. The connection is established using a common network protocol known by both the client and server software. Thus, the client and server software can be from different sources.

2. Network services are established using a common network protocol. The protocol specifies which TCP or UDP port number is used for communications.

3. Lion supports Bonjour and Server Message Block (SMB), including support for legacy Network Basic Input/Output and Windows Internet Naming Service (NetBIOS and WINS) dynamic network service discovery protocols.

4. Devices providing a network service advertise their availability via a dynamic network service discovery protocol. Clients that are looking for services request and receive this information to provide the user with a list of available network service choices.

5. From the Finder's Connect to Server dialog, you can connect to Apple File Protocol (AFP), Server Message Blocks/Common Internet File System (SMB), Network File System (NFS), Web-based Distributed Authoring and Versioning (WebDAV), and File Transfer Protocol (FTP) network file services.

6. The Finder populates the Network folder using information provided by the dynamic network services discovery protocols. Computers providing services appear as resources inside the Network folder, while service discovery zones or workgroups appear as folders. Any currently connected servers will also appear in the Network folder.

7. AirDrop provides a quick and easy method to share files locally via Wi-Fi. AirDrop creates a secure peer-to-peer network between local Macs. You can verify that a Mac supports AirDrop from the Finder's Go menu.

8. To provide services to other network clients, you first set your Mac's network identification, then enable the desired network file service, and finally define access to file system resources.

9. To support SMB authentication to a Mac client providing file sharing services, users' passwords must be stored in a special format, which must be enabled in Sharing preferences.

10. Administrators who connect to your Mac via AFP or SMB have access to any locally mounted volume. By default, standard users can only access their home folder and other users' Public folders.

11. The items shared by all users by default are the local users' Public folders inside their home folders.

12. Mac OS X's client sharing services include screen sharing, remote login, remote management, remote Apple Events, and Xgrid sharing.

13. If a client sharing service is compromised, an unauthorized user can control your Mac and execute unwanted applications or processes.

14. Lion's built-in firewall inspects each incoming network connection to determine if it's allowed. Connections are allowed or denied on a per-application basis. The advanced firewall settings let you control whether signed applications are automatically allowed through the firewall, control the list of allowed (or denied) applications, and enable stealth mode (which means your Mac will not respond to any unsolicited connections).

15. Files with metadata may cause problems for NFS or WebDAV network file systems. Also, avoid AFP 2 services when provided by Windows file servers.

16. Review the Network preferences, review the Network Utility statistics, and attempt to connect to different network services.

17. A directory is a database of information that in some cases can be shared to the network. The most commonly accessed directory resource is account information.

18. Common directory resources that Lion can access include user accounts, user groups, computer accounts, computer groups, network file mounts, and management settings.

19. Local accounts are available only to a single Mac; network accounts are available to Macs connected to a network directory service; and mobile accounts are network accounts that are cached to the local Mac for offline use.

20. Four advantages of using network directory services to store account information are: 1) user accounts are no longer tied to individual Macs; 2) the same user account information can be used for multiple network services; 3) you can use Kerberos to provide secure single-sign-on authentication; and 4) you can define user and computer settings from a centralized location.

21. The directory service types that can be used in Lion are Local, Network Information Systems (NIS), Lightweight Directory Access Protocol version 3 (LDAPv3), and Active Directory (AD).

22. Authentication is the process of proving your identity to the computer; authorization defines which items or services you are allowed to access.

23. Three common authentication methods are basic or clear-text passwords, encrypted passwords, and Kerberos ticket–based authentication.

24. Kerberos tickets are used to validate an account's identity. Kerberos uses ticket-granting tickets (TGTs) and service tickets. Kerberos requires a special trusted service known as the KDC. In most cases, the KDC service is running alongside the network directory service.

25. Kerberos can only be used to authenticate kerberized services and is often managed on a networkwide scale. The keychain system can be used to save a wide variety of authentication information, but saved keychain information is accessible only to the local Mac.

26. Common directory services and authentication services troubleshooting techniques are: 1) attempting to authenticate with another user account; 2) resetting the account password; 3) verifying network directory service connectivity and configuration; 4) verifying Kerberos authentication and configuration; and 5) checking the directory service log files.

8

Time

This chapter takes approximately 2 hours to complete.

Goals

Understand, manage, and troubleshoot peripheral connectivity

Pair Bluetooth devices to your Mac

Understand, manage, and troubleshoot printing, scanning, and faxing systems

Chapter 8

Peripherals and Printing

Apple pioneered the concept of automatic peripheral support with the original Macintosh. This feature, commonly known as plug-and-play, is now supported with varying success in all modern operating systems. Peripheral hardware has also improved, as now the most common connectivity standards support hot-pluggable or even wireless connections. Lion supports all popular modern peripheral standards, demonstrating Apple's continued commitment to making peripheral use as easy as possible.

Similarly, Apple and Adobe pioneered the desktop publishing revolution by introducing the first high-quality printing solution for personal computers. Although Adobe created the PostScript printing system, Apple was the first to include it in both the Macintosh operating system and the first PostScript printer, the Apple LaserWriter. Apple has continued to pioneer advancements in printing software with Mac OS X by adopting a printing workflow based on Adobe's Portable Document Format (PDF) and the Common UNIX Printing System (CUPS).

At the start of this chapter, you'll learn how Lion supports different peripheral technologies, and then you'll manage and troubleshoot peripherals connected to your Mac. You'll also learn how Lion supports different print, scan, and fax technologies and how to manage and troubleshoot printers and multifunction devices connected to your Mac.

Understanding Peripherals

For the purposes of this chapter, a peripheral is any non-networked device to which your computer system can be directly connected. A peripheral is also controlled by the Mac, whereas network devices are shared.

Given the wide range of devices included in this definition, this chapter shows you how to categorize devices based on their connectivity type and device class. Understanding the available connection methods and device types is necessary to manage and troubleshoot peripherals, which is your goal in the first half of this chapter.

> **NOTE ▸** This chapter will only cover connection technologies included with Mac systems that support OS X Lion.

Understanding Peripheral Connectivity

Most peripherals communicate with the Mac system via a connection mechanism commonly known as a bus. Bus connections are the most common peripheral connection type because they allow multiple peripherals to connect to your Mac simultaneously. In fact, the only connection types that are not buses are those used strictly for audio and video connectivity. Even then, your Mac is connected via a peripheral bus to intermediary hardware responsible for encoding or decoding the audio and video signals.

We can categorize peripheral connectivity into four types:

▸ Peripheral buses—General-purpose buses primarily used to connect an external device to your Mac.

▸ Expansion buses—Designed to expand your Mac's hardware capabilities, often by adding extra connectivity options.

▸ Storage buses—Used only for accessing storage devices.

▸ Audio and video connectivity—Standard interfaces used to send audio or video signals from one device to another.

Each connection is specialized for a particular type of communication, so a combination of technologies is often required to use a peripheral. For example, your Mac's graphics hardware is obviously designed to output a standard video signal, but it communicates with the processor via an expansion bus. You'll see many examples of combined connection types as you explore various peripheral devices.

Given this, it's a good thing Lion includes the System Information application to help you identify connected peripherals, including their connection types. Access System

Information by holding the Option key and choosing Apple menu > System Information. Once System Information is open, select a hardware interface from the Contents list to view its information. Using System Information for further troubleshooting peripherals is covered in this chapter's "Troubleshooting Peripherals" section.

Peripheral Buses

Peripheral buses are the connection type most commonly associated with computer peripherals. Because they are designed to provide a general-purpose communications link between the computer and the peripheral, a variety of devices can use them. There have been dozens of peripheral connectivity standards developed over the years, but in the last decade three have dominated the market: Universal Serial Bus (USB), FireWire, and Bluetooth.

Universal Serial Bus (USB) 1.1/2.0

Standard on every Mac that supports Lion, USB is by far the most popular peripheral connection. In fact, every single type of peripheral can be found in USB versions. You're probably already aware of the external USB ports on your Mac, but you may not know that Intel-based Macs also use USB for internal connectivity. For example, the MacBook's keyboard, trackpad, infrared receiver, iSight camera, and Bluetooth controller are all connected via internal USB connections.

USB was originally designed by Intel and is a hot-pluggable interface that allows the user to connect and disconnect devices while they are on, or "hot." USB is also a highly expandable connection platform that allows for daisy-chained connections. So, you can connect one USB device to your Mac, then connect another USB device to the first, and so on. The USB specification allows for up to 127 simultaneous devices per host controller. Most Macs have at least two externally accessible USB host controllers.

A USB port may supply up to 2.5 watts of power (500 mA of current at 5 volts) to the connected devices, which is all that some types of devices need to operate. Unpowered hubs, including those built into many USB keyboards, split the available power between their ports, usually supplying only 0.5 watts (100 mA) to each, enough for only very low-power devices. When the system detects that there is not enough power for a connected device, it displays a low-power warning and disables the device.

If you see this dialog, you can verify the power issue by opening /Applications/Utilities/ System Information and selecting USB from the report list. Selecting any USB device will display the electric current available to, and desired by, the device.

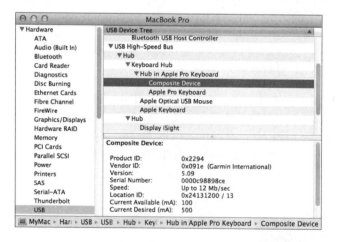

You can try resolving USB power issues by connecting the peripheral directly to the Mac or through a powered hub, which uses an external power connection to supply full power to the attached device. Peripherals that require even more power to operate, such as printers or large disk drives, generally also include a separate power source.

At the time of this writing, there are two USB versions supported by Apple hardware: USB 1.1 and USB 2.0. USB 2.0 ports are backward-compatible with USB 1.1 cabling and devices. USB 1.1 supports low-speed connections at 1.5 megabits per second (Mbit/s) and full-speed connections at up to 12 Mbit/s. USB 2.0 supports high-speed connections up to a theoretical maximum of 480 Mbit/s. In practice, though, high-speed USB 2.0 connections fall short of the theoretical maximum. (At the time of this writing, no Mac includes support for USB 3.0.) If you require a higher-performance peripheral connection bus, consider the next two technologies: FireWire and Thunderbolt.

> **MORE INFO** ▶ You can find out more about USB at the official USB Implementer's Forum website: www.usb.org.

FireWire

Also standard on many Macs that support Lion, FireWire is a high-speed, general-purpose peripheral connection originally developed by Apple. FireWire has been ratified as an Institute of Electrical and Electronics Engineers (IEEE) standard known as IEEE-1394 and has been adopted as a standard interface for many digital video devices. Like USB, FireWire supports hot-pluggable and daisy-chained connections. Using hubs, each FireWire host controller can support up to 63 devices simultaneously.

FireWire

FireWire has several advantages over USB. FireWire's primary advantage is that its host controllers work without placing a burden on your computer's main processor, allowing for higher overall performance compared with USB. These sophisticated FireWire host controllers also allow your Mac to be used in target disk mode without the need for a functional operating system, as covered in Chapter 3, "File Systems."

All Macs with FireWire ports support FireWire 400 with a maximum transfer rate of up to 400 Mbit/s, and most newer Macs support FireWire 800 with a maximum transfer rate of up to 800 Mbit/s. These two FireWire standards use different port connections, but Macs with FireWire 800 ports can connect to FireWire 400 devices with the appropriate adapter.

Because FireWire is designed to move large quantities of data efficiently, FireWire 400 typically outperforms high-speed USB 2.0 even though the latter has a higher theoretical maximum throughput.

Also, Apple's FireWire ports generally supply about 7 watts per port, compared with USB's 2.5 watts. This increased power capacity makes FireWire ideal for use with external portable hard drives, as no additional power source is required to run the drive. But the additional cost and complexity of FireWire host controllers makes the technology overkill for many simple peripherals, such as mice, keyboards, and flash drives, which are well served by USB.

> **MORE INFO** ▶ You can find out more about FireWire at the official 1394 Trade Association website: www.1394ta.org.

Thunderbolt

Originally designed by Intel, then later in collaboration with Apple, Thunderbolt represents the latest in peripheral connectivity. This new standard folds PCI Express and DisplayPort data into a single connection and cable. One Thunderbolt host computer connection supports a hub or daisy chain of up to six devices, with up to two of these devices being high-resolution displays. Further, Macs with Thunderbolt can be used in target disk mode without the need for a functional operating system, as covered in Chapter 3, "File Systems."

Thunderbolt provides for unmatched peripheral flexibility given its mix of PCI Express and DisplayPort connectivity. As detailed later in this chapter, PCI Express is actually an expansion bus and DisplayPort provides digital video and audio connectivity. With the appropriate adapters, a single Thunderbolt connection can provide access to any other networking, storage, peripheral, video, or audio connection. For example, Apple's Thunderbolt display not only provides a high-definition digital display, but also a built-in camera, audio speakers, a three-port USB hub, a FireWire port, a Gigabit Ethernet port, and an additional Thunderbolt port for another display—all this through a single Thunderbolt cable from the Mac to the display.

All this connectivity through one cable means that Thunderbolt provides significant data rates. In fact, Thunderbolt is the fastest external peripheral bus to date, providing two bidirectional 10 Gbit/s (10 gigabits per second, or 10,000 Mbit/s) channels. This means a total of 20 Gbit/s outbound and 20 Gbit/s inbound. Thunderbolt also supplies up to 10W of power to connected devices, again providing more power than any previous external peripheral bus. Future versions of Thunderbolt are supposed to provide up to 100 Gbit/s channels and optical cable lengths of up to 100 meters. While this technology isn't available yet, the plan bodes well for Thunderbolt's prospects for future expansion.

Apple's contribution to the Thunderbolt standard brought the inclusion of DisplayPort connectivity and use of the Mini DisplayPort connection. Thunderbolt connections are physically identical to Mini DisplayPort connections, but they provide both PCI Express and DisplayPort data via this single connection. As a result, Thunderbolt devices and cables provide full support for DisplayPort data. However, older Mini DisplayPort devices and cables don't support the additional PCI Express data. Thus, items that only support Mini DisplayPort should be the last connection in a Thunderbolt daisy chain. You can identify items compatible with Thunderbolt by an icon that looks like a thunderbolt, while items compatible with only Mini DisplayPort feature an icon that looks like a flat-panel display.

> **MORE INFO** ► You can find out more about Thunderbolt at Intel's official website: www.intel.com/technology/io/thunderbolt/index.htm.

Bluetooth

Bluetooth is a short-range wireless peripheral connection standard originally developed by Ericsson for cell phone headsets. Most Bluetooth devices have a range of only 1 to 10 meters, ideal for peripherals but inadequate for wireless networking. Further, it's not nearly as fast as wireless Ethernet; Bluetooth 1.2 has a maximum transfer speed of up to 721 kilobits per second (kbit/s) and Bluetooth 2.0 + Extended Data Rate (EDR) a maximum transfer speed of up to 3.0 Mbit/s. However, Bluetooth's primary advantage is that it works with low-power devices.

As Bluetooth increased in popularity, computer manufacturers adopted it for wireless peripherals as well. In addition to providing a wireless connection between your Mac and cell phone, Bluetooth allows your Mac to use wireless headsets, mice, keyboards, and printers. Most Macs that support Lion include Bluetooth wireless, and for those that don't, you can easily add it with a USB-to-Bluetooth adapter. You can find out if your Mac has Bluetooth support by opening the System Preferences application and looking for the Bluetooth icon in the Internet & Wireless section. You may also see a small Bluetooth icon in the menu bar near the clock. Configuring Bluetooth is covered in the "Using Bluetooth Peripherals" section later in this chapter.

MORE INFO ▶ You can find out more about Bluetooth at the official Bluetooth Technology Information website: www.bluetooth.com.

Expansion Buses

With expansion buses, you can add hardware functionality to your Mac, usually in the form of a small computer board, often referred to as a card. Expansion buses are only found built into the main computer board inside your Mac. Though designed to allow for the addition of any type of technology, they are most often used to add support for another type of bus or connection. For example, most graphics cards are connected to your Mac via an expansion bus. Other common expansion cards add network ports, peripheral bus ports, storage bus connections, or audio and video input/output connections.

Even if you never add an expansion card to your Mac, several internal components are actually connected via an expansion bus. Many Mac computers feature a space-saving design that accommodates most users' needs without additional expansion connections. Yet, for those who require hardware expansion, certain Lion-compatible computers have additional expansion bus connections: Mac Pros, older model 15-inch MacBook Pros, and 17-inch MacBook Pros. The specific type of expansion ports varies by Mac model. As always, you can use the System Information application to identify your Mac's expansion bus capabilities.

As of this writing, the three main expansion buses supported by Lion compatible hardware are:

▶ PCI Express 1.x (PCIe)—This more recent version of the PCI standard supports a maximum connection bandwidth of up to 32 Gbit/s, depending on configuration.

All Intel-based Macs use PCIe internally, and Mac Pro features PCIe expansion ports.

▶ PCI Express 2.x (PCIe)—This latest version of the PCI standard supports a maximum connection bandwidth of up to 64 Gbit/s, depending on configuration, and is backward compatible with PCIe 1.0 cards. The latest Mac Pros feature PCIe 2.0 expansion ports.

▶ ExpressCard 34—Based on PCIe and USB technology, this expansion format is primarily designed for portable computers and features a maximum connection bandwidth of up to 2.5 Gbit/s. The slot supports both PCIe and USB signaling, so it will use whichever is most appropriate for the inserted card. Some MacBook Pro models feature a single ExpressCard 34 slot.

NOTE ▶ Some MacBook Pro models feature an SD card slot. While convenient for those needing regular access to SD cards, this is not an expansion-bus technology, as it only allows for connections to SD cards.

Storage Buses

Storage buses are designed to connect your computer to disk or optical storage drives. The age and model of your Mac determines which storage bus technologies are used. But if your Mac features free expansion bus connections, you can generally add any storage bus connections you require via an expansion card.

Some storage buses are designed for internal use, and others can be used externally as well. It's important to know that external storage disk and optical drives connected via USB or FireWire are still using a dedicated storage bus inside the external drive case. So, every disk or optical drive is designed to use a specific storage bus, but those signals can also be retransmitted via a USB or FireWire connection. Therefore, you can purchase empty external drive enclosures that include hardware that bridges the storage bus connection to USB or FireWire, and then install your own internal drive in the case. This is extremely useful for recovering data from a Mac with a functional internal hard drive but otherwise inoperable hardware.

Storage buses supported in various Mac hardware include:

▶ Advanced Technology Attachment (ATA)—Sometimes called Parallel ATA, this storage bus was the most common standard for internal storage for many years and supports a maximum connection bandwidth of up to 133 megabytes per second (MB/s). ATA host controllers are inexpensive because they support only two drives per controller. Some Macs still use ATA-based internal optical drives to reduce product costs.

▶ Serial ATA (SATA)—This improvement on ATA is now the most common storage bus for internal storage. Most current Macs support SATA 3 Gbit/s, which sports a maximum connection bandwidth of up to 384 MB/s. SATA host controllers are also inexpensive, but they support only a single drive per controller. All Intel-based Macs use SATA-based internal disk drives. External SATA connectivity can be added to your Mac via an expansion bus.

▶ Small Computer System Interface (SCSI)—Sometimes also called Parallel SCSI, this was the original drive interface designed for personal computers. Over the years SCSI has evolved to become the most common storage bus for use in high-end or server computers, and though it supports internal storage, it's more often used for external storage. The latest SCSI supports a maximum connection bandwidth of up to 320 MB/s and up to 16 drives per controller. SCSI connectivity can be added to the Mac Pro via an expansion card.

▶ Serial Attached SCSI (SAS)—This improvement on SCSI is becoming a popular storage bus for use in high-end or server computers. SAS also allows internal and external connections and currently supports a maximum connection bandwidth of up to 3Gbit/s or 384 MB/s and up to 16,384 devices through the use of expanders. The Intel-based Xserve supports internal SAS drives, but again, you can add SAS connectivity to your Mac via an expansion card.

▶ Fibre Channel—This networking technology is most often used for high-end SCSI connectivity. Fibre Channel can offer speeds up to several gigabytes per second (GB/s) depending on the specification and adds features important for large-scale storage solutions such as long-distance cabling and packet-based communication switching. Fibre Channel host controllers are more complicated than other storage controllers, so they are relatively expensive and only available via an expansion card or Thunderbolt adapter. Apple's Xsan network storage technology is built around Fibre Channel hardware.

Audio and Video Connectivity

Most dedicated audio and video connections are point-to-point and don't support multiple devices. An audio or video signal is typically output from one device and directly connected to another single device designed to receive the signal.

All Macs, with the exception of some Xserve computers, have a variety of audio and video output connections. Most Macs also include audio input connections that allow you to record audio to digital files. Conversely, no Mac includes built-in support for direct video input. Nevertheless, a wide variety of video input options allow you to capture video files to your Mac via USB, FireWire, or an expansion card.

Audio connections supported by various Macs include:

▶ Analog stereo audio—The standard stereo signal used by most consumer-grade audio equipment, which takes the form of either the 3.5 mm minijack or twin RCA connectors. Nearly every device made by Apple features built-in analog stereo output via minijack, and most Macs also feature analog stereo input.

▶ TOSLINK digital audio—This optical connection has become the most common digital audio connection for consumer-grade audio equipment. While both analog and digital audio connections support varying audio resolutions, digital audio connections do not suffer from electromagnetic interference; thus they typically provide a much clearer audio signal. Most Intel-based Macs feature digital audio input and output. The Mac Pro uses standard TOSLINK ports, while all other Macs use special audio ports that support both analog stereo minijack and mini-TOSLINK connections.

Video connections supported by various Macs include:

▶ Composite video—This RCA connection is the most common connection for analog standard-definition consumer-grade video. Many older Intel-based Macs can output a composite video signal using an Apple video adapter. However, composite video has an effective resolution of only 640 × 480 pixels, so it's not ideal for computer use.

▶ S-Video—This mini-DIN connection is also a common connection for analog standard-definition consumer-grade video, but it provides a slightly better picture than composite video. Many older Intel-based Macs can output an S-Video signal using an Apple video adapter. S-Video is also hindered by an effective resolution of 640 × 480 pixels.

▶ Video Graphics Array (VGA)—This is the most common connection used for analog computer video displays. Most Macs can output a VGA signal up to a resolution of 1600 × 1200 pixels, with some going as high as 2048 × 1536 pixels. Although older Macs feature built-in VGA ports, Intel-based Macs all require an Apple VGA adapter.

▶ Digital Video Interface (DVI)—This is the most common connection used for digital computer video displays and high-definition televisions. DVI supports resolutions of up to 1920 × 1200 pixels. For a while Apple used smaller connections for DVI on some Macs to save space. These connections, known as mini-DVI and micro-DVI, are electronically identical to DVI; they simply use smaller connections. Many older Macs feature built-in DVI ports, but more recent Macs require an Apple DVI adapter.

▶ Dual-Link DVI (DVI-DL)—This is an extension to the DVI standard that supports resolutions of up to 2560 by 1600 pixels. Older high-end Macs directly support DVI-DL connections, while some newer Macs support this through an Apple DVI-DL adapter.

▶ Mini DisplayPort—The most recent display standard used by Apple, this is based on a smaller connector version of the DisplayPort standard. DisplayPort is quickly becoming the standard connection for computer-based digital displays because of its support of new technologies and less complicated, ultimately less expensive, display hardware. Apple has stated that going forward, all Macs will be compatible with Mini DisplayPort for external displays. Both Apple and third parties have created adapters for Mini DisplayPort to allow the use of most other video standards.

NOTE ▶ The Mini DisplayPort connector is also used for Thunderbolt; however, Thunderbolt provides more than just video connectivity. Details regarding compatibility between these two technologies is covered previously in this chapter.

▶ High-Definition Multimedia Interface (HDMI)—This is fast becoming the standard connection for consumer-grade digital audio and high-definition video equipment. HDMI combines a DVI-based digital video signal with multichannel digital audio signals in a single, inexpensive copper connection. Although no Mac features built-in HDMI ports, you can convert any DVI or Mini DisplayPort connection to HDMI by using an inexpensive cable adapter. However, all DVI connections and certain older Macs with Mini DisplayPort do not support HDMI audio. For a full list of Macs with Mini DisplayPort that support HDMI audio, please refer to Apple Knowledge Base article HT4241, "About Mini DisplayPort to HDMI adapters."

MORE INFO ▶ To identify the various Apple video adapters available, see Apple Knowledge Base article HT3235, "Monitor and Display Adapter Table."

Using Bluetooth Peripherals

Because Bluetooth is a wireless technology, some configuration is required to connect your Mac to a Bluetooth peripheral. The process of connecting Bluetooth devices is known as pairing. Once two devices are paired, they will act as if they were directly connected to each other. Lion's Bluetooth interface makes the process of configuring peripherals easy.

NOTE ▶ Desktop Macs can be purchased with only Bluetooth wireless input devices. If this is the case, you will have already paired these devices during first startup with the Lion Setup Assistant.

To set up and manage Bluetooth peripherals:

1   Select the Bluetooth menu extra near the clock on the right side of the menu bar.

Make sure your Mac's Bluetooth is turned on. It's also advisable to disable Discoverable mode, as leaving it enabled is a potential security risk.

NOTE ▶ Discoverable mode advertises your Mac as a Bluetooth resource to any device within range, which could invite unwanted attention to your Mac. The only time you should enable Discoverable mode is when you are having difficulty pairing your Mac to a Bluetooth peripheral; then you can try it the other way around and attempt to pair the peripheral to your Mac.

2   Enable Discoverable mode on the Bluetooth peripheral you're going to pair with your Mac.

Each device is different, so you may need to consult the device's user guide to enable Discoverable mode. In this example we will be using an Apple Bluetooth keyboard, which is automatically discoverable any time it's not paired to a Mac.

3   From the Bluetooth menu extra, select Set Up Bluetooth Device to open the Bluetooth Setup Assistant, which walks you through the setup process.

4   Once open, the Bluetooth Setup Assistant scans for any Bluetooth peripherals in range that are in Discoverable mode. It may take several moments for the device's name to appear; once it does, select it and click Continue.

5   For Bluetooth peripherals, a passkey must be used to authorize pairing. Depending on the device, you will perform one of the following:

▶   The paring will automatically complete in the background with an automatically generated passkey. This is often the case for a device that has no method to verify the passkey, such as a Bluetooth mouse.

▶   On your Mac, enter a predefined passkey as given in the device's user guide, and click Continue to authorize the pairing.

▶   Allow the Bluetooth Setup Assistant to create a random passkey that you then enter or verify on the Bluetooth device to authorize the pairing. In this example of pairing to an iPhone, the passkey is generated for you automatically.

6 The Bluetooth Setup Assistant will automatically detect the capabilities of your Bluetooth peripheral and may present you with additional configuration screens. Continue through these screens until you complete the setup process.

7 When the pairing is complete, you can choose Quit the Bluetooth Setup Assistant or Set Up Another Device.

8 You can verify that your Mac is paired to the device by again selecting the Bluetooth status menu.

Notice that the Bluetooth status menu indicates a connected device by using bold letters; in this case, the Magic Mouse is connected, but the iPhone is not. You can adjust settings such as the peripheral's name from the Bluetooth preferences.

9 To access all the Bluetooth management settings, open Bluetooth preferences from either the Apple menu > System Preferences or the Bluetooth status menu > Open Bluetooth Preferences.

10 To manage a Bluetooth peripheral, select it from the list, and then click the Action (gear icon) button to reveal a pop-up menu with management choices.

Note the option to show more information about the Bluetooth devices. You can also use the plus and minus keys at the bottom of the Bluetooth devices list to add or delete peripheral pairings.

11 Optionally, click the Advanced button to reveal a dialog allowing you to adjust additional Bluetooth settings.

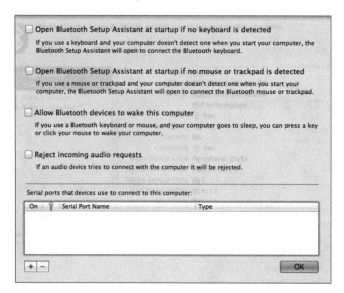

12 Optionally, click the Sharing Setup button to open the Bluetooth pane of the Sharing preferences, which allows you to adjust Bluetooth sharing settings.

Troubleshooting Peripherals

Troubleshooting peripheral issues can be difficult because of the wide variety of devices out there. However, peripheral issues can usually be categorized as either software related or hardware related. The first part of this section looks at how the system software interacts with peripherals and how to identify peripheral issues related to software. As for peripheral hardware issues, ultimately replacing or repairing the peripheral or its connections usually resolves the issue. Yet a few general troubleshooting techniques can help you identify and possibly resolve the problem.

Peripheral Device Classes

Peripherals are divided into device classes based on their primary function. Lion includes built-in software drivers that allow your Mac to interact with peripherals from all device classes. While these built-in drivers may provide basic support, many third-party devices require device-specific drivers for full functionality. Detailed information about software drivers is covered in the next section.

Device classes as defined in Lion include:

► Human input devices (HID)—Peripherals that allow you to directly input information or control the Mac's interface. Examples are keyboards, mice, trackpads, game controllers, tablets, and even braille interfaces.

► Storage devices—Disk drives, flash drives, optical drives, and iPods. Storage peripherals are covered in Chapter 3, "File Systems."

► Printers—Printers of all types, plotters, and fax machines. Printing is covered later in this chapter.

► Scanners—Flatbed, negative, slide, and drum scanners. Lion supports scanners via the Image Capture framework, which allows you to control scanners from /Applications/Image Capture or any other compatible third-party capture application, such as Photoshop.

TIP The Image Capture application supports both locally attached scanners and scanners being shared via the network. Further, the Sharing preferences also allow you to share a locally attached scanner to the network. Network scanner discovery is accomplished using Bonjour, so usually no additional setup is required to locate shared scanning resources.

▶ Digital cameras—These peripherals include both directly connected cameras and camera storage cards mounted to the Mac's file system. Recall that many digital cameras, when connected to a computer, simply extend their internal storage to the computer. In this case, Lion accesses the camera's internal storage, or any directly attached camera storage cards, as it does any other storage device. Applications like iPhoto or Aperture then take over to essentially copy the picture files from the camera storage to the Mac's storage. Some cameras support a tethered capture mode in which they are directly controlled by the Mac and send the captured picture data directly to the Mac. Lion supports this type of camera connection via the Image Capture framework, which also allows you to use /Applications/Image Capture or another compatible third-party capture application.

▶ Video devices—These peripherals include video cameras and video converters connected via USB, FireWire, or an expansion bus. Lion supports these video devices via the QuickTime framework, which allows you to use /Applications/QuickTime Player or any other compatible video application, such as iMovie or Final Cut Pro.

▶ Audio devices—These peripherals include external audio interfaces connected via USB, FireWire, or an expansion bus. Lion supports these audio devices via the Core Audio framework, so you can use any compatible audio application, such as GarageBand or Logic Pro.

Peripheral Device Drivers

One of the primary responsibilities of the system software is to act as an intermediary between peripherals and applications. If an application supports a general device class, the operating system handles all the technical details of communicating with each model of peripheral in that class. Here's an example: For an application to receive user input, it needs to receive information from the keyboard, mouse, trackpad, or the like, but it doesn't need to know any details about how to interpret the electrical signals from that device because that's handled by the operating system. This separation of peripherals and applications by the operating system allows you to use nearly any combination of the two with few incompatibilities.

Lion supports peripherals using device drivers, specialized pieces of software that allow peripherals to interoperate with the system. Some peripherals are supported via a generic driver, but many require a device driver created specifically for the peripheral. Although Lion includes a decent selection of common device drivers, you may have to install third-party device drivers to support your peripherals. Nearly all device drivers are installed using an installer utility that places the driver software in the correct resource folder on your Mac. Device drivers are implemented in one of three ways: kernel extensions, framework plug-ins, or applications.

> NOTE ▶ Lion will only use a driver if it's already installed. In other words, if you're adding support for a new third-party peripheral that requires custom drivers, install those drivers first before you connect the peripheral to the Mac.

> NOTE ▶ It's always best to check the peripheral manufacturer's website to obtain the latest version of the driver software.

Device driver implementations in Lion include:

▶ Kernel extensions (KEXTs)—This is a special type of software created to add peripheral support at the lowest level of Lion: the system kernel. KEXTs load and unload from the system automatically, so there's no need to manage them aside from making sure they are installed in the correct locations. While some KEXTs are hidden inside application bundles, most are located in the /System/Library/Extensions or /Library/Extensions folders. Remember, in general, nearly all the items in the /System folder are part of the standard Lion install. Examples of peripherals that use KEXTs are human input devices, storage devices, audio and video devices, and other expansion cards.

▶ Framework plug-ins—This type of device driver adds support for a specific peripheral to an existing system framework. For example, support for additional scanners and digital cameras is facilitated via plug-ins to the Image Capture framework.

▶ Applications—In some cases a peripheral is best supported by an application written just for that peripheral. Examples are the iPod, iPhone, and iPad, which are managed by the iTunes application.

Inspecting Loaded Extensions

Even though the Lion kernel is designed to manage KEXTs without user interaction, you may still need to verify that a specific KEXT is loaded. You can view currently loaded KEXTs from the System Information application (while holding the Option key, choose Apple menu > System Information). Once System Information is open, select the Extensions item in the Contents list; it may take a few moments for the system to scan all currently loaded KEXTs. Once the list appears, you can further inspect individual KEXTs by selecting them from this list.

A key feature of Lion is support for a 64-bit kernel, thus necessitating 64-bit KEXTs. From System Information, you can easily identify which loaded extensions support 64-bit mode. Lion starts up the kernel in 64-bit mode by default; you can force it to start up the kernel in 32-bit mode as outlined in Chapter 9, "System Startup." Using the kernel in 64-bit mode helps performance with certain applications, but with this mode enabled, some third-party KEXTs may not work. Any KEXTs that don't support 64-bit mode will simply be ignored when starting up the kernel in 64-bit mode.

General Peripheral Troubleshooting

General peripheral troubleshooting techniques include:

▸ **Always check System Information first.** If you remember only one peripheral troubleshooting technique, it should be this: Connected peripherals appear in System Information regardless of functioning software drivers. In other words, if a connected peripheral does not show up in System Information, then you are almost certainly experiencing a hardware failure. If a connected peripheral appears as normal in System Information, you are probably experiencing a software driver issue. In that case, use System Information to validate whether the expected extensions are loaded.

▸ **Unplug and then reconnect the peripheral.** Doing this will reinitialize the peripheral connection and force Lion to reload any peripheral-specific drivers.

▸ **Plug the peripheral into a different port or use a different cable.** This will help you rule out any bad hardware, including host ports, cables, and inoperable hubs.

- ▶ **Unplug other devices on the same bus.** Another device on the shared bus may be causing an issue.

- ▶ **Resolve potential USB power issues.** As covered previously in this chapter, the USB interface can prove problematic if devices are trying to draw too much power. Try plugging the USB device directly into the Mac instead of any USB hubs.

- ▶ **Shut down and then restart the Mac.** This tried-and-true troubleshooting technique reinitializes all the peripheral connections and reloads all the software drivers.

- ▶ **Try the peripheral with another Mac.** This helps you determine whether the issue is with your Mac or the peripheral. If the device doesn't work with other computers, your Mac is not the source of the issue.

- ▶ **Check for system software and driver software updates.** Software bugs are constantly being fixed, so it's always a good time to check for software updates. You can use Lion's built-in Software Update application, but you should also check the peripheral manufacturer's website for the latest driver updates.

- ▶ **Check for computer and peripheral firmware updates.** Like software updates, firmware updates may also be necessary to resolve your peripheral issue. This possibility is especially likely for more sophisticated devices like iPods, iPhones, and iPads, which have their own internal firmware.

Understanding Printing, Scanning, and Faxing

Robust printing has always been an important part of the Mac operating system because of its popularity with graphic design users. Lion continues this tradition with an updated printing system featuring redesigned and simplified printing interfaces.

Print and Fax Technology Architecture

Lion uses the open source Common UNIX Printing System 1.5 (CUPS) to manage local printing and faxing. Originally an independent product, CUPS was purchased by Apple and remains an open source project. Architecturally, CUPS uses the Internet Printing Protocol (IPP) standard as the basis for managing printing and faxing tasks and uses PostScript Printer Description (PPD) files as the basis for printer drivers. Though still used by CUPS, the PPD name is a bit of a misnomer, as non-PostScript printers can also be described by these files.

A print or fax job starts when a user prints from either an application in the graphical user interface or the print commands in the Terminal. When you print from an application, Lion's Quartz graphics system generates a Portable Document Format (PDF) file. When you print from the command line, a PostScript (PS) file is generated. In either case, the file created is called a spool file and is placed inside the /var/spool/cups folder. The CUPS background process, cupsd, takes this spool file and passes it through a series of filter processes known as the print chain. These processes convert the spool file to a format that is understood by the destination printer or fax, and then ultimately communicate this information to the printer (or in the case of a local fax, your Mac's modem).

> **MORE INFO ▶** CUPS provides capabilities beyond the scope of this text. To find out more, visit the official CUPS website at www.cups.org.

Printing, Scanning, and Faxing Drivers

Before you can print or fax, you must configure printer or fax modem settings, which includes associating an appropriate printer driver with the printing device. This association happens automatically as you configure a new printing device; however, the system must have the printer driver installed before it can use the printer. Apple supplies printer drivers for most popular models, among them Brother, Canon, Epson, Fuji-Xerox, Hewlett-Packard, Lexmark, Ricoh, and Samsung.

> **MORE INFO ▶** For a complete list of printer and scanner drivers available from Apple for Mac OS X, refer to Knowledge Base article HT3669, "OS X Lion, Mac OS X v10.6: Printer and scanner software."

The Lion installer is designed to save space on the system volume and will avoid installing unnecessary print drivers. New installations of Lion include only Apple and generic print drivers. Lion upgrade installations will only install drivers for printers in use by the Mac. It's expected that additional print drivers will be acquired via the Internet.

If you attempt to add a printer that the Mac does not have the driver for and you are connected to the Internet, the system will prompt you to automatically download and install the driver using Apple's Software Update service. You can also manually download and install printer drivers from Apple's support website.

NOTE ▶ You should always attempt to use Apple's collection of printer drivers. These drivers provide the most Mac-native experience and will automatically update via the Software Update mechanism.

NOTE ▶ You must log in or authenticate as an administrative user to install printer drivers either manually or via Software Update.

NOTE ▶ The automatic printer driver installer from Software Update will often install multiple printer drivers from the same manufacturer simultaneously.

Obviously, if you aren't connected to the Internet, then you will have to acquire the printer driver manually, though some standard PostScript and PCL printers can use the built-in generic printer drivers. Also, if Apple doesn't provide the printer driver via its Software Update mechanism, you will have to manually acquire the appropriate driver, often directly from the printer's manufacturer.

A few of the built-in Apple printer drivers are installed in /System/Library/Printers, but all of the third-party printer drivers will be installed to the /Library/Printers folder. The primary folder for drivers is the PPD folder, but you may notice other vendor folders that contain ancillary printer driver resources.

Once you've added a printer or fax configuration, a copy of the PPD with the name of the device is placed in the /etc/cups/ppd folder and two configuration files are modified: /etc/cups/printers.conf and /Library/Preferences/org.cups.printers.plist. Finally, the first time a user prints or accesses a printer or fax queue, the system will create a printer or fax queue application, again with the name of the device, in the ~/Library/Printers folder in the user's home folder.

Configuring Printing, Scanning, and Faxing

In this part of the chapter, you will configure printers, scanners, and faxes, as well as manage print jobs. You will also learn how to troubleshoot printing issues.

> **TIP** ▶ When adding supported multifunction printers, scanning and faxing services will also be configured along with general printing services.

Configuring a Directly Attached Printer

If your Mac already has the correct printer driver for a directly attached USB or FireWire printer, the system automatically detects the appropriate settings and configures the new printer for you as soon as you plug it in. If the printer provides fax and scan support, the system should automatically configure this as well. It's important to note, however, that this automatic configuration only occurs if an administrative user is currently logged into the Mac. You can verify the printer has been added by simply opening the Print dialog from any application (File > Print in the menu bar) or the Print & Scan preferences. In the Print & Scan preferences, you can tell which printers are locally connected if their location is shown as the same name as the local Mac's sharing name.

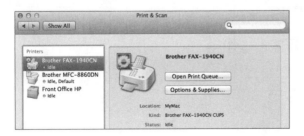

If the driver isn't installed but is available from Apple, you will be prompted with the automatic Software Update install mechanism when you plug the printer in. If an administrative user chooses to install the printer driver, after installation the printer will be automatically configured as well. Finally, if a printer driver for a directly attached printer is unavailable from Apple, then nothing will happen automatically when you plug it in. You will have to manually acquire and install the printer driver to get it working.

Configuring a Local Network Printer

Network printer and all fax configurations have to be manually added, but Apple has made this process incredibly easy for locally networked printers. If the printer you wish to add is on the local network, either as a standalone printer advertising via Bonjour or shared via another Mac or AirPort base station, then all you need to do is select it from the Print dialog (File > Print in the menu bar) from any application. Once in the Print dialog, select the Printer pop-up menu, and the system will scan the local network for available printers to select from. As covered previously, the Mac will either configure the printer with a preinstalled driver or prompt to download the driver from Apple's Software Update service. Again, the system should also configure fax and scan support for multifunction devices. Also, again note that only administrative users can add printers.

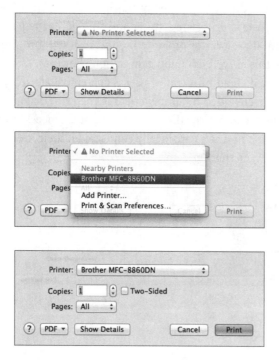

NOTE ▶ If a network printer requires authentication, you may be presented with an authentication dialog in order to print to the shared printer.

NOTE ▶ Your Mac will automatically acquire the appropriate printer drivers from any Mac that is sharing a printer via the network. In other words, the Mac hosting a shared printer will automatically send your Mac the drivers if they aren't preinstalled.

Manually Configuring a Printer

If the network printer doesn't support automatic network discovery via Bonjour, then you will have to configure it manually via the Add Printer window. Also, if a directly attached printer does not automatically configure, then you can manually add it. You can open the Add Printer window at any time to manually add new printers, faxes, or multifunction devices. Again, nonadministrative users will have to provide administrator authentication to access the Add Printer window.

NOTE ▶ Mac OS X v10.6 and later does not support the AppleTalk network protocol and thus does not support printing via AppleTalk network printers.

NOTE ▶ Bluetooth printers are configured via the Bluetooth Setup Assistant as covered in the "Using Bluetooth Peripherals" section earlier in this chapter.

To manually add a new printer, fax, or multifunction device:

1   Open the Add Printer window via one of the following methods:

▶ From any application, open a Print dialog by choosing File > Print from the menu bar. Next, from the Printer pop-up menu, select Add Printer.

▶ Open the Print & Scan preferences by choosing Apple menu > System Preferences, then clicking the Print & Scan icon. Click the lock icon in the bottom-left corner and authenticate as an administrative user to unlock the Print & Scan preferences. Finally, click the small plus button at the bottom of the Printers list.

▶ From the Finder, open the /System/Library/CoreServices/AddPrinter application. This application's icon can also be placed in your Dock.

2 The Add Printer window features several panes for selecting a printer or fax. These panes are accessed by clicking the following buttons in the toolbar:

▶ Default—This browser lets you select directly attached USB and FireWire printers and network printers discovered using Bonjour or network directory services.

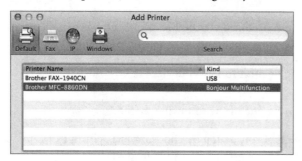

▶ Fax—This browser allows you to select the specific modem port that will be used for incoming and outgoing fax transmissions. Configuring your Mac to act as a fax is covered in the next section of this chapter.

▶ IP—This dialog allows you to manually enter the IP address or DNS host name of a Line Printer Daemon (LPD), IPP, or HP JetDirect printer. You must select the appropriate protocol from the pop-up menu and enter the printer's address. Entering a printer queue is usually optional.

▶ Windows—This browser lets you select printers shared via the Server Message Block (SMB) printer sharing protocol. Double-click on a SMB server and authenticate to access the server's shared printers.

3 Once you have selected a printer or fax modem from the top half of the new printer configuration dialog, the system will complete the bottom half for you using information it has discovered. This includes automatically selecting the appropriate printer driver if possible.

Often this information isn't ideal, and you can easily change it. The Name and Location fields are only there to help you identify the device, so you can set those to anything you like.

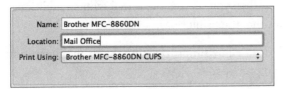

4   If you're configuring an LPD printer connection, you will also have to manually specify the appropriate printer driver. This is also often the case with HP JetDirect and SMB printer connections.

To specify a specific printer driver, choose Select Printer Software from the Print Using pop-up menu. You can manually scroll through the list of installed printer drivers, but using the Spotlight field to narrow the search is much quicker.

5   Once you have selected and configured the new printer or fax, click the OK button to finish the printer's configuration.

If you are configuring an IP printer, then you may be presented with an additional dialog to select any special options that the printer has.

6   You can verify the printer has been added by simply opening the Print dialog from any application or the Print & Scan preferences.

In the Print & Scan preferences, you can tell which printers are connected via network if their location is shown as something different than your local Mac's sharing name. Also note that multifunction devices will show a Scan tab, indicating the system has also configured the scanning driver software.

Configuring Fax Services

Creating a fax printer configuration, similar to adding a printer, is all that's required to prepare your Mac to send faxes. However, a few more steps are required to configure your Mac to *receive* faxes.

> **TIP** You can also share your Mac's faxing capabilities via the network as detailed in the "Sharing Printers" section later in this chapter.

To configure your Mac to send faxes:

1 Open and unlock the Print & Scan preferences, and then click the small plus button at the bottom of the Printers list to open the Add Printer dialog.

2 From the Add Printer dialog, click the Fax button in the toolbar, and then select a fax connection.

You will be able to choose either using Bluetooth DUN for faxing via a paired Bluetooth-enabled mobile phone or External Modem for faxing via the Apple USB Modem. The system will automatically complete the lower half of the Add Printer dialog, but you can change both Name and Location to whatever is most convenient.

3 After you have selected a fax configuration, click the Add button to add the fax printer to your printer list.

4 Back at the Print & Scan preferences, you should at least enter the fax number for the line configured as your Mac's fax.

TIP ▶ Quickly view the status of your Mac's fax configuration by selecting "Show fax status in menu bar," which enables the fax status menu item on the far-right side of the menu bar near the time.

At this point, you can send faxes from any application that can print. From any Print dialog, simply start a print job that specifies the fax printer you just created. The Print dialog will automatically expand and allow you to enter a phone number for the destination fax and optionally create a fax cover page. To enable your Mac to receive faxes, you must perform a few more configuration steps.

MORE INFO ▸ Detailed print job settings are covered in "Managing Print Jobs" later in this chapter.

To configure your Mac to receive faxes:

1   Open and unlock the Print & Scan preferences, and then select a fax printer from the Printers list.

2   Click the Receive Options button to reveal a dialog where you'll enable and configure your Mac to receive incoming faxes. At the very least, you must select the "Receive faxes on this computer" checkbox.

You can also define the number of rings before the fax will answer, and the destination folder for the received fax documents, which are saved as PDF files. Optionally, you can have the Mac automatically print or email received fax documents.

3   Click OK when you have completed your configuration options, and the Mac will wait patiently for incoming faxes as long as it's powered on and awake.

NOTE ▸ Your Mac can't receive faxes in sleep mode. You can disable your Mac's automatic sleep activation or enable wake for network access from the Energy Saver preferences.

Modify an Existing Printer or Fax

You may find it necessary to edit a printer or fax configuration after you set it up. From the Print & Scan preferences, you can:

▸   Delete a printer or fax configuration—Select the item you wish to delete from the printer and fax list, and then click the small minus button at the bottom of the list.

▶ Set printing defaults—From the two pop-up menus at the bottom of the Print & Scan preferences, select the default printer and paper size. Use caution when setting the default printer for Last Printer Used; because you will effectively have no permanent default printer, the default destination for print jobs may constantly change.

▶ Open the print or fax queue— Select a printer or fax from the list, and then click the Open Print Queue or Open Fax Queue button. Details regarding print queues are covered in the "Managing Printer and Fax Queues" section later in this chapter.

▶ Edit an existing configuration and check supply levels—Select a printer from the list, and then click the Options & Supplies button. In the resulting dialog, you can easily edit the printer's configuration including changing the selected printer driver and, if available, check the printer supply levels and open the printer's hardware configuration utility.

NOTE ▶ The only way to edit a fax configuration is by accessing its fax queue application, as covered in the "Managing Printer and Fax Queues" section later in this chapter.

▶ Manage scanning—Select a multifunction device from the list and then select the Scan tab. From this interface, you can open the scanner image capture interface or enable local network scanner sharing.

Managing Print Jobs

Lion features a unified Print dialog that combines previously separate Page Setup and Print dialogs. The Page Setup dialog typically contains document size, orientation, and scale settings, and the Print dialog has all other printer settings. For backward compatibility, Lion allows older applications to continue to use separate Page Setup and Print dialogs, but older apps will still be able to use the new unified printing interface when you open a Print dialog. In other words, some older applications will have document settings in both the Page Setup and Print dialogs.

This unified Print dialog also features two modes: The basic mode allows you to quickly preview and start a print job based on default settings, and the details mode allows you to specify any page or print option and manage print setting presets.

> **NOTE** ▶ Some applications, especially graphic design and desktop publishing applications, use custom dialogs for printing that may look different from the standard Print dialog covered in this chapter.

> **NOTE** ▶ If a network printer requires authentication, you may be presented with an authentication dialog in order to print to the shared printer.

Basic Printing

To start a print job based on default print settings:

1   From an application, start a print job by choosing File > Print or by pressing the Command-P keyboard shortcut.

NOTE ▶ Some applications will bypass the Print dialog and issue a print job to your default printer when you use Command-P.

The Print dialog appears. In some cases it will slide out of the application's window title bar; in other cases it will appear as its own dialog window. Most applications will show a print preview, but some may just show the basic print options.

2   The default printer and print preset will be selected, but you can choose the number of pages, copies, and duplex (two-sided) options.

Customizing printer presets is covered in the next section of this chapter.

3   Click the Print button to start the print job.

The system will automatically open the print queue application associated with the destination printer. Though no window will open if the print job is successful, you will be able to click on the print queue in the Dock.

Detailed Printing and Print Presets

To start a print job based on custom print settings:

1   From an application, open the Print dialog by choosing File > Print or by pressing Command-P.

2   The default printer and print preset will be selected, but you can choose any other configured printer or preset from the associated pop-up menu.

3   Click the Show Details button, and the Print dialog will expand to its details mode.

The arrow button will toggle the Print dialog between basic and advanced modes. The Print dialog also remembers which mode you were in last for each application. In other words, every application will start with a basic Print dialog the first time you print, but for subsequent print jobs, the Print dialog will open to the mode last used for each individual application.

4   On the left side of the details Print dialog, you can page through a preview of the print job. Any changes you make to the page layout settings are instantly reflected in the preview.

5   On the right side of the dialog, you can configure all possible print settings for most applications. The top half features basic page setup and print settings.

Settings on the bottom half vary based on the application you're printing from and your selected printer's driver. You can select a category of print settings to modify by choosing it from the pop-up menu that separates the print settings from top to bottom. The settings list and configuration options within will vary based on the application, selected printer, and selected printer driver.

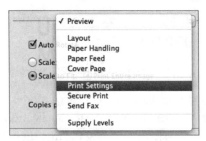

TIP ▶ If the selected printer is a multifunction device that provides fax support, one of the items in the Print Settings pop-up menu will be Send Fax. From here, you can define fax settings that will be used on the multifunction device to send a fax instead of printing a document.

6 To save the current print settings as a preset, choose Save Current Settings as a Preset from the Presets pop-up menu. Select if you want this preset to apply to all printers or just the currently selected printer. Give the preset a name in the resulting dialog and click OK to save it.

NOTE ▶ Print presets do not save application-specific settings.

The preset will now be accessible from the Presets pop-up menu in the details view of any Print dialog. The print presets are saved to the ~/Library/Preferences/com.apple. print.custompresets.plist file, so each user has her own custom print presets.

7   To manage existing print presets, choose Show Presets from the Presets pop-up menu.

The print Presets dialog, new in Lion, will appear, allowing you to manage all print presets for this user account. Select a preset to see its settings and values, and optionally use the Delete and Duplicate buttons at the bottom of the presets list. Double-clicking a print preset allows you to rename the preset. When you are done managing print presets, click the OK button to return to the Print dialog.

8   Click the Print button to start the job based on your print settings.

Using PDF Tools

Lion includes a built-in PDF workflow architecture and editing tools. The full Adobe Acrobat suite has more advanced PDF features, but Lion includes all the tools to create PDF documents or perform basic editing. Any application that can print can also use Lion's Quartz imaging system to generate high-quality PDF documents. In any Print dialog, click the PDF button. A pop-up menu will appear where you can choose a PDF workflow destination, including the ability to save a PDF to any location.

From the PDF pop-up menu, you can also specify a PDF workflow designed to accept and automatically process PDF files. Some preset workflows are built in, but you can add your own PDF workflows by choosing Edit Menu from the PDF pop-up menu. Alternately, you can manually add PDF workflows to the /Library/PDF Services or the ~/Library/PDF Services folders, depending on who needs access to the PDF workflows. To create custom PDF workflows, you can use either the /Applications/Utilities/AppleScript Editor application or the /Applications/Automator application.

Lion's /Applications/Preview application also offers comprehensive PDF editing functionality—you can edit and adjust individual elements, reorder pages, crop the document, add annotations, and fill out form data. From Preview, you can also convert PDF files to other formats or resave the PDF file using more appropriate settings.

Managing Printer and Fax Queues

As stated previously, when a print or fax job is started, the spool file is placed inside the /var/spool/cups folder, and then CUPS takes over to process the file and send it to the printer or fax modem. When you print from the graphical interface, Lion opens a print queue application to manage the print job. If a job completes quickly, the file will only be in the print or fax queue for a few moments, and the print queue application will quit when done. However, printers always seem to be the most problematic of peripherals, so often your Mac will not be able to complete the print job. The printer or fax queue application will remain open until the print job finishes or you resolve the print issue.

NOTE ▶ If the system detects an error with the printer or fax modem, it will stop all print jobs to that device. You will still be able to issue print jobs, but they will simply fill up in the device's queue.

To manage print and fax job queues:

1 You can access the print or fax queue application using one of the following methods:

▶ If a printer or fax queue is already open, simply click on its icon in the Dock. In the example screenshot, the printer queue's Dock icon is indicating that there are currently two jobs in queue and that the printer is disconnected.

▶ You can manually open a fax or print queue from the Print & Scan preferences by selecting the device from the printer and fax list, and then clicking the Open Print Queue or Open Fax Queue button.

▶ You can manually open a fax or print queue from the ~/Library/Printers folder.

2 When the printer or fax queue opens, you will immediately see the current status of the printer and any currently queued print jobs.

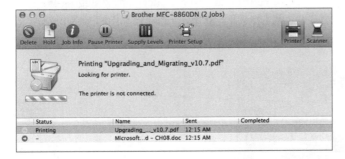

A typical example of a print queue you'll see when the printer is offline is multiple versions of the same job because the user has incorrectly assumed sending the print job again would fix the issue. The system will automatically detect when the printer becomes available again, assuming the queue isn't paused.

3 To pause or resume the printer queue, click the Pause Printer or Resume Printer button in the queue application toolbar.

4   To hold or resume a specific print job, select it from the job list and then click the Hold or Resume button in the queue application toolbar.

You can also delete a job by selecting it from the job list and then clicking the Delete button in the queue application toolbar.

TIP▶ Selecting a job and pressing the Space bar will open a Quick Look preview window of the print job.

Once you are done managing a printer or fax queue, it's acceptable to leave the application running. You may find it useful to leave often-used print and fax queues in the Dock for direct access. Simply right-click or Control-click on the queue application's Dock icon and from the shortcut menu choose Options > Keep in Dock.

You can also provide quick access to all your print and fax queues by dragging the ~/Library/Printers folder to your Dock. Clicking on this folder in your Dock reveals all configured devices.

Some other features are also available in the printer queue application's toolbar. For instance, to check the printer's supplies, click the Supply Levels button. You can also reconfigure nearly all of the printer's settings by clicking the Printer Setup button in the toolbar. Finally, if the queue is for a supported multifunction printer, you can click the Scanner button in the toolbar to change the printer queue window into an image capture window. Lion supports scanning to multifunction devices both locally and via the network.

Sharing Printers

It's very easy to share printer and fax configurations with Lion. Your Mac's shared print service is made available via the IPP and SMB printer sharing protocols. While Macs and Windows PCs technically support both printing protocols, Macs are more likely to use IPP, and Windows PCs are more likely to use SMB. As a bonus, the IPP protocol supports automatic printer driver configuration and installation for Mac systems, so when another Mac user connects to your Mac's shared print service, her system will automatically select, and download if necessary, the appropriate printer drivers.

The CUPS shared print service also allows other network clients to easily locate your shared printer and fax configurations with Bonjour for IPP or NetBIOS/WINS for SMB. Again, Macs and Windows PCs support both discovery protocols, but Macs are more likely to use Bonjour, and Windows PCs are more likely to use NetBIOS/WINS. Or, network clients can manually enter your Mac's IP address or DNS host name to access your Mac's shared print service. Configuring your Mac's identification for providing network services is covered in Chapter 7, "Network Services."

NOTE ► Users will not be able to access shared print services on a Mac in sleep mode. You can disable your Mac's automatic sleep activation or enable wake for network access from the Energy Saver preferences.

To share printers and faxes from your Mac:

1   Open and unlock the Sharing preferences.

2   Select the Printer Sharing checkbox to enable printer and fax sharing.

Selecting this checkbox tells the cupsd process (which is always running in the background) to listen for IPP print service requests on TCP port 631. By default, only locally connected printers will be shared.

3   To enable sharing for additional printer or fax configurations, simply select the checkboxes next to the printers or faxes you wish to share.

You can also enable specific printing devices for sharing from the Print & Scan preferences.

NOTE ► To avoid confusion, you shouldn't reshare network printers using your Mac's shared print services if network printers are already available on your network.

4   Optionally, you can limit who is allowed to print to your shared printers or faxes. By default, all users are allowed access to your shared printing devices. To limit access, select a shared device from the Printers list, and then click the small plus button at the bottom of the Users list.

A dialog will appear, allowing you to select user or group accounts that you wish to grant access to the printing device. When adding accounts, you can also choose to deny access to guest users by selecting No Access to Everyone in the Users list. Also, with limited printing access enabled, all users will have to authenticate in order to print to your shared printer.

5   If you need to enable authenticated print sharing via the SMB protocol, you must also enable the relevant user's passwords in the SMB sharing settings of the Sharing preferences.

From the Sharing preferences, select File Sharing in the Service list, then click the Options button.

In the resulting dialog, select the "Share files and folders using SMB (Windows)" checkbox.

NOTE ▶ SMB file sharing does not need to be enabled for SMB print sharing.

Finally, you'll select and enter passwords for the user accounts you wish to allow to connect to your SMB shared resources. Click the Done button once you have made your selections.

The launchd control process will now listen for SMB service requests on TCP port 139, and automatically start the smbd background process as necessary to handle any requests.

Advanced Printing Management

All these CUPS attributes—being server-based, UNIX-based, and open source—led to the need for a common interface to manage the CUPS system that doesn't require specific system software. While it's true that all CUPS-compatible systems have a command line, most users simply aren't comfortable navigating the command line, especially for something as fundamental as printing. Thus, CUPS also includes a web server that provides a full web-based graphical administration interface.

You can access your Mac's CUPS web interface by opening a web browser and entering the following URL: http://localhost:631/. This URL essentially tells the browser to request a website on your local Mac via TCP port 631. The CUPS web interface home page lists the available documentation. While the documentation is great, the really interesting features from a management perspective are the rest of the tabs across the top of the page, including Administration, Jobs, and Printers.

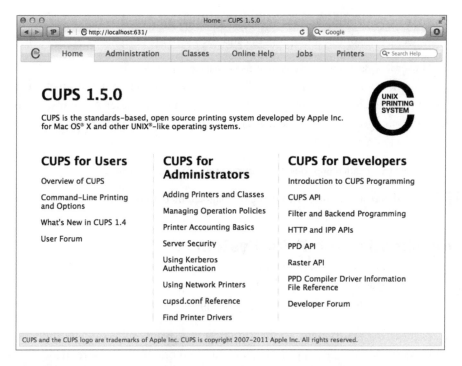

Exploring the details of the CUPS web interface is beyond the scope of this guide, but the page is well documented and is the best place to start digging deeper into CUPS. A few of the web interface highlights include the ability to enable remote CUPS administration, essentially allowing you to access the Mac's CUPS web interface from another computer. Also, CUPS has the ability to create web RSS feeds with print accounting information. This allows you to use an RSS aggregator application to keep tabs on printing statistics.

Modifying Printer Administration Rights

As stated previously, by default, you must be an administrative user to make changes to printer and fax settings. However, you can change this default and give any number of specific users and groups the ability to administrate printer and fax settings. With CUPS, only those belonging to the system group _lpadmin can do this. You can't edit this group using the Users & Groups preferences, so if you want to grant additional administration rights for printing and faxing, you will have to use the command-line group editor dseditgroup.

In the following example, Michelle, as an administrative user, adds the Logan user account to the _lpadmin group using the dseditgroup command. Thus, Michelle is giving Logan the ability to manage printing and fax settings. Note that Michelle has to put her account name in the dsedigroup command arguments and then provide her password.

MyMac:~ michelle$ dseditgroup -o edit -u michelle -a logan _lpadmin

Here is a different example in which Michelle uses the same command, but this time adds the staff group to the _lpadmin group. As covered in Chapter 2, "User Accounts," all local users are in the staff group. Thus, Michelle is effectively giving local users the ability to manage printing and fax settings.

MyMac:~ michelle$ dseditgroup -o edit -u michelle –t group -a staff _lpadmin

TIP ⯈ To delete a user or group using dseditgroup, instead of using -o edit, use -o delete.

Troubleshooting the Print System

You will probably experience more printing issues caused by hardware than by software. However, this being a reference about Lion, the following is a series of mostly software-based general print system troubleshooting techniques.

▶ **Always check the print queue application first.** The print and fax queue application will always show the first symptoms of an issue, and odds are you were made aware of the issue by the queue. The print queue will let you know if there is a printer connection issue, but you should also check to make sure that the queue is not paused and that none of the jobs are on hold. Sometimes deleting old print jobs from the queue will help clear the problem.

▶ **Double-check page and print settings.** If the job is printing but doesn't print correctly, double-check page and print settings using the Print dialog's details mode.

▶ **Review the PDF output of the application.** Remember that the CUPS workflow is application > PDF > CUPS > printer. Thus, verifying if the PDF looks correct will let you know if the source of the problem is with the application or the printing system.

▶ **Print from another application.** If you suspect the application is at the root of the problem, try printing from another application. You can also print a test page while in the printer queue application by choosing Printer > Print Test Page.

▶ **Check the printer hardware.** Many modern printers have diagnostic screens or printed reports that can help you identify a hardware issue. Many also have a software utility or a built-in webpage that may report errors. Clicking the Printer Setup button in the printer queue application's toolbar will access these management interfaces. Also, don't forget to double-check cables and connections. Finally, you may be well served by contacting the printer manufacturer to diagnose printer hardware issues.

▶ **For fax issues, check phone line and phone settings.** As with any fax system issue, you need to check for modem and phone line problems. When sending faxes via the print system, you may encounter issues that are outside your control because you are relying on the phone system and another user's fax hardware.

▶ **For directly connected printers, use peripheral troubleshooting techniques.** For printers connected via USB or FireWire, use the peripheral troubleshooting techniques outlined earlier in this chapter.

▶ **For network printers, use network troubleshooting techniques.** For printers connected via a network connection, use the network troubleshooting techniques described in Chapter 6, "Network Configuration."

▶ **Delete and then reconfigure printers or faxes.** From the Print & Scan preferences, delete and then reconfigure a troublesome printer or fax using the techniques outlined earlier in this chapter. This will reset the device's drivers and queue.

▶ **Reset the entire print system.** Sometimes it's necessary to reset the entire printing system. From the Print & Scan preferences, right-click or Control-click anywhere in the printers and fax list, and choose "Reset printing system" from the shortcut menu. Click OK in the verification dialog. Next you'll have to authenticate as an administrative user. This clears all configured devices, shared settings, custom presets, and queued print jobs. While this may seem drastic, it's likely to clear up any software-related printing issues.

▶ **Review CUPS log files.** Like other system services, CUPS writes all important activity to log files. You can access these logs while in any printer queue application by choosing Printer > Log & History. This opens the Console utility to the CUPS error_log file. While in the Console, you can also check the CUPS access_log and page_log files located in /private/var/log/cups.

NOTE ▶ The CUPS error_log file may not exist if the CUPS service hasn't yet logged any serious print errors.

▶ **Reinstall or update printer drivers.** Again, software bugs are always being fixed, so it's always a good time to check for printer driver updates. You can use Lion's built-in Software Update application to check for system updates and many printer updates. However, be sure to also check the printer manufacturer's website for the latest printer driver updates.

▶ **Repair installed software disk permissions.** Third-party installers tend to sometimes mess up system software permissions. Use Disk Utility's Repair Permissions feature to resolve permissions issues with printer drivers and other print system files (see Chapter 3, "File Systems").

What You've Learned

▶ Lion supports a wide variety of peripherals, expansion cards, storage devices, and audio and video connections.

▶ Bluetooth peripherals require pairing for the Mac to securely access their services.

▶ These devices are supported in groups of device classes, and Lion includes a selection of generic software drivers.

▶ Built-in and third-party drivers are supported via kernel extensions, framework plug-ins, and standalone applications.

▶ Lion uses CUPS to provide print and fax services for both local and shared users.

▶ A rich PDF workflow capability is also built into Lion.

▶ You learned a variety of peripheral and printing troubleshooting techniques.

References

Check for current Knowledge Base documents at www.apple.com/support.

Peripherals

HT1151, "USB and FireWire Quick Assist"

TA26476, "FireWire: Frequently Asked Questions"

HT3039, "What you can do with Bluetooth wireless technology"

HT4241, "About Mini DisplayPort to HDMI adapters"

HT3235, "Monitor and Display Adapter Table"

HT3783, "Mac OS X v10.6.x and OS X Lion: About Sync Diagnostics assistant"

HT3825, "Mac OS X v10.6: Digital camera RAW formats supported"

HT4614, "About Thunderbolt to Thunderbolt cable (2 m)"

Printing

HT3771, "Mac OS X v10.6: Mac 101—Printing"

HT3669, "OS X Lion, Mac OS X v10.6: Printer and scanner software"

URLs

Official USB Implementer's Forum resource website: www.usb.org

Official 1394 Trade Association (FireWire) website: www.1394ta.org

Official Intel Thunderbolt website: www.intel.com/technology/io/thunderbolt/index.htm

Official Bluetooth Technology Information website: www.bluetooth.com

Official CUPS print server resource website: www.cups.org

Your Mac's local CUPS management website: http://localhost:631

Review Quiz

1. Which peripheral, expansion, and storage buses are supported by Lion?
2. What is a device driver? What three primary types of device drivers are there?
3. How does Lion support third-party devices without needing third-party device drivers?
4. What does CUPS do?
5. What are PPD files responsible for?
6. How do you share printers with other Mac and Windows users?

Answers

1. Lion supports Universal Serial Bus (USB), FireWire, Thunderbolt, and Bluetooth peripheral buses; PCI Express (PCIe), PC Card, and ExpressCard 34 expansion buses; and Advanced Technology Attachment (ATA), Serial ATA (SATA), Small Computer System Interface (SCSI), Serial Attached SCSI (SAS), and Fibre Channel storage buses.
2. A device driver is software specially designed to facilitate the communication between Lion and a peripheral. Device drivers can be kernel extensions, framework plug-ins, or standalone applications.
3. Lion uses built-in generic drivers based on each device class. For example, there are generic drivers for scanners and printers that can be used in lieu of official third-party drivers.
4. Common UNIX Printing System (CUPS) manages all printing and faxing for Lion, including both local and shared printing.
5. PostScript Printer Description (PPD) files are printer driver files that instruct the CUPS system on how to communicate with specific printer models.
6. You can enable printer sharing for Mac clients from the Print & Scan or Sharing preferences, but to enable authenticated print sharing to Windows clients, you must also enable users' passwords in the SMB file sharing settings from the Sharing preferences.

9

Time   This chapter takes approximately 1 hour to complete.

Goals   Understand the Lion startup process

Identify the essential files and processes required to successfully start up Lion

Troubleshoot the startup and login processes

Chapter 9

System Startup

System startup certainly isn't the most glamorous part of Lion, but it's clearly important and technically quite impressive. Apple has improved startup and runtime processes with every revision of Mac OS X. When things work correctly, the startup process is often under 30 seconds. Obviously, users appreciate a quick startup, but most don't and shouldn't have to care what goes on during system startup because they expect their Macs to work properly.

However, when things do go wrong during system startup, users often fear the worst. Novice users may assume that if their Macs won't start up, they will lose important documents. But the system startup process can fail due to many issues that probably won't result in any user data loss. So, it's important to properly diagnose startup issues so you can get the Mac up and running, or at least try to recover data.

This chapter focuses on the process that your Mac goes through from the moment you press the power button until you ultimately reach the Finder. First you will identify the essential files and processes required to successfully start up Lion. This allows you to effectively troubleshoot startup and login issues covered in the remaining portion of this chapter.

Understanding the Startup Sequence

This section examines the main stages of the Lion system startup procedure. The stages of system startup can be categorized into either *system initiation*, the processes required to start the operating system, or *user session*, the processes required to initialize the user environment. At each stage the Mac will present an audible or visual cue to help you validate startup progress. The startup cues discussed here are what you'll experience during a typical startup. Any deviation will be covered throughout this section as you learn more about the startup process.

System Initialization

Firmware

Booter

Kernel

System launchd

User Session

loginwindow

User launchd

User environment

The four main Lion system initialization stages are, in order:

▶ Firmware—At this stage the Mac's hardware is tested and initialized, and then the booter is located and started. Successfully completing this stage results in an audible startup chime and a bright flash from the power-on light, and all displays show a light gray background.

▶ Booter—The booter's main job is to load the system kernel and essential hardware drivers, known as kernel extensions (KEXTs), into main memory and then allow the kernel to take over the system. The booter stage is indicated by a dark gray Apple logo on the main display.

▶ Kernel—The kernel provides the system's foundation and loads additional drivers and the core BSD UNIX system. It is indicated by a dark gray spinning gear below the Apple logo on the main display.

▶ System launchd—Once the core operating system is loaded, it starts the first nonkernel process, the system launchd, which is responsible for loading the remainder of the system. This stage is indicated by the disappearance of the dark gray spinning gear and a white background on all displays. Successful completion of this stage results in either the login screen or the Finder, if the user is set to automatically log in.

The three main Lion user environment stages are, in order:

▶ loginwindow—This is the process responsible for presenting the login screen and eventually logging the user into the system. Successful completion of this stage results in initialization of the user environment, thus allowing user applications to run.

▶ User launchd—This process works in conjunction with the loginwindow process to initialize the user environment and start any user processes or applications.

▶ User environment—This is the "space" the user's processes and applications exist in when she is logged into the system. Obviously, the user environment is maintained by the loginwindow and user launchd processes.

System Initialization: Firmware

Your Mac's firmware, also called BootROM, resides on flash memory chips built into the Mac's main computer board. This way, when you power on your Mac, even before it starts a "real" operating system, the firmware acts as a mini-operating system with just enough software to get things going. Specifically, the firmware tests and initializes the hardware, and then locates and starts the system software booter.

Intel-based Macs feature firmware based on Intel's Extensible Firmware Interface (EFI) technology. Aside from supporting Intel's processor hardware, EFI is what allows your Mac to start up from Lion, Windows, or any other Intel-compatible operating system.

> **MORE INFO** ▶ EFI is an extremely flexible boot architecture and is now managed by the Unified EFI Forum. In fact, EFI will soon be known as Unified Extensible Firmware Interface (UEFI). You can find out more at www.uefi.org.

Power-On Self-Test

The first thing your Mac's firmware does at power on is the Power-On Self-Test (POST). The POST tests built-in hardware components such as processors, system memory, network interfaces, and peripheral interfaces. When your Mac passes the POST, you hear the startup chime and see a light gray background on all displays. After a successful POST, the firmware will go on to locate the booter file.

If your Mac fails the POST, the displays will remain blank or off, and you may get hardware error codes. Depending on the age and model of your Mac, these error codes may manifest as audible tones, a series of flashes from the external power-on light, or internal diagnostic lights illuminating. You may even see a combination of these things. Regardless of which error code you experience, it indicates that a hardware problem exists outside of Lion's control. You can visit Apple's support website at www.apple.com/support to identify your specific Mac's error code, or you can take your Mac to an Apple Authorized Service Provider.

Booter Selection

By default, the firmware will pick the system booter file that was last specified from the Startup Disk preferences in Lion or the Boot Camp control panel in Windows. The booter file's location is saved in your Mac's nonvolatile RAM (NVRAM) so that it remains persistent across system restarts. If the booter file is found, EFI will start the booter process and Lion will begin to start up. This is indicated by the dark gray Apple logo in the center of the main display.

If the firmware cannot locate a booter file, you will see a flashing folder icon with a question mark. Troubleshooting this issue will be covered in the second portion of this chapter.

FileVault 2 Unlock

If the system drive is protected with FileVault 2 encryption, the Lion booter cannot be accessed until the system drive is unlocked by a user. If this is the case, the system will instead begin initial startup from the Lion Recovery HD, where a special EFI booter resides that presents the user with an authentication screen much like the login window.

The FileVault 2 authentication unlock screen appears just a few seconds after POST and has a much lighter background than the standard Lion login window.

Once the user successfully authenticates and unlocks the encrypted system drive, the EFI firmware will be granted access to the system volume containing the Lion booter. Startup will continue as normal, with one exception. Because the user has already authenticated to unlock the drive, he will automatically log into his session without having to authenticate again at the login window. This will only happen once per startup and only for the user who unlocked the encrypted system drive.

Startup Shortcuts

Your Mac's firmware also supports many keyboard shortcuts, which, when pressed and held during initial power-on, allow you to modify the startup process. Some of these shortcuts modify the booter selection, while others modify how Lion starts up. Alternate Lion startup modes are covered later in the "Troubleshooting Startup" section.

> **NOTE** ▶ If the Mac has a firmware password set, then all the startup shortcuts will be disabled save for the Option key (Startup Manager), which will prompt for the firmware password. Using a firmware password is covered in Chapter 2, "User Accounts."

> **NOTE** ▶ Some hardware does not support startup shortcuts, including some third-party keyboards and keyboards connected via some USB hubs or a keyboard-video-mouse (KVM) switch. Also, Bluetooth wireless keyboards may not work either.

> **NOTE** ▶ Startup volumes selected with a shortcut are not saved in NVRAM, so this setting will not persist between system restarts.

Mac startup shortcuts that allow you to select another system include:

▶ Option—Starts up into the Startup Manager, which allows you to select any volume containing a valid system to start up from. This includes internal volumes, optical drive volumes, some external volumes, and, on later Macs, Wi-Fi networks and NetBoot images.

▶ C—Starts up from a bootable CD or DVD in a supported optical drive.

▶ D—Starts up from the Apple Hardware Test partition on the first restore DVD included with your Intel-based Mac. Later models also include this diagnostic built into the hardware ROM and thus don't require the DVD.

▶ Command-Option-D—Starts up from the Apple Hardware Test via an Internet connection to Apple's servers. This option is only available to Mac models released after July 19, 2011.

▶ N—Starts up from the last-used NetBoot server, or the default NetBoot server if none was previously used. The Mac will show a flashing or spinning globe icon in the center of the main display until it locates the NetBoot server, at which point it will show the dark gray Apple logo.

▶ Option-N—Similar to holding the N key, but this shortcut will always start up from the default NetBoot server instead of the last-used NetBoot server.

▶ Command-R—Starts up from the local Lion Recovery HD, if available. If the Mac was released after July 19, 2011, and no local Lion Recovery HD was found, the Mac will automatically attempt to start up from Lion Internet Recovery. Lion Recovery is detailed in Chapter 1, "Installation and Configuration."

▶ Command-Option-R—Forces startup to Lion Internet Recovery. This option is only available to Mac models released after July 19, 2011.

Mac startup shortcuts that modify Lion's default startup:

▶ Shift—Starts up Lion in Safe mode.

▶ Command-V—Starts up Lion in Verbose mode.

▶ Command-S—Starts up Lion in single-user mode.

▶ 6 and 4—Starts up Lion with a 64-bit kernel on supported Mac hardware. The 64-bit kernel mode is covered in the "System Initialization: Kernel" section later in this chapter.

▶ 3 and 2—If your Mac has been set to always start in 64-bit kernel mode, this will force it back to the standard 32-bit kernel mode.

Other useful Mac startup shortcuts:

▶ T—For Macs with built-in Thunderbolt or FireWire ports, holding this key powers on the Mac in target disk mode, allowing other computers to access your Mac's internal drives. Target disk mode details are covered in Chapter 3, "File Systems."

▶ Command-Option-P-R—Resets NVRAM settings and restarts the Mac.

▶ Eject key, F12 key, mouse or trackpad button—Ejects any removable media, including optical discs.

Firmware Updates

Boot read-only memory, or boot ROM, refers to older versions of firmware technology that are not upgradable. Your Mac's firmware, however, is upgradable, and on Intel-based Macs it's even replaceable if it has become damaged. Lion's Software Update service may automatically update some Macs' firmware, but you can also check Apple's Knowledge Base for the latest list of Mac firmware updates. Document HT1237, "EFI and SMC firmware updates for Intel-based Macs," maintains a list of Mac firmware updates. You can replace your Intel-based Mac's firmware using a firmware restoration CD as outlined in document HT2213, "About the Firmware Restoration CD (Intel-based Macs)."

> **MORE INFO** ▶ You can easily extend your Intel-based Mac's EFI capabilities using the open source rEFIt toolkit available at http://refit.sourceforge.net.

System Initialization: Booter

The booter process is launched by your Mac's firmware and is responsible for loading the Lion kernel and enough essential kernel extensions, or KEXTs, so the kernel can take over the system and continue the startup process. Your Mac's firmware also passes on any special startup mode instructions for the booter to handle, such as when the user is holding down the Shift key, indicating that Lion should start up in Safe Mode. The booter process itself resides at /System/Library/CoreServices/boot.efi.

To expedite the startup process, the booter will load cached files whenever possible. These files contain an optimized kernel and KEXTs that load much quicker than if the system had to load them from scratch. These caches are located in the /System/Library/Caches/com.apple.kernel.caches folder. If the system detects a problem or you start Lion in Safe Mode, these caches will be discarded and the kernel-loading process will take much longer.

As covered previously, the booter process is indicated at startup by the dark gray Apple icon in the center of the main display. If the booter successfully loads the kernel, this will be indicated by a small, dark gray spinning gear icon below the Apple icon.

If your Mac is set to NetBoot and the firmware successfully locates the booter file on the NetBoot server, you will again see the dark gray Apple icon. However, in this case the booter and the cached kernel information must be downloaded from the NetBoot server. This process is indicated by a small, dark gray spinning globe icon below the Apple icon.

The globe icon will be replaced by the standard spinning gear icon once the kernel has been successfully loaded from the NetBoot server.

Finally, if the booter is unable to load the kernel, a dark gray prohibitory icon will take the place of the Apple icon. Again, troubleshooting this issue will be covered later in this chapter.

System Initialization: Kernel

Once the booter has successfully loaded the kernel and essential KEXTs, the kernel itself takes over the startup process. The kernel has now loaded enough KEXTs to read the entire file system, allowing it to load any additional KEXTs and start the core BSD UNIX system. A spinning gray gear icon below the Apple icon indicates the kernel's startup progress. Finally, the kernel starts the first normal (nonkernel) process, the system launchd, which is ultimately the parent process for every other process. The appearance of anything besides the white startup screen with the Apple logo is an indication that the kernel has fully loaded and the launchd process is starting other items.

Again, in most cases the kernel is loaded by the booter from cached files. However, the kernel is also located on the system volume at /mach_kernel. This file is normally hidden from users in the graphical user interface, because they don't need access to it. Many other hidden files and folders at the root of the system volume are necessary for the BSD UNIX system, and again the average user doesn't need access to these items. As covered in Chapter 8, "Peripherals and Printing," KEXTs reside in the /System/Library/Extensions and /Library/Extensions folders.

64-Bit Kernel Mode

The default for Lion is to start the kernel in 64-bit mode on any hardware that supports it. However, Lion's 64-bit kernel will prevent you from using any 32-bit KEXT. Many third-party KEXTs only support 32-bit mode. As covered in Chapter 8, "Peripherals and Printing," you can use /Applications/Utilities/System Information to identify which installed KEXTs support 64-bit mode.

To resolve incompatible 32-bit-only KEXTs, you can force Lion to start up in 32-bit kernel mode by holding down the 3 and 2 keys during system startup. As with all startup modifiers, this is not a permanent solution. To permanently configure 32-bit kernel mode, you will need to use the systemsetup command. Specifically, from the Terminal, enter sudo systemsetup -setkernelbootarchitecture i386 to set the default startup for 32-bit kernel mode. Conversely, you can set the default back to 64-bit kernel with sudo systemsetup -setkernelbootarchitecture x86_64. Finally, you can verify that your Mac is running with a 64-bit kernel by opening System Information and selecting the Software overview.

System Initialization: System launchd

Once the kernel is up and running, the Mac is ready to start running processes at the behest of the system and eventually human users. The first normal (nonkernel) process started is the system launchd, located at /sbin/launchd, which runs as root and is given the process identification number of 1. In UNIX terms, the system launchd is the first parent process that spawns all other child processes, and those processes go on to spawn other child processes.

The first task for the system launchd process is to complete the system initialization by starting all other system processes. Previous versions of Mac OS X show the "Welcome to Mac OS X" dialog with a progress bar to indicate system initialization status as the various system processes start up. However, beginning with Mac OS X v10.5, the launchd process was highly optimized, so the system initialization process takes only a few moments and is indicated by a white background on all displays. This white background is actually a result of launchd starting the WindowServer process, which is responsible for drawing the Lion user interface, but it's still a good indication that things are progressing through the system startup process.

The launchd process is designed to expedite system initialization by starting multiple system processes simultaneously whenever possible and starting only essential system processes at startup. After startup, the system launchd process automatically starts and stops additional system processes as needed. By dynamically managing system processes, launchd keeps your Mac responsive and running as efficiently as possible.

> **MORE INFO** ▶ launchd is an extremely powerful open source system for managing services. Learn more about launchd by reading its manual page in the Terminal.

System launchd Items

As covered in Chapter 4, "Data Management," launchd manages system processes as described by launchd preference files in the /System/Library/LaunchDaemons folder. Third-party processes can also be managed when described by launchd preference files in the /Library/LaunchDaemons folder.

Apple strongly encourages all developers to adopt the launchd system for all automatically started processes. But the system launchd process also supports legacy startup routines. This includes support for running the traditional UNIX /etc/rc.local script during system initialization if present, though this script is not included on Lion by default. The system launchd process also starts the /sbin/SystemStarter process, which manages system processes as described by legacy Mac OS X startup items. Lion does not include any built-in startup items, but SystemStarter will still look in the /System/Library/StartupItems and /Library/StartupItems folders for third-party startup items.

Viewing the launchd Hierarchy

The /Applications/Utilities/Activity Monitor application lists all processes along with their identification numbers and parent/child relationships. In the Activity Monitor, you can sort the process list by clicking on the title of the Process ID column, and you can view a process's parent process by double-clicking on its name in the list. You will find it beneficial to open Activity Monitor and examine the process listing as you learn about how Lion starts up the user environment. Detailed information about using Activity Monitor is covered in Chapter 5, "Applications and Processes."

User Session

Eventually, after enough system processes have started, the system launchd process will start /System/Library/CoreServices/loginwindow.app. The loginwindow process has the ability to run as both a background process and a graphical interface application. The loginwindow coordinates the login screen and, along with the opendirectoryd process, authenticates the user. After authentication, the loginwindow, in conjunction with the user's launchd, also initializes the graphical interface user environment and continues to run as a background process to maintain the user session.

A user can authenticate manually using the login screen, or the loginwindow can be set to automatically authenticate a user at startup. As covered previously, the system will also automatically log in a user if she provided authentication to unlock FileVault 2 during startup. The loginwindow settings are stored in the /Library/Preferences/com.apple.loginwindow.plist preference file. As covered in Chapter 2, "User Accounts," you can configure loginwindow settings from the User & Groups preferences.

If no users are logged into the Mac, the loginwindow process is owned by the root user. Once a user successfully authenticates, the loginwindow process switches ownership to this user and then proceeds to set up the graphical interface user environment with help from the user's launchd. In fact, the system launchd process starts another instance of launchd that is also owned by the authenticated user. All user processes and applications, even those that the user manually opens, will be started by the user-specific launchd process. If fast user switching is enabled, the system launchd process will start additional loginwindow and launchd processes to initialize and maintain each user's environment.

Initialize the User Environment

The user's loginwindow and launchd processes set up the graphical interface user environment by:

▶ Retrieving the user account information from opendirectoryd and applying any account settings

▶ Configuring the mouse, keyboard, and system sound using the user's preferences

▶ Loading the user's computing environment: preferences, environment variables, devices and file permissions, and keychain access

▶ Opening the Dock (responsible for Mission Control), Finder, and SystemUIServer, which is responsible for user interface elements like menu extras on the right side of the menu bar

▶ Automatically opening the user's login items

▶ By default in Lion, automatically resuming any application that was open before the last logout

It's important to understand the differences between the various autostarting mechanisms in Lion: launch daemons, startup items, launch agents, and login items. Again, launch daemons and startup items are started during system initialization by the system launchd process on behalf of the root user. On the other hand, launch agents and login items are only started on behalf of a specific user. In other words, launch daemons and startup items affect the system as a whole, while launch agents and login items affect individual users.

Specifically, launch agents are started by the user's launchd process on behalf of the user. Launch agents can be started at any time as long as the user's launchd process is running. Most launch agents are started during the initialization of the user environment, but they could also be started afterward or on a regular repeating basis depending on need. Launch agents provided by the system can be found in /Library/LaunchAgents, whereas third-party launch agents should be located in either /Library/LaunchAgents or ~/Library/LaunchAgents.

Finally, login items are started only at the very end of the initialization of the user environment. The loginwindow process, again with help from the user's launchd process, is responsible for starting a user's login items. The user's login item list is stored in the ~/Library/Preferences/loginwindow.plist preference file. As covered previously in Chapter 2, "User Accounts," you can configure a user's login item list from the Users & Groups preferences.

Maintaining the User Environment

The user-owned launchd and loginwindow processes will continue to run as long as the user is logged in to the session. The user's launchd process will start all user processes and applications, while the user's loginwindow process will monitor and maintain the user session.

The user's loginwindow process monitors the user session by:

▶ Managing logout, restart, and shutdown procedures

▶ Managing the Force Quit Applications window, which includes monitoring the currently active applications and responding to user requests to forcibly quit applications

▶ Writing any standard-error output to the user's console.log file

While the user is logged in to the session, the user's launchd process automatically restarts any user application that should remain open, such as the Finder or the Dock. If the user's loginwindow process is ended, whether intentionally or unexpectedly, all the user's applications and processes will also immediately quit without saving changes. If this happens, the system launchd process will then automatically restart the loginwindow process as if the Mac had just started up. In other words, the loginwindow will, depending on configuration, either display the login screen or automatically log in the specified user.

Sleep Modes, Logout, and Shutdown

At the other end of the spectrum, but still related, are the processes required to pause or end the user session. The main distinction is that your Mac's sleep function does not quit any open processes, whereas the user logout and system shutdown functions will quit open processes. In most cases, the user manually issues a sleep, logout, or shutdown command from the Apple menu or by pressing the Mac's power button.

NOTE ▶ New in Lion is the automatic Resume feature, enabled by default for all users. Upon login the user's items will reopen to their previous state. This feature works in conjunction with application Auto Save as covered in Chapter 5, "Applications and Processes."

However, other processes and applications can also initiate sleep, logout, or shutdown commands. For instance, the Installer and Software Update applications can request a restart when the installation of new software requires it. Further, you can configure the Mac to automatically perform certain commands such as put the system to sleep after a period of inactivity with settings in the Energy Saver preferences; set a schedule to sleep, shut down, or start up the Mac with settings in the Schedule dialog of the Energy Saver preferences; automatically log out users after a period of inactivity with settings in the Security & Privacy preferences; and automatically log out managed users with settings in the Parental Controls preferences. Many of these settings can be managed remotely from Apple Remote Desktop or from managed client settings hosted on a network directory server.

Sleep Modes

Your Mac's sleep function is convenient because it does not quit any active processes or applications. Instead, the system kernel pauses all processes and then essentially shuts down all the hardware except for system memory and power to the USB and FireWire ports. This greatly reduces the amount of power used; as an example, portable Macs can remain in sleep mode for several days on a single battery charge. Waking your Mac from sleep mode restarts all hardware, and the kernel will resume all processes and applications from the point where you left them.

All Intel-based portable Macs support a safe sleep mode. When these Macs go to sleep, they also copy the entire contents of system memory to an image file on the system volume. This way, if these Macs stay in sleep mode long enough to completely drain the battery, no data is lost when the system has to fully shut down.

When you restart a Mac from safe sleep mode, the booter process will reload the saved memory image from the system volume instead of proceeding with the normal startup process. The booter process indicates that the Mac is restarting from safe sleep mode by showing a light gray version of your Mac's screen when it was put to sleep and a small progress bar at the bottom of the main display. It should take only a few moments to reload system memory, and the kernel will resume all processes and applications. If FileVault 2 is enabled, the safe sleep-wake process will be preceded by the FileVault 2 authentication unlock screen.

Logout

Users can log out any time they want to end their user session, but they also have to log out to shut down or restart the Mac. When the currently logged-in user chooses to log out, the user's loginwindow process manages all logout functions with help from the user's launchd process. Once the user authorizes the logout, the user's loginwindow process issues a Quit Application Apple event to all applications. Applications that support Lion's new Auto Save and Resume features will immediately save changes to any open documents and quit. Applications that do not support these features will still respond to the Quit event, but they are programmed to ask the user if changes should be saved. If the application fails to reply or quit itself after 60 seconds, the logout process will be stopped and loginwindow will display an error message.

If all the user's applications successfully quit, the user's loginwindow process will then forcibly quit any background user processes. Finally, the user's loginwindow process will close the user's graphical interface session, run any logout scripts, record the logout to the main system.log file, and reset device permissions and preferences to their defaults. If the user chose only to log out, as opposed to shutting down or restarting, the user's loginwindow and launchd processes will quit, the system launchd process will restart a new loginwindow process owned by the root user, and the login screen will appear.

Shutdown and Restart

When a logged-in user chooses to shut down or restart the Mac, again the user's loginwindow process manages all logout functions with help from the system launchd process. First the user's loginwindow process logs out the current user. If other users are logged in via fast user switching, the loginwindow process will ask for administrative user authentication and, if granted, will forcibly quit all other users' processes and applications, possibly losing user data.

After all user sessions are logged out, the user's loginwindow process tells the kernel to issue the quit command to all remaining system processes. Processes like loginwindow should quit promptly, but the kernel must wait for processes that remain responsive while they are going through the motions of quitting. If system processes don't respond after a few seconds, the kernel will forcibly quit those processes. Once all processes are quit, the kernel will stop the system launchd process and then shut down the system. If the user chose to restart the Mac, the Mac's firmware will begin the system startup process once again.

Troubleshooting Startup

The most important part of troubleshooting system startup is fully understanding the startup process. Once you can identify the various stages—and know which processes and files are responsible for each—you are well on your way to diagnosing any startup issue. In the second portion of the chapter, you'll troubleshoot each of these stages as well as investigate logout and shutdown problems.

Here you will learn about the three primary Lion diagnostic startup modes: Verbose mode, Safe mode, and single-user mode. These three modes are initiated at the firmware stage but can affect the remaining startup process at each stage. The ramifications of each diagnostic startup mode are covered with each stage throughout this section.

The Lion diagnostic startup modes are:

▶ Verbose mode—This mode is initiated by holding down Command-V during system startup. In Verbose mode, the system will not hide the startup progress from you with the light gray or blue screens. Instead, you will see a black background with white text showing all details of the startup process.

▶ Safe Boot/Safe Mode/Safe Login—This mode is initiated by holding down the Shift key during system startup and user login. Safe Boot occurs when the system is starting up; Safe mode is when the system is actually running; and Safe Login is when the system starts up the user session. During Safe Boot, the system will clear specific caches, carefully test startup procedures, and limit automatically launched processes during each stage.

▶ Single-user mode—This mode is initiated by holding down Command-S during system startup. When starting up in single-user mode, the system will only start core kernel and BSD UNIX functionality. You must be familiar with the command-line interface to use single-user mode. Using the command line is detailed in Appendix B, "Command-Line Essentials."

Troubleshooting the Firmware

Issues at the firmware stage are indicated by an inability of your Mac to reach the light gray screen with the dark gray Apple icon. The key to troubleshooting at this point is to determine whether this issue is related to the Mac's hardware or system volume.

Hardware Issues

If you don't hear the startup chime or see the power-on light flash, the Mac's hardware did not pass the POST. You may also hear a series of diagnostic tones or see a series of power-on flashes. If this is the case, your Mac has a fundamental hardware issue.

To troubleshoot hardware issues:

▶ Always check for simple things first. Is the Mac plugged into an electrical outlet? Are the keyboard and mouse working properly?

▶ Run the Apple Hardware Test (AHT) included on the first restore disc packaged with your Mac. Insert the disc in the optical drive, and start up holding down the D key to automatically select the AHT volume.

▶ You can also attempt to reset your Mac's firmware by using a firmware restoration CD as outlined in Apple Knowledge Base document HT2213, "About the firmware restoration CD (Intel-based Macs)."

▶ Ultimately, if this is a serious hardware issue, you will have to take your Mac to an Apple Authorized Service Provider.

System Volume Issues

If your Mac passes the POST but you are left with a flashing dark gray question mark folder icon, it means the firmware cannot locate a valid system volume or booter file. The Mac's main processor and components are probably working correctly, and you may only have a software issue. Hold down the Option key during startup and use the Startup Manager to locate system volumes.

To troubleshoot system volume issues:

▶ If the original system volume appears, select it to start up from. If your Mac starts up from the system on the volume, open the Startup Disk preferences to reset the volume as the startup disk. You can also attempt to define the startup disk when booted from another system volume like Lion Recovery HD, as covered in Chapter 1, "Installation and Configuration."

▶ If the original system volume appears but your Mac still cannot find a valid system or booter, you may need to reinstall Lion on that volume. As always, back up any important data from that volume before you make significant changes.

▶ If your original system volume does not appear, the issue lies with that storage device. Start up from another system, like the Lion Restore HD, and use the storage troubleshooting techniques outlined in Chapter 3, "File Systems."

Troubleshooting the Booter

Issues at the booter stage are indicated by a flashing dark gray prohibitory icon—evidence of a failure to load the kernel.

To troubleshoot the booter:

▶   If you're starting up the Mac from a volume containing a system this Mac has never booted from, the prohibitory icon usually indicates that the version of Lion on the volume is not compatible with your Mac's hardware.

▶   Start up the Mac while holding down the Shift key to initiate a Safe Boot. The booter will first attempt to verify and repair the startup volume, indicated by a dark gray progress bar across the bottom of the main display. If repairs were necessary, the Mac will automatically restart before continuing. If this happens, continue to hold down the Shift key. The booter will verify the startup volume again, and if the volume appears to be working properly, the booter will attempt to load the kernel and essential KEXTs again. The booter uses the most judicial, and slowest, process to load these items and will clear both the KEXT and font caches. If successful, the booter will pass off the system to the kernel, which will continue to safe-boot.

▶   If the booter cannot find or load a valid kernel, you may need to reinstall Lion on that volume.

Troubleshooting the Kernel

Issues at the kernel stage are indicated by an inability to reach the bright blue screen, as evidence of a failure to load all KEXTs, the core BSD UNIX system, and ultimately the system launchd process. If this is the case, your Mac is stuck at the light gray screen with the dark gray spinning gear icon.

To troubleshoot the kernel:

▶   Start up the Mac while holding down the Shift key to initiate a Safe Boot. In addition to the Safe Boot procedures covered in the "Troubleshooting the Booter" section earlier, this will force the kernel to ignore all third-party KEXTs. If successful, the kernel will start the system launchd process, which will continue to safe-boot. Completing the kernel startup stage via a Safe Boot indicates the issue may be a third-party KEXT, and you should start up in Verbose mode to try to identify the problem KEXT.

▶   Start up the Mac while holding down Command-V to initiate Verbose mode. The Mac will show you the startup process details as a continuous string of text. If the text stops, the startup process has probably also stopped, and you should examine the end of the text for troubleshooting clues. When you find a suspicious item, move it to a quarantine folder and then restart the Mac without Safe Boot, to see if the problem was resolved. This may be easier said than done, as accessing the Mac's drive to locate and remove the item may not be possible if the Mac is crashing during startup. This is an example of where target disk mode really shines. As covered in Chapter 3, "File Systems," you can easily modify the contents of a problematic Mac's system volume using target disk mode and a second Mac.

NOTE ▶ If your troublesome Mac successfully starts up in Safe Boot mode and you're trying to find the issue, do not use Safe Boot and Verbose mode at the same time. If the startup process succeeds, Verbose mode will eventually be replaced by the standard startup interface and you will not have time to identify problematic items.

▶ If the kernel cannot completely load while safe-booting or you are unable to locate and repair the problematic items, you may need to reinstall Lion on that volume.

Troubleshooting the System launchd

Issues at this stage are indicated by an inability to reach the login screen or log in a user (evidence of a failure by the system launchd process). If the system launchd process is not able to complete the system initialization, the loginwindow process will not start. Your Mac will be either stuck with a black screen or a white screen, depending on how far the system launchd got.

To troubleshoot system launchd issues:

▶ Start up the Mac while holding down the Shift key to initiate a Safe Boot. In addition to the Safe Boot procedures covered earlier in the "Troubleshooting the Booter" and "Troubleshooting the Kernel" sections of this chapter, this will force the system launchd process to ignore all third-party fonts, launch daemons, and startup items. If successful, the system launchd process will start the loginwindow. At this point the Mac system has fully started up and is now running in Safe Mode. Completing the system initialization process via Safe Boot indicates the issue may be a third-party system initialization item, and you should start up in Verbose mode to try to identify the problematic item.

▶ Start up the Mac while holding down Command-V to initiate Verbose mode. Again, if the text stops, examine the end of the text for troubleshooting clues; if you find a suspicious item, move it to a quarantine folder and then restart the Mac normally.

▶ At this point you might be able to successfully safe-boot into the Finder. If so, use the Finder's interface to quarantine suspicious items.

▶ While working in Safe Mode, you may also consider removing or renaming system cache and preference files, as they can be corrupted and cause startup issues. Begin by removing /Library/Caches because those files contain easily replaced information.

As far as system preferences go, you can remove any setting stored in the /Library/ Preferences or /Library/Preferences/SystemConfiguration folders you're comfortable with having to reconfigure. A much safer solution would be to simply rename individual system preference files in these folders. Once you have moved or replaced these items, restart the Mac, and the system will automatically replace these items with clean versions.

▶   If Safe Boot continues to fail or you have located a suspicious system item that you need to remove, start up the Mac while holding Command-S to initiate single-user mode. You'll see a minimal command-line interface that will allow you to move suspicious files to a quarantine folder. If you want to modify files and folders in single-user mode, you will have to prepare the system volume. Start by entering /sbin/fsck -fy to verify and repair the startup volume. Repeat this command until you see a message stating that the drive appears to be OK. Only then should you enter /sbin/mount -uw / to mount the startup volume as a read and write file system. Use the techniques covered in Appendix B, "Command-Line Essentials," to deal with potentially troublesome files. Once you have made your changes, you can exit single-user mode and continue to start up the system by entering the exit command, or you can shut down the Mac by entering the shutdown -h now command.

   TIP ▶ If you find single-user mode daunting, then you may want to install AppleJack, which is a third-party command-line interface that makes running common troubleshooting commands easy. Find it at http://applejack.sourceforge.net.

▶   If the system initialization process cannot complete while safe-booting or you are unable to locate and repair the problematic items, you may need to reinstall Lion on that volume.

Troubleshooting User Initialization

If the loginwindow process is not able to initialize the user environment, the user will never be given control of the graphical interface. You may see the user's desktop background picture, but no applications will load, including the Dock or the Finder. Or it may appear that the user session starts, but then the login screen will reappear. At this point you should first attempt a Safe Login, which is initiated by holding down the Shift key while you click the Log In button at the login screen. Safe Login is also part of the Safe Boot startup mode.

With Safe Login enabled, the loginwindow process will not automatically open any user-defined login items or applications set to resume. Further, the user's launchd process will not start any user-specific LaunchAgents. Obviously, if a Safe Login resolves your user session issue, you need to adjust this user's Login Items list from the Users & Groups preferences or any items in the /Library/LaunchAgents or ~/Library/LaunchAgents folders.

If a Safe Login doesn't resolve your user session issue, there are other troubleshooting sections in this book you should refer to. Primarily, you should follow the troubleshooting steps outlined in Chapter 2, "User Accounts." Additionally, the loginwindow process relies heavily on directory services, so you may also be well served by the troubleshooting steps outlined in Chapter 7, "Network Services."

Troubleshoot Logout and Shutdown

An inability to log out or shut down is almost always the result of an application or process that refuses to quit. If you're unable to log out, as long as you still maintain control of the graphical interface, you can attempt to forcibly quit stubborn processes using the techniques outlined in Chapter 5, "Applications and Processes." You may find that the loginwindow process has closed your user session but the Mac refuses to shut down. This is indicated by a small spinning gear icon on top of your desktop background or a white screen after all your applications have quit. You should let the system attempt to shut down naturally, but if it takes longer than a few minutes, it means a system process is refusing to quit. You can force your Mac to shut down by holding down the power-on key until the Mac powers off, as indicated by a blank display.

> **NOTE ▶** When you restart the Mac, the firmware does not perform a full POST during the subsequent startup process. Thus, if you're troubleshooting hardware issues, you should always shut down and then start up, never restart.

What You've Learned

▶ The Lion system initialization happens in four stages: firmware, booter, kernel, and system launchd. The Lion user environment happens in three stages: loginwindow, user launchd, and the user environment.

▶ At each stage there are audible or visual cues that help you recognize startup progress.

▶ Your Mac's firmware features a variety of startup modes that help you administer and troubleshoot the system.

▶ The launchd and loginwindow processes are primarily responsible for managing the user environment, including processes such as system initialization, graphical interface user session setup, and login, logout, and shutdown.

▶ Safe Mode, Verbose mode, and single-user mode are the three primary Lion startup diagnostic modes.

References
Check for current Knowledge Base documents at www.apple.com/support.

Firmware
HT1547, "Power On Self-Test Beep Definition—Part 2"

HT2341, "Intel-based Mac Power-On Self-Test RAM error codes"

HT1533, "Startup key combinations for Intel-based Macs"

HT1343, "Mac OS X keyboard shortcuts"

HT1310, "Startup Manager: How to select a startup volume"

HT1237, "EFI and SMC firmware updates for Intel-based Macs"

HT2213, "About the firmware restoration CD (Intel-based Macs)"

General Startup
TS1892, "Mac OS X: 'Broken folder' icon, prohibitory sign, or kernel panic when computer starts"

HT2674, "Intel-based Mac: Startup sequence and error codes, symbols"

HT1564, "What is Safe Boot, Safe Mode?"

HT1757, "Progress bar appears after waking from sleep"

TS1388, "Isolating issues in Mac OS X"

URLs
Official Unified Extensible Firmware Interface (UEFI) resource website: www.uefi.org

rEFIt alternative EFI booter with advanced features website: http://refit.sourceforge.net

Easy-to-use single-user mode software: http://applejack.sourceforge.net

Review Quiz

1. What are the primary system initialization stages and user environment stages in Mac OS X, and in what order do they start?

2. What are the visual and/or audible cues of the stages of system initialization?

3. What does the firmware do? What is the POST?

4. What role does the system launchd process serve during system startup?

5. What items are automatically started by the system launchd during the system initialization process?

6. What role does the loginwindow process serve in system startup?

7. What is the difference between launch daemons, startup items, launch agents, and login items?

8. What happens during user logout?

9. What happens during system shutdown?

10. What is the difference between Safe Boot, Safe Mode, and Safe Login?

11. Which items are not loaded when Mac OS X safe-boots?

12. What keyboard shortcut is used to safe-boot Mac OS X?

13. How do you further resolve an issue that disappears when the Mac successfully safe-boots?

Answers

1. The primary system initialization stages are: firmware, booter, kernel, and system launchd (in that order). The primary user environment stages are loginwindow, user launchd, and user environment.

2. Each stage is indicated by the following: firmware, startup chime or bright flash of the power-on light followed by a light gray screen on the primary display; booter, a dark gray Apple logo on the primary display; kernel, a small dark gray spinning gear or spinning earth icon below the Apple logo; and system launchd, a white screen on all displays followed by the login screen.

3. The firmware initializes the Mac's hardware and locates the booter file on a system volume. The Power-On Self-Test (POST) checks for basic hardware functionality when your Mac powers on.

4. The system launchd process is ultimately responsible for starting every system process. It also manages system initialization and starts the loginwindow process.

5. During system initialization the system launchd process automatically starts /System/ Library/LaunchDaemons, /Library/LaunchDaemons, /Library/StartupItems (via SystemStarter), and the /etc/rc.local UNIX script if it exists.

6. The loginwindow process displays the login screen that allows the user to authenticate, and then sets up and manages the graphical interface user environment.

7. Launch daemons and startup items are opened during system initialization by the system launchd process on behalf of the root user. Launch agents and login items are opened during the initialization of the user environment by the user's specific launchd process.

8. During user logout the user's loginwindow process does the following: requests that all user applications quit; automatically quits any user background processes; runs any logout scripts; records the logout to the main system.log file; resets device permissions and preferences to their defaults; and quits the user's loginwindow and launchd processes.

9. At system shutdown the loginwindow process logs all users out and then tells the kernel to quit all remaining system processes. Once the kernel quits all system processes, the Mac will shut down.

10. Safe Boot refers to when the system is starting up; Safe Mode is when the system is actually running; and Safe Login is when the system starts up the user session.

11. When Mac OS X safe-boots, it will not load third-party KEXTs, third-party launch agents, third-party launch daemons, third-party startup items, third-party fonts, any user login items, or any user-specific launch agents.

12. A Safe Boot is initiated by holding down the Shift key during system startup.

13. If an issue disappears when the Mac successfully safe-boots, then you must find and remove or quarantine the third-party startup resource that caused the issue. The best way to isolate the problematic item is to start up the Mac in Verbose mode and then observe where the startup process fails. Verbose mode is initiated by holding down Command-V during system startup.

General Mac Troubleshooting

Each lesson in this guide features troubleshooting information specific to the technologies covered in that lesson. This appendix serves as a supplementary quick reference to general Mac troubleshooting techniques.

Troubleshooting Workflow

Always remember that the two primary goals of troubleshooting are to fix the issue properly and to fix it quickly. Following a systematic troubleshooting process will let you consistently achieve both of these goals. Even if you or your organization already have a preferred troubleshooting process, you will still find the following workflow useful.

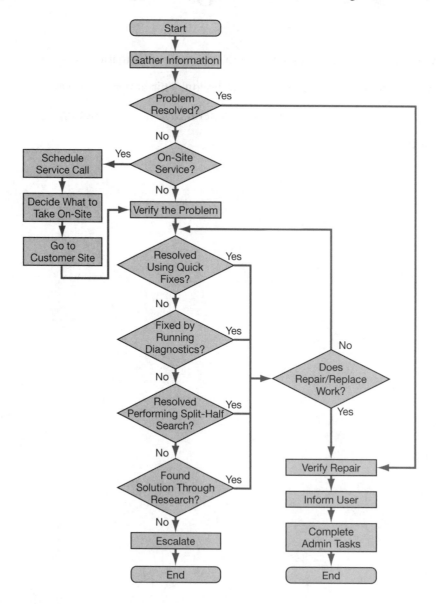

The AppleCare support group uses this workflow to ensure that all customer issues are properly handled. The beginning steps involve gathering information and verifying the problem. The end steps involve verifying the solution and informing the user, or escalating the problem to a higher support level. This appendix focuses on the four primary troubleshooting steps in the diagram: quick fixes, diagnostic tools, binary (or split-half) search, and research resources.

Quick Fixes

The quick fixes applicable to troubleshooting OS X Lion range from innocuous to invasive; it's usually best to try fixes from the innocuous end of the spectrum first.

Innocuous Fixes (Consider These First)

The following general troubleshooting steps have little impact on the computer, and may fix transient issues:

▶ Choose Force Quit from the Apple menu if an application is not responding.

▶ Shut down and then restart the Mac.

▶ Disconnect all external devices.

▶ Run Software Update to check for any uninstalled updates.

When you begin troubleshooting, you might try these innocuous tactics to assess the problem:

▶ Try the same task in another application if available.

▶ If you're experiencing a network issue, double-check physical connectivity, then try connecting to another network service.

▶ Check other Macs to see if they are experiencing the same problem, indicating a possible network issue.

▶ Inspect your Mac using System Information.

▶ Review logs using Console.

▶ Perform a safe boot by holding down the Shift key during startup; then you will be running Lion in Safe mode. After a successful safe boot, restart the Mac normally to see if it works better after the repairs completed by a safe boot.

▶ Start in single-user mode by pressing Command-S during startup.

▶ Start in verbose mode by pressing Command-V during startup.

▶ Start from another known good system such as Lion Recovery. You may need to use an external copy of Lion Recovery if the Mac's internal drive is unreachable.

Less Innocuous Fixes (Consider Next)

The following fixes have a moderate impact on the computer or the user environment. They are also somewhat more time-consuming, so use caution and document your work:

▶ Adjust user-specific settings in System Preferences.

▶ Log in with another user account or with an administrative user account. Remember that it's easy to create a new account for testing and delete it when you are finished.

▶ Delete saved application state files from the ~/Library/Saved Application State/ folder.

▶ Delete cache files from the ~/Library/Caches and /Library/Caches folders.

▶ Move, rename, or delete suspect user preference files in ~/Library/Preferences.

▶ Try a different network interface or port.

▶ Verify network settings using the Network, Sharing, and Security preferences.

▶ Create a new test network location, and then test with that location.

▶ Update peripheral and printer drivers.

▶ Try another known good peripheral.

▶ Check the settings in the Startup Disk preference.

▶ Fix permissions using Disk Utility.

▶ Repair disk volumes with Disk Utility.

▶ Check for firmware updates by visiting Apple's support website.

Invasive Fixes (Consider Last)

The following fixes have a more substantial impact on the system:

▶ Move, rename, or delete suspect system preference files in /Library/Preferences.

▶ Reinstall the suspect application.

▶ Reset parameter random-access memory (PRAM) or nonvolatile RAM (NVRAM) by pressing Command-Option-P-R at startup until you hear the startup chime twice. Note that after resetting NVRAM, you should reselect the boot volume in Startup Disk preferences.

▶ Remove non-Apple internal hardware upgrades from your computer, including memory or expansion cards.

▶ Reinstall Lion over the current installation.

▶ Back up important user data, use Disk Utility to erase the system volume, perform a "new" installation of OS X Lion, reconfigure the system, and restore the user's data.

Diagnostic Tools

The following tools are often used for diagnostics in Lion:

▶ Activity Monitor

▶ System Information

▶ Console

▶ Network Diagnostics, accessed from the Network preferences

▶ Network Utility

▶ Directory Utility

▶ Disk Utility

▶ Apple Hardware Test. For older Mac models this is accessed by inserting the restore disc that came with your Mac, and then restarting while holding down the D key. Newer Mac models don't require the restore disc as they include the diagnostics in hardware ROM.

▶ A variety of diagnostic tools are available to Apple Authorized Service Providers. For certain hardware-related issues, taking your Mac to a service provider may be your only option.

Binary Search

When you cannot quickly isolate the cause of a problem, a technique known as a binary or split-half search can be helpful. Binary searches can take a bit of time, so you should exhaust any quick-fix techniques before proceeding. The aim of a binary search is to isolate an issue by systematically eliminating variables that could be its cause. You must temporarily remove half the variables, and then try to re-create the problem. When you discover which half contains the problem-causing item, you again halve the set of variables with the issue. Repeat to get successively smaller sets of variables. With each subsequent split you come closer to the source, ultimately narrowing down to the problematic item.

The following are common binary search techniques:

▶ Start using Safe Boot by pressing Shift during startup.

▶ Start in single-user mode by pressing Command-S during startup.

▶ Systematically remove potential problem files such as third-party system items, cache files, or preference files.

▶ Disconnect peripherals.

▶ Use Network Utility to evaluate connectivity to other devices and computers on a network.

Research Resources

The best problem-solving experts don't necessarily know every answer; instead, they know where to *find every answer.*

Common resources to consult for troubleshooting Lion issues are:

▶ User documentation

▶ Read Me files

▶ The Mac Help menu

- ▶ Command man pages viewable using the Terminal
- ▶ Log files viewable using Console
- ▶ The Apple support website: www.apple.com/support
- ▶ Internet support communities
- ▶ Results gathered from a well-queried Google search (specific error messages in quotation marks are often good search terms)
- ▶ Apple's Service Source, which is available to Apple Authorized Service Providers

Appendix **B**
Command-Line Essentials

The analogy goes like this: You can spend your entire life driving cars without having any idea how to fix them, but if you plan on being a mechanic, then you need to know how things work under the hood. The same is true of OS X Lion: You can spend years using Macs without having any idea how to fix them, but if you plan to administer and troubleshoot issues, you need to know how things work "under the hood." In the case of Lion, because UNIX is what provides the foundational technologies, "under the hood" means working with the command-line interface.

First, there are a great many indispensable management and troubleshooting tools that are available only at the command line. And once you become comfortable with the command line, you'll find many tasks are actually much more quickly done there than in the graphical interface. In this appendix you will be introduced to the Mac command-line environment. You will learn the basics of using commands and command-line navigation, along with other general-use commands.

Command-Line Basics

Aside from impressing all your geek friends, there are several legitimate advantages to using the command line:

▶ Additional options—Many additional administrative and troubleshooting options are available from the command line that are not available from the graphical interface. For example, the following applications have command-line equivalents with more options (commands in parenthesis): System Information (system_profiler), Installer (installer), Software Update (softwareupdate), Disk Utility (diskutil), and Spotlight (mdfind). These are just a few instances, as nearly every administrative function has both a graphical and a command-line tool.

▶ Finder limitations—From the command line you have unfettered access to the file system, unlike with the Finder, which intentionally limits a user's ability to access the full file system. For example, the Finder hides many files and folders that are easily visible at the command line. Also, there are many file system permissions settings that the Finder is incapable of displaying properly. File system permissions are detailed in Chapter 3, "File Systems."

▶ Remote access—You can remotely log in to a Mac's command-line environment using the secure shell (SSH) protocol. This allows administrators to make changes at the command line without alerting the user to their work. Using SSH remote login is detailed in Chapter 7, "Network Services."

▶ System user (root) access for administrators—By using the sudo command, any administrator can masquerade as the system user, also known as root. This allows for great administrative flexibility at the command line, as covered later in this appendix.

▶ Easily scriptable—If you understand how to interactively work at the command line, then you can apply the same syntax to a command-line script. This allows you to easily automate repetitive tasks.

▶ Administer multiple Macs simultaneously—If you combine command-line instructions with Apple Remote Desktop (ARD), you can remotely administer multiple, even thousands, of Macs simultaneously. Essentially the ARD application allows you to remotely send the same command to any number of Mac computers with the click of a button. Obviously, this can save a tremendous amount of time for anyone who has to administer multiple Macs.

MORE INFO ▶ The ARD application is not included with Lion, but your Mac does include the client-side half of ARD with the Remote Management service. You can find out more about ARD in Chapter 7, "Network Services," or at www.apple.com/ remotedesktop.

Accessing the Command Line

You may hear the term "shell" kicked around when the command line is discussed. A shell is the first command that runs automatically when you access the command line, and it provides you with the actual interactive command-line interface. Many types of shells are available, but Lion will start the bash shell by default.

Although most people access the Lion command line using the Terminal application, there are multiple methods for accessing it:

▶ Terminal application—The main application on Lion for accessing the command line is /Applications/Utilities/Terminal. The Mac's Terminal application is quite sophisticated and has gained many convenient features over the years, including highly customizable interface settings, a tabbed interface for quickly handling multiple command-line sessions, multiple split panes for easily viewing your history, and, in Lion, support for full-screen mode.

▶ Enter >console at the login screen—This method bypasses the graphical interface entirely and takes over the whole screen with a simple black background and white text. You will still have to log in with a user account, but this is a convenient method for testing login issues as the standard login screen doesn't provide much in the way of error reporting. When you want to log out of this mode, simply use the exit command to return to the standard login screen.

NOTE ▸ Only if you can manually enter a user name at the login screen will you be able to use console mode. You can make the login screen default to the "show name and password" mode from the login options of Users & Groups preferences. Alternately, you can change the login screen to this mode by pressing the Command-Option-Arrow-Enter keyboard shortcut.

▸ Startup in single-user mode—This is a troubleshooting mode enabled by holding the Command-S keyboard shortcut at system startup. This mode starts the minimum system required to provide you with a command-line prompt so you can enter commands in an attempt to repair a system that cannot fully start up. Using single-user mode is detailed in Chapter 9, "System Startup."

▸ SSH remote login—This allows you to securely log in from a remote computer to access your Mac's command line. SSH is a common standard, so any operating system that supports SSH can remotely log into your Mac. Using SSH remote login is detailed in Chapter 7, "Network Services."

Working at the Command Line

When opening the Terminal for the first time, many approach the command line with unnecessary caution. Even though the command line offers nearly limitless capability, getting started with the basics is not that complicated.

Command-Line Prompt

The first thing you'll see at the command line is the *prompt*. The prompt is presented to you by the computer to let you know that it's ready for your command. By default, the prompt will always show you the name of the computer you're using, followed by where you are in the computer's file system, followed by your current user account name, and ending with a $. The use of $ at the end of the prompt is an indication that you are using the standard bash shell. Where you are in the computer's file system is referred to as the *working directory,* and it will change as you navigate through the file system.

> **NOTE** ▶ While Mac systems have traditionally called file system containers "folders," the command line's UNIX heritage prefers to use the word "directory." In the context of this appendix, these two words are synonymous.

At the prompt you enter your command string, often more than one word, and then press the Return key to initiate or execute the command you entered. Depending on the command entry you chose, it will either take over the Terminal window with a text interface, show the results of the command and then return to the prompt, or simply perform some work and then return to the prompt when the command is complete. Many commands display results only if there was a problem; it's worth reading what the command returns to make sure it doesn't indicate that something went wrong.

> **NOTE** ▶ Some commands can take a while to execute and may not give any sort of progress indication. Generally, if you don't see a new prompt, you should assume your last command is still running.

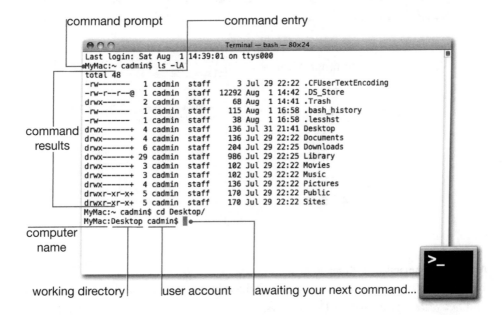

Command String

As for the command string, it is generally composed of only a few parts:

▶ Command name—Commands are just like applications, but they are more focused; many commands provide very specific functionality. Some commands just need you to enter their name to execute.

▶ Command options (sometimes called "flags")—After the command, you may specify some options that will change the command's default behavior. These items are not required and can be different for every command. Options start with one or two dashes to distinguish them from arguments. Many commands allow several single-letter options to be combined after a single dash. For example, ls -lA is the same as ls -l -A.

▶ Arguments (sometimes called "parameters")—After the command and its options, you will typically specify the argument, which is the item that you want the command to modify. Again, this is only necessary if the command requires an item to act upon.

▶ Extras—Extras are not necessary, but they can greatly enhance the capabilities of your command. For example, you could add items that redirect the command output, include other commands, or generate a document.

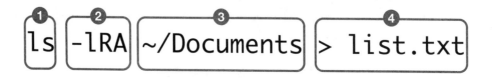

1—**Command Name**	In this example the "ls" command displays a list of a folder's contents
2—**Command Options**	Options add conditions, limits, or other modifiers to the command
3—**Arguments**	This is the recipient of the action, often specified as a file or folder path
4—**Extras**	Redirected output, or other commands, as needed... In this example a text file is created from the list output

A Simple Command-Line Example

Here is an example in which the user Michelle is working on a computer called MyMac and her working directory is Documents. She is deleting an application called Junk inside the /Applications folder. It is assumed that Michelle will press the Return or Enter key once she has entered her command.

```
MyMac:Documents michelle$ rm -R /Applications/Junk.app
MyMac:Documents michelle$
```

In this case the command was entered and executed properly, and the computer simply returns to a new prompt. This is an example of a command that only returns information if the command didn't execute properly. The computer will usually let you know if you entered something improperly by returning some sort of error message or help text. Nevertheless, the computer will not prevent you from doing something stupid at the command line, such as accidentally deleting your home folder. If you remember only one rule about using the command line, it should be this one: Always double-check your typing.

Learning About Commands

There are literally thousands of commands, each with dozens of options or requirements for proper usage. In fact, most users are overwhelmed by the command line simply because they think they have to memorize commands in order to use them. In reality, all you need to know is one command: man.

Most commands have manuals that tell you everything you need to know about them. Simply enter man followed by the name of the command you are curious about, and you will be shown its manual page. Manual pages include command usage and, at the bottom of the page, often include references to other related commands. Once inside the manual page viewer (which automatically redirects to the less command), you can use a few navigation shortcuts to quickly move through the manual:

▶ Use the Up Arrow and Down Arrow keys to scroll through the manual.

▶ Use the Space bar to move down one screen at a time.

▶ Search through the manual page by entering / and then a keyword.

▶ Exit the manual page by simply pressing the Q key.

What if you don't even know the name of the command you're looking for? Simply enter man -k and then a keyword to search the command manual database. For example, entering man -k owner will return a short list of the commands used for changing file and folder ownership, including the command chown. Using the chown command to change file and folder ownership is covered in Chapter 3, "File Systems."

> **NOTE ▶** In addition to commands, the manual database also includes scripting and programming functions and file format documentation; hence, a man -k *search* may give results besides the relevant commands.

Command-Line Navigation

If knowing how to use commands is the first part of conquering the command line, the second part is learning how to navigate the file system effectively at the command line. Once you master navigation at the command line, you'll find that it can be much faster than navigation using the Finder.

> **NOTE ▶** The command line is case-sensitive and requires that you use full filenames with filename extensions. In other words, the command line will not be able to locate the "itunes" application, but it will easily locate the "iTunes.app" application.

Understanding Navigation Concepts

First, a few common navigation terms must be clearly defined. While Mac systems have traditionally called file system containers "folders," the command line's UNIX heritage prefers to use the word "directory." Though the terms can be used interchangeably, this book will continue to favor the word "folder" to describe file system containers, as the word "directory" is often used for other nonfolder items. For example, network databases used to store user information are often referred to as "directory databases." Furthermore, the process in Lion for accessing these user databases is called opendirectoryd.

A new term you'll see in this appendix is *path*. A path represents a file or folder's location in the file system, described by the path taken to reach it. You have already seen paths in this book used to describe the specific location of an application or utility. For instance, the Disk Utility application's file system path is /Applications/Utilities/Disk Utility.app. The command line uses pathnames exclusively for navigating and locating items in the file system.

There are two types of file system pathnames: absolute paths and relative paths. Either type is valid for navigating or locating items at the command line, but they differ in where they start:

▶   Absolute paths—These are full descriptions of an item's location starting from the root, or beginning, of the system (startup) volume. Thus, an absolute path will always begin with a forward slash to indicate the beginning of the file system. This book uses absolute paths to describe the location of items. An example of the absolute path to the user Michelle's Drop Box folder would be /Users/michelle/Public/Drop Box. A plain English translation of this path would be: "Starting from the startup volume, go into the Users folder, then into the michelle subfolder, then the Public subfolder, and select the item named Drop Box."

▶ Relative paths—Relative paths are partial descriptions of an item's location based on where you're currently working in the file system from the command line. When you first open the Terminal application, your command-line session starts out working from your home folder. Therefore, the relative path from your home folder to your Drop Box would be Public/Drop Box. A plain English translation of this would be: "From where you are now, go into the Public subfolder, and then select the item named Drop Box."

Using Navigation Commands

You will use three basic commands for navigating the file system at the command line: pwd, ls, and cd.

pwd

Short for "print working directory," this command will report the absolute path of your current working location in the file system:

```
MyMac:~ michelle$ pwd
/Users/michelle
```

ls

Short for "list," ls will list the folder contents of your current working location. Entering a pathname following the ls command will list the contents of the specified item. The ls command has many additional options for listing file and folder information that will be covered throughout this book.

```
MyMac:~ michelle$ ls
Desktop Library Pictures
Documents Movies Public
Downloads Music Sites
MyMac:~ michelle$ ls Public
Drop Box
```

cd

Short for "change directory," cd is the command you will use to navigate at the command line. Entering a pathname following the cd command will change your current working location to the specified folder. Entering cd without specifying a path will always return you to your home folder. In the following example, Michelle will use the cd command to navigate to her Drop Box folder, and then she will navigate back to her home folder:

```
MyMac:~ michelle$ cd Public/Drop\ Box/
MyMac:Drop Box michelle$ pwd
/Users/michelle/Public/Drop Box
MyMac:Drop Box michelle$ cd
MyMac:~ michelle$ pwd
/Users/michelle
```

Using Special Characters

At this point you may have noticed that the command line uses special characters in the command prompt and pathnames. Many of these special characters are used as shortcuts to save time. On the other hand, one special character isn't a time-saver; it's an unfortunate necessity. The backslash character "\" is used before a space in a path or filename. This practice is necessary because the command line often uses the spaces between items to parse the command entry into separate logical pieces. A space in a filename without the backslash may confuse the command line, and your command will not execute properly.

There are other methods for entering filenames and paths with spaces. One alternative is to surround filenames and paths with quotation marks:

```
MyMac:~ michelle$ cd "Public/Drop Box"
MyMac:Drop Box michelle$ pwd
/Users/michelle/Public/Drop Box
```

Another solution involves dragging and dropping items from the Finder to the Terminal window. The Terminal automatically enters the item's absolute path with the appropriate backslash characters before spaces in names. The most efficient solution, though, is to use the tab complete feature built into Lion's command line to automatically complete filenames and pathnames for you. Saving time by using tab completion is covered next in this section of the appendix, so be sure to check it out.

> **NOTE ▶** The space is not the only character that needs to be treated specially at the command line. Others include !, $, &, *, ;, |, and \, as well as parentheses and all types of quotes and brackets. Both Finder's drag-and-drop capability and tab completion deal with these characters appropriately.

When navigating the file system, you can also save time by using the double period ".." shortcut to indicate the parent folder. In other words, if you were working in your home folder located at /Users/username, entering cd .. would tell the command line that you want to navigate to the /Users folder. In the following example, Michelle navigates to her Drop Box folder, backs up to her Public folder, and then finally backs up twice to the /Users folder:

```
MyMac:~ michelle$ cd Public/Drop\ Box/
MyMac:Drop Box michelle$ pwd
/Users/michelle/Public/Drop Box
MyMac:Drop Box michelle$ cd ..
MyMac:Public michelle$ pwd
/Users/michelle/Public
MyMac:Public michelle$ cd ../..
MyMac:Users michelle$ pwd
/Users
```

Finally, there is the tilde (~). This little guy is used as shorthand to describe the current user's home folder in a pathname. Once again using the example from earlier, the current user's Drop Box is located at ~/Public/Drop Box. This also helps to explain the tilde you see in the default command prompt. For example, if Michelle opened the Terminal on a computer called MyMac, the following would be the command prompt:

```
MyMac:~ michelle$
```

> **TIP** ▶ You can also use the tilde to specify another user's home folder. For example, ~logan/Public would specify Logan's Public folder.

If Michelle navigated to her Drop Box, the command prompt would change. Note that the prompt only shows the current working location and not an absolute or even relative path:

```
MyMac:Drop Box michelle$
```

Using Tab Completion

Tab completion is the command line's absolute top time-saving feature. Not only does using tab completion save time by automatically finishing filenames, pathnames, and command names for you, it also prevents you from making typographical errors and verifies that the item you're entering exists.

Using tab completion couldn't be simpler. Start from your home folder by entering cd, then P, and then press the Tab key. The Terminal window will flash quickly and you may hear an audible error sound, letting you know there is more than one choice for items that begin with "P" in your home folder. Press the Tab key again, and the computer will display your two choices, Pictures and Public. Now, enter a u after the initial P, then press the Tab key again and the computer will automatically finish Public/ for you. Finally, enter a D and press the Tab key one last time, and the computer will finish the path with Public/Drop\ Box/.

> **NOTE ▶** When tab completion fills in a folder name, it automatically puts a forward slash (/) at the end (assuming you want to continue the path from there). Most commands will ignore this trailing slash, but a few will behave differently if it's there. When in doubt, it's usually safest to delete a leftover / at the end of a path.

Even in this small example, tab completion turned a pathname that would take 17 keystrokes (Public/Drop\ Box/) into just 5 (Pu<tab>D<tab>). Further, tab completion helped you avoid mistakes by essentially spell-checking your typing and verifying that the item is where you expected it to be. Making tab completion a habit when using the command line can easily shave hours off the time you have to spend there. Thus, if you remember only two rules about using the command line, it should be these two: Always double-check your typing, and always use tab completion to help make sure you spell correctly and to save time.

> **NOTE ▶** Tab completion cannot read into folders you don't have permissions to. Thus, you may run into issues trying to use tab completion for items that are only readable by the root user. This is often the case when you're trying to use the sudo command.

Viewing Invisible Items

To simplify navigation in the file system, both the command line and the Finder hide many files and folders from your view. Often these are system support items that are hidden for good reason. While there is no easy way to make the Finder reveal hidden items, it is quite simple to view hidden items at the command line. The first reason for this is that many items hidden by the Finder are set this way via the hidden file flag. The command line ignores the hidden file flag, so it will show these items regardless. However, the ls command will hide items that have a filename beginning with a period, but even these items can be easily revealed.

To view hidden items at the command line, simply add the -a option to the -l option when using the ls command:

```
MyMac:~ michelle$ ls -la
total 32
drwxr-xr-x  15 michelle  staff  510 Aug 20 17:33 .
drwxr-xr-x   8 root      admin  272 Aug 20 17:05 ..
```

```
-rw-------   1 michelle  staff     3 Aug 20 01:08 CFUserTextEncoding
-rw-------   1 michelle  staff  2666 Aug 20 16:42 .bash_history
-rw-------   1 michelle  staff    48 Aug 20 17:19 .lesshst
-rw-------   1 root      staff   632 Aug 20 14:25 .viminfo
drwx------+  5 michelle  staff   170 Aug 20 15:49 Desktop
drwx------+  3 michelle  staff   102 Aug 20 01:08 Documents
drwx------+  3 michelle  staff   102 Aug 20 01:08 Downloads
drwx------  19 michelle  staff   646 Aug 20 01:08 Library
drwx------+  3 michelle  staff   102 Aug 20 01:08 Movies
drwx------+  3 michelle  staff   102 Aug 20 01:08 Music
drwx------+  4 michelle  staff   136 Aug 20 01:08 Pictures
drwxr-xr-x+  7 michelle  staff   238 Aug 20 15:29 Public
drwxr-xr-x   5 michelle  staff   170 Aug 20 01:08 Sites
```

NOTE ▸ While ls -a shows all items in the folder, including ".." (a shortcut to the parent folder) and "." (a shortcut to the current folder), another option, ls -A, shows all invisible items except for these two folder shortcuts.

As you can see from Michelle's home folder, any item that has a period at the beginning of its name will be hidden by default in both the command line and the Finder. These items are created and used by the operating system, so they should be left alone.

MORE INFO ▸ Managing hidden items is detailed in Chapter 4, "Data Management."

Navigating to Other Volumes

At the command line, the system volume is also known as the root volume, and it's identified by the lone forward slash. It may come as a surprise to you, however, that at the command line other nonroot volumes appear as part of the main file system in a folder called Volumes. In the following example, Michelle will start in her home folder, navigate to and list the items in the /Volumes folder, and then finally navigate into a volume named "Backup Drive" that is connected to this Mac via FireWire:

```
MyMac:~ michelle$ pwd
/Users/michelle
MyMac:~ michelle$ cd /Volumes/
MyMac:Volumes michelle$ pwd
/Volumes
MyMac:Volumes michelle$ ls
Backup Drive        Macintosh HD
```

MyMac:Volumes michelle$ cd Backup\ Drive/
MyMac:Backup Drive michelle$ pwd
/Volumes/Backup Drive

Command-Line File Manipulation

Basic file management is also a much richer experience from the command line than it is from the Finder. Consequently, basic file management from the command line can lead to increased opportunities for user error. Once again, always make sure to thoroughly check your typing before you execute a command.

File Examination Commands

There are a variety of basic commands for locating and examining files and folders from the command line, including cat, less, which, file, and find. As always, you can get more detailed information about each one of these commands by reading their manual entries.

cat

Short for "concatenate," this command will read a file sequentially to the standard output, often the Terminal window. The syntax is cat followed by the path to the item you wish to view. The cat command can also be used to append to text files using the >> redirect operator. In the following example, Michelle uses the cat command to view the content of two text files in her Desktop folder, TextDocOne.txt and TextDocTwo.txt. Then she uses the cat command with the >> redirect operator to append the second text file to the end of the first text file.

MyMac:~ michelle$ cat Desktop/TextDocOne.txt
This is the contents of the first plain text document.
MyMac:~ michelle$ cat Desktop/TextDocTwo.txt
This is the contents of the second plain text document.
MyMac:~ michelle$ cat Desktop/TextDocTwo.txt >> Desktop/TextDocOne.txt
MyMac:~ michelle$ cat Desktop/TextDocOne.txt
This is the contents of the first plain text document.
This is the contents of the second plain text document.

less

A play on words from the previously popular text-viewing command more, the less command is much better for viewing long text files, as it will let you interactively browse and search through the text. The syntax is less followed by the path to the item you wish to view. The less viewer command is actually the same interface used to view manual pages, so the navigation shortcuts are identical to what you find when you use the man command:

▶ Use the Up and Down Arrow keys to scroll through the text.

▶ Use the Space bar to move down one screen at a time.

▶ Search through the text by entering /, then a keyword.

▶ Type the "v" key to automatically redirect the text file to the vi text editor. Using vi is covered later in this appendix.

▶ Exit the less viewer command by simply pressing the Q key.

> **NOTE** ▶ In Lion, attempting to run the more command will actually run the less command instead, but with slightly different options. For example, the more command will automatically quit when it gets to the end of a document, while the less command requires you to explicitly quit.

which

This command will locate the file path of a specified command. In other words, it will show you which file you're actually using when you enter a specific command. The syntax is which followed by the command or commands you wish to locate. In the following example, Michelle uses the which command to locate the file path of the man, ls, pwd, and cd commands:

```
MyMac:~ michelle$ which man ls pwd cd
/usr/bin/man
/bin/ls
/bin/pwd
/usr/bin/cd
```

Using this command, you'll notice that most commands are found in one of four folders; "/usr/bin" for most commands, "/usr/sbin" for system-oriented commands, "/bin" for critical commands the system needs during the startup process, and "/sbin" for critical system-oriented commands.

file

This command will attempt to determine a file's type based on its content. It is useful for identifying files that do not have a filename extension. The syntax is file followed by the path to the file you're attempting to identify. In the following example, Michelle uses the file command to locate the file type of two documents in her Desktop folder, PictureDocument and TextDocument:

MyMac:~ michelle$ ls Desktop/

PictureDocument TextDocument

MyMac:~ michelle$ file Desktop/PictureDocument

Desktop/PictureDocument: TIFF image data, big-endian

MyMac:~ michelle$ file Desktop/TextDocument

Desktop/TextDocument: ASCII English text

find

This command is used to locate items in the file system based on search criteria. The find command does not use the Spotlight search service, but it does allow you to set very specific search criteria and use filename wildcards. (Filename wildcards are covered in the next section.) The syntax is find followed by the beginning path of the search, then an option defining your search criteria, and then the search criteria within quotation marks. In the following example, Michelle uses the find command to locate any picture files in her home folder by searching only for files with names ending in *.tiff*:

MyMac:~ michelle$ find /Users/michelle -name "*.tiff"

/Users/michelle/Desktop/PictureDocument.tiff

/Users/michelle/Pictures/FamilyPict.tiff

/Users/michelle/Pictures/MyPhoto.tiff

TIP ▶ When using the find command to start a search at the root of the system drive, you should also use the -x option to avoid searching through the /Volumes folder.

TIP ▶ To use the Spotlight search service from the command line, use the mdfind command. The syntax is simply mdfind followed by your search criteria.

Using Wildcard Characters

One of the most powerful features of the command line is the ability to use wildcard characters, also known as "globs," to define path name and search criteria. Here are three of the most commonly used ones:

▶   Asterisk (*)—The asterisk wildcard is used to match any string of characters. For instance, entering * matches all files, while entering *.tiff matches all files ending in *.tiff*.

▶ Question mark (?)—The question-mark wildcard is used to match any single character. For example, entering b?ok matches *book* but not *brook*.

▶ Square brackets ([ ])—Square brackets are used to define a range of characters to
match in that specific space. For example, [Dd]ocument would locate any item named
"Document" or "document," and doc[1-9] matches any file named "doc#" where # is
any number between 1 and 9.

Combining filename wildcards can be used to great effect. Consider a collection of five
files with the names "ReadMe.rtf", "ReadMe.txt", "read.rtf", "read.txt", and "It's All About
Me.rtf". Using wildcards to specify these files:

▶ *.rtf matches ReadMe.rtf, read.rtf, and It's All About Me.rtf

▶ ????.* matches read.rtf and read.txt

▶ [Rr]*.rtf matches ReadMe.rtf and read.rtf

▶ [A-Z].* matches ReadMe.rtf, ReadMe.txt, and It's All About Me.rtf

Using Recursive Commands

When you direct a command to execute some task on an item at the command line, it will
touch only the specified item. If the specified item is a folder, the command line will not
automatically navigate inside the folder to execute the command on the enclosed items. If
you require that a command be executed on a folder and its contents, you have to tell the
command to run recursively. "Recursive" is a fancy way of saying, "Execute the task on
every item inside every folder starting from the path I specify." Most commands accept -r
or -R as the option to indicate that you want the command to run recursively.

In the following example, Michelle will list the contents of her Public folder normally, and
then recursively using the -R option. Notice that when she lists the contents of the Public
folder recursively, the system also lists the contents of the Drop Box and Drop Folder:

```
MyMac:~ michelle$ ls Public
Drop Box PublicFile1 PublicFile2 PublicFile3
MyMac:~ michelle$ ls -R Public
Drop Box PublicFile1 PublicFile2 PublicFile3

Public/Drop Box:
Drop Folder DroppedFile1 DroppedFile2

Public/Drop Box/Drop Folder:
DropFolderFile1 DropFolderFile2
```

Modifying Files and Folders

A variety of basic commands let you modify files and folders from the command line, including mkdir, cp, mv, rm, rmdir, and vi.

mkdir

Short for "make directory," this command is used to create new folders. The syntax is mkdir followed by the paths of the new folders you want to create. An often-used option is -p, which will tell mkdir to create intermediate folders that don't already exist in the paths you specify. In the following example, Michelle uses the mkdir command with the -p option to create a folder called Private with two folders inside it called Stocks and Bonds:

```
MyMac:~ michelle$ ls
Desktop Downloads Movies Pictures Sites
Documents Library Music Public
MyMac:~ michelle$ mkdir -p Private/Stocks Private/Bonds
MyMac:~ michelle$ ls
Desktop Downloads Movies Pictures Public
Documents Library Music Private Sites
MyMac:~ michelle$ cd Private/
MyMac:Private michelle$ ls
Bonds Stocks
```

TIP ▶ You can use the mkdir command to quickly create temporary folders for command-line testing. You can also use the touch command followed by a filename to quickly create temporary files for command-line testing. While the original purpose of the touch command was to update the modification date of the specified item, it will also create an empty file if it doesn't already exist.

cp

Short for "copy," this command will copy items from one location to another. The syntax is cp followed by the path to the original item, ending with the destination path for the copy. In the following example, Michelle uses the cp command to create a copy of testfile located at the root of her home folder and place the copy, testfile2, in her Desktop folder.

NOTE ▶ Remember, if you want to copy a folder and its entire contents, you must tell the cp command to run recursively by adding the -R option.

```
MyMac:~ michelle$ ls
Desktop Library Pictures testfile
Documents Movies Public
Downloads Music Sites
MyMac:~ michelle$ cp testfile Desktop/testfile2
MyMac:~ michelle$ ls Desktop/
testfile2
```

When working with the cd command, specifying a destination folder but no filename will make a copy with the same name as the original. Specifying a destination filename but not a destination folder will make a copy in your current working folder. Further, unlike copying with the Finder, the cp command will not warn you if your copy will replace an existing file. It will simply delete the existing file and replace it with the copy you told it to create. This behavior is true of most commands.

> **TIP** You can use the secure copy command scp to copy files between networked Macs via SSH remote login. Enabling SSH remote login is covered in Chapter 7, "Network Services."

mv

Short for "move," this command will move items from one location to another. The syntax is mv followed by the path to the original item, ending with the new destination path for the item. In the following example, Michelle uses the mv command to move testfile2 from her Desktop folder to the root of her home folder:

```
MyMac:~ michelle$ ls Desktop/
testfile2
MyMac:~ michelle$ ls
Desktop Library Pictures testfile
Documents Movies Public
Downloads Music Sites
MyMac:~ michelle$ mv Desktop/testfile2 testfile2
MyMac:~ michelle$ ls
Desktop Library Pictures testfile
Documents Movies Public testfile2
Downloads Music Sites
```

The mv command uses the same destination rules as the cp command. Since the destination filename was specified without a folder, it moves it into the current working folder. The mv command also happens to be the rename command. After all, moving an item into the same folder with a different name is the same as renaming it. In the following example, Michelle, working in her home folder, uses the mv command to rename testfile to testfile1:

```
MyMac:~ michelle$ ls
Desktop Library Pictures testfile
Documents Movies Public testfile2
Downloads Music Sites
MyMac:~ michelle$ mv testfile testfile1
MyMac:~ michelle$ ls
Desktop Library Pictures testfile1
Documents Movies Public testfile2
Downloads Music Sites
```

rm

Short for "remove," this command will permanently delete items. There is no Trash folder at the command line. The rm command removes items forever. The syntax is rm followed by the paths of the items you wish to delete. In the following example, Michelle uses the rm command to delete testfile1 and testfile2.

NOTE ▶ Remember, if you want to delete a folder and its entire contents, you must tell the rm command to run recursively by adding the -R option.

```
MyMac:~ michelle$ ls
Desktop Library Pictures testfile1
Documents Movies Public testfile2
Downloads Music Sites
MyMac:~ michelle$ rm testfile1 testfile2
MyMac:~ michelle$ ls
Desktop Downloads Movies Pictures Sites
Documents Library Music Public
```

TIP Items deleted with the rm command are recoverable to a degree using drive recovery tools. Thus, to securely erase an item, you can use the srm command. Secure erasure is further detailed in Chapter 3, "File Systems."

rmdir and rm -R

Short for "remove directory," this command will permanently delete folders. Again, there is no Trash folder in the CLI. The rmdir command removes folders forever. The syntax is rmdir followed by the paths of the folders you want to delete. The rmdir command cannot remove folders with any items in them, so in many ways the rmdir command is superfluous, as you can easily remove folders and their contents by using the rm command with the recursive option.

In the following example, Michelle tries to use the rmdir command to delete the Private folder but is unable to because it contains items. She then attempts to use the rm command, but again she is unable to because the folder contains items. Finally, she uses the rm command with the recursive option, -R, to remove the Private folder and all its contents.

```
MyMac:~ michelle$ rmdir Private/
rmdir: Private/: Directory not empty
MyMac:~ michelle$ rm Private/
rm: Private/: is a directory
MyMac:~ michelle$ rm -R Private/
MyMac:~ michelle$ ls
Desktop Downloads Movies Pictures Sites
Documents Library Music Public
```

vi

For many this command, short for "visual," has the most ironic of names, as it's probably the least visually engaging text editor they have ever come across. However, vi is the most common text editor you'll find at the command line. To open a text document for editing with this command, simply enter vi followed by the path or name of a text file.

> **TIP** ▶ Lion automatically redirects vi to the newer improved version, vim. However, for basic functionality you probably won't notice the difference.

> **TIP** ▶ Lion includes nano, a more modern, and by many accounts easier to use, text editor. For example, it features a cheat sheet of commonly used commands at the bottom of the screen. However, vi is the default editor in some situations, as when editing some system files, so it behooves you to learn at least basic vi techniques.

Much like the less command, vi takes over the entire Terminal window with the contents of the text file. When vi first opens, it's in command mode and is expecting you to type predefined characters that tell vi which operation you want to complete next. You can also browse through the file in command mode by using the arrow keys. When starting out with vi, simply enter the letter a to begin editing the text.

In this mode, vi will insert new text into the document wherever the cursor is. You can move the cursor using the arrow keys. When you are done with your edits, you then need to save the changes. This requires you to get back to vi command mode first. You can re-enter vi command mode at any time by pressing the Esc (Escape) key. Once in command mode, you can simultaneously save changes and quit vi by entering ZZ.

In summary, you really only need to know three keyboard commands to get by in the vi text editor; a to begin inserting text, Esc to re-enter command mode, and ZZ to save your changes and quit (think "a to z"). There is one more vi command you should learn in case you make serious mistakes while editing text. In command mode, you can quit vi without saving any changes by entering :quit! (think "quit now!").

Command-Line Administration

Perhaps the most powerful feature in the command line is the ability to quickly invoke the access of another user account or even the system root user account. In this section you will look at a few commands that are very useful to administrators, as they allow you to access items normally restricted by file system permissions.

> **MORE INFO** ▶ A full discussion of file system permissions is available in Chapter 3, "File Systems."

Using su

The su command, short for "substitute user identity," will allow you to easily switch to another user account at the command line. Simply enter su followed by the short name of the user you want to switch to, and then enter the account password (the command line will not show the password in the Terminal). The command prompt will change, indicating that you have the access privileges of a different user. You can easily verify your currently logged-on identity by entering who -m at the command line. You will remain logged on as the substitute user until you quit the Terminal or enter the exit command. In the following example, Michelle will use the su command to change her shell to Kevin's account, and then she will exit back to her account:

```
MyMac:~ michelle$ who -m
michelle ttys001 Aug 20 14:06
MyMac:~ michelle$ su kevin
```

```
Password:
bash-3.2$ who -m
kevin ttys001 Aug 20 14:06
bash-3.2$ exit
exit
MyMac:~ michelle$ who -m
michelle ttys001 Aug 20 14:06
```

Using sudo

An even more powerful command is sudo, which is short for "substitute user do," or more appropriately, "super user do." Preceding a command with sudo instructs the computer to execute the command that follows using root account access. The only requirements to use sudo in Lion are that it's initiated and authenticated from an administrative account (again, the command line will not show the password in the Terminal).

In other words, by default in Lion, any administrative user can use sudo to evoke root access at the command line. Further, sudo works even if the root user account is disabled in the graphical interface. This access is one of the primary reasons that, in many environments, granting administrative access to every user is insecure. You can, however, adjust the sudo command's configuration file to further restrict its usage, as described later in this section.

> **TIP** The sudo command can also be used to execute a command as a specific nonroot user. Before a command, simply enter sudo -u username, where username is the short name of the user you wish to execute the command as.

In the following example, Michelle is not normally allowed to read the text file named Secrets, using the standard command-line text reader command cat. She uses the sudo command to enable root access for the cat command so she can see the contents of the Secrets text file:

```
MyMac:~ michelle$ cat Secrets.txt
cat: Secrets.txt: Permission denied
MyMac:~ michelle$ sudo cat Secrets.txt
Password:
```

This is the contents of the Secrets.txt text file that the user account Michelle does not normally have access permissions to read. However, because she is an administrative user, she can use the sudo command to envoke root user access and thus read the contents of this file.

TIP ▶ If the command line returns an error because you forgot to use sudo, at the next prompt simply enter sudo !! to run the previous command entry preceded by sudo.

Remember, with great power comes great responsibility. Using the power of sudo with an improperly typed command can easily wreak havoc on your operating system. The command line will only warn you the first time you attempt to use sudo that you could cause serious damage. After that, the command line assumes you know what you're doing. If you remember only three rules about using the command line, it should be these: Always double-check your typing, always use tab completion to help make sure you spell correctly and to save time, and, when using sudo, always triple-check your typing.

Switching the Shell with sudo

If, as an administrative user, you need to execute more than one command with root account access, you can temporarily switch the entire command-line shell to have root level access. Simply enter sudo -s and then your password to switch the shell to have root access. You can easily verify your currently logged-in identity by entering who -m at the command line. You will remain logged in as the root user until you quit the Terminal or enter the exit command. In the following example, Michelle will use the sudo command to switch her shell to the root user, and then she will exit back to her own account:

```
MyMac:~ michelle$ who -m
michelle ttys001 Aug 20 14:31
MyMac:~ michelle$ sudo -s
Password:
bash-3.2# who -m
root ttys001 Aug 20 14:31
bash-3.2# exit
exit
MyMac:~ michelle$ who -m
michelle ttys001 Aug 20 14:31
```

Managing sudo Access

Again, by default, any administrative user can use the sudo command to access resources as the system administrator (root). Additionally, once you initially authenticate the sudo command, it will remain "open" for five minutes, so you do not have to reauthenticate subsequent sudo usage during that time. Further, using sudo -s could leave an open Terminal with root access indefinitely.

For these reasons you should consider limiting sudo access. You can, of course, choose to allow only standard user accounts on your Mac system. This would limit more than sudo access, but as covered in Chapter 2, "User Accounts," this is the safest general-use account for users.

> **TIP** ▶ All usage of the sudo command is written to the system.log file, so you can check in to see if a user is improperly wielding his administrative power. You can view system.log from the /Applications/Utilities/Console application.

Alternately, you can manage the sudo configuration file /etc/sudoers. This file contains the rules by which the sudo command determines allowable actions. As an administrative user, you can read this configuration file using the cat or less commands. In the following example, Michelle uses cat to read the sudo configuration file. Note that she must preface the cat command with sudo because the sudoers file is protected by root access. Also, the output of the less command has been truncated to show only the most interesting bits of the sudoers file.

```
MyMac:~ michelle$ sudo cat /etc/sudoers
Password:
# sudoers file.
#
# This file MUST be edited with the 'visudo' command as root.
# Failure to use 'visudo' may result in syntax or file permission errors
# that prevent sudo from running.
#
# See the sudoers man page for the details on how to write a sudoers file.
#
...
# User privilege specification
root            ALL=(ALL) ALL
%admin          ALL=(ALL) ALL
...
```

As you can see from the "User privilege specification" section of this file, the root user or anyone in the admin group is allowed unrestricted sudo access to all commands. You can edit this file, but note that the document states you must use a special version of the vi command known as visudo. Using vi to edit text files is covered earlier in this appendix.

Once you are familiar with vi usage, editing the sudoers file with visudo is quite easy. To disable administrative user sudo access, simply add a hash mark (#) to the beginning of the

%admin line, and the sudo command will ignore that line. You can add users or groups for sudo access by duplicating the existing user privilege lines with alternate account names. Just remember to use only the account's "short" name and to use the percent symbol (%) to specify any group names.

Command-Line Tips and Tricks

Here are a few command-line tips that will help you customize your experience and save a lot of time typing:

▶ The single best command-line tip is to always use tab completion when entering file paths. Tab completion was covered previously in this appendix.

▶ Drag and drop files and folders from the Finder to the Terminal window to automatically enter their locations at the command line.

▶ Use open . at the prompt to open your current command-line location in the Finder.

▶ Thoroughly explore the Terminal's preferences (Terminal > Preferences from the menu bar) to customize the look and feel of your command line.

▶ To cancel a command gone awry or clear your current command entry, use the Control-C keyboard shortcut.

▶ You can edit commands before submitting them. The Left and Right Arrow keys and the Delete key work as you would expect, but the mouse will not.

▶ At the command prompt, use the Up Arrow and Down Arrow keys to travel through and reuse your command history. This also includes the ability to edit old commands before rerunning them. You can also simply enter the history command to see your recent command history.

▶ To clear the Terminal screen enter the clear command or use the Control-L keyboard shortcut.

▶ To move the cursor to the beginning of the current line, use the Control-A keyboard shortcut.

▶ To move the cursor to the end of the current line, use the Control-E keyboard shortcut.

▶ To move the cursor forward one word, use the Esc-F keyboard shortcut.

▶ To move the cursor back one word of the line, use the Esc-B keyboard shortcut.

Index

Numbers

6 to 4, 376
32-bit mode, 287, 294–295
64-bit mode, 294–295, 543, 582–583
128-bit encryption, 260, 265
256-bit encryption, 260
802.1X protocol, 389, 395, 399–400

A

About This Mac dialog, 43–44
Absolute paths, 616–617
AC power, 6
Access control lists. See ACLs (access control lists)
Access rules, for file sharing, 458–464
Accessibility. See Universal Access
Account passwords, 89
ACE (Access Control Entry), 191
ACLs (access control lists)
    clearing from Terminal, 203–204
    overview of, 174–175
    resetting home folder ACLs, 205–207
    viewing from Terminal, 191–192
Acrobat, Adobe, 561
Active Directory. See AD (Active Directory)
Activity Monitor
    as diagnostic tool, 605
    forcing applications to quit, 333
    monitoring processes with, 326–329
    process list in, 584
AD (Active Directory)
    configuring binding for, 503–505
    directory services supported by Lion, 499
    KDC (Key Distribution Center) and, 509
    verifying authentication, 510–511
Ad hoc messaging, iChat and, 438
Ad hoc networks, disabling on Wi-Fi, 397
Address Book 6, 435–437

Address Resolution Protocol (ARP), 359–360
Admin group, 69
Administrative commands, in Terminal, 630–634
Administrative users
    account vulnerabilities, 86–87
    in admin group, 69
    authorization as, 300
    creating initial account, 38
    deleting user accounts, 75
    file sharing access rules, 459
    modifying printer administration rights, 569–570
    quick fixes, 604
    resetting passwords, 110–111
    resetting primary administrator password, 114–116
    sudo command and, 632–634
    system user (root) and, 610
    types of user accounts, 61
Advanced Technology Attachment (ATA), 531
Advanced Wi-Fi settings, 397–399
AES encryption, 260, 265
AFP (Apple Filing Protocol)
    access rules, 458–460
    authorizing file sharing, 458
    backing up to, 267
    browsing file services, 441–445
    enabling file sharing, 457
    file services support in Lion, 439
    file sharing support in Lion, 455
    manually connecting to, 445–447
    troubleshooting file sharing issues, 494
Agents, background processes and, 286
AirDisk volumes, 252
AirDrop
    overview of, 452–453
    sharing files between Macs that support, 453–455
    Wi-Fi sharing and, 397
Aliases, 228–233

Analog modems. See Modems (external analog)
Analog stereo audio, 533
Apache 2.2 web server, 464–465
APM (Apple Partition Map), 123, 261
App Store
    browsing, searching, and installing from, 302–306
    installing applications from, 299–300
    limiting access or disabling, 300–302
    Lion available from, 13–14
    managing accounts, 306–309
    removing installed software, 311
    updating and managing purchases, 310–311
Apple Authorized Service Providers, 606–607
Apple Filing Protocol. See AFP (Apple Filing Protocol)
Apple Hardware Test, 605
Apple ID
    authentication via, 306
    creating, 304, 308
    for installing from App Store, 300
    making changes to, 309
    registration process and, 36
    updating and verifying, 307
    validating, 305
    viewing items purchased via, 310
Apple Partition Map (APM), 123, 261
Apple Remote Desktop. See ARD (Apple Remote Desktop)
Apple Service Source, 607
Apple Software Update
    command-line access, 610
    downloading printer drivers from, 546, 548
    migration of data and, 33, 77
    overview of, 50–51
    as quick fix, 603
    running in preparing for upgrade installation, 6–7

setting update preferences, 52–54
viewing software update details,
    51–52
Apple Support, 8, 10, 607
AppleDouble files, 238–240
AppleScripts, 470
AppleTalk, 353, 388, 549
Application environments
    BSD, 292
    Carbon, 290
    Classic and Roseta, 293
    Cocoa, 289–290
    Java, 290–292
    overview of, 289
    X11, 292
Application Support folder, 215
Applications. See also Software
    64-bit vs. 32-bit, 294–295
    accessibility preferences, 314–315
    adding widgets to Dashboard,
        342–345
    Auto Save, 315–317
    browsing, searching , and installing
        from App Store, 302–306
    common items in user's home
        folder, 74
    contention issues in fast user
        switching, 83
    Dashboard interface for mini-
        applications, 341–342
    as device driver, 542
    diagnostic reports, 335–337
    drag-and-drop installation,
        296–298
    forcing quit, 85, 333–335
    installation packages, 298–299
    installing from App Store, 299–300
    limiting access or disabling App
        Store, 300–302
    locating application information
        using Finder, 324–326
    locking documents, 320–322
    managing App Store accounts,
        306–309
    managing widgets manually, 345
    open source, 293
    overview of, 285–286
    preference troubleshooting,
        337–340
    registering using Launch Services,
        241–242
    reinstalling, 605
    removing installed, 311–312
    resource troubleshooting, 340–341
    Resume feature, 322–323
    review quiz, 349–351

standards supported by Lion, 3
summary and reference
    information, 347–349
troubleshooting, 331–333
troubleshooting widgets, 346–347
updating and managing App Store
    purchases, 310–311
updating installed, 299
verifying compatibility of, 8–9
Versions, 318–320
VoiceOver access to, 313–314
widget architecture, 345–346
Applications folder, system root, 214
Applications, network
    Address Book 6 for contacts,
        435–437
    iCal for calendaring, 434–435
    iChat for Instant Messaging,
        437–438
    Mail 5 for email and Exchange,
        432–434
    Safari 5.1 for web browsing,
        431–432
    troubleshooting, 492–494
Architecture
    for printing, scanning, and faxing,
        544–545
    security, 288
    widget, 345–346
Archives
    compared with disk images, 256
    creating zip archives, 256–258
    expanding zip archives, 258–259
    overview of, 255–256
    saving home folders as disk image,
        75, 78
    saving to Mac OS Extended
        volumes, 266
ARD (Apple Remote Desktop)
    administering multiple Macs
        simultaneously, 610
    controlling another computer via
        screen sharing, 474–477
    enabling remote management,
        483–485
    overview of, 470
ARP (Address Resolution Protocol),
    359–360
Asterisk (*) wildcard, 624
ATA (Advanced Technology
    Attachment), 531
Attributes
    accessing hidden account
        attributes, 71
    extended attributes, 234–235
    of privileges, 191

for refining Spotlight searches, 248
of user accounts, 62–64
Audio, 524, 532–533, 541
Authentication
    802.1X protocol. See 802.1X
        protocol
    App Store purchases and, 306
    configuring VPNs, 381–382
    keychains for protecting
        authentication assets, 98–99
    verifying user authenticity, 88
    Wi-Fi (Wireless Ethernet) and, 395
Authentication, of network services
    Kerberos commands, 513
    Kerberos for, 508–510
    Kerberos Ticket Viewer application,
        511–513
    overview of, 507–508
    verifying Kerberos authentication,
        510–511
Authorization, 300, 458, 507
Auto Save and Versions feature
    locking documents, 320–322
    overview of, 315–317
    using Auto Save, 317–318
    using Versions, 318–320

B

Back ups
    automating, 256
    configuring, 268–273
    quick fixes, 605
    during upgrade, 9
    using Time Machine for, 266–268
Backslash character (\), 618
bash shell, 613
Berkeley Software Distribution (BSD),
    292
Binary searches, 606
Binding methods, directory services,
    501–505
Bitmaps, 220
Bluetooth
    DUN (dial-up networking),
        406–407
    Lion support for, 370
    managing and setting up, 535–539
    overview of, 529–530
    PANs (personal area networks)
        and, 407
    printers and, 549
    sharing via, 471
Bonjour
    configuring network identification,
        430
    configuring printers and, 549–550

dynamic network service discovery, 427

network identification methods, 428–429

Booter
   initializing, 581–582
   selecting, 578
   stages of, 576
   troubleshooting, 592–593

BOOTP (Bootstrap Protocol), 363

BootROM. See Firmware

BSD (Berkeley Software Distribution), 292

Bundles, software, 236–238

Burn folders, 157–160

C

Cables, troubleshooting peripherals and, 543

Cache files, deleting, 332, 604

CalDAV, 435–436

Calendars, iCal for, 434–435

Carbon, as application environments, 290

cat (concatenate) command, 622

cd (change directory) command, 617

CDFS (Compact Disk File System), 126

CDs. See also optical media, 159–160, 469

Cellular network connections, 389, 406–408

Certificates, VPN authentication and, 382

Chat services, 437

chflags command, 195–196, 227–228

chmod command, 193–194, 203–204

chown command, for changing ownership, 192

Classic Mac OS X, as application environments, 293

Client management settings, 498

Client/server model, in network communication, 425

Cocoa, as application environments, 289–290

Code signing, for signed applications, 288

Command line. See Terminal

Command strings, 614

Commands, applications compared with. See also Terminal, 286

Common UNIX Printing System. See CUPS (Common UNIX Printing System)

Communication
   network services for, 425

troubleshooting shared services, 495

web communication via HTTP/ HTTPS, 432

Compact Disk File System (CDFS), 126

Compatibility, 8–9, 331

Composite video, 533

Compressed files. See Zip archives

Compression, disk image options, 260

Computer accounts, 498

Computer names, 428–429

Concatenated disk sets, 148

Configuration, documenting critical settings during upgrade, 9–10

Configured devices, viewing in Dock, 564

Configuring
   calendar accounts, 434
   directory services, 500–501
   host sharing, 468–471
   networks. See Network configuration
   personal application firewalls, 487–490
   Time Machine, 268–273

Configuring directory services
   AD binding, 503–505
   advanced configuration, 505–506
   OD binding, 501–503

Configuring fax services
   receive, 555
   send, 553–554

Configuring OS X Lion
   account creation, 37–38
   getting information about Mac (About This Mac dialog), 43–44
   migrating data from previous system, 33–35
   mouse scrolling settings, 40
   network settings, 31–33
   registering, 36–37
   Setup Assistant, 30–31
   System Information application, 45–46
   System Preferences, 41–43
   time zone settings, 39

Configuring printers
   directly attached, 547–548
   local network, 548–549
   manually, 549–553

Configuring websites
   computer websites, 465–466
   personal websites, 466–468
   web sharing of computer sites, 465–466
   web sharing of personal sites, 466–468

Connectivity
   checking as quick fix, 603
   evaluating, 606
   standards supported by Lion, 3
   troubleshooting shared services, 496

Connectivity, of peripherals
   audio and video connectivity, 532–534
   Bluetooth connections, 529–530
   expansion buses, 530–531
   FireWire connections, 527–528
   overview of, 524–525
   storage buses, 531–532
   Thunderbolt connections, 528–529
   USB connections, 525–527

Console, 605, 607, 612

Contacts, 434–437

cp (copy) command, 626–627

CPUs. See Processors

Crashes, diagnostic reports, 335

CUPS (Common UNIX Printing System)
   Logs/logging, 571
   in print and fax technology architecture, 544–545
   printing support and, 523
   sharing printers and, 565
   web server for managing, 568–569

D

Daemons, 286

Darwin, based on FreeBSD, 292

Dashboard
   64-bit and 32-bit applications and, 295
   adding widgets to, 342–345
   managing widgets manually, 345
   for mini-applications, 341–342
   troubleshooting widgets, 346–347
   widget architecture, 345–346

Data management
   AppleDouble file format, 238–239
   application registration, 241–242
   archives compared with disk images, 256
   backing up using Time Machine, 266–268
   bundles and packages and, 236–238
   changing Launch Service settings, 242–245
   comparing file system shortcut types, 232–233
   configuring Time Machine, 268–273
   creating aliases, 229–231

creating disk images from selected items, 263–265
creating empty disk images, 260–263
creating symbolic links, 231–232
creating zip archives, 256–258
disk images and, 259–260
expanding zip archives, 258–259
file flags and extended attributes, 234–235
file system shortcut types, 228–229
file system structure, 214–215
file type identification, 240–241
files system metadata, 234
hiding/unhiding items, 227–228
Launch Services, 240
Mac OS Extended metadata, 234
managing fonts, 220–223
managing hidden items, 223–224
managing Spotlight settings, 253–255
managing Time Machine, 265–266
manually restoring from Time Machine, 276–278
open command and, 225–226
opening hidden items from Terminal, 226–227
opening hidden items in Finder, 224–225
overview of, 213
Quick Look previews, 249–251
restoring entire system from Lion Restore, 276
restoring from Time Machine, 273–275
restoring using Migration Assistant, 275
review quiz, 280–283
Spotlight plug-ins, 252–253
Spotlight searches, 246–249
Spotlight security, 252
summary and reference information, 279–280
system resource hierarchy, 216–218
system resource troubleshooting, 219
system resource types, 215–216
Time Machine flaws, 278–279
viewing AppleDouble files from Terminal, 239–240
viewing metadata from Terminal, 235–236
Date & Time preferences, 39
DDNS (Dynamic DNS), 401
Desktop, default items in user's home folder, 72–73

Developers folder, system root, 214–215
Device drivers
    manually configuring printers, 552
    for peripherals, 541–542
    for printers, 571
    for printing, scanning, and faxing, 545–547
Devices, peripheral classes of, 539–541
DHCP (Dynamic Host Configuration Protocol)
    client ID settings, 390
    link aggregation and, 388
    network settings, 31
    overview of, 363–364
    VLANs (virtual LANs) and, 385
Diagnostics
    reports, 335–337
    tools, 605–606
    troubleshooting applications, 332
Dial-up networking (DUN), 406
Digital cameras, 541
Digital Video Interface (DVI), 533
Directory binding
    AD, 503–505
    defined, 500
    methods, 501
    OD, 501–503
Directory services
    AD binding, 503–506
    advanced configuration, 505–506
    advantages of, 499–500
    binding methods, 501
    configuring, 500–501
    OD binding, 501–503
    overview of, 497
    resources, 497–498
    troubleshooting, 513–515
    troubleshooting network access issues, 496
    types supported by Lion, 498–499
    user account types and, 500
Directory Utility, 506, 605
Discoverable mode, managing and setting up Bluetooth peripherals, 535
Discovery, network services for, 426–427
Disk drives. See Drives
Disk images
    archives compared with, 256
    burning to optical disc, 160–161
    changing format of, 263
    creating empty, 260–263
    creating from selected items, 263–265
    data management and, 255–256

making content available to Finder, 297
    overview of, 259–260
    saving home folders as, 75, 78
Disk Utility
    burning disk image to optical disc, 160–161
    changing disk image format, 263
    command-line access to, 610
    creating disk images, 260–263
    creating disk images from selected items, 263–265
    creating RAID sets, 149–152
    data recovery options, 202
    as diagnostic tool, 605
    erasing drives or volumes, 135–138
    erasing files securely, 139–140
    erasing/repartitioning drives, 11, 18
    erasing rewriteable optical media, 162
    formatting/reformatting drives, 127–130
    gathering file system information, 196–198
    managing file systems, 126
    managing volume mounts, 142–144
    preparing drive for new installation of Lion, 23
    quick fixes, 604–605
    rebuilding RAID sets, 153–154
    Repair Disk Permissions, 571
    repartitioning drives, 131–134
    troubleshooting drives, 198
    verifying/repairing disk permissions, 205
    verifying/repairing drives, 198–200
    viewing mounted volumes, 141
DisplayPort, 529, 534
DNS (Domain Name System)
    configuring network identification, 429–430
    dynamic network service discovery, 426–427
    host names, 426
    looking up DNS names, 414–415
    manually configuring, 389–393
    network identification methods, 428–429
Dock, 333, 564
Documents
    Auto Save and Versions feature, 315–317
    contention issues in fast user switching, 84
    default items in user's home folder, 73

locking, 320–322
managing, 315
standards supported by Lion, 3
using Auto Save, 317–318
using Versions, 318–320
Domain Name System. See DNS (Domain Name System)
Double period (."”), indicating parent folder, 618–619
Drag-and-drop method
for installing applications, 296–298
moving files and folders to Terminal window, 634
moving files to remote desktop, 477
removing installed software, 311–312
Drives
ejecting, 141–142
erasing, 134–138
formatting/reformatting, 127–130
gathering file system information, 196–198
repartitioning, 130–134
troubleshooting, 198
verifying/repairing, 198–200
virtual, 258
DriveSavers, 196
du command, 126
Dual-Link DVI (DVI-DL), 534
DUN (dial-up networking), 406
Duplicate options, documents, 318
DVDs. See also optical media, 155, 159–160, 469
DVI (Digital Video Interface), 533
DVI-DL (Dual-Link DVI), 534
Dynamic DNS (DDNS), 401
Dynamic Host Configuration Protocol, DHCP (Dynamic Host Configuration Protocol)
Dynamic memory allocation, 287

E

EDR (Extended Data Rate), Bluetooth and, 529
EFI (Extensible Firmware Interface), 7, 577
Email. See Mail
Encryption
authentication via encrypted password, 508
choosing option for, 262, 265
disk image options, 260
of email protocols, 433
FileVault 2 and, 97, 163–164
Legacy FileVault and, 96

Ethernet
built-in support for Ethernet hardware, 389
Lion support for, 370, 372
manually configuring, 405–406
network settings, 32
VLANs as Ethernet interface, 385
wireless. See Wi-Fi (Wireless Ethernet)
Everyone setting, in permission ownership structure, 173
EWS (Exchange Web Services), 432–434, 436–437
Exchange Server 2010, 433–434, 435, 436–437
Exchange Web Services (EWS), 432–434, 436–437
ExFAT (Extended FAT), 125
Expansion buses, 524, 530–531
ExpressCard 34, 530–531
Extended attributes, metadata, 234–235
Extended Data Rate (EDR), Bluetooth and, 529
Extended FAT (ExFAT), 125
Extensible Firmware Interface (EFI), 7, 577
Extensions, file, 215, 240–241

F

Fast user switching
login options, 81
overview of, 81–82
resolving issues in, 84–86
resource contention issues in, 83–84
FAT (File Allocation Table), volume formats, 125
Fax services
adding manually, 549
configuring receiving, 555
configuring sending, 553–554
device drivers for, 545–547
managing job queues, 562–565
modifying existing settings, 555–557
options for starting, 545
selecting port for transmissions, 550
Send Fax option on Print Settings pop-up menu, 560
sharing fax devices, 566
troubleshooting, 571
Fibre Channel, 532
file command, for determining file type, 623–624

File flags, metadata, 234–235
File sharing
access, 458–460
AirDrop, 452–455
authorizing, 458
automatically connecting network volumes, 451–452
browsing file services, 440–445
customizing access to, 460–464
enabling, 456–458
managing connected volumes, 450–451
manually connecting file services, 445–450
overview of, 438–439
providing file services, 455
web sharing, 464–468
File systems
ACLs (access control lists), 174–175
burn folders and, 157–160
burning optical discs using Disk Image, 160–161
burning optical discs using Finder, 155–157
clearing ACLs from Terminal window, 203–204
components of, 122
creating RAID sets, 149–152
disk image options, 260
ejecting drives, 141–142
ejecting in-use volumes, 144–146
enabling FileVault 2 for use with, 165–169
erasing drives or volumes, 134–138
erasing files securely, 138–140
erasing rewriteable optical media, 162
FileVault 2 options, 163–164
FileVault 2 recovery keys, 169–171
formatting/reformatting drives, 127–130
gathering information regarding, 196–198
locked item management from Terminal, 195–196
locked item management with Finder, 186–187
managing, 126–127
metadata. See Metadata
optical media, 154–155
overview of, 121
partitions, 123
permission modification from Terminal, 192–194

permission modification with Finder, 183–186
permission ownership, 173
permissions, 171–172, 458
permissions for external volumes, 187–188
permissions for sharing, 178–182
permissions hierarchy, 176–178
rebuilding RAID sets, 153–154
recovering data using target disk mode, 201–202
repairing disk permissions, 204–205
repartitioning drives, 130–134
resetting home folder permissions and ACLs, 205–207
review quiz, 209–211
securing new items, 182
software RAID, 146–149
standard (POSIX) permissions, 174
standards supported by Lion, 3
sticky bit permission in sharing, 194–195
structure of, 214–215
summary and reference information, 207–209
Target Disk Mode button, 200–201
troubleshooting, 196
troubleshooting permissions issues, 202–203
verifying/repairing drives, 198–200
viewing ACLs, 191–192
viewing permissions, 172–173, 189–190
volume formats, 124–126
volume mounts, 142–144
File Transfer Protocol (FTP), 439, 447–450
Filenames, backslash character (\) in, 618
Files
Auto Save and Versions feature, 316–317
backing up during upgrade, 9
command-line options for examining, 622–624
command-line options for modifying, 626–630
determining file type, 623
dragging and dropping to Terminal window, 634
groups for controlling sharing, 69
identifying file type with Launch Services, 240–241
keychain file types, 99–100
previewing installer package, 49

replacing corrupted, 333
FileVault 2
enabling, 165–169
encryption, 97
options, 163–164
recovery keys, 169–171
unlocking during system startup, 578–579
FileVault, legacy version
encryption, 96
home folders, 96–98
keychain file types, 99
Migration Assistant and, 275
resetting master passwords, 107–108
resetting passwords, 111–113
Time Machine and, 275
turning off/switching to FileVault 2, 97–98
find command, for locating items in file system, 624
Finder
assigning standard permissions, 174
automatically connecting network volumes, 451–452
browsing file services, 440–445
burn folders, 157–160
burning data to optical disc, 155–157
changing Launch Service settings, 243–245
command line compared with, 610
connecting to network file systems, 439
creating aliases, 229–231
creating zip archives, 257–258
customizing file sharing access, 461–462
data recovery options, 202
ejecting drives, 141–142
ejecting in-use volumes, 144–146
expanding zip archives, 258
extended attributes used with, 235
hiding/unhiding extensions, 241
hiding/unhiding items, 227–228
honoring ownership on external volumes, 187–188
locating application information, 324–326
locking files or folders, 186–187
making disk image content available to, 297
managing network-connected volumes, 450–451
modifying file permissions, 183–186

open command and, 225–226
opening current command-line location in Finder, 634
opening hidden items, 224–225
parental controls and, 67
Quick Look and, 250
refining Spotlight searches, 247–248
restoring from Time Machine and, 274
securely erasing files, 138–139
selecting fonts, 221
viewing file system permissions, 172–173
viewing mounted volumes in, 141
viewing package content, 237–238
viewing system root folders, 214–215
Finger section, of Network Utility, 411
Firewalls, 486–490, 495
FireWire
configuring directly attached printers, 547
configuring local network printers, 550
Lion support for, 371
overview of, 527–528
recovering data from non-starting system, 201–202
target disk mode and, 200–201
Firmware
booter selection, 578
checking for updates, 7–8
initializing in system startup, 577
POST (Power-On Self-Test), 577–578
quick fixes, 604
stages of system initialization, 576
startup shortcuts, 579–580
troubleshooting peripherals, 544
troubleshooting system startup, 591–592
unlocking FileVault 2 and, 578–579
updating during system startup, 581
Firmware Password Utility, 24, 95–96
Firmware passwords, 89, 94–96
Firmware Restoration CDs, 8
Flags, file flags, 234–235
Folders, 634
backing up during upgrade, 9
burn folders, 157–160
command-line options for examining, 622–624
command-line options for modifying, 626–630

groups for controlling sharing, 69
home folder. See Home folder
legacy FileVault folders and, 96–98
library folders, 214–216, 337–338
locked folders, 186–187
shared folders, 181–182, 194
Smart Folders, 248
Font Book, 219, 220–223
Font Validation window, 222
Fonts, 215, 220–223
Force Quit, 333–335, 603
Formatting/reformatting drives,
127–130
Forward lookup, DNS names and, 414
Framework plug-ins, 542
Frameworks folder, 215–216
FreeBSD, 292
FTP (File Transfer Protocol), 439,
447–450

G

Generated Unique ID (GUID), 63
Get Info window, of Finder
comparing file system shortcut
types, 233
locating application information,
324–326
matching disk image file to disk
image target volume, 262
overriding Launch Services'
defaults, 242
overview of, 186–190
sharing files and folders and,
178–179
Google, as research resource, 607
GPT (GUID Partition Table), 10–11,
18, 123
Groups
account attributes, 63
creating, 69–70
directory resources used by Lion,
498
in permission ownership structure,
173
Guest users
account vulnerabilities, 87–88
creating, 66
file sharing access rules, 459
types of user accounts, 61–62
GUID (Generated Unique ID), 63
GUID Partition Table. See GPT (GUID
Partition Table)

H

Hangs, diagnostic reports about, 335
Hard links, 229, 232–233

Hardware
Apple Hardware Test, 605
expansion buses for adding,
530–531
preferences, 42
preventing failure using target disk
mode, 200
quick fixes, 605
serial number for, 44
storage buses, 531–532
troubleshooting firmware,
591–592
troubleshooting printers, 570
HDMI (High-Definition Multimedia
Interface), 534
hdutil command, for managing disk
images, 263
Hearing, accessibility options related
to, 312
Help, getting online help, 23
HID (human input devices), 540
Hidden items
hiding/unhiding, 227–228
open command and, 225–226
opening from Terminal, 226–227
opening in Finder, 224–225
overview of, 223–224
viewing from Terminal, 620–621
High-Definition Multimedia Interface
(HDMI), 534
Home Directory, user account attributes,
64
Home folder
contents, 72–74
contents of, 72–74
deleting, 74–75
legacy FileVault folders and, 96–98
moving or restoring manually,
77–80
moving or restoring with Migration
Assistant, 76–77
overview of, 71
resetting home folder permissions,
205–207
sharing and, 179–182
Host names, DNS, 428–430
Host network identification, network
services for, 428
Hosting sharing services
ARD remote management,
483–485
iChat screen sharing, 478–480
overview of, 468–471
remote login, 480–483
screen sharing, 471–472
system screen sharing, 472–477

Hot-pluggable interfaces, 526
HTTP (Hypertext Transfer Protocol),
432
HTTPS (Secure HTTP), 432, 434
Human input devices (HID), 540

I

iCal, 434–435
iChat, 437–438, 478–480, 493
IDs (identifiers), user accounts, 63
iDVD, burning data to optical disc, 155
IEEE 802.1Q (VLAN), 384
IEEE 1394. See FireWire
Image Capture application, supporting
scanners, 540
Image formats, 259
IMAP (Internet Message Access
Protocol), 433
Info section, of Network Utility,
410–412
Input devices, 540
Inspector, keyboard shortcut for
opening, 178–179
Installation packages, 298–299
Installer. See Lion Installer
Installer packages, 236
Installing applications
drag-and-drop method, 296–298
installation package approach,
298–299
overview of, 295–296
Installing/configuring OSX Lion
account creation, 37–38
acquiring Lion Installer, 13–14
advanced Installer features, 48–50
Apple Software Update and, 50–51
creating full Lion Recovery drive,
28–30
creating minimal Lion Recovery
drive, 25–27
getting information about Mac,
43–44
install destination, 17–18
install process, 14–17
Installer application, 47–48
Lion Recovery utilities, 22–25
logging installation, 19–21
migrating data from previous
system, 33–35
mouse scrolling settings, 40
network settings, 31–33
OS X Lion introduction, 2–3
partitioning options, 11–12
preparing for upgrade, 5–10
registration, 36–37
review quiz, 56–57

Setup Assistant and, 30–31
standards supported, 3
starting up from Lion Recovery, 21–22
summary and reference information, 54–56
system drive preparation for, 10–11
System Information application, 45–46
System Preferences, 41–43
time zone settings, 39
troubleshooting installation, 18–19
update preferences, 52–54
upgrade installations, 3–4
verifying installation requirements, 5–6
viewing software update details, 51–52
Instant Messaging, 437–438
Interface bonding. See Link aggregation
Interface option, Network Utility, 411–412
Internet, 42, 470–471, 607
Internet Message Access Protocol (IMAP), 433
Internet Printing Protocol (IPP), 544, 565
Internet Protocol addresses. See IP addresses
IP addresses
6 to 4, 376
configuring, 356–357
configuring network identification, 429–430
correspondence to DNS names, 363
DHCP servers and, 364
dynamic network service discovery, 426–427
LAN traffic and, 359–360
for multiple network interfaces, 372
network identification methods, 428–429
network services identification, 426
overview of, 356–357
for printers, 550
returning from host name, 414
for routers, 357–358
subnet masks and, 357
viewing interface information with Network Utility, 412
IP proxies. See Proxy servers
ipfw firewall, 487
iPhoto, 155
IPP (Internet Printing Protocol), 544, 565
IPSec, 379–380

J
Java, 290–292
JavaScript, 291

K
KDC (Key Distribution Center), 509–510
Kerberos
advantages of network directory services, 499
authentication via, 508
bypassing authentication dialogs when using, 452
commands, 513
Kerberos Ticket Viewer application, 511–513
overview of, 508–510
verifying authentication, 510–511
Kernel, 577, 582–583, 593–594
KEXTs (Kernel extensions)
booter initialization and, 581
inspecting loaded extensions, 542–543
kernel initialization and, 582
peripheral support, 542
troubleshooting kernel issues, 593–594
Key Distribution Center (KDC), 509–510
Keyboards, accessibility options, 312
Keychain Access tool, 100–104
Keychain passwords, 89, 113–114
Keychains
file types, 99–100
Keychain Access tool, 100
managing keychain files, 102–104
managing keychain items, 100–102
protecting authentication assets, 98–99
resetting keychain passwords, 113–114
saving authentication information to, 452
Keychains folder, 216
kill command, 334–335
killall command, 334–335

L
L2TP (Layer 2 Tunneling Protocol), 379–380
LANs (Local Area Networks), 359–360
Launch Services
application registration, 241–242
changing settings, 242–245
file type identification, 240–241
overview of, 240

LaunchAgents, Library folders, 216
launchd
enabling remote management, 484
Library folder for, 216
System launchd initialization, 583–585
System launchd stage of system initialization, 577
troubleshooting system launchd issues, 594–595
User launchd initialization, 586–587
User launchd stage of system initialization, 577
Layer 2 Tunneling Protocol (L2TP), 379–380
LDAP (Lightweight Directory Access Protocol), 436, 499
Legacy FileVault. See FileVault, legacy version
less command, for viewing long files, 622–623
Library, default items in user's home folder, 73
Library folder, 214, 337–338
Licensing agreement, 15
Lightweight Directory Access Protocol (LDAP), 436, 499
Link aggregation, 376, 386–388
Link Speed, viewing interface information with Network Utility, 412
Link Status, viewing interface information with Network Utility, 412
Lion Installer
acquiring, 13–14
advanced features, 48–50
checking information on Installer log, 19–21
command-line access to, 610
install process, 14–17
installing software, 47–48
opening/running, 15–17
reinstalling Mac OS X, 23
selecting install destination, 17–18
troubleshooting installation with, 17–18
Lion Recovery
creating full Lion Recovery drive, 28–30
creating minimal Lion Recovery drive, 25–27
FileVault 2 and, 164
managing firmware passwords, 94–96
quick fixes, 604

Reset Password utility. See Reset Password utility
resetting primary administrator password, 114–116
running Installer from, 16
starting up from, 21–22
utilities on, 22–25
Lion Restore
creating restore system on destination drive, 16–17
restoring entire system from, 276
ln command, for creating symbolic links, 231–232
Local accounts, 500
Local Area Networks (LANs), 359–360
Local, resource domain, 217
LocalTalk, 353
Locked items, 186–187, 195–196
Locking documents, 320–322
Login
managing user login items, 66–67
options, 80–81
resetting passwords at, 108–110
VoiceOver enabled at, 314–315
Login shell, user account attributes, 64
loginwindow
initializing user environment, 585–586
logout and, 589–590
maintaining user environment, 587
shutdown and restart, 590
troubleshooting logout and shutdown, 596
troubleshooting user initialization, 595–596
user session stages, 577
Logout, 589–590, 596
Logs/logging
CUPS (Common UNIX Printing System), 571
firewalls, 488
installation, 19–21
Installer log, 48–49
Library folders, 216
reviewing as quick fix, 603
troubleshooting applications, 332
viewing with Console, 607
Lookup section, of Network Utility, 411, 414–415
LPD printers, 551–552
ls (list) command
overview of, 617
viewing hidden files, 224, 226–227
viewing hidden items, 620–621
viewing metadata, 235–236

M
MAC addresses, 355–356, 360, 364
Mac computers, migrating data from, 34
Mac OS Extended, 124, 234, 266
Mac OS Extended (Case-Sensitive), 124
Mac OS Extended (Journaled), 124, 261
Mac OS Extended (Journaled, Encrypted), 125, 134, 163, 267
Mac OS Standard, 124
Mail
iChat and, 437
preferences, 434
troubleshooting network applications, 493
using Mail 5 email and Exchange, 432–434
man pages, as research resource, 607
Master Boot Record (MBR), 122–123
Master passwords, 89, 105–108
MBR (Master Boot Record), 122–123
MDM (Mobile Device Management), 400, 431, 501
mds, background process for metadata server, 251
Media Access Control addresses. See MAC addresses
Memory, 287, 327
Messaging services, iChat and, 437–438
Metadata
AppleDouble file format, 238–239
bundles and packages and, 236–238
file flags and extended attributes, 234–235
overview of, 234
viewing AppleDouble files from Terminal, 239–240
viewing from Terminal, 235–236
Microsoft Exchange Server 2007
collaborative calendaring, 435
contact sharing, 436–437
support for, 433–434
Migration Assistant
data recovery options, 202
migrating data from previous system, 33–35
moving or restoring user accounts, 76–77
restoring from, 275
Mini DisplayPort, 529, 534
Mirroring (RAID 1), 148
mirroring (RAID 1), 153–154
mkdir (make directory) command, 626
Mobile accounts, 500

viewing standard permissions, 189–190

Mobile Device Management (MDM), 400, 431, 501
Modems (external analog), 370–371, 389, 410
Monitoring processes, 326–331
Mouse, 40, 312
Movies, in home folder, 73
MP3s, 155
Multiprocessing, symmetric, 287
Multitasking, preemptive, 287
Music, in home folder, 73
mv (move) command, 627–628

N
Names
account names, 38
computer names, 428–429
filenames, 618
user account attributes, 63
Navigation commands, 617–618
Nested groups, 70
Nested RAID, 148
NetBIOS (Network Basic Input/Output System)
built-in support for, 389
configuring, 400–402
network identification methods, 428–429
NetBoot, 581–582
Netstat section, of Network Utility, 410
Network Basic Input/Output System. See NetBIOS (Network Basic Input/Output System)
Network configuration
802.1X protocol, 399–400
advanced Wi-Fi settings, 397–399
Bonjour for network identification, 430
cellular Internet connections, 406–408
DHCP (Dynamic Host Configuration Protocol), 363–364
DNS (Domain Name System), 361–363
DNS host name, 429–430
Ethernet settings, 405–406
interface option of Network Utility, 411–412
IP (Internet Protocol) addresses, 356–357
LAN (Local Area Network) traffic, 359–360
link aggregation settings, 386–388
lookup option of Network Utility, 414–415

MAC (Media Access Control)
    addresses, 355–356
MDM (Mobile Device
    Management), 431
multiple network interfaces
    simultaneously, 371–372
NetBIOS and WINS settings,
    400–402
Network Diagnostics Assistant,
    409–410
network interface settings,
    373–375
network interfaces, 370–371
network location settings, 367–370
network protocols, 388–389
network status indicators, 409
network terminology, 354–355
Network Utility, 410–411
overview of, 31–33, 353–354
ping option of Network Utility,
    412–413
PPPoE settings, 377–379
proxy server settings, 402–404
review quiz, 418–421
router addresses, 357–358
Setup Assistant for basic settings,
    365–366
subnet masks, 357
summary and reference
    information, 416–418
TCP/IP and DNS settings, 389–393
TCP (Transmission Control
    Protocol), 358
traceroute option of Network
    Utility, 415–416
troubleshooting network
    configuration, 408
URLs (Uniform Resource
    Locators), 432
virtual network services, 376
VLAN settings, 384–386
VPN settings, 379–384
WAN (Wide Area Network) traffic,
    360–361
Wi-Fi settings, 393–397
Network Diagnostics Assistant, 409–
    410, 605
Network file mounts, 498
Network File System. See NFS (Network
    File System)
Network Information Systems (NIS),
    498
Network interfaces
    configuring, 373–375
    hardware interfaces supported,
        370–371

multiple network interfaces
    simultaneously, 371–372
overview of, 354
viewing interface information with
    Network Utility, 411–412
Network locations
    changing, 369–370
    configuring, 367–369
Network preferences
    advanced Wi-Fi settings, 397–399
    changing network locations,
        369–370
    configuring network locations,
        368–369
    configuring network service
        interfaces, 373–375
    configuring VLANs, 384–386
    Ethernet settings, 405–406
    link aggregation settings, 386–388
    NetBIOS and WINS settings,
        401–402
    network status indicators, 409
    overview of, 365–366
    PPPoE settings, 377–379
    proxy server settings, 403–404
    quick fixes, 604
    TCP/IP and DNS settings, 389–393
    VPN connection settings, 379–384
Network printers, 548–549
Network protocols
    802.1X protocol, 399–400
    advanced Wi-Fi settings, 397–399
    cellular Internet connections,
        406–408
    Ethernet settings, 405–406
    NetBIOS and WINS settings,
        400–402
    overview of, 354–355, 388–389
    proxy server settings, 402–404
    TCP/IP and DNS settings,
        389–393
    Wi-Fi settings, 393–397
Network services
    AD (Active Directory) binding,
        503–505
    Address Book 6 for contacts,
        435–437
    AirDrop, 452–455
    ARD remote management,
        483–485
    authentication of, 507–508
    automatically connecting network
        volumes, 451–452
    browsing file services, 440–445
    communication, 425

configuring directory services,
    500–501
configuring network identification,
    429–430
configuring network interfaces,
    373–375
customizing file sharing access,
    460–464
directory binding methods, 501
directory service advantages,
    499–500
directory service resources,
    497–498
directory service types, 498–499
discovery, 426–427
enabling file sharing, 456–458
file sharing, 438–439
file sharing access, 458–460
file sharing authorization, 458
file sharing issues, 494
host network identification, 428
host sharing services, 468–471
iCal for calendaring, 434–435
iChat for Instant Messaging,
    437–438
iChat for screen sharing, 478–480
identification, 425–426
Kerberos authentication, 508–510
Kerberos commands, 513
Kerberos Ticket Viewer application,
    511–513
Mail 5 for email and Exchange,
    432–434
managing connected volumes,
    450–451
manually connecting file services,
    445–450
OD (Open Directory) binding,
    501–503
overview of, 355, 423–424
personal application firewalls
    protecting, 486–490
port scanning, 490–492
providing file services, 455
remote login, 480–483
resource domain, 217
review quiz, 517–521
Safari 5.1 for web browsing,
    431–432
screen sharing, 471–472
security of, 486
software, 424
standards supported by OS X
    Lion, 3
status indicators, 409

summary and reference information, 515–517
system screen sharing, 472–477
terminology, 354–355
troubleshooting directory services, 513–515
troubleshooting network applications, 492–494
troubleshooting shared services, 495–497
UPD (User Datagram Protocol) and, 358
user account types, 500
verifying Kerberos authentication, 510–511
virtual. See Virtual network services
web sharing, 464–468
Network user accounts, 60, 72, 81, 500
Network Utility
as diagnostic tool, 605
evaluating connectivity, 606
interface option, 411–412
Lion Recovery utilities, 24
lookup option, 414–415
overview of, 410–411
ping option, 412–413
port scan option, 491
traceroute option, 415–416
NFS (Network File System), 439, 447–450, 494
NIS (Network Information Systems), 498
No Access, standard (POSIX) permissions, 174
NTFS (NT File System), 125
NVRAM (nonvolatile RAM), 578, 605

O

OD (Open Directory)
authentication, 507
configuring binding for, 501–503
directory services supported by Lion, 498
KDC (Key Distribution Center) and, 509
troubleshooting directory services, 513–514
verifying authentication, 510–511
Online gaming, 358
open command, 225–226, 634
Open Directory. See OD (Open Directory)
Open source software, 293
opendirectoryd daemon, 497

OpenSSH, 480
OpenType fonts, 220
Optical media
burning data to using Finder, 155–157
burning disk image to using Disk Image, 160–161
deploying drag-and-drop software via, 296
erasing rewriteable, 162
overview of, 154–155
sharing, 469
types of, 122
Ownership
changing from Terminal, 192
honoring ownership on external volumes, 187–188
of permissions, 173
troubleshooting network service access issues, 496

P

Packages, 236–238, 298–299
PANs (personal area networks), 407–408
Parallel ATA, 531
Parameter RAM (PRAM), 605
Parental controls, 67–69, 300–301
Partition Layout pop-up menu, 128
Partitions
formatting/reformatting drives, 128–130
options, 11
repartitioning drives, 130–134
schemes, 122–123
single partition vs multiple partitions, 11
Passkey, for pairing Bluetooth devices, 536
Password Assistant, 92–94
Password hints, 108–109
Passwords
administrator resetting, 110–111
authentication via, 508
checking strength of, 92–94
creating initial account, 38
creating user accounts, 64–66
firmware passwords, 94–96
login options, 81
resetting at login, 108–110
resetting keychain passwords, 113–114
resetting legacy FileVault passwords, 111–113
resetting logged-in user's password, 85

resetting master passwords, 107–108
resetting primary administrator password, 114–116
security and privacy preferences, 90
setting or changing master password, 105–107
user account options, 88–89
Wi-Fi (Wireless Ethernet) and, 394
Paths, 616–618
PCIe (PCI Express), 530–531
PCs, migrating data from, 34
PDF (Portable Document Format), 545, 561–562, 570
Performance features, processes, 287
Peripheral buses
Bluetooth, 529–530
FireWire, 527–528
overview of, 524
Thunderbolt, 528–529
troubleshooting peripherals and, 544
USB, 525–527
Peripherals
audio and video connectivity, 532–534
Bluetooth connections, 529–530
connectivity of, 524–525
contention issues in fast user switching, 84
device classes, 539–541
device drivers, 541–542
expansion buses, 530–531
FireWire connections, 527–528
inspecting loaded extensions, 542–543
managing and setting up Bluetooth peripherals, 535–539
overview of, 523–524
printing interfaces. See Printing/printers
quick fixes, 604
review quiz, 573
storage buses, 531–532
summary and reference information, 572–573
Thunderbolt connections, 528–529
troubleshooting techniques, 543–544
USB connections, 525–527
Permissions
ACLs (access control lists), 174–175
for external volumes, 187–188
file system, 458
hierarchy of, 176–178

managing locked items from
Terminal, 195–196
modifying file permission with
Finder, 183–186
modifying from Terminal, 192–194
modifying locked items with
Finder, 186–187
overview of, 171–172
ownership, 173
quick fixes, 604
resetting home folder permissions
and ACLs, 205–207
for sharing, 178–182
Spotlight security and, 252
standard (POSIX) permissions, 174
sticky bit permission in sharing,
194–195
troubleshooting file systems,
202–203
troubleshooting network service
access issues, 496–497
viewing, 172–173
viewing ACLs from Terminal,
191–192
viewing standard permissions from
Terminal, 189–190
Personal application firewalls, 486–490
Personal area networks (PANs),
407–408
Personal preferences, 42
Pictures, in home folder, 73
PIDs (process identifiers), 327
Ping section, of Network Utility, 410,
412–413
Plug-and-play, peripheral support, 523
Plug-ins, 251–253, 294–295
Point-to-Point Protocol over Ethernet
(PPPoE), 376, 377–379
Point-to-Point Protocol (PPP), 389, 406
Point-to-Point Tunneling Protocol
(PPTP), 379, 380
POP (Post Office Protocol), 433
Port-based firewalls, 487
Port scans, 411, 490–492, 496
Portable Document Format. See PDF
(Portable Document Format)
Ports
email, 433–434
FireWire, 527–528
iCal, 435
troubleshooting peripherals and,
543
USB, 526
Post Office Protocol (POP), 433
POST (Power-On Self-Test), 577–578
PostScript, 220, 523, 545

PostScript Printer Description (PPD),
544, 547
Power-On Self-Test (POST), 577–578
PPD (PostScript Printer Description),
544, 547
PPP (Point-to-Point Protocol), 389, 406
PPPoE (Point-to-Point Protocol over
Ethernet), 376, 377–379
PPTP (Point-to-Point Tunneling
Protocol), 379, 380
PRAM (Parameter RAM), 605
Preemptive multitasking, 287
Preference files, in Library folder,
337–338
PreferencePanes, 216
Preferences. See System Preferences
Presets Pop-up menu, 561
Previews, Quick Look, 249–251
Print & Scan preferences
configuring directly attached
printers, 547
configuring fax services, 553–555
managing queues, 562–565
modifying existing settings, 555–557
Printing/printers
advanced printing, 568–569
architecture of, 544–545
configuring directly attached
printers, 547–548
configuring local network printers,
548–549
device drivers for, 545–547
as Lion device class, 540
managing job queues, 562–565
manually configuring printers,
549–553
modifying existing, 555–557
modifying printer administration
rights, 569–570
overview of, 544
quick fixes, 604
review quiz, 573
sharing, 469
sharing printers, 565–568
starting basic print job, 557–558
starting custom print job, 559–561
summary and reference
information, 572–573
troubleshooting, 570–571
working with PDFs, 561–562
Privacy preferences, user accounts,
89–91
Privately hosted messaging services, 438
Privileges. See also Permissions, 185,
191, 193–194
Process identifiers (PIDs), 327

Processes
memory management features, 287
monitoring from command line,
329–331
monitoring with Activity Monitor,
326–329
overview of, 285–286
performance features, 287
review quiz, 349–351
summary and reference
information, 347–349
viewing with Activity Monitor, 584
Processors, 121, 287, 327
Property list files, in XML format, 339
Protected memory, 287
Protocols, network. See Network
protocols
Proxy servers, 389, 402–404
ps command, for monitoring processes,
330–331
Public files, 73
Public messaging services, 437
pwd (print working directory)
command, 617

Q
Quarantine, 288, 297
Quartz graphics system, 545
Question mark (?) wildcard, 625
Queues, printer or fax, 556, 562–565, 570
Quick fixes, 603–605
Quick Links, managing App Store
accounts and, 306, 309
Quick Look
overview of, 246
plug-ins, 251
previewing common file types, 242
previewing documents, 317
previewing print jobs, 564
previews generally, 249–251
restoring from Time Machine and,
274
revealing location information
for, 247

R
RAID (Redundant Array of
Independent Disks)
creating RAID sets, 149–152
increases in storage capacity and,
121
levels of, 148
overview of, 146–147
rebuilding RAID sets, 153–154
Read & Write permissions, 174, 176–178
Read attributes, privileges, 191

Read Me files, 606
Read Only permissions, 174, 176–178
Recovery. See Lion Recovery
Recovery Disk Assistant, 27
Recovery keys, 166–168, 169–171
Recursive commands, 625
Red status, network status indicators, 409
Redundant Array of Independent Disks. See RAID (Redundant Array of Independent Disks)
Registration, of OS X Lion, 36–37
Relative paths, in navigation, 617
Remote Disk services, 469
Remote login
    enabling Remote Login service (SSH), 481–482
    overview of, 480
    remotely accessing host, 482–483
    using SSH, 470, 610
Remote management, via ARD, 470
Removing installed software, 311–312
Repair Disk Permissions, of Disk Utility, 204–205, 571
Repartitioning drives, 130–134
Requirements, verifying installation requirements, 5–6
Research resources, 606–607
Reset Password utility, 115–116, 205–207
Resetting account passwords
    administrator passwords, 114–116
    administrator role in, 110–111
    keychain passwords, 113–114
    legacy FileVault passwords, 111–113
    logged-in user's password, 85
    at login, 108–110
    master passwords, 107–108
    overview of, 104–105
Resource passwords, 89
Resources
    contention issues in fast user switching, 83–84
    directory services, 497–498
    font resources, 220–223
    replacing corrupted, 333
    system resource hierarchy, 216–218
    system resource types, 215–216
    troubleshooting, 340–341
    troubleshooting system resources, 219
Restart, login options, 81
Restores
    manual restore from Time Machine, 276–278

standard fonts, 223
    system restore using Lion Restore, 276
    using Migration Assistant, 275
    using Time Machine, 273–275
Resume feature, for maintaining application state, 322–323
Reverse lookup, DNS names and, 414
Rewriteable optical media, erasing, 162
Rights, modifying printer administration rights. See also Permissions, 569–570
rm (remove) command, 628
rmdir (remove directory) command, 629
Root domain, in DNS, 362
Root users, 62, 88
Roseta, as application environments, 293
Routers, 357–358, 416

S

S-Video, 533
Safari, 296–297, 431–432, 493
Safe Boot, 593–595, 606
Safe Login, 595–596
Safe Mode, 581, 594–595, 604
Sandboxing, application and process, 289
SAS (Serial Attached SCSI), 532
Scanners
    adding manually, 549–553
    device drivers for, 545–547
    as Lion device class, 540
    managing, 556
    sharing, 469–470
Screen sharing
    controlling another computer via, 474–477
    defined, 469
    enabling, 472–474
    iChat screen sharing, 478–480
    overview of, 471–472
Scripts, 470, 610
Scrolling options, for mouse, 40
SCSI (Small Computer System Interface), 532
SD cards, support for, 531
Search options
    binary searches, 606
    find command, 624
    Finder. See Finder
    Quick Look. See Quick Look
    Spotlight. See Spotlight
Secure HTTP (HTTPS), 432, 434
Secure Shell. See SSH (Secure Shell)
Secure Sockets Layer (SSL), 432

Security & Privacy preferences
    disabling automatic reports, 336
    enabling FileVault 2, 165
    quick fixes, 604
    user accounts, 89–91
Seeing/vision, accessibility options, 312
Self-Monitoring, Analysis, and Reporting Technology (SMART), 198
Serial ATA, 532
Serial Attached SCSI (SAS), 532
Server Message Block. See SMB (Server Message Block)
Server software, 424–425
Service Source, Apple, 607
Services for Macintosh (SFM), 494
Setup Assistant
    Bluetooth settings, 535–539
    calendar account settings, 434
    changing to Migration Assistant, 33–35
    initial account settings, 37–38
    mouse scrolling settings, 40
    network settings, 31–33, 365–366
    overview of, 30–31
    registering OS X Lion, 36–37
    time zone settings, 39
SFM (Services for Macintosh), 494
Shared folders, 181–182, 194
Sharing
    file sharing access rules, 459
    groups for controlling, 69
    home folder and, 179–182
    permissions for managing, 178–182
    printers, 565–568
    securing new file system items, 182–183
    sticky bit permission and, 194–195
    troubleshooting network service access issues, 496
Sharing only users, 62, 88
Sharing preferences
    Bluetooth, 538–539
    file sharing, 463–464
    host sharing, 468–471
    printer and fax sharing, 566–568
    quick fixes, 604
    troubleshooting shared services, 495
Shut Down, login options, 81
shutdown command, 595
Shutdown/Restart, 544, 590, 596, 603
Signed applications, 288
Simple Mail Transfer Protocol (SMTP), 434
Single-sign on. See also Kerberos, 508

Single-user mode (Command-S), 595, 604, 606, 612
Sites. See Websites
Sleep, login options, 81
Sleep mode, 469, 588–589
Smart Folders, 248
SMART (Self-Monitoring, Analysis, and Reporting Technology), 198
SMB (Server Message Block)
    access rules, 458–460
    authorizing file sharing, 458
    browsing file services, 441–445
    dynamic network service discovery, 427
    enabling file sharing, 456–457
    Lion support for file services, 439
    Lion support for file sharing, 455
    manually connecting, 445–447
    sharing printers and, 565–568
SMC (System Management Controller), 7
SMTP (Simple Mail Transfer Protocol), 434
Snapshots, Time Machine, 267–268
Software. See also Applications
    advanced Installer features, 48–50
    Apple Software Update, 50–51
    Installer application for, 47–48
    installing, 47
    network services, 424
    open source, 293
    setting update preferences, 52–54
    verifying compatibility, 8–9
    viewing update details, 51–52
Software RAID
    creating RAID sets, 149–152
    overview of, 146–149
    Rebuilding RAID sets, 153–154
Software Update. See Apple Software Update
Solid-state disks (SSDs), 122
Special characters, used in commands, 618–619
Spotlight
    command-line access, 610
    filtering running processes, 328
    overview of, 245–246
    plug-ins, 252–253
    restoring from Time Machine and, 274
    searches with, 246–249
    searching App Store, 303
    security, 252
    settings, 253–255
    understanding, 251–252
Square brackets ([]) wildcard, 625

SSDs (solid-state disks), 122
ssh command, 480, 482
SSH (Secure Shell)
    accessing command line from, 612
    remote login, 470, 480–483, 610
SSL (Secure Sockets Layer), 432
Staff group, standard users in, 69
Standard (POSIX) permissions, 174–175, 189–190
Standard users
    account vulnerabilities, 86
    file sharing access rules, 459
    in staff group, 69
    types of user accounts, 61
Standards, supported by OS X Lion, 3
Startup Disk preferences, 200, 604
Startup items, Library folders, 216
Sticky bit permission, in sharing, 194–195
Stings, command strings, 614
Storage buses, 524, 531–532
Storage capacity, of drives, 121
Storage devices, as Lion device class, 540
Striping (RAID 0), 148
su command, for switching user accounts, 630–631
Subnet masks, 357
Subscriptions, iCal managing, 435
sudo command, 631–634
Symbolic links, 228–232
Symmetric multiprocessing, 287
System
    build number, 44
    keychain file types, 99
    navigating system volume to other volumes, 621–622
    preparing system drive for installation, 10–11
    resource domain, 217
    restoring entire system from Lion Restore, 276
    screen sharing, 472–477
    version number, 44
System Administrator. See also Root users, 62
System folder, 214
System Information
    application for, 45–46
    command-line access to, 610
    as diagnostic tool, 605
    Lion Recovery utilities, 25
    as quick fix, 603
    troubleshooting drives, 198
    troubleshooting peripherals, 543
System initialization phase, of startup, 576

System launchd, 577, 583–585, 594–595
System Management Controller (SMC), 7
System Preferences
    64-bit and 32-bit applications and, 295
    accessibility, 314–315
    Bluetooth, 537
    configuring, 41–43
    Date & Time, 39
    file sharing, 456
    fonts, 220
    Library folders, 216
    Mail, Contacts & Calendars, 434
    network. See Network preferences
    parental controls, 68–69
    Print & Scan, 547, 549, 552–553
    quick fixes, 604–605
    replacing corrupted files, 333
    resolving corrupted preferences, 338–339
    Security & Privacy. See Security & Privacy preferences
    sharing. See Sharing preferences
    software updates, 52–54
    Spotlight, 253–255
    Startup Disk, 200, 604
    Terminal, 634
    Time Machine, 269
    Users & Groups. See Users & Groups
    viewing and editing, 339–340
    wireless, 42
System Profiler, 5
System resources, 215–219
System startup
    booter initialization, 581–582
    booter selection, 578
    firmware initialization, 577
    firmware updates, 581
    kernel initialization, 582–583
    logout, 589–590
    overview of, 575
    POST (Power-On Self-Test), 577–578
    review quiz, 598–599
    sequences in, 576–577
    shortcuts, 579–580
    Shutdown/Restart, 590
    sleep modes, 588–589
    summary and reference information, 596–597
    system launchd initialization, 583–585

troubleshooting booter issues, 592–593

troubleshooting firmware issues, 591–592

troubleshooting kernel issues, 593–594

troubleshooting logout and shutdown, 596

troubleshooting system launchd issues, 594–595

troubleshooting user initialization, 595–596

unlocking FileVault 2, 578–579

user session initialization, 585–587

System user (root), 610

T

Tab completion, 619–620

Target disk mode, 200–202

TCP/IP (Transmission Control Protocol/Internet Protocol)

built-in support for, 388

DHCP for preliminary configuration of, 363

DNS and, 362

history of networking, 353–354

LANs and, 359–360

link aggregation and, 388

manually configuring, 389–393

NetBIOS and WINS running on top of, 400

packet-basis of, 358

VLANs (virtual LANs) and, 385

WANs and, 361

TCP (Transmission Control Protocol), 358, 425, 492

Terminal

accessing command line in, 611–612

administrative commands, 630–634

advantages of command line, 610

changing ownership, 192

changing privileges, 193–194

clearing ACLs from, 203–204

command strings in, 614

comparing file system shortcut types, 232–233

creating symbolic links, 231–232

example of command line, 614–615

file and folder modification commands, 626–630

file examination commands, 622–624

forcing quit, 334–335

hiding/unhiding items, 227–228

interface to UNIX command-line environment, 24–25

learning command options, 615–616

Lion Recovery utilities, 24

login shell and, 64

man pages for research from, 607

managing disk images, 263

managing locked items, 195–196

monitoring processes from command line, 329–331

navigating command line, 616–617

navigating to other volumes, 621–622

navigation commands, 617–618

open command and, 225–226

opening hidden items, 226–227

overview of, 609

recursive commands, 625

remote login from, 480, 482

resetting primary administrator password, 115–116

special characters used commands, 618–619

staring print or fax jobs, 545

tab completion, 619–620

tips for working with command line, 634–635

viewing ACLs, 191–192

viewing AppleDouble files from, 239–240

viewing hidden files, 224

viewing invisible items, 620–621

viewing metadata, 235–236

viewing standard permissions, 189–190

wild card characters in commands, 624–625

working with command-line prompt, 612–613

TextEdit, 317

TGT (ticket-granting ticket), in Kerberos, 509–510

Threads, 327

Thunderbolt, 200–202, 528–529

Ticket-granting ticket (TGT), in Kerberos, 509–510

Tilde (~), for specifying home folder, 619

Time Capsule wireless base stations, 267, 271

Time Machine

backing up files and folders during upgrade, 9

backing up using, 266–268

configuring, 268–273

flaws in, 278–279

managing, 265–266

manually restoring from, 276–278

migrating data with, 35

Migration Assistant and, 77

restoring from, 23, 273–275

Spotlight service indexing, 252

Time zone settings, 39

TLDs (top-level domains), 362

top command, for monitoring processes, 330

Top-level domains (TLDs), 362

TOSLINK digital audio, 533

Traceroute section, of Network Utility, 411, 415–416

Trackpad, accessibility options, 312–313

Transmission Control Protocol. See TCP (Transmission Control Protocol)

Transmission Control Protocol/Internet Protocol. See TCP/IP (Transmission Control Protocol/Internet Protocol)

Trash, 138–140, 311–312

Troubleshooting

binary searches, 606

diagnostic tools for, 605–606

directory services, 513–515

installation, 18–19

printing, scanning, and faxing, 570–571

quick fixes, 603–605

research resources, 606–607

system resources, 219

VPN connections, 383

widgets, 346–347

workflow for, 602–603

Troubleshooting applications

diagnostic reports, 335–337

forcing quit, 333–335

overview of, 331–333

preference troubleshooting, 337–340

resource troubleshooting, 340–341

Troubleshooting file systems

clearing ACLs from Terminal, 203–204

gathering file system information, 196–198

overview of, 196

permissions issues, 202–203

recovering data using target disk mode, 201–202

Repair Disk Permissions feature of Disk Utility, 204–205

Resetting home folder permissions and ACLs, 205–207

Target Disk Mode button, 200–201

verifying/repairing drives, 198–200
Troubleshooting network configuration
  interface option of Network Utility,
    411–412
  lookup option of Network Utility,
    414–415
  Network Diagnostics Assistant,
    409–410
  network status indicators, 409
  Network Utility, 410–411
  overview of, 408
  ping option of Network Utility,
    412–413
  traceroute option of Network
    Utility, 415–416
Troubleshooting network services
  file sharing issues, 494
  network applications, 492–494
  port scanning, 490–492
  shared services, 495–497
Troubleshooting peripherals
  basic techniques in, 543–544
  device classes, 539–541
  device drivers, 541–542
  inspecting loaded extensions,
    542–543
Troubleshooting system startup
  booter issues, 592–593
  firmware issues, 591–592
  kernel issues, 593–594
  logout and shutdown, 596
  system launchd issues, 594–595
  user initialization, 595–596
TrueType fonts, 220

U

UDF (Universal Disk Format), 126
UDP (User Datagram Protocol), 425,
  427, 492
UFS (UNIX File System), 125
Uniform Resource Locators (URLs), 432
Uninstaller programs, 312
Universal Access
  accessibility preferences, 314–315
  managing application accessibility,
    312–313
  VoiceOver options, 313–314
Universal Disk Format (UDF), 126
Universal Serial Bus. See USB (Universal
  Serial Bus)
Universally Unique ID (UUID), 63
UNIX
  as foundation of Lion's multiple-
    user environment, 59
  hard links, 229
  hidden items required by, 223–224

history of networking and, 354
Lion compatibility with, 292
open source foundation for Mac
  OS X, 2
printing system. See CUPS
  (Common UNIX Printing
  System)
symbolic links, 228–229
UNIX File System (UFS), 125
unzip command, 258
Up Arrow and Down Arrow, navigating
  command history, 635
UPD (User Datagram Protocol), 358
Updates. See also Apple Software
  Update, see
  firmware updates, 7–8, 580
  of installed software, 299
  quick fixes, 603–604
  troubleshooting peripherals and,
    544
Upgrade installation
  backing up important files and
    folders, 9
  checking for firmware updates, 7–8
  checking for software updates, 6–7
  documenting critical settings
    during, 9–10
  install options, 14
  overview of, 3–4
  plugging portable Macs into AC
    power, 6
  preparing for, 5–10
  staying current with installation
    information, 10
  verifying application compatibility,
    8–9
  verifying installation requirements,
    5–6
URLs (Uniform Resource Locators), 432
USB (Universal Serial Bus)
  Bluetooth adapter, 530
  cellular network adapters, 407
  configuring directly attached
    printers, 547
  configuring local network printers,
    550
  Lion support for network
    interfaces, 371
  overview of, 525–527
  power issues, 544
  versions supported by Lion, 527
User accounts
  accessing hidden attributes, 71
  administrator role in resetting
    passwords, 110–111

advantages of network directory
  services, 499
attributes of, 62–64
creating, 64–66
deleting, 74–75
directory resources used by Lion,
  498
fast user switching, 81–82
firmware passwords, 94–96
groups accounts, 69–70
home folder contents, 72–74
initial account setup, 37–38
Keychain Access tool, 100
keychain file types, 99–100
keychains for protecting
  authentication assets, 98–99
legacy FileVault folders and, 96–98
location options, 500
login options, 80–81
managing keychain files, 102–104
managing keychain items, 100–102
managing user login items, 66–67
moving or restoring manually,
  77–80
moving or restoring with Migration
  Assistant, 76–77
network users. See Network user
  accounts
overview of, 59–60
parental controls, 67–69
Password Assistant options, 92–94
password options, 88–89
resetting administrator password,
  114–116
resetting keychain password,
  113–114
resetting legacy FileVault password,
  111–113
resetting master password, 107–108
resetting passwords at login,
  108–110
resolving fast user switching issues,
  84–86
resource contention issues in fast
  user switching, 83–84
review quiz, 117–119
Security & Privacy preferences,
  89–91
setting or changing master
  password, 105–107
summary and reference
  information, 116–117
troubleshooting network service
  access issues, 496
types of, 60–62, 500

vulnerabilities, 86–88
User Datagram Protocol. See UDP (User Datagram Protocol)
User environment, 577, 586–587
User launchd, 577, 586–587
User session
    initializing user environment, 586–587
    maintaining user environment, 587
    phase of system startup, 576
    stages of, 577
    troubleshooting system startup, 595–596
Users & Groups
    accessing hidden attributes, 71
    AD (Active Directory) binding, 503–505
    creating user accounts, 64–66
    deleting user accounts, 74–75
    directory binding method, 501
    login options, 80–81
    managing login items, 66–67
    OD (Open Directory) binding, 501–503
    Password Assistant, 92
    preferences, 69–70
    resetting Legacy FileVault passwords, 111–113
    restoring user accounts and, 79
Users folder, 214–215
Users resource domain, 217
UUID (Universally Unique ID), 63

V

Verbose mode (Command-V), 604
Versions, document. See also Auto Save and Versions feature, 318–320
VGA (Video Graphics Array), 533
vi command, for accessing Vi text editor, 629–630
Video, 532–534, 541
Video Graphics Array (VGA), 533
Virtual LANs (VLANs), 376, 384–386
Virtual Network Computing (VNC), 471–472, 474–477
Virtual network services
    link aggregation settings, 386–388
    overview of, 376

PPPoE settings, 377–379
VLAN settings, 384–386
VPN settings, 379–384
Virtual private networks (VPNs), 376, 379–384
VLANs (virtual LANs), 376, 384–386
VNC (Virtual Network Computing), 471–472, 474–477
Voice Over IP (VoIP), 358
VoiceOver, 81, 313–315
VoIP (Voice Over IP), 358
Volumes
    automatically connecting network volumes, 451–452
    disk images containing virtual volumes, 258
    ejecting in-use, 144–146
    erasing, 134–138
    formats, 122, 124–126
    managing network-connected, 450–451
    managing volume mounts, 142–144
    navigating to other, 621–622
    permissions for external, 187–188
    quick fixes, 604
    resizing, adding, deleting, 132–133
    troubleshooting system volume issues, 592
    unmounting with Finder, 141–142
VPNs (virtual private networks), 376, 379–384
Vulnerabilities, user accounts, 86–88

W

WANs (Wide Area Networks), 360–361
WAP, for wireless authentication, 395
Web-based Distributed Authoring and Versioning. See WebDAV (Web-based Distributed Authoring and Versioning)
Web browsing. See also Safari, 431–432
Web publishing, iCal managing, 435
Web sharing, 455, 464–468
WebDAV (Web-based Distributed Authoring and Versioning)
    iCal managing, 435
    Lion supported file services, 439

manually connecting, 447–450
troubleshooting file sharing issues, 494
Websites, 74, 465–468
which command, for locating file path, 623
Whois section, of Network Utility, 411
Wi-Fi (Wireless Ethernet)
    built-in support for, 389
    configuring, 393–397
    link aggregation and, 388
    Lion support for network interfaces, 371–372
    network settings, 32
    overview of, 361–363
    PANs (personal area networks), 407–408
    UDP used by, 358
    VLANs (virtual LANs) and, 385
Wide Area Networks (WANs), 360–361
Widgets, 342–347
Wild card characters, in commands, 624–625
Windows PCs, migrating data from, 34–35
WINS (Windows Internet Naming Service), 400–402, 428
Wireless Ethernet. See Wi-Fi (Wireless Ethernet)
Wireless preferences, 42
Workflow, in troubleshooting, 602–603
Working directory, 613
WPA, 802.1X authentication, 399
Write attributes, 191
Write Only permissions, 174

X

X11, as application environments, 292
Xcode Developer Tools, 238
Xgrid system, 470
XML format, 339
XTS-AES 128 encryption, 163

Y

Yellow status, network status indicators, 409

Z

Zip archives, 256–259, 296–297

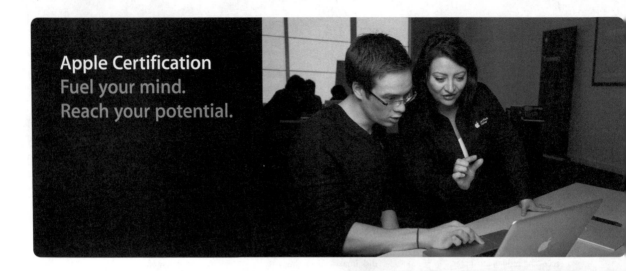

Apple Certification
Fuel your mind.
Reach your potential.

Stand out from the crowd. Differentiate yourself and gain recognition for your expertise by earning Apple Certified Pro status to validate your OS X Lion skills.

This book prepares you to pass the OS X Support Essentials 10.7 Exam and earn Apple Certified Support Professional (ACSP) status. The exam is available at Apple Authorized Training Centers (AATCs) worldwide. ACSP certification is designed for the help desk professional, technical coordinator or power-user who supports Mac OS X users, manages networks or provides technical support for Macs in your organization.

Three Steps to Certification

1 Choose your certification path.
  More info: training.apple.com/certification.

2 All Apple Authorized Training Centers (AATCs) offer all Mac OS X and Pro Apps exams, even if they don't offer the corresponding course. To find the closest AATC, please visit training.apple.com/locations.

  ster for and take your exam(s).

tion places you in a unique class of professionals.
   that you care enough about what you do to
       get certified, it also demonstrates that you

       Sheehan, Multimedia Studio Manager,
                    MFS Investment Management

Reasons to Become an Apple Certified Pro

- **Raise your earning potential.** Studies show that certified professionals can earn more than their non-certified peers.

- **Distinguish yourself from others in your industry.** Proven mastery of an application helps you stand out from the crowd.

- **Display your Apple Certification logo.** Each certification provides a logo to display on business cards, resumes and websites.

- **Publicize your Certifications.** Publish your certifications on the Apple Certified Professionals Registry to connect with schools, clients and employers.

Training Options

Apple's comprehensive curriculum addresses your needs, whether you're an IT or creative professional, educator, or student. Hands-on training is available through a worldwide network of Apple Authorized Training Centers (AATCs). Self-paced study is available through the Apple Pro Training Series books, which are also accessible as eBooks via the iBooks app. Video training and video training apps are also available for select titles. Visit training.apple.com to view all your learning options.

The Apple Pro Training Series

Apple offers comprehensive certification programs for creative and IT professionals. The Apple Pro Training Series is the official training curriculum of the Apple Training and Certification program, used by Apple Authorized Training Centers around the world

To find an Authorized Training Center near you, visit: **www.apple.com/software/pro/training**

**Apple Pro Training Series:
Final Cut Pro X**
0321774671 • $54.99
Diana Weynand

**Apple Pro Video Series:
Final Cut Pro X**
0321809629 • $59.99
Steve Martin

**Apple Pro Video Series:
Final Cut Pro X
(Streaming Only)**
0132876302 • $39.99
Steve Martin

**Apple Pro Training Series:
Final Cut Pro X Quick-
Reference Guide
(E-book Only)**
0132876345 • $19.99
Brendan Boykin

**Apple Pro Training Series:
Final Cut Pro X Advanced
Editing**
0321810228 • $59.99
Michael Wohl

**Apple Pro Training Series:
Motion 5**
032177468X • $54.99
Mark Spencer

**Apple Pro Training Series:
Aperture 3**
0321647440 • $54.99
Dion Scoppettuolo

**Apple Pro Training Series:
OS X Lion Support Essentials:
A Guide to Supporting and
Troubleshooting OS X Lion**
0321775074 • $64.99
Kevin M White

**Apple Pro Training Series:
OS X Lion Server: A Guide
to Using and Supporting
OS X Lion Server**
0321775082 • $64.99
Arek Dreyer, Ben Greisler

**Apple Training Series:
iLife '11**
032170097X • $39.99
Scoppettuolo / Plummer

**Apple Training Series:
iWork 09**
0321618513 • $39.99
Richard Harrington

To see a complete range of Apple Pro Training Series books, videos and apps visit:
www.peachpit.com/appleprotraining

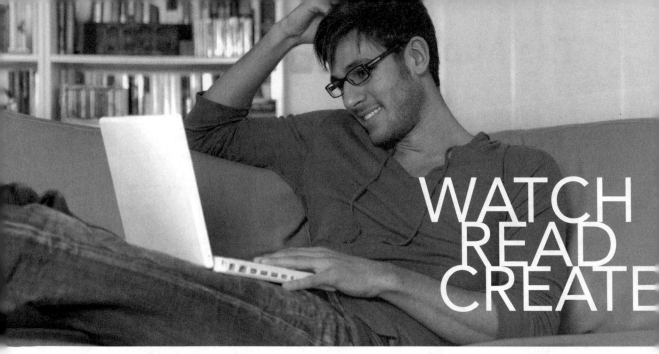

WATCH
READ
CREATE

Meet Creative Edge.

A new resource of unlimited books, videos and tutorials for creatives from the world's leading experts.

Creative Edge is your one stop for inspiration, answers to technical questions and ways to stay at the top of your game so you can focus on what you do best—being creative.

All for only $24.99 per month for access—any day any time you need it.

creative edge

creativeedge